GLOBEMASTER DOWN

GLOBEMASTER DOWN

SOVIET ESPIONAGE AND THE DOOMED AMERICAN ATTEMPT TO SNEAK NUKES INTO EUROPE

TOD ROBBERSON

CITADEL PRESS
Kensington Publishing Corp.
kensingtonbooks.com

CITADEL PRESS BOOKS are published by

Kensington Publishing Corp.
900 Third Avenue
New York, NY 10022

All Kensington titles, imprints, and distributed lines are available at special quantity discounts for bulk purchases for sales promotions, premiums, fund-raising, educational, or institutional use. Special book excerpts or customized printings can also be created to fit specific needs. For details, write or phone the office of the Kensington sales manager: Kensington Publishing Corp., 900 Third Avenue, New York, NY 10022, attn Sales Department; phone 1-800-221-2647.

10 9 8 7 6 5 4 3 2 1

First Citadel hardcover printing: April 2026

Printed in the United States of America

ISBN: 978-0-8065-4460-1

ISBN: 978-0-8065-4462-5 (e-book)

Library of Congress Control Number: 2025950975

The authorized representative in the EU for product safety and compliance
is eucomply OU, Parnu mnt 139b-14, Apt 123,
Tallinn, Berlin 11317; hello@eucompliancepartner.com

To Catherine and Fiona
and all the friends and family members
who kept the faith

CONTENTS

CAST OF CHARACTERS

Samuel E. Anderson: Air Force major general, commander of Eighth Air Force Division

Henry H. "Hap" Arnold: General of the Air Force, former General of the Army

Frederick Ashworth: Navy commander and weaponeer on the Nagasaki bombing

Clement Attlee: Prime minister of Britain

Winston Churchill: Former and future prime minister of Britain

Paul T. Cullen: Brigadier general, commander of newly created Seventh Air Force Division

Reva Joy Hurwitz Cullen: Paul Cullen's co-wife, Operation Crossroads Red Cross liaison

Ruth Gravett Cullen: Paul Cullen's co-wife of sixteen years

Dwight Eisenhower: Supreme Commander, North Atlantic Treaty Organization

John Faherty: Farmer in Renvyle, Ireland who discovered mysterious Globemaster note

Hunter Harris, Jr.: Brigadier general commanding Walker Air Force Base

James I. Hopkins: Lieutenant colonel, operations officer, 509th Bomb Wing

William L. Laurence: *New York Times* correspondent

Curtis E. LeMay: Lieutenant general, commander of the Strategic Air Command

Oswald W. Lunde: Air Force attaché, U.S. Embassy, Dublin, Ireland

Lauris Norstad: Commander in chief, U.S. Air Forces Europe

Arthur Quinlan: Reporter, *The Irish Times*

Lawrence Rafferty: Captain, passenger aboard Globemaster 49-244

Joseph Stalin: Premier, Union of Soviet Socialist Republics

Charles "Chuck" Sweeney: Major, command pilot of the Nagasaki mission

Paul W. Tibbets: Colonel, commander of Hiroshima, Nagasaki atomic missions

Lee Van Atta: Radio correspondent

Arthur Vandenberg: U.S. Senator from Michigan, 1928–1951

Hoyt S. Vandenberg: U.S. Air Force Chief of Staff

Kenneth S. Wherry: U.S. Senator from Nebraska, 1943–1951

Ben Wyatt: Commodore, Marshall Islands

GLOBEMASTER 49-244 PASSENGERS AND CREW

Name	Rank	Rating	Assignment
CREW			
Amsden, Robert D.	Staff Sgt	Flight engineer	509th Bomb Wing Second Strategic Support Squadron
Armstrong, Jr., Karl R.	2nd Lt	Navigator	509th Bomb Wing Second Strategic Support Squadron
Bell, Robert J.	Maj	Pilot	509th Bomb Wing Second Strategic Support Squadron
Collins, Emmett E.	Capt	Pilot	509th Bomb Wing Second Strategic Support Squadron
Crow, Jack R.	Cpl		509th Bomb Wing Second Strategic Support Squadron
Davies, Francis N.	Capt	Navigator	509th Bomb Wing Second Strategic Support Squadron
Green, Charles E.	TSgt	Flight engineer	509th Bomb Wing Second Strategic Support Squadron
Jones, Jr., Homer	Staff Sgt	Radio operator	509th Bomb Wing Second Strategic Support Squadron
Mathers, Howard P.	2nd Lt	Pilot	509th Bomb Wing Second Strategic Support Squadron

Name	Rank	Rating	Assignment
PASSENGERS			
Adler, Glenn E.	Staff Sgt		509th Bomb Wing 830th Bomb Squadron
Adrean, Phil B.	Capt	Pilot	509th Bomb Wing 830th Bomb Squadron
Ambrose, George W.	Sgt		509th Bomb Wing 4013th Maintenance Squadron
Ambrose, Sterling L.	Cpl		509th Bomb Wing 715th Bomb Squadron
Bemis, Bartin C.	Staff Sgt		509th Bomb Wing Second Strategic Support Squadron
Berenberg, Dwight A.	Pvt	Radio operator	509th Bomb Wing 830th Bomb Squadron
Bristow, Robert R.	Sgt	Radio operator	509th Bomb Wing 393rd Bomb Squadron
Broussard, Joseph D.	Sgt		509th Bomb Wing Second Strategic Support Squadron
Chute, Arthur F.	Cpl		509th Bomb Wing Second Strategic Support Squadron
Counsell, John E.	Capt	Bombardier	509th Bomb Wing 393rd Bomb Squadron
Cullen, Paul T.	Brig Gen	Commander	SAC Second Air Force Seventh Air Division
Dubach, Mark O.	Capt	Navigator	509th Bomb Wing 715th Bomb Squadron
Dudek, Miezyslaw	Capt	Bombardier	509th Bomb Wing 393rd Bomb Squadron
Dughman, Gene D.	Staff Sgt		509th Bomb Wing 393rd Bomb Squadron
Fife, Jack R.	1st Lt	Pilot	509th Bomb Wing 715th Bomb Squadron
Fisher, Jr., William E.	2nd Lt	Navigator	509th Bomb Wing 715th Bomb Squadron
Gray, Kenneth N.	Col		SAC Second Air Force Seventh Air Division

Name	Rank	Rating	Assignment
Greene, Thomas E.	Staff Sgt		509th Bomb Wing 4013th Electrical Maintenance Squadron
Hopkins, James I.	Lt Col	Pilot	SAC Second Air Force Seventh Air Division
Kampert, Robert F.	Capt	Bombardier	509th Bomb Wing 393rd Bomb Squadron
Kelly, Thomas R.	Capt	Bombardier	509th Bomb Wing 830th Bomb Squadron
Krawiec, Carl N.	Capt	Bombardier	509th Bomb Wing 715th Bomb Squadron
Lee, Max D.	2nd Lt	Navigator	509th Bomb Wing 830th Bomb Squadron
Lengua, Nicolo A.	Staff Sgt	Radio operator	509th Bomb Wing 830th Bomb Squadron
Lutjeans, Samuel P.		Bombardier	509th Bomb Wing 715th Bomb Squadron
McGee, Ronald D.	Sgt	Radio operator	509th Bomb Wing 393rd Bomb Squadron
McKoy, Edwin A.	Lt Col	Pilot	SAC Second Air Force Seventh Air Division
Meckler, Frank A.	Sgt	Flight engineer	509th Bomb Wing 830th Bomb Squadron
Peterson, Walter T.	Capt	Pilot	509th Bomb Wing 393rd Bomb Squadron
Porter, Calvin	Capt	Bombardier	509th Bomb Wing 393rd Bomb Squadron
Rafferty, Lawrence E.	Capt	Pilot	509th Bomb Wing 715th Bomb Squadron
Scarbrough, Everett D.	Master Sgt		509th Bomb Wing Second Strategic Support Squadron
Stoddard, Gordon H.	Maj	Pilot	SAC Second Air Force Seventh Air Division
Swisher, Clarence G.	Cpl		509th Bomb Wing 393rd Bomb Squadron
Thomas, Bobby G.	Cpl		509th Bomb Wing 715th Bomb Squadron

Name	Rank	Rating	Assignment
VanGilder, Taylor H.	Master Sgt		509th Bomb Wing 509th Aviation Squadron
Vincent, Roger S.	Capt	Pilot	509th Bomb Wing 830th Bomb Squadron
Wagner, Jr., Walter A.	Capt	Pilot	509th Bomb Wing 830th Bomb Squadron
Williamson, H. C.	Master Sgt		509th Bomb Wing 509th Aviation Squadron
Witkowski, Raymond L.	Capt	Bombardier	509th Bomb Wing 715th Bomb Squadron
Zabawa, Edwon D.	Capt	Bombardier	509th Bomb Wing 830th Bomb Squadron
Zalac, Frank B.	Capt	Pilot	509th Bomb Wing 715th Bomb Squadron
Zweygartt, John C.	Capt	Bombardier	509th Bomb Wing 830th Bomb Squadron

INTRODUCTION

ON MARCH 23, 1951, THE U.S. AIR FORCE SUFFERED THE WORST air disaster in its short history. A C-124 Globemaster cargo plane, tail number 49-244, carrying fifty-three passengers and crew, was crossing the Atlantic en route to Mildenhall Royal Air Force Base, north of London, when it disappeared. As far as the American public was concerned, it was just a routine flight. The disaster was easily dismissed by authorities as perhaps the result of bad weather or maybe an equipment failure. After all, Americans had been steeped in the news of one disaster after another in World War II. Military planes go down. Men die. The U.S. Air Force was perfectly happy to cultivate that storyline and ensure it was repeated so often that newspaper editors grew tired of it and moved on to more important events of the day: spy scandals, the war in Korea, the Red Scare, and the constant churn of American domestic politics. After about a week of front-page attention, the story of Globemaster 49-244 steadily drifted onto the inside pages, then into the briefs, followed by no coverage at all.

There were, however, a few details that kept the story alive before it fell into a historical black hole. For one thing, there was a brigadier general onboard, Paul T. Cullen, who had garnered heavy attention in World War II for a series of dangerous reconnaissance flights that provided crucial photographic mapping details of enemy emplacements. One of those flights took place when Cullen was based in the Soviet Union with the rare permission of Soviet dictator Joseph Stalin. Cullen became the first American military pilot to take off from a Russian base and land in Ukraine. His mission was to demonstrate to Stalin the value of America's most modern aerial photographic reconnaissance technology. Cullen's photo, in his crisp officer's uniform, accompanied many, if not most, of the early stories about the disappearance of 49-244.

Another key bit of news was that the plane had inexplicably veered almost 300 miles off course before ditching in the Atlantic. For two days, newspaper coverage focused on a single report from a B-29 search plane that survivors on one or more life rafts had been spotted amid a field of wreckage. (Actually, multiple reports came in of survivors, but those reports were kept confidential.)

There were flares and SOS signals. But when U.S. and British ships arrived at the ditching site, they found nothing more than several small pieces of charred, splintered wood, a canvas satchel full of documents, and a *Collier's* magazine belonging to Captain Lawrence Rafferty, who had been one of the passengers onboard. The search, probably the largest in U.S. naval history at the time, turned up no evidence of survivors. No bodies floated to the surface. Not even life vests. Aside from Rafferty's satchel, it was hard to identify anything in the wreckage that spoke to passengers and crew having been aboard the Globemaster. They had simply vanished.

The Air Force maintained a tight hold on information about the passengers' and crew's backgrounds. Only the basic information—names, ranks, hometowns—were released to the news media. The Air Force did allow the release of information about three officers onboard who were described as traveling to England on routine temporary duty from their base at the headquarters of the Strategic Air Command. As far as the public was concerned, that was the only connection to the SAC. The rest were just on an assortment of transfers and short-duty assignments. Nothing out of the ordinary in this picture.

What the Air Force didn't tell the public was this: All fifty-three aboard were attached to the Strategic Air Command on a classified mission related to General Curtis LeMay's effort to install an atomic attack force in Britain in preparation for imminent war against the Soviet Union. The Globemaster carried two supposedly empty KB-29 aerial-refueling tanks along with assorted cargo items that, on the plane's manifest, were listed as weighing roughly the same as a "Fat Man" atomic bomb.

These were the kinds of details the Air Force probably had good reason to withhold from the public for fear of creating a panic. Nothing speaks of global catastrophe like the threat of an atomic deployment against Russia, which was the only other atomic superpower in the world at the time. The Soviets were known to have amassed an estimated 1.5 million troops near the eastern edge of Europe, and fears were running high among European leaders that a military sweep across the continent could happen at any moment. America's atomic weaponry was viewed by many leaders as Europe's bulwark against a Soviet onslaught.

Perhaps the biggest fear in President Harry Truman's administration was that any leakage of the true mission of Globemaster 49-244 would provoke a backlash in Britain, the extremely nervous host of U.S. training missions in preparation for retaliatory strikes should the Soviets invade. Britain had not yet formally agreed to host an American atomic bomb, nor had its leaders prepared the public for any such eventuality.

General Cullen was on the Globemaster flight because he had just been appointed to command the first-ever foreign SAC base, to be headquartered at Mildenhall. Also aboard was Lieutenant Colonel James I. Hopkins, one of the Air Force's top atomic-certified pilots and the only pilot to have participated in a wartime atomic bombing. He had been the operations officer for the atomic missions against Japan and flew on the mission to drop the Fat Man on Nagasaki, which effectively brought World War II to a close.

For the seventy-five years following the ditching of 49-244 and disappearance of all onboard, the Air Force kept tight control over key details about the mission. Some items, particularly those contained in a 42,500-page investigative file still under U.S. Air Force wraps from the early Cold War era,[1] remain classified to this day. What could be so sensitive that it justified keeping a seventy-five-year-old secret from the American people? The full story of Globemaster 49-244 cannot be told unless and until that information is released.

Over the years, in the absence of information, all sorts of conspiracy theories have developed about the flight. This book seeks to dispel some of the myths while, perhaps more importantly, providing the historical context that surrounded the Globemaster mission. What was the background of the key decision-makers and their motivations? Why did America's military commanders believe that war with Russia was imminent? How did spies and sabotage play a potential role? What did the Atlantic search reveal at the time? And why was it so important that an entire atomic attack force, headed by a brigadier general, needed to accompany a cargo listed as two KB-29 tanks across the ocean?

The reader should be forewarned: This book does not solve the mystery behind the disappearance of Globemaster 49-244. It does seek to clarify circumstances by laying out what is known from the historical record hidden in thousands of pages of archival records provided by the Library of Congress Manuscript Reading Room and the Department of the Air Force Historical Research Agency, among hundreds of other sources.

Writing this book required reducing thousands of pages of research material into a readable, engaging format. That necessarily entails reducing highly complex decisions and military operations into a few phrases or sentences. Those decisions were hardly that simple. Leaders had to weigh a wide variety of factors before making any move. No one should be fooled into thinking, for example, that Curtis LeMay was the only decision-maker regarding the movement of atomic weaponry, or that he merely had to snap his fingers to make a deployment happen. This book makes an effort to describe the complexities of his life and the various pressures bearing down on him. The other major figures faced their own pressures, doubts, and fears. The Globemaster's disappearance itself might have been misconstrued over time because of all the evidence, presented here and elsewhere, pointing to something nefarious.

It remains entirely possible that the plane experienced a catastrophic series of communication and mechanical failures that caused it to go down all on its own, without the intervention of some external force. That is unlikely, but possible.

Once the historical context comes into focus, substantial evidence—albeit circumstantial in many cases—comes into better focus, helping explain why investigators into the ditching spent inordinate amounts of time looking into possible sabotage as the cause of the plane's disappearance. The historical context also explains the armed confrontations that led U.S. commanders to conclude, ten years before the Cuban Missile Crisis, that this was no longer a cold war but rather a hot one that deserved a forceful American response. The world was on the verge of a nuclear war, and Curtis LeMay, among others, privately pushed to make it happen. The Soviets were overtly shooting down American military planes over international territory. They were disguising their pilots as Koreans and painting MiG jet fighters with North Korean flags in order to engage U.S. planes in combat. Soviet naval vessels, as we will find, were believed by the Pentagon to have been stationed in the very area where Globemaster 49-244 went down.

Then comes the question of the cargo onboard the plane. The Truman administration, at the highest levels, had approved the transfer of atomic components for preplacement in Britain with the objective of using them immediately upon the start of hostilities should Russia invade Europe. LeMay, among others, was arguing that it made no sense to wait for the start of hostilities, and that striking a preemptive first blow might be necessary to send a clear message to Russia about American military supremacy.

Stalin, of course, had his own messages that he wanted the Americans to receive. He wanted them to know his spies could infiltrate the most top secret U.S. and British missions with ease. His forces were capable of sophisticated forms of sabotage. He was not above capturing American military men for interrogation and imprisonment. Foremost, Stalin's message was that there was no such thing as American military supremacy.

Finally, there is the question of how a crucial mission like that of Globemaster 49-244's final flight could have been infiltrated and sabotaged, if indeed that's what caused the diversion and ditching. This book will examine in detail one of the most bizarre aspects of the Globemaster story: that Brigadier General Paul T. Cullen was married to two women at the same time and might have compromised the very atomic mission he was chosen to command.

These are the elements behind the unsolved, untold mystery of Globemaster 49-244.

CHAPTER 1

Heady Days

PRECIOUS FEW PEOPLE REMAIN ALIVE TODAY WHO CAN RECALL the heady days after the end of World War II. It was a time of unbridled celebration in the streets and bars and dance halls of cities and towns across America. Wives were reuniting with husbands in anticipation of long sessions of lovemaking to catch up for years of war-imposed celibacy. Children were finally able to hug their daddies again or, in some cases, shyly meet them for the first time. The long years of rationing and self-sacrifice for the war effort were finally over. Americans wanted to dance, drink, have fun, and enjoy the fruits of their sacrifice. Germany had been defanged and wrestled into submission. The atomic bomb, which followed months of firebombing that had already reduced Japan to smoldering cinders, had finally forced Japan's submission to the will of the world's only atomic superpower. Americans weren't just celebrating the end of the war—they were celebrating the dawn of a new age: the age of unquestionable, unchallengeable American military and economic supremacy. The atom bomb, and America's monopoly over it, ensured that a new era of global peace would reign across the world because no other nation would dare risk provoking the ire of the one nation in possession of nuclear weaponry. Or so Americans thought.

Deep inside the Pentagon and National Security Council, analysts were coming to a far darker and more ominous conclusion. While all the other belligerents in the war were rapidly demobilizing their armed forces and devoting resources to rebuild their war-ravaged economies, the Soviet Union showed no sign of relaxing its war footing. The number of Communist Bloc troops still in arms along the European front dwarfed that of the Soviet Union's former allies. Analysts at the Pentagon asked: If Joseph Stalin truly was interested in peace, why was he not demonstrating it with a good faith gesture of demobilization? Moscow had opted to maintain a standing army of nearly 4.5 million men and women spread across 113 divisions,[1] even if the cost of maintaining those forces meant prolonged devastation and hardship at home.

Viewed from the United States' intelligence perspective, there could be only one interpretation of Stalin's continued war footing. He adhered to the doctrine that the Communist mission could never be regarded as complete unless the philosophy had been adopted throughout the world, be it by the voluntary embrace of the people, by internal revolution, or by external coercion. Russia had every intention, American intelligence analysts concluded, of using military force to conquer the world. And the immediate goal was to unite all of Europe under the banner of Marxism.

From the Soviet perspective, however, the conclusion of World War II didn't bring the promised peace and stability that the American and British leadership had promised. Rather, the world had been rendered dangerously unstable because of the atomic technology that the United States had wielded with brutal efficiency to subdue Japan while deliberately keeping this new weaponry secret in order, perhaps, to deploy against the Soviet Union if Moscow failed to kneel before the capitalist king. The accident of geography had heavily favored America in the war, sparing it the kinds of devastation that had cost an estimated 27 million Russian lives and left the country in ruins.[2] Starvation in Russia was rampant in the immediate postwar period. Stalin, mindful of the heavy losses Russia had suffered to fend off Hitler, was determined to ensure that his proud nation would never face that kind of threat again, much less be forced to submit to the dominance of any outside power. Communism might not be able to solve the massive domestic problems facing the Soviet people, but if Stalin could deliver some kind of humiliation to the capitalist swine in Washington, perhaps the people's discomfort could be assuaged. If the war had proven anything, especially given the way it ended, it was that brutal military might was what commanded global fear and respect. The generalissimo kept his armed forces mobilized and ready because, in Stalin's mind, there was still a war to be fought.

Stalin had good reason to be resentful and distrustful of his former allies. While Franklin Roosevelt and Winston Churchill made a show of partnering with him during their meetings at Yalta, followed by the meeting of the three powers at Potsdam with Roosevelt's soon-to-be successor, Harry S. Truman, sitting in, Stalin was keenly aware that the other two men at the table were keeping important, world-changing secrets from him. They knew about the crash program to develop an atomic bomb, but they had deliberately kept Stalin in the dark.

Stalin knew this because he was being fed intelligence on a nearly daily basis about every key aspect of the Manhattan Project. The intelligence was of such high quality and specificity that it would soon enable Russia to embark on its own atomic weaponry program and explode a crude bomb before the decade was finished—and years ahead of American intelligence experts' best estimates of Soviet capabilities.[3] The near-total and unchallenged infiltration of America's most cherished, top secret military project gave Stalin a level of confident defiance that left his U.S. counterparts confounded. The Soviet economy was a mess. Russia's infrastructure was in tatters. Its people were exhausted from war and starvation. And yet the Soviet leader seemed unyielding and willing to constantly prod and provoke the West, even to the point from 1945 to 1951 of allowing Soviet pilots to engage in dogfights with their U.S. counterparts and shoot them out of the sky. Stalin strong-armed neighboring states, crushed a guerrilla uprising in Ukraine, engineered a coup in Czechoslovakia, assassinated critics, and staged the ultimate act of defiance by blocking the United States and Britain from accessing Berlin.

Before that happened, the Pentagon and the newly created Central Intelligence Agency disagreed about how serious the threat was from the Soviet Union. The civilian leadership acknowledged Stalin as an irritant but discounted his ability or desire to provoke another war. But by the end of the 1940s, military generals became increasingly vocal in their belief that something bad was brewing. The CIA concluded that, despite the tensions in Czechoslovakia and the Berlin blockade, the Soviets were not on a war footing.

"The Air Force disagreed with both [Pentagon and CIA] assessments, predicting that war was imminent.... Since 1945 the Air Force had taken the position that the Soviet Union posed a threat to the United States, and in 1947 and 1948 believed there was nothing to prevent the Soviets from attempting to utilize their superior ground forces in Europe."[4]

The detection of the Soviet atomic explosion in August 1949 couldn't have come at a worse time for the Truman administration. The previous year, Chinese Communists had overwhelmed Nationalist forces in that nation's civil war, pushing the Nationalists completely off the mainland and onto the island to the east known at the time as Formosa, now Taiwan. The Truman administration was already defending itself for having "lost China." Now the Soviets were a nuclear-armed superpower, meaning Truman was also on the verge of sacrificing the U.S. status of global military superiority. At the same time, Truman had bowed to congressional pressure to cut back on armed forces spending, "reducing the defense budget from $45 billion in 1946 to $13 billion by 1949. The result was a drastic drop in the Army and Navy and near total reliance on the Air Force to protect the nation."[5]

Since General Curtis E. LeMay led the only command in the Air Force trained and authorized to conduct atomic attacks, the vast bulk of the responsibility for containment of the Soviet threat fell on his shoulders. His was among the few commands that actually saw its budget increase at a time when the others were having to impose drastic cuts.

Air Force intelligence, even without knowledge of the extent of Soviet spying on the Manhattan Project, correctly predicted a Soviet atomic breakthrough sometime between 1949 and 1951. Among the most outspoken skeptics of Soviet postwar intentions was LeMay, who had witnessed firsthand the extent of Stalin's treachery during the war and was the Air Force's choice to come up with a plan to thwart Stalin by commanding the Berlin Airlift. LeMay had commanded the Army Air Forces 509th Composite Group that dropped the atomic bombs on Hiroshima and Nagasaki, as well as the hundreds of B-29 bombers that pummeled Japan with incendiary bombs during the weeks immediately preceding the August 1945 atomic attack. LeMay was a firm believer in the doctrine of overwhelming, brutal force to vanquish an enemy as quickly and efficiently as possible, reasoning that the short-term, heavy casualty tolls that such an attack would inflict, horrifying as they might be, ultimately would save lives on both sides of the conflict by cutting it short rather than allowing it to degrade into a war of attrition.

LeMay's views on how to fight a war were almost diametrically opposite to the philosophy advanced by Stalin. In the Soviet leader's view, attrition was the goal, especially when faced with a superior fighting force. Wear them out. Grind them down. Whittle down their will to fight. The horrors of LeMay's firebombings, followed by the one-two punch of Hiroshima and Nagasaki, worked entirely in favor of Stalin's propaganda efforts. Americans increasingly challenged LeMay's assertion that lives were ultimately saved with his tactics. Britons were even more horrified and had grown adamant that their country should have nothing to do with the use of their soil to store American atomic bombs. Scientists who worked on the Manhattan Project concluded that the physics behind splitting the atom were too precious, too valuable to be left solely in the hands of one nation. So a few among them took it upon themselves to share not only what they held in their brains but also what documentation they could smuggle out of the research facilities at Los Alamos to be passed by intermediaries to Stalin's scientists. An emboldened Stalin not only embarked on a crash course to develop the bomb, he doubled down on his defiance of Western attempts to hold Communist expansionism in check.

Americans came to know this period as the Cold War even though it was, in reality, a very hot armed conflict with direct confrontations between the two superpowers—confrontations kept almost entirely out of public view for fear that public knowledge of what was really happening could lead to outright war—a war in which both sides possessed an ability to deploy atomic weaponry and inflict thousands, if not millions, of casualties. The direct confrontations began around the time of the Berlin blockade. The United States was developing new technologies to conduct photographic reconnaissance flights identifying Soviet installations and troop formations on the East European front. The Soviets were at the same time making dramatic advances in the development of war-weapon rocketry and MiG jet fighters. Suddenly, the two former allies found themselves in direct armed conflict in the skies over Eastern Europe exactly as the Berlin blockade was taking hold. From 1945 through early 1951, twenty-two U.S. or Allied aircraft went down along the dividing line between Soviet and Western forces in Europe.[6] The Soviets also started challenging American pilots over the Sea of Japan.

The Korean War underscored Soviet defiance. Stalin had his pilots dress in North Korean flight suits before boarding MiGs painted with North Korean flags in order to confront American pilots in the skies. No one was fooled into believing that North Korea, until then having minimal war-fighting experience on the ground and probably none in the air, was suddenly so flush with flying expertise that its pilots were capable of besting American bombers and fighters in direct aerial combat. But North Korean planes were scoring major victories, and American officials were having a hard time coming up with a plausible explanation that didn't involve publicly identifying the Soviets as the culprit. Because once that identification was made, there could be no more denying that this was a hot, not cold, war. A groundswell of public outrage would be certain to follow, along with demands by hawks for retaliatory strikes that threatened to prompt yet another world war. Generals like LeMay were privately salivating over the prospect of direct confrontation,[7] but the leadership in Washington was adamant that the Korean conflict stay limited to Korea, and that the conduct of the war be limited to conventional weaponry and tactics. The president nonetheless wanted the Air Force to prepare for the worst.

The Joint Chiefs of Staff supported the deployment and use of atomic weaponry against China should it be determined that Beijing was directly involved in launching airstrikes against U.S. forces, followed by a decision by the Truman administration to transfer nine Mark 4 Fat Man bombs, with their fissile cores, from Atomic Energy Commission control to the military.[8] But top officials decided that it would be too reckless to entrust those weapons to the mercurial commander of U.S. forces in Korea, General Douglas MacArthur. Truman ordered that the Strategic Air Command be given sole authority over the atomic deployment.

By this time, China and the Soviet Union had signed a mutual defense pact, meaning that if one was attacked, it would be regarded as an attack on the other as well. Since LeMay was in charge of the SAC, the atomic deployment decision empowered LeMay with unprecedented authority to launch World War III. The great irony was that LeMay's attention was not focused on Korea or China but rather on Europe and the rising Soviet threat there. He regarded the SAC's involvement in Korea more as an inconvenient distraction, if not annoyance.[9] But the authority granted him regarding the use of atomic weapons was significant. LeMay didn't just want authority to deploy the atomic bomb in the Asian theater but also, if necessary, on the European front.

The Korean War helped LeMay hone the doctrine he had so carefully crafted against Japan and Germany: If the enemy's industrial complex is what is feeding the war, attack those industrial centers aggressively. Restrained by the Truman administration from exercising the nuclear option, LeMay proposed the very tactic that nearly brought him a nonatomic success in Japan: napalm incendiary bombs dropped from B-29 bombers. The administration rejected that approach as too harsh and effectively handcuffed his ability to prosecute the air war over Korea in a way that he believed would ultimately save lives and bring it to a quicker close. His frustrations were acute, as he later articulated in a 1975 oral history he recorded for the Air Force: "What I'm trying to say is, if once you make a decision to use military force to solve your problem, then you ought to use it and use an overwhelming military force. . . . Deliberately use too much so that you don't make an error on the other side and not quite have enough. . . . You save resources, you save lives—not only your own but the enemy's, too. And the recovery is quicker, and everybody's back to peaceful existence hopefully in a shorter period of time."[10]

LeMay's outspoken advocacy of using all-out force made its way into the intelligence briefings the KGB sent to Moscow, making him one of the most feared U.S. military leaders in Soviet eyes because he was so demonstrably dangerous. Even worse, he did not subscribe to the widely held view that preemptive strikes were somehow beneath the dignity of civilized nations. That view, embraced and enforced by the Truman administration, held that the nation would have to be attacked first, and with a level of force justifying an atomic-level response, before any such counterattack could be authorized. The best the nation could do was be ready.

LeMay regarded such attitudes as weakness and folly. "I believe our national leaders must be impressed with the need for taking the following specific steps. First, provide an overriding priority for the establishment of an intelligence system which will tell us the where and when of the enemy's atomic force. Second, place the Air Force on a war footing without further delay. Third, provide funds in such quantities as may be needed to ensure that the striking force will be operational as a long-range intercontinental force not later than July 1952, and fourth, reexamine present policies which imply that we must absorb the first atomic blow."[11] In other words, perhaps striking the first blow, rather than waiting for it to come to you, would be the smarter approach.

"LeMay left little doubt as to his belief that attacking first in a war, specifically a nuclear war, was warranted and necessary."[12]

Despite the distraction of Korea, LeMay remained devoted to what he regarded as the primary mission of countering the broader Soviet threat beyond Asia and preparing for the possibility of direct confrontation. The administration, all the way to Truman himself, concurred with LeMay's assessment that the Korean War was designed to be a sort of decoy, as if to draw the United States into Asia and concentrate its forces there, leaving Europe unguarded or underprotected. In June 1950, the president authorized the transfer of ninety Mark 4 nonnuclear atomic bomb assemblies[13] for military training at secret sites code-named Able, Baker, and Charlie, but better known, respectively, as Kirtland Air Force Base in New Mexico, Fort Hood in Texas, and Clarksville Base at Fort Campbell in Kentucky.[14] Three months later, North Korea invaded the south.

"Truman smartly worried that the Soviets would think that America was dropping its guard in Europe and see that as an opportunity to make a land grab. Truman agreed with a recommendation made by the Joint Chiefs to send two groups of B-29s to Europe as a show of force and as a quick reaction capability should it become necessary."[15] It was LeMay who urged that the Air Force deploy not just any B-29s but rather the nuclear-capable Silverplate B-29s designed specifically for the atomic missions over Japan. LeMay was pushing for an atomic-strike capability. Further, LeMay sought the deployment of Fat Man bombs to Europe, but the administration, aware of the heightened sensitivities should this plan become public knowledge, arranged to transfer Fat Man casings separately from their atomic cores. In order to help disguise what was happening, the Air Force began referring to those bombs more innocuously as M107s.[16]

Although other nations were approached, England was the only nation willing to entertain the idea of atomic preparedness. British Prime

Minister Clement Attlee, himself a socialist and loath to take measures that could be deemed by Moscow as provocative, was acutely concerned about British public reaction to a U.S. atomic deployment on his shores and insisted on total confidentiality. The absence of an atomic core also gave him plausible deniability: Without the core, the Fat Man was just another big, conventional bomb. What neither the Americans nor the Brits knew, however, was that a spy network at the most senior echelons of MI-6, Britain's foreign intelligence agency, was feeding details of American plans directly to Moscow. From an American perspective, the leaks were unforgivable and became fodder for those who argued that the British simply could no longer be trusted—especially given that an avowed socialist was now the head of government there. Even Attlee doubted the trustworthiness of his own cabinet members and forbade the discussion of nuclear matters during regular cabinet sessions.[17]

From a historical perspective, though, the infiltration by the so-called Cambridge Five British spies—Kim Philby, Guy Burgess, Anthony Blunt, John Cairncross, and Donald Maclean—might well have contributed mightily to the prevention of World War III. The fact that Moscow was made fully aware of the American deployment plans in Britain, coupled with the knowledge that LeMay was in control of it and that he subscribed to the doctrines of preemption and overwhelming use of force, likely convinced Stalin to think twice about a military incursion into Europe. Had Stalin not been informed of the American deployment plans, he might have been willing to risk a Europe invasion, reasoning that Soviet occupation forces would already be too well entrenched by the time the United States organized a response. Though it was not public knowledge at the time, LeMay and other American leaders were more than willing to launch a full-blown nuclear attack on Moscow if such an invasion happened.

Because of the threat posed by Stalin, the Truman administration took LeMay's side and supported his approach regarding pre-deployment of atomic attack forces and nuclear-capable weaponry. The National Security Council had come to the same conclusions in its now declassified NSC-68 study of Soviet military strength and expansionist intentions—and the assessment that the United States needed to prepare for a war involving atomic weapons.

The Soviets knew that their technological capabilities to compete in a nuclear war were years behind those of the United States. The Americans were well aware of their technological superiority but were nonetheless nervous about having so badly misjudged the status of Soviet atomic research and development. If they didn't know about this, what else didn't they know?

By 1950, the Americans were also keenly aware that their most secret atomic programs had been infiltrated, and that Communist spies seemed to be lurking everywhere. Because the priority in World War II was the defeat of Germany and Japan, which were thus the focus of espionage efforts, almost no effort had been put forth to develop a workable pro-U.S. spy network within the Soviet Union. So the Americans were flying blind in Russia, while Stalin had a crystal-clear view of everything the Americans were planning.[18]

Former Secretary of State Dean Acheson gave a prescient speech at the White House in 1950 that warned of the growing Soviet menace and counseled his compatriots to recognize that "the only way to deal with the Soviet Union, we have found from hard experience, is to create situations of strength. Wherever the Soviet detects weakness or disunity—and it is quick to detect them—it exploits them to the full." The experience to which he was referring was not just the Berlin blockade or the Soviet sweeps into Czechoslovakia, Hungary, and Bulgaria but also what was, in retrospect, the clear and obvious weakness in American security that allowed the KGB to infiltrate the Manhattan Project while inserting spies into the global security apparatus being devised by the United States and Great Britain.

Stalin saw weakness and exploited it. Did that make him devious and evil, or did it make the Americans and their British counterparts look weak and stupid? Acheson's assessment seemed to point to the latter, and he was among a growing host of military and political leaders, including LeMay, demanding a tighter hold over security. The ink was barely dry on Acheson's speech when congressional investigations began uncovering the vast extent of Soviet spy rings within the federal government. Alger Hiss was convicted in January 1950, while British atomic scientist Klaus Fuchs was disclosed the following month as having shared an enormous trove of Manhattan Project secrets with Moscow. Many more espionage revelations were soon to come.

So the two nations were locked in a competition in which each opted to play on a different playing field from the other. The Americans concentrated on developing and publicly displaying their overwhelming military capabilities, particularly on the nuclear front. The Soviets opted not to play to American strengths but rather to continue exploiting the nation's weaknesses.[19] Moscow concentrated on chipping away at American leaders' confidence by preventing them from obtaining an accurate intelligence assessment of Moscow's military capabilities and intentions while steadily infiltrating U.S. military programs and stealing secrets. The more the Americans learned about the extent of this infiltration, the less confident they became of the nation's ability to cow a defiant Moscow into submission.

LeMay was never among those who wavered in his confidence. He took control of the SAC ready to instill a mindset from the start: "We are at war now. So that, if actually we did go to war the very next morning or even that night, we would stumble through no period in which preliminary motions would be wasted. We would be ready to go *then*."[20] And he was absolutely ready. So ready, in fact, that he began drawing up plans to open the first Strategic Air Command base on foreign shores.

Britain agreed, albeit with a measure of reluctance, to host the first base. Attlee was, however, adamant from the start that any such basing plan be carried out in secret, with American forces maintaining the lowest profile possible, given domestic sensitivities over atomic weaponry and the prospect of accidentally provoking a war with the Soviets. Britons, like the rest of Europeans, were still far too weary of war to contemplate fighting for their survival once again. They needed time to rebuild and recuperate. Like their American civilian counterparts, Britons wanted to dance, dine, celebrate peace, and enjoy life without the constant burdens imposed by shortages and rationing.

British ambivalence led the United States to cast its net more widely into Europe in search of a more receptive, if not enthusiastic, basing site. One offshoot of NSC-68 was Operation Offtackle in 1949, which presented a more moderate assessment of Soviet military capabilities, perhaps as a way of convincing European governments that they could afford the risks of standing up to help. Offtackle was based on the assumption that, as of July 1, 1949, "war has been forced upon the United States by acts of aggression by the USSR and/or her satellites." Soviet allies were listed as Bulgaria, Romania, Hungary, Poland, Albania, Czechoslovakia, and China.

Then came even worse news: "Although the following countries would desire to ally with the Anglo-American powers their political or strategic situation would be so precarious that they could not be relied upon and would be likely to be rapidly overrun by the Soviet Union: Austria, Greece, Iran, Finland, West Germany, South China, and South Korea." France, Canada, Australia, and New Zealand could be relied upon as allies, but France would be too easily overrun in a war, making it infeasible as an atomic base, while the other three were too distant to provide the rapid-deployment capability the United States needed. The only country deemed steadfast from start to finish and ideally situated to host LeMay's SAC base was Britain.

"While the countries which have signed the Atlantic Pact will have improved economically and militarily, they will be unable, with the exception of the United Kingdom, to effectively resist being overrun and occupied by Soviet Forces," the Offtackle plan stated. "High governmental approval will be obtained and atomic weapons will be used by the United States. Atomic weapons will be used by the USSR if available. (Intelligence estimates indicate that the USSR will have no atomic bombs available in fiscal year 1950.)"[21]

Negotiations with Attlee over the SAC base were often tense and riddled with delays as the British government weighed the pros and cons. The cons were considerable, including that Attlee would face a possible vote of no confidence if the U.S. atomic forces deployment went public. There was also the possibility of a preemptive attack by the Soviets. The Joint Chiefs deemed that latter option a significant factor for political leaders to weigh. The pros were mainly that the United States would have a ready attack force in the event the Soviets launched a full-scale invasion. Pre-deployment meant the crucial difference between instant readiness versus waiting days to obtain Atomic Energy Commission transfer clearance, then load a Fat Man bomb onto a U.S.-based bomber, hopscotch the bomber and crew into an appropriate location in Europe, then launch the actual attack.

By that time, the Joint Chiefs predicted Soviet forces would have swept across Europe and become entrenched to the point that even an atomic attack could fail to dislodge them.

Additional cons listed by the Joint Chiefs included:

- "Destruction or neutralization of all forces of the Allies on the Eurasian land mass."
- "Disruption of the Allied war-making capacity by subversion and sabotage."
- "Disruption of vital Allied lines of communication by aggressive submarine warfare, mining and air operations."
- "Accomplishment of diversionary attacks on Allied-held territory for the purpose of causing mal-deployment of Allied forces."[22]

The Joint Chiefs began advocating a far more aggressive campaign for a preemptive first strike, arguing that "the atomic bomb would be a major element of Allied military strength in any war with the USSR, and would constitute the only means of rapidly inflicting shock and serious damage to vital elements of the Soviet war-making capacity. In particular, an early atomic offensive will facilitate greatly the application of other Allied military power with prospect of greatly lowered casualties. Full exploitation of the advantages to be obtained is dependent upon the adequacy and promptness of associated military and psychological operations. From the standpoint of our national security, the advantages of its early use would be transcending. Every reasonable effort should be devoted to providing the means to be prepared for prompt and effective delivery of the maximum numbers of atomic bombs to appropriate target systems."[23]

These were serious considerations for LeMay to take into account after he received the go-ahead from the Truman administration following heated negotiations with Attlee. The accord they ultimately reached was for the disassembled components of an atomic bomb to be transferred secretly to the SAC base in Britain, which was to be established at Mildenhall Royal Air Force Base with auxiliary bases spread across the country. The SAC already had deployed personnel at Mildenhall and nearby Lakenheath Royal Air Force Base, but Mildenhall was to be the first official base abroad for the U.S. atomic command (officially, that is, without an assembled atomic bomb).[24]

Among the thirteen crew members and forty SAC specialists chosen for the inaugural basing were Brigadier General Paul Thomas Cullen, a rising star in the Air Force whose exploits in aerial reconnaissance were world renown—celebrated by even Stalin himself—and Lieutenant Colonel James I. Hopkins, SAC's most senior B-29 atomic pilot and the only member of LeMay's staff who had actually commanded a plane on a wartime atomic mission—the U.S. attack on Nagasaki that effectively ended World War II.

Leaving LeMay behind at his command center outside Omaha, Nebraska, Hopkins and his team climbed aboard C-124 Globemaster No. 49-244 at Walker Air Force Base in New Mexico. Walker was a 200-mile drive southeast of Albuquerque, where Kirtland Air Force Base served as one of three secret repositories for the nation's growing arsenal of nuclear bombs. The Globemaster's cargo consisted of two large crates, each big enough to fully contain a Fat Man, along with assorted items that, on the manifest, almost exactly matched the weight of a Fat Man atomic bomb. On March 21, 1951, they departed Walker for Barksdale Air Force Base in Louisiana, where they picked up Cullen and a few others, then took off for a refueling and rest stop at Limestone Air Force Base in Maine. From there, they departed for the jump across the Atlantic to Mildenhall.

Ground crew members watched as the lumbering Globemaster disappeared into the nighttime darkness over Maine. The C-124 would never be seen again.

The Soviet Union had the intelligence capability to learn about this flight in advance. The Soviet Union had a strong motivation to make sure the Globemaster never reached its destination. Moscow had a strong motivation to capture not only the cargo aboard 49-244 but also the two most prominent personalities onboard—Cullen and Hopkins—because of their highly valued expertise in areas where the Soviets were far behind their American counterparts. The Soviet Union had the capability to intercept the flight in midair and force it to ditch in the Atlantic using various means, including sabotage. But an unfortunate, though unlikely, series of disastrous mechanical and equipment failures also could have led to the same result.

The unanswered questions remain to this day: What brought down Globemaster 49-244? And even though survivors were spotted by at least one search plane, why did they disappear without a trace?

CHAPTER 2

A General's General

IF THERE WERE ONE WORD THAT COULD BEST DESCRIBE GENERAL Curtis LeMay's military philosophy, it would be *preemption*. The general's upbringing and grounding in war-fighting strategies pointed to the singular, unifying understanding of the consequences when an enemy is allowed to gain the element of surprise. Aggressors advance their cause most effectively by striking first and striking hard. Hitler overwhelmed Europe by striking overwhelmingly before his target nations even knew what hit them. Japan gained the upper hand in the Pacific by attacking Pearl Harbor and decimating the American naval fleet even before the United States had joined the Second World War on the side of the Allies. One way of looking at it, from LeMay's perspective, is that the ability to strike first and strike hard is the best way to disarm an enemy before it has a chance to fight back. If you know who the enemy is and what it is capable of—and that it is preparing to strike at you—then it didn't make any sense in LeMay's way of thinking to wait for that strike to happen. Another way of looking at it, based on his own experience growing up during World War I and entering battle in World War II, was that of understanding the consequences of complacency and hesitation. If you maintain a no-first-strike posture and wait for the enemy to attack, you automatically put your forces at a strategic disadvantage.

"I will know from my own intelligence whether or not the Russians are massing their planes . . . for a massive attack against the United States," LeMay stated in a closed-door briefing of two Eisenhower administration officials in 1957. "If I come to that conclusion, I'm going to blow the shit out of them before they get off the ground." One of the two administration officials, Robert C. Sprague, challenged LeMay by saying this was not the administration's policy. He recalled LeMay replying, "No, it's not national policy, but it's my policy."[1]

LeMay's policy when speaking in public was that he had no policy nor any position regarding preemption versus no-first-strike. His job, he stated publicly, was to carry out the orders of the commander in chief. But privately, he made clear exactly where he stood, including at a top secret 1950 meeting of Air Force generals, where he made a lengthy and impassioned argument for the Air Force command jointly to press the Truman administration to "re-examine present policies which imply that we must absorb the first atomic blow."[2]

LeMay also believed that the very nature of war required brutality. Enemies don't drop to their knees because a nation waves its weaponry and merely threatens severe consequences. Enemies who are given a chance to brace themselves and absorb the early blows are more likely to endure and live to fight again than an enemy attacked with such overwhelmingly brutal force that it has no chance to get to its knees, much less stand and fight back. The firebombing of Germany, followed by the firebombing of Japan, followed by the nuclear bombing of Hiroshima and Nagasaki, bore the trademarks of LeMay's war-fighting philosophy. He may well go down in history as the most brutal, mass-murdering general ever to command an American fighting force. He didn't give a rat's ass what history had to say about his methods. LeMay also might go down in history as the most effective—that is, victorious—general ever to lead an American fighting force. For that, he would no doubt have been proud, though he would never have admitted it. His public and private statements indicated he cared little about fame or worried about infamy. What Curtis LeMay cared about were results. The public and, more importantly, multiple U.S. presidents had come to know him as a general who delivered results when others couldn't.

What the public has known far less about, however, are LeMay's failures and shortcomings. The disappearance of Globemaster 49-244 is perhaps the most glaring example. Rather than openly acknowledge that a mission went badly awry on his watch, LeMay strived to get as far away from accountability as he could. He made not a single public comment, not even to express sympathy for the families of the victims. He wrote two blandly worded letters of condolence. Even in cases where he personally knew the men onboard and had socialized with them, as was the case with Lieutenant Colonel Hopkins, LeMay responded to the tragedy with complete, almost cowardly, silence. Because his Strategic Air Command was headquartered outside Omaha, the Nebraska newspapers covered virtually every appearance and statement by LeMay (as well as his wife's social engagements). Yet they carried not even a whisper or hint of sympathy from LeMay or anyone else in his command when Globemaster 49-244 disappeared. In fact, unlike virtually every other newspaper in the country, those newspapers barely covered the disaster at all.

While the biggest naval and air search in U.S. history took place to scour the North Atlantic for survivors in the week after the Globemaster went down, the *Omaha World-Herald* focused on the Air Force's appreciation for the financial support the local business community had shown to help upgrade housing at Offutt Air Force Base. LeMay himself even made a statement calling the community's $40,000 donation an "outstanding example" of public support for the SAC base.[3] Yet LeMay offered not a word about the missing Globemaster or the fifty-three men who had been aboard.

A mere three days after the plane's disappearance, the *World-Herald* did turn its focus on Air Force atomic missions and LeMay's role in commanding the nation's only nuclear force. Except the story offered not even a sentence about the Globemaster disaster, dealing instead with the complications of operating and crewing the Air Force's new B-36 bomber.[4] The front page of the *World Herald* that Sunday—a day when most major newspapers around the country and Britain were devoting above-the-fold, front-page coverage to the Globemaster search—seemed entirely uninterested in it. There was an above-the-fold story about a bizarre claim by Argentina's Juan Perón that his country had produced atomic energy using the same technology employed to create the American atom bomb. There was another story about the clear skies and nice weather expected for Easter, and another about a mother reported to be the smallest woman in the world who had given birth to a four-pound baby boy. And just above that, occupying about two inches of column space at the bottom of the page, was a brief about a valise that was found in the Atlantic belonging to one of the fifty-three men onboard the Globemaster. The article mentioned nothing about the Strategic Air Command's connection to the flight. The newspaper was all but disavowing any knowledge of the mission. The next sixty pages of the *World-Herald* offered nothing. If determined readers made it all the way to page 63, there they would find a story about the Strategic Air Command and its new mission in Europe. But, again, the story was not about the disappeared Globemaster. Rather, it was about the importance the SAC was placing on accompanying its big bombers with fighter jets to keep them safe from would-be aggressors.[5]

In fact, the only day when the newspaper devoted significant coverage to the plane's disappearance was on March 24, 1951, when a search plane reported sighting a life raft, flares, and wreckage nearly 600 miles off the coast of Ireland. The front-page Associated Press story, whose headline offered no hint of any local connection, did note that a brigadier general was onboard along with what it said were four officers from the Strategic Air Command. At the bottom, five other Air Force members "from this area" also were listed as being aboard. And that was all the newspaper had to report on the incident.[6] It was almost as if some influential person in the area had lobbied for the hometown newspaper of the Strategic Air Command not to make a big deal out of the plane's disappearance. *The New York Times*, by contrast, carried the story as its front-page lead that day. But even *The Times* was unable to get a comment from the cigar-chomping general in command of the botched Globemaster mission.

LeMay's response in this case merits a close examination and perhaps a reexamination of his other wartime exploits to determine whether the hero's mantle he assumed was entirely warranted or simply served to hide a record pockmarked with deadly serious flaws. Not everything involving Curtis LeMay was imprinted with his golden touch.

Make no mistake, LeMay was exactly the kind of brash, bold, confident leader the Army Air Forces and, subsequently, the U.S. Air Force needed to win World War II and serve warning to the Soviet Union in the early days of the Cold War. Like General George Patton, LeMay cultivated the image of a fearless wild man who could wreak havoc on enemy forces with whatever resources the military command put at his disposal. The Soviet leadership didn't know what to make of him, which forced them to assume more of a defensive posture when they contemplated any moves that risked tangling with LeMay's bomber fleet. In many ways, he was a smarter tactician than Patton and was certainly more adept at controlling his emotions and public statements. Almost to a fault.

Whereas Patton slapped a battle-addled soldier and inflicted serious diplomatic damage with his well-publicized anti-Soviet remarks at a moment when the White House was trying hard to hold its fragile World War II alliance together, LeMay chose his words cautiously, employing every bit the precision with which he planned out his bombing campaigns. Sometimes, though, he was a little too precise, too focused. He was so mission driven that he tended to forget the emotions of the people living out there in the real world. The move of the Strategic Air Command to Offutt, deep in the middle of the country and designed to be beyond range of any Soviet attack force, was one such case where LeMay could have mustered just a modicum of zeal for his new home when local reporters came looking for a good quote about any positive effect the city of Omaha might enjoy from being chosen as SAC's new headquarters.

Omaha wasn't just proud to have been chosen; it was ecstatic. Political and business leaders saw the basing decision as a boon to the war-ravaged economy and a way to put Nebraska on the map as something more than a way station for cattle heading to slaughter. Leaders wanted to know that the World War II hero coming to their town shared their enthusiasm. Instead, LeMay replied gruffly to reporters, "It doesn't mean a damn thing to Omaha, and it doesn't mean a damn thing to me."[7] The comment apparently was designed to convey that the mission of protecting the United States from attack would proceed regardless of where the SAC was based. LeMay later clarified, somewhat clumsily after being admonished by his wife, that the SAC was in such a state of disrepair and disorganization at the time, he didn't think the basing decision would be an asset for Omaha.[8] Even that pseudo-apologetic explanation fell flat.

LeMay almost immediately recognized the gravity of his mistake when he assessed that one of his first priorities after taking up command was to upgrade the housing available to officers and airmen at the base. Just like the decrepit conditions the 509th Composite Group had to endure during their pre-Hiroshima Fat Man training at Wendover, Utah, the tar-paper-and-cinder-block design of housing at Offutt was cutting into morale and making life difficult for his officers at home. The military could no longer get away with asking wives to keep sacrificing at a time when the rest of the country was indulging in the bounty of a booming postwar economy. The Air Force denied his request for a greater budgetary outlay to upgrade housing, so the general took the unusual step of appealing to the Omaha community for help—that is, the same community he appeared to have dismissed with his "doesn't mean a damn thing" quote. Shrugging off the insult, the business community rallied on his behalf to come up with the $40,000 in donations that dominated the local news and helped distract local readers from the Globemaster debacle that had just unfolded in the North Atlantic.

That episode with reporters underscored one of the most obvious weaknesses in LeMay as a military leader: the ability to emote. A person responsible for sending thousands of his airmen to their deaths and for raining terror upon hundreds of thousands on the ground below should have been able to articulate some kind of basic human empathy for the tragedy he helped inflict on their lives. But from LeMay, they got nothing.

Even his own daughter, Jane, complained of his long absences as a father and his almost frigid responses when she and her mother greeted him after his return home. She resorted to insisting that her father sit with her on the front porch of their home in Omaha, despite the cold temperatures at the time, just so the other kids on the block could see that she had a father, just like them. "I had made such a big deal about sitting on the porch because I wanted everybody to know: Yes, I really did have a father. So, I remember that he sat out on the porch. It was below-zero weather, but we sat out. I don't think anybody else saw us. We were the only ones sitting out on the porch."[9]

LeMay's image as a hard-ass—and "hard-ass" was one of the nicknames his airmen gave him—was bolstered by the near-constant presence of the cigar he kept tucked between his lips and jowl. LeMay even posed for military portraits with the cigar in place. To the public, it seemed as if he was using the cigar to cultivate the tough-guy image, but the simple fact was that he suffered from Bell's palsy, which caused the muscles on the right side of his face to relax slightly. He had physical difficulties showing what he was thinking through facial expressions. Although Sigmund Freud might have offered a different explanation about the cigar, it served in large part to exercise his cheek muscles and keep his face from drooping farther. The palsy also served to limit LeMay's ability to smile, again conveying the image of someone for whom emotions were a waste of time and energy.

The bottom line is that emotions and emotional expressions were not LeMay's strong suit. He had a way of reducing complex equations involving noncombatant death tolls and collateral damage to a simple question: What would this versus that action yield in terms of advancing the quest for victory? If the answer meant a hard, cold acceptance that thousands of airmen would die or be maimed because of his air-attack strategies, or tens of thousands of noncombatants would die in an atomic holocaust, or that tens of thousands more would die horribly painful firebombing deaths by being coated with napalm, LeMay seemed not to struggle emotionally as long as the chosen option yielded victory.

In that sense, yes, he was, indeed, one coldhearted son of a bitch, and LeMay himself would probably have agreed with that assessment.

LeMay had the rare ability to sweep aside emotions when it came to undertaking a mission. He sifted through any thoughts or concerns about human life to boil the issue down to its essence: What is the fastest and clearest route to winning the war? If the sacrifice of life, be it tens of thousands of civilians or thousands more of his own men, was what it took to yield that victory, in LeMay's eyes, it was worth it. He left it to history to decide whether his judgment was correct, and to this day, history has yet to reach a verdict.

A Pulitzer Prize–winning photograph attributed to Nick Ut during the Vietnam War brought home the realities of napalm's brutality to an American audience that had rarely borne witness to the horrors inflicted by LeMay's blind quest-for-victory mentality. It was June 8, 1972. A little girl, Phan Thi Kim Phuc, was running naked down Highway 1, clearly screaming in pain and terror. Her clothing had burned off; her skin was melting away after having been caught in a napalm bombing by the South Vietnamese Air Force. Behind her, soldiers nonchalantly strolled, either unaware of her pain or so numbed by the human suffering they had witnessed in the war that this scene posed nothing new to them.

Although the napalm used against Phan and her family was dropped by a South Vietnamese unit, the use of the chemical as a mass destruction firebombing tool was masterminded decades earlier by Curtis LeMay. He also rationalized its use, deadly and destructive as it was, as a means to *save* lives in the long run—the same rationale he used to justify the atomic bombings of Hiroshima and Nagasaki. In his book, *Mission With LeMay: My Story*, the explanations for his resort to firebombings and nuclear warfare seem plausible. In the case of Japan, LeMay argued, all indications from that country's military leadership were that they planned to keep fighting to the death—even after at least 100,000 were killed in LeMay's intensive firebombing campaign, followed by the deaths of 165,000 more in the Hiroshima and Nagasaki bombings.[10] LeMay also cited the willingness of 10,000 civilians and 97% of military personnel to choose suicide over surrender on the island of Saipan as an indication of the horrors to come if the United States was forced to conduct a ground invasion of the Japanese mainland.[11] By the estimates he cited, tens of thousands more U.S. troops would likely have been killed if the ground invasion had occurred. In that regard, LeMay's claim seems at least plausible that the net result of the atomic bombing and firebombing of Japan was, ultimately, a far lower death toll on both sides.

In the case of Germany, the napalm firebombing of Dresden in February 1945 wiped out thirteen square miles of the city and killed up to 40,000 civilians. That joint operation by British and American bombers provided LeMay with the blueprint of success he was looking for to justify what he accomplished later that year in Japan. The general abandoned the idea of precision targeting to take out, say, a ball-bearing factory that kept German tanks and military vehicles rolling in favor of carpet-bombing across a vast expanse. The toll in terms of military casualties and material damage was unprecedented while the cost in terms of collateral noncombatant deaths was extreme.

By today's standards, the bombings would likely constitute prosecutable war crimes, but they were considered a legitimate option by LeMay.[12] Still, he was keenly aware of the U.S. civilian leadership's strong objections to firebombing. Some had labeled it "terror bombing." Five years after Japan's surrender, North Korea launched an invasion that prompted the United States and United Nations to intervene in South Korea's defense. Drawing from his experience in Japan, LeMay advocated a similar firebombing strategy but it was rejected outright as inhumane. Napalm saw a brief resurgence in the Vietnam War, only to disappear when photos such as the one of Phan Thi Kim Phuc exposed the horror it inflicted. LeMay remained adamant that the horror of mass bombings, bad as it was, ultimately reduced the human toll by ending wars sooner.

"Once you are in a position where you are compelled to use military force, or in a position where you decide that military force is the only solution to the problem, then you resort to military force. The quicker you complete that military action, the better for all concerned."[13]

All that said, LeMay wasn't interested in victory at any cost, no matter the war the United States was fighting. He clearly had his doubts, for example, about the way the war was being prosecuted in Korea. LeMay was uninspired by the justification for intervening and even less inspired by the man prosecuting the war, General Douglas MacArthur. He was careful not to antagonize MacArthur but perhaps equally careful not to further empower him. When the appeal came for the Strategic Air Command to supply bombers for the Korean effort, LeMay complied, sending some of his older B-29s and making sure none of them were the Silverplate variety capable of dropping an atomic bomb. MacArthur's appeals for access to the bomb went largely ignored. On this, LeMay and Truman were in lockstep. MacArthur, in Truman's opinion, was too unhinged to be trusted with the most powerful weapon in human existence. LeMay was happy to keep MacArthur immersed in Korea because it allowed the SAC commander to focus on what he deemed the far bigger threat: the growing potential of a Soviet invasion of Europe.

LeMay's perspective changed when it came to the war in Vietnam. He was now the top commander, meaning he could no longer choose which wars he wanted to support versus those he would watch as an observer. By this time, "Bombs-Away LeMay" had gained a reputation as the top hawk among hawks, criticized even by Defense Secretary Robert McNamara—himself no wallflower when it came to inflicting mass casualties—as being perceived as "brutal."[14] LeMay also did himself no favors on the public relations front by agreeing to run for vice president on Alabama Governor George Wallace's third-party ticket in 1968. The juxtaposition of napalm, mass civilian casualties in Asia, and a right-wing retired general campaigning alongside a presidential candidate known for having racist views gave LeMay the public image of someone who placed a low value on certain types of human life.

Even in 1951, few aside from perhaps his wife and daughter would have mistaken LeMay for an empathetic handwringer when it came to large-scale deaths among those who served under his command. Where it matters in terms of Globemaster 49-244 and its fifty-three passengers and crew, however, boiled down to a question of accountability.

It was one thing for LeMay to rationalize their disappearance as a cost of war or a necessary sacrifice to hold the Soviets in check. But he never appears to have held himself even slightly accountable for the egregious security flaws that left this top secret mission vulnerable to infiltration and sabotage. Those flaws could be traced back to LeMay's decision to elevate a man whose personal life was a legal trainwreck and a security nightmare.

It was on LeMay's watch that a brigadier general, Paul Thomas Cullen, was brought onboard to head up the transfer of an atomic attack force to Britain even though some in the command were aware that Cullen had been up to activities that certainly merited deeper investigation, including an off-the-books trip to Mexico for the purpose of secretly marrying a second wife without the benefit of having divorced his first wife.

The fact that Cullen was capable of lying about the affair, engaging in egregious acts of marital infidelity, and sneaking outside the country to hide his bigamy merited far more scrutiny than occurred under LeMay's command. Someone on the senior staff should have asked the simple question: If this man could so wantonly violate military code, be so disloyal to his wife, and engage in such blatant acts of legal evasion, could he also be disloyal to his country? Then there's the question of his second wife's background and familial roots in Lithuania. None of this is to suggest that Cullen and his second wife, Reva Joy Hurwitz Cullen, did anything to deliberately betray their country, only that LeMay, as the commander whose primary duty was to manage deployment of the nation's atomic arsenal, should have placed security and background checks at the top of his list of priorities. LeMay did not. Or he delegated that responsibility to others who neglected to do their jobs. Either way, the buck should have stopped with the commander. LeMay took no responsibility.

At the time he took over the SAC in 1948, the U.S. Air Force was confronting a serious recruitment and morale crisis, and the nuclear forces under LeMay's command proved no exception. Their equipment was in terrible shape. The pilots and crew members were undertrained, unprepared for war, and out of shape as a fighting unit. They couldn't come even slightly close to hitting a target. SAC, LeMay wrote, "in its infant stages was one shockingly ill-organized, ill-equipped, nonfunctioning military operation, and everyone in the upper echelons of the Air Force knew it. It is no coincidence that SAC had an appalling accident rate. Worse, nobody seemed to care. In 1947, SAC ran a simulated test. Out of the 180 planes in its command, 101 could not even get off the ground."[15]

People inside and outside the military were tired of being in a constant state of wartime readiness, and even those who shared LeMay's concern about the Soviet menace seemed to regard his zeal for action as bordering on irrational. He wanted his fighting forces to embrace his sense of urgency, of crisis, over the potential of a Communist invasion of Europe. What he got in reply from his men, along with the general public, was a collective yawn. The public was done with war and the stresses and sacrifices it imposed.

The families of the men who opted to stay in the military after the war found their patience tested at every turn. "'Genteel poverty' was a term used to describe the threadbare existence of military families; vacations, good schools, elective orthodontia for children, and other perks enjoyed by civilians in comparable positions were not available to those in the military," LeMay wrote of the difficulties he faced in persuading talented people to choose the Air Force over civilian life.[16] The U.S. Air Force, preceded by the Army Air Forces, had spent hundreds of millions of dollars training the pilots who survived the missions over Europe, Africa, and the Pacific. And now those experienced pilots had the option of jobs in the private sector flying commercial passenger planes. Perhaps there was still some sexy allure in this new Air Force thing, but they couldn't make the argument to their wives and children that the sacrifice was worth it if the military continued to impose upon them the decrepit conditions that existed on bases like Offutt.

Various forces and pressures were pushing and tugging and demanding his attention all at once. He had priorities to keep men (and their wives) happy on his bases. He had to help prosecute a hot war in Korea. And the threat of a Soviet sweep across Europe demanded that he rush into existence a new SAC command to be based in Britain and equipped to launch an atomic strike at a moment's notice.

Somehow in all this, LeMay's attention appears to have wandered, and a planeload of his handpicked officers and enlisted atomic specialists experienced some kind of disastrous encounter over the Atlantic on the eve of the new command's establishment. LeMay had a lot to answer for, but he had no answers whatsoever.

CHAPTER 3

International Man of Mystery

PAUL THOMAS CULLEN POSSESSED TALENTS AND INSIGHTS THAT few others in the Army Air Forces could claim back in the early 1940s. He not only was an ace pilot whose exploits over Europe, Ukraine, and Africa were well documented in Army records and newspaper coverage, but he also had devised new technologies to map war zones using aerial photography that would later generate their own accolades.

Up to his date of entry into the Army Air Forces in 1928 and even a decade beyond, more than 90% of the world had remained uncharted.[1] The flat-grid maps that existed at the time were largely useless in terms of providing pilots with the specificity required to navigate accurately and drop a bomb squarely on target. Pilots understood the concept of lead time, that is, releasing a bomb long before the plane was overflying the intended target because of the arc that the bomb would have to travel, given the speed of the plane and the pull of gravity toward the target. They even understood the drift coefficient caused by wind. But to come even close to hitting the target from the much higher elevations required of bombers in World War II, pilots needed detailed maps and photos of identifiable features on the ground miles before they were over their target. Identifying those ground features was how pilots, navigators, and bombardiers knew they were on or off track.

No technology existed to give them the specificity they required. Which meant that thousands upon thousands of bombs hit far off their mark, leading to untold collateral damage, civilian casualties, expensive waste, and, worst of all, the survival of the target itself. Enemy fighters survived to fight again. Fuel and weapons depots went untouched. A bomb that missed its target was worse than useless, especially when the enemy was as formidable as Germany as it swept across Europe, the Middle East, and North Africa.

Cullen completed his first course in aerial photography in July 1931 and subsequently assumed command roles with the various squadrons to which he was assigned. A year later, Cullen experienced his first of three crash landings—an unusually high number for any airman. In this case, he was not piloting the plane but nonetheless experienced that shock of a forced landing in heavy fog on a cornfield in New York State while conducting aerial photographic work. His story of survival was retold in news accounts, the first among hundreds to come focusing on Cullen's exploits. He was a true survivor.

In 1933, the *Pittsburgh Sun-Telegraph* carried a feature photo of then-Lieutenant Cullen brandishing a giant aerial camera with the unprecedented ability to take an amazing "110 pictures with one loading."[2] The Army in 1935 assigned him to head up the first publicized case of high-altitude aerial photography being used to map a key ground feature, in this case the New York State barge canal system near Syracuse.[3]

In 1938, Cullen was appointed chief instructor of the photo department at Lowry Field in Denver. That's where he met Ruth Gravett, the daughter of a local minister. They married, and the couple moved into a tiny, single-story house on Olive Street. The newly built, treeless neighborhood with a view of the distant Rocky Mountains was just within walking distance of Cullen's air base.

After war broke out in Europe and Axis forces swept into North Africa, Cullen received a secret commission in mid-1941 to perform photo reconnaissance work for the British Royal Air Force. The mission involved some of the most dangerous work any airman could undertake because the planes were unarmed, unescorted, and had to fly close enough to Axis positions to photograph their ground installations. If Cullen's plane were shot down and he was captured, the United States would probably have had to disavow any association with his activities since, at the time, America was officially uninvolved in the war.

Ruth Cullen stayed behind in Denver, no doubt spending weeks or months at a time knowing nothing of her husband's whereabouts—or whether he was even still alive. After Cullen returned, he received a new assignment in Washington, where he and Ruth rented a house on Twenty-Eighth Street Southeast.

The Japanese attack on Pearl Harbor in December 1941 marked America's official entry into World War II. Again leaving Ruth behind, Cullen flew across the Atlantic to head up a series of clandestine reconnaissance missions over Africa the following January. It was during this phase that Cullen found himself in command of an equally dashing, attention-grabbing personality: Elliott Roosevelt, son of President Franklin Delano Roosevelt.

The two were assigned to carry out a mission that came from the president himself, dubbed Project Rusty. When Elliott Roosevelt was first briefed about it by his father, the young Army airman balked and protested. He wanted action and excitement. Project Rusty sounded like an assignment taking photos of Saharan sand, Eliott complained. He accused his father of deliberately arranging the assignment to keep him out of dangerous combat and as far away as possible from the headlines. "It seemed so tame to me that it was more than rusty, it was broken," Elliott recalled. His father quickly countered that this reconnaissance work was absolutely critical to the war effort by preventing the Germans from gaining control of the Suez Canal, denying them a jumping-off point to cross the Atlantic and occupy Brazil, and clearing a land-sea bridge to link up with allies Russia and China. Without this crucial preliminary effort, Germany and Italy could solidify their foothold in North Africa. Project Rusty had to be done.[4]

Elliott accepted, although he didn't seem entirely convinced. As fate would have it, Elliott was assigned as navigator/photographer aboard Paul Cullen's plane. As the pilot and senior officer aboard, Cullen bore an awesome responsibility as commander to the commander in chief's son.

It's unclear why Cullen took such an intense interest in photo reconnaissance, as opposed to favoring the bombing exploits of the pilots who trained on the same B-17s and, later, B-29s that he had learned to fly. The War Department no doubt had an ample supply of bomber pilots but precious few who understood the technology behind aerial photo reconnaissance. The Army—and the president—regarded his mission to be among the most important of the war and, despite the secrecy surrounding his work, saw to it that Cullen's name appeared regularly in news headlines.

Suddenly the Army had a breakthrough mapping technique that gave pilots a far greater ability to track their progress on a bombing run and deliver their bombs much closer to the target.

Few would've imagined that Cullen, this nerdy specialist in aerial photography, would find himself anointed with power and virtually untouchable by the military hierarchy because of the extraordinarily high level of contacts he established starting with Project Rusty. Cullen, as a mere lieutenant colonel in the Second World War, would find himself dining at the White House as the guest of President Franklin Delano Roosevelt. He would receive requests for demonstrations of his reconnaissance capabilities from the highest echelons of the U.S. military. Even Soviet dictator Joseph Stalin would take an interest in his technology, with the U.S. military's strong encouragement. What Paul Cullen said he wanted—in terms of personnel, the most modern equipment and aircraft, and plum assignments—he got.

No small portion of that special status was due to the fact that he commanded (and kept alive) the president's son. They became the daring dynamic duo, racing their small spy planes across North Africa in search of German installations and troop concentrations at a time when public discovery of involvement by the president's son on such dangerous clandestine missions—including some that occurred before America's formal entry into the war—would have been scandalous. Shooting down those planes or capturing the American president's son would have handed the Germans a propaganda coup of world-shaking proportions.

There were moments when such Axis efforts nearly came to fruition, but Cullen's expert piloting skills got them out of one mess after another. Where Elliott swashed, Cullen buckled. Cullen's natural tendency to lie low and avoid the spotlight enabled Elliott, described as a "born salesman,"[5] to claim all the glory for himself from their exploits during Project Rusty.

The Army Air Forces dispatched its best fighter pilots to North Africa under the command of Major General Russell Maxwell, based in Cairo. It was there, in early 1942, that Lieutenant Colonel Paul Cullen first crossed paths with a young B-25 fighter pilot, Captain James I. Hopkins. The goal was to use pilots like Hopkins to harass German ground forces and provide a diversion so that the unarmed planes flown by Cullen could perform their vital reconnaissance work.

It was no easy task to deploy these forces to their secret bases in Khartoum and Accra. Long accustomed to flying the route from U.S. air bases to England, or due east across the Atlantic to Lagens in the Azores, the Army command decided the risks of German detection and interception were growing too great. General Henry H. "Hap" Arnold, commander of the Army Air Forces, shut down the North Atlantic route in early 1942. That's when a far safer route was devised using friendly bases in South America as a stopover point for the easy jump from Brazil to Liberia or Khartoum and points farther east.

The reconnaissance team's job was to utilize a complex series of slightly offset cameras aboard their stripped-down B-17 to shoot stereographic images of the widest expanses of terrain they could cover. They would track back and forth, slightly overlapping the terrain they had just covered, until they had photographed all terrain in an entire region. The stereographic images helped mappers create more realistic 3D-style images to help pilots visualize mountains and valleys while making note of any German installations or encampments captured in the images. The plane, which flew as high as 30,000 feet, was painted sky blue to help it blend in with the background and make it harder for ground forces to pinpoint.[6]

Occasionally, they would encounter antiaircraft fire, but since their plane had been stripped of its defensive weaponry to reduce weight and save space for photographic equipment, the only option was to dip and dive and climb in hopes of evading the enemy. They returned stateside with death-defying stories that enraptured anyone with the clearance to qualify for a briefing, including the president and Eleanor Roosevelt.

The unveiling of their talents at melding maps with stereographic, geo-located photos could not have occurred at a more opportune time for Cullen's career. After the Japanese bombing of Pearl Harbor prompted America's formal entry into the war, British Prime Minister Winston Churchill received an almost unprecedented invitation to address a joint session of Congress during Christmas week of 1941. President Roosevelt invited Churchill to stay in the White House during his visit, and they conferred constantly about next steps in the war. Churchill had made an unusual request, which Roosevelt accommodated, to set up a separate room on the second floor of the White House devoted solely to the display of the prime minister's prized global maps, upon which he tracked the deployment of ships and troops to counter German, Italian, and Japanese offensives.[7] Once Roosevelt saw the maps and noted Churchill's attention to detail, he became hooked. The president no doubt delighted in revealing to Churchill that Roosevelt's son was now on the cutting edge of aerial photographic reconnaissance and producing new kinds of maps that would put Churchill's collection to shame.

Despite the high-level attention, the work itself was numbingly routine, if not outright boring. "It meant several months of painstaking work, mapping the whole of northwestern Africa from the air, by photographs, occasionally running into Fascist patrol planes, occasionally under fire, but by and large just getting a hot, dry job over with as expeditiously as possible," Elliott wrote.[8]

Barely five months after the U.S. entry into the war, when the top brass was scrambling to put together fighting forces capable of fending off enemies on two distant war fronts, memos from lower-ranking officers tended to be short and to the point, mainly for fear of testing the generals' patience and wasting their time with excess verbiage. In May 1942, Cullen submitted an unusually long, four-page, single-spaced memo to the commanding general of the Army Air Forces summarizing the status of German and Vichy French defenses in North Africa. It detailed the use of aircraft basing facilities in West and Central Africa and provided photographic intelligence of unprecedented quality and detail to assist with the command's planning. He identified airports and landing fields that American forces could utilize should the command decide to stage a surprise attack from the south on German installations farther north. He outlined what the Vichy French capabilities were and how the capture of their facilities would ease the burden on Allied forces to construct their own bases.

A separate section outlined Cullen's assessment of British capabilities, given their long-established colonial military presence in the region. Cullen went a bold step further, recommending "Logistical Requirements (Equipment, Supplies and Bases)" that the U.S. military would need to establish in Africa to counter the German buildup.[9] Cullen's correspondence detailed the sightings of more than 100 German military installations in North Africa that were previously unmapped and were identified either as worthy of attack or capture for reuse as an Allied asset.

The memo, written in the dry, unemotional style that characterized much of Cullen's prose, created a buzz among the command and served as the reference point for multiple follow-up memos among the senior command, including General Dwight Eisenhower. The attention Cullen received underscored his unique position as someone who could provide a rare service deemed absolutely essential to countering the German military's advance.

Cullen's reconnaissance missions continued through 1943 to 1944 over North Africa, providing crucial, real-time data pinpointing the location of Field Marshal Johannes Erwin Rommel's troop and tank placements so that American and British air forces could more effectively attack from the air while Allied artillery and ground forces proceeded with ground offensives. The result was the first German retreat of the war, and the top generals did not hold back in their assessment of the importance of Cullen's reconnaissance.

Cullen became a star in the news media as well, garnering the kinds of newspaper headlines that few military men of his rank could compete with. Rarely during the war did the news coverage reflect the top secret technology he was working on, only the flying exploits that put him and his crews in extreme danger. Referring to Cullen's back-and-forth flights sweeping the expanse of desert terrain and overflying German positions from Casablanca eastward to Tunis, the War Department stated "that the mission brought back the first complete photographs of Northern Africa expanses, and was one of the most significant examples of the importance of aerial photography in modern times," The Associated Press reported in 1943.[10] The AP account was published in scores of American dailies. Not once did Cullen raise objections to the publicity his missions were generating. All indications were that he basked in the attention. The photos that accompanied the articles depicted him as dark, handsome, and extremely serious.

One of the biggest difficulties in the Army Air Forces' effort to keep this mission secret was the fact that Elliott Roosevelt was a part of it. Unless Cullen and his crew confined themselves to the most obscure airstrip outposts in the African outback, they ran the constant risk of being spotted by outsiders who recognized the president's son. Perhaps because of an Elliott sighting, *The New York Times*'s prolific foreign correspondent C. L. Sulzberger managed to track the patterns and locations of the reconnaissance flights and publish them in a *Times* report that noted that "America's immense, if slow-moving, war effort" was "making itself more and more evident in Africa."

Sulzberger managed to identify many of the very bases where the American reconnaissance crews were landing or overflying, then offered the caveat, "While it would be indiscreet for obvious military reasons to describe in any detail the exact course of the air-transport route as traveled by the writer [Sulzberger], certain broad descriptions are permitted." He listed the "jungles and deserts of the vast area between the Niger delta and the Nile," followed by Khartoum, Liberia, the Gold Coast, Eritrea, and Sudan.[11] These were the exact areas being photographed by Cullen and his crew.

In another dispatch, he wrote about a joint Allied spying and transport network, adding, "Whether this information is correct cannot be ascertained, but it is no secret that the United Nations [the Allies united against Germany and Italy] are keeping up a steady watch abetted by occasional aerial reconnaissance."

While other American officers traveled in blissful anonymity, Elliott Roosevelt found that his every move was recorded in print under headlines such as "Elliott Roosevelt Is in Africa," "Elliott Roosevelt in Hospital," "Elliott Roosevelt Leaves Cairo," and "Elliott Roosevelt in London" (this latter headline occurred in *The New York Times* a full four months before the United States entered the war). The newspaper reports typically described him as leading or commanding a photographic reconnaissance group, clearly ignoring the fact that the actual commander was Cullen. The latter had every reason to be bitter at the way his hard work was credited to someone who owed his rise through the military ranks less to talent than heritage.

American reporters were hardly the only ones paying attention to Cullen and Elliott Roosevelt's exploits. Soviet analysts also were reporting on the significance of aerial photo reconnaissance as a game changer in the war. Writing years later about this era, Red Army officers Y. G. Makarov and N. P. Rozhdestvin cited multiple wartime successes against German offensives and attributed those successes to aerial reconnaissance. They quoted one field officer as saying, "Photo reconnaissance is our mainstay, for without it we are virtually blind. Ground observation cannot furnish a commanding officer all the information he needs; only when I have before me aerial mosaics showing me not only the front line but the depth of the terrain ahead can I properly make tactical decisions based on these and other intelligence available."[12] The Soviets, envious of American advances, began looking for ways to copy Cullen's technology for their own use. American libraries and newspaper coverage provided them with a road map of sources to get what they needed. Just as Paul T. Cullen was gaining attention at the highest echelons of the U.S. government and military, so was his fame resonating in Moscow. Elliott Roosevelt would wind up being among those who brought Cullen's talents directly to Joseph Stalin's attention.

Cullen returned to Washington in July 1942 to become commander of the Army Air Forces' First Mapping Group. On June 9, 1943, he was piloting a modified B-17 bomber, outfitted with surveillance equipment, when he overshot the runway at St. Louis Lambert Field and crashed into nearby Coldwater Creek.[13] The plane was a total loss, and two of his crew members were seriously injured. The St. Louis newspapers covered the crash heavily, with unflattering front-page photos appearing in both the *St. Louis Globe-Democrat* and *St. Louis Post-Dispatch*. Cullen suffered back injuries severe enough to prevent him from flying, and the Army Air Forces relieved him of his command. He returned to Washington, where Ruth spent the next several months nursing him back to health.

His recovery was quick enough to not completely derail his career, but the pause allowed others to advance in his absence. Elliott Roosevelt, eight years Cullen's junior and far less experienced in the field, leapfrogged over his former commander to become a full colonel. Now Elliott was the boss, meaning Cullen had to answer to him. Such were the perks of being the president's son.[14]

CHAPTER 4

Frantic Joe

IN EARLY 1944, THE TOP COMMANDER OF THE ARMY AIR FORCES, General Hap Arnold, devised a pre–D-Day plan to attack German forces in Europe by staging an aerial assault from Germany's less-protected eastern flank. The idea was to put German forces on the defensive and force them to divert crucial assets to protect the eastern flank, leaving their forces in France and Belgium more vulnerable to U.S. and British forces preparing for the D-Day invasion.

The problem Arnold's idea sought to solve was that too many strategic sites deep behind German lines were going to be untouched by Allied bombers because of the distance the bombers had to traverse before running out of fuel and having to return to base. The logistical problem underscored the limited distance a B-29 could fly without running low on fuel. Those sites would be more accessible if bombers could take off, say, from Soviet bases, attack their targets, then continue directly to Allied bases on the other side rather than have to turn around and traverse the same primed German defenses they had just escaped in order to return to base. Or, conversely, the missions could originate from Britain, bomb German targets, then land on the Soviet side. The shuttle strategy would be safer for the crews and save fuel by dramatically cutting thousands of miles from the distance flown.[1]

For the plan to work, Stalin needed to be convinced that it was not only viable, but, more importantly, that the Americans could be trusted if they were allowed access to Soviet bases. Some deft diplomacy was required to bring Stalin around. President Roosevelt organized a meeting in Tehran with Stalin and British Prime Minister Winston Churchill to discuss strategies and visions for a postwar division of regional influences. In a highly unusual move, Roosevelt decided that Elliott needed to be included as a military adviser in the official delegation.

The American president entrusted his son with the mission of pulling Stalin aside for private chats, building as much of a sense of trust as was possible with the Soviet dictator so he would reverse a long-standing policy that no foreign forces would be allowed to conduct wartime operations against Hitler's forces from Soviet territory.

To change Stalin's mind, Elliott Roosevelt captivated him with stories of derring-do from the North African front, which naturally would have meant bragging about what he and Cullen had been up to. Elliott worked hard to convince Stalin that the same positive results that aerial photographic reconnaissance had yielded in North Africa could be applied against Hitler's forces in Eastern Europe. It's not clear how detailed Elliott was allowed to get regarding the highly classified results of Cullen's work, but whatever he divulged was sufficient to change Stalin's mind. The Soviet dictator approved the flight of a limited American reconnaissance mission from a base in Russia to Ukraine for a demonstration of what this new American technology might yield.

Stalin remained skeptical of the merits of the next step, an aerial bombing campaign, but he needed little convincing of the merits of aerial reconnaissance. This was cutting edge, and it was clear from his perspective that the more Stalin could glean from this most advanced of American technology, the better for his long-term plans. Arnold chose Cullen to conduct the historic first shuttle flight of a U.S. combat plane into the Soviet Union, from England to Poltava, Ukraine.

Amid the deft diplomacy at Tehran before the flight, British Prime Minister Winston Churchill pulled the American president aside to warn him specifically not to divulge or cede too much to the Soviet dictator. President Roosevelt later recounted to his son about Churchill: "Trouble is, the P.M. is thinking too much of the *post*-war, and where England will be. He's scared of letting the Russians get too strong. Maybe the Russians will get strong in Europe. Whether that's bad depends on a whole lot of factors."[2]

It turned out to be very, very bad. Churchill was 100% correct in his assessment, and Cullen may well have wound up paying the price for Roosevelt's failure to take the British prime minister seriously.

Stalin wasn't as concerned about the threat from Hitler as he was obsessed with gaining access to American technological and spying secrets. This new method of aerial photographic reconnaissance seriously caught his attention. Stalin quickly approved Elliott's proposal for a series of test flights to demonstrate how the technology could work. But the American and British sides insisted the test flights would be meaningless unless they were followed by aerial bombardments using the new technology to pinpoint the geocoordinated Axis positions. That necessarily required the positioning of American and British bombers on Soviet soil. Stalin recoiled at the idea.

In February 1944, Stalin finally relented, but the only flight Stalin permitted in the beginning was a B-17 flown by Cullen along with Colonel John S. Griffith, the photo wing's overall commander. They arrived in Moscow on February 25, 1944, with reporters waiting on the ground to record what was a historic moment for both countries. Another colonel, Alfred Kessler, was to join them, but a bout of severe bronchitis and/or pneumonia delayed his departure from Cairo for ten days.

The mission had the express support of General Carl Spaatz, commander of the Army's Strategic Air Force and the top commander of the top secret Manhattan Project developing the two atomic bombs later deployed against Japan. Spaatz told Cullen and Griffith in no uncertain terms that they were to sell the combo reconnaissance–shuttle bombing plan to their Soviet hosts as the next crucial step in halting Hitler's advance.[3] But it was only after Cullen and Griffith had arrived in Moscow, where they received briefings from U.S. Ambassador Averell Harriman and Major General John R. Deane, that the two airmen became aware of another motive behind the operation code-named Frantic: to establish U.S. bases in Siberia for use in opening a new route to attack Japan (a tricky prospect since Stalin had yet to declare war against Japan). It was clear that senior-level talks with the Soviets were not delivering the results the Americans sought, so they put it on Cullen's shoulders to wow them with his reconnaissance technology, along with the results it delivered in terms of more accurate bombings of Axis targets.

Major General Fred Anderson, deputy commander of U.S. Army Strategic Air Forces, noted in his diary at the time: "This move is much larger than meets the eye. The establishment of bases in Russia for use in shuttle-bombing and shuttle-reconnaissance is a minor factor. If we are successful in this effort it may be of vital importance when we shift our entire attention to Japan and the Far East."[4]

When Cullen's decked-out reconnaissance plane landed in Russia, Griffith took the highly unusual step of allowing his Soviet counterparts to tour the American team's B-17, even permitting the Russians to examine the cherished, top secret Norden bombsight. The bombsight consisted of 2,000 cams, wheels, dials, lenses, and gauges to let a bombardier zero in on a target and simultaneously take control of the plane to guide it on a path to deliver the bomb directly on target. Crew members who boarded planes equipped with the Norden were required to sign a pledge that they would destroy it, and their plane if necessary, to prevent it from falling into enemy hands. Inventor Carl Norden was deemed such an essential asset to the war effort that he was provided a full-time government guard detail.

That's how precious his secret technology was. And yet, Cullen and Griffiths were handing it over for Soviet inspection. Perhaps it was a calculated risk, assuming that the device was so complicated that no one would be able to copy it, even if the Soviets were carrying hidden cameras.[5] But this access was precisely what Stalin was hoping for. The entire Soviet mission, it seemed, was to let the Americans do all the hard work of developing the world's most sophisticated weaponry and technology. Moscow's mission was to steal it by any means necessary.

The next step was for Cullen to demonstrate his spying technology, which involved another first: He piloted a flight on May 26, 1944, overflying German positions to land at a base in Ukraine. The flight, only days before the D-Day invasion, also required overflying Soviet military positions, which meant Cullen had to trust that his host forces wouldn't turn their guns on him, mistaking him for a German invader. Cullen was quoted telling Spaatz during a preflight meeting: "Usually all I have to worry about are enemy guns. Now I have to worry about the Russian guns, too."[6]

The headlines Cullen garnered across the country marked an almost unprecedented level of fame, access, and power for an Army officer of such a relatively low rank. Cullen was still just a lieutenant colonel. Because of Elliott Roosevelt's promotion to full colonel, he was now issuing orders to Cullen regarding the entire Poltava mission. By all accounts, Cullen was a man of few words, especially when it came to commentary about his relationship with Elliott and the fact that his subordinate—a mere navigator, no less—had leapfrogged him to become a photo reconnaissance wing commander. Cullen, blinded by resentment, seemed not to appreciate all the professional perks that accompanied an assignment with the president's son.

Cullen would later express his bitterness privately during an extramarital love affair. Elliott Roosevelt seemed fully aware that it was upon Cullen's shoulders that he had climbed and saw to it that Cullen received some of the most coveted and high-profile assignments any pilot could ask for. Others also noted the injustice of Elliott's promotion over his previous commander.

"In reference to Col. Paul T. Cullen, I know him personally and he is the officer that normally would have been promoted to Brigadier General if Elliott had not been around. I am not familiar with the background of his story, except that when I first met him I asked him if he knew Elliott. He looked me in the eye and said, 'I gave him his star' and then changed the subject," Major Joseph E. Benoit wrote in a letter to columnist Westbrook Pegler in 1947.[7]

The story of Cullen's flight was noteworthy not just because it was a historic first but also because it demonstrated the ability of two highly distrusting allies, Russia and the United States, to cooperate in the sharing of highly secret reconnaissance information for the sake of defeating Germany. That level of cooperation would prove to be short-lived, yet it served not only to put Paul Cullen's name in the headlines but to place him squarely on the radar of Soviet intelligence as a rising personality in the U.S. military renowned for his courage and reconnaissance expertise. He was a person to be watched, for sure. And the newspaper coverage was so thorough, articles even listed his parents' address at the time: 855 N. Sultana Avenue, San Gabriel, California, as well as his and Ruth Cullen's address in Washington.

Months later, Cullen's name again exploded into newspapers across the country when the Second Bombardment Group he commanded flew its 300th mission, no small feat for any unit in a war that typically saw the ranks decimated by daily downings from German flak and fighter planes. More nationwide headlines came when the same unit flew its 400th mission in May 1945. (The *Memphis Belle*, subject of a 1990 film, flew twenty-five combat missions.)

The fact that Cullen performed his missions to the full satisfaction of the Army's senior command while delivering the president's son back to the White House in one healthy, albeit exhausted, piece helped establish the high-level professional protections that would allow Cullen anointed status as one of the military's untouchables. Hap Arnold quickly rose through the senior ranks to become a five-star general of the Army in 1944 and general of the Air Force in 1949, the only person to have ever held that latter status and also the only person to have held more than one five-star rank. Arnold's embrace of Cullen and his photo-reconnaissance advancements, combined with enthusiastic endorsements from Generals Jimmy Doolittle and Hoyt Vandenberg, ensured Cullen a level of protection from any would-be predators among his peers as they clawed their way up the ranks. He had a comfort level enjoyed by few others at his level, even as others such as *Enola Gay* pilot Paul Tibbets found themselves constantly fending off challenges and surreptitious career-sabotage campaigns.

There also were precious few competitors for Cullen's job because, as Elliott Roosevelt so keenly observed, the world of photo reconnaissance was tainted with the aura of inconspicuous boredom—the exact opposite of the glamorous challenges most wartime pilots were seeking to burnish their air combat résumés.

Add to those endorsements the extraordinary access Cullen had to the president of the United States, through Elliott, and it soon became clear to Army officers at every rank that this was not someone to mess with. Generals fawned over him. Newspaper articles were replete with photos of him briefing the top brass about his new photographic toys. Cullen had lunch at the White House with the president and his son. He also dined with General Spaatz in London while commanders heard a briefing from Elliott about the meeting he had with Stalin in Tehran.

As a result of that London meeting, Cullen was handed responsibility for on-site management of the Frantic operation in Poltava as deputy commander of the Eastern Front, based in the Soviet Union. His reconnaissance reports on German activities along the front were delivered straight to General Spaatz in London,[8] making the general the only person standing between Cullen and Spaatz's immediate superior, Supreme Allied Commander Dwight D. Eisenhower.[9]

Stalin and his top generals also received Cullen's intelligence reports, further elevating his stature among his Communist hosts. His work involved daily interactions with his Russian counterparts working out the specifics of missions as well as finding solutions to the vast array of complaints registered by soldiers on Cullen's side and Russian civilians on the other. The tedium took a heavy toll on Cullen's morale.

Cullen ran into one roadblock after another while based behind Soviet lines. His Russian counterparts insisted on receiving no less than twenty-four hours' notice for any American military flights that crossed over the war front, a demand that was impossible to meet given the constant weather variations and equipment snafus that regularly altered the timing of a bombing run. The two sides finally reached a compromise of twelve hours' notice. (That accord was actually the genesis of Cullen's historic solo flight from Moscow to Kiev: to test the notification system and make sure it could be completed without the plane being subjected to Soviet ground fire.)

After being briefed about Cullen's flight, Stalin finally agreed to permit the American shuttle-bombing program using five specified air corridors and a ten-hour minimum advance advisory. But his generals were so unenthusiastic that they repeatedly neglected to inform their ground commanders about the flights. When the American shuttle-bombing planes flew over their positions, the Russian forces opened fire. Russian generals initially refused to modify a standing order that troops basically should shoot down anything that passed over them across the battle lines. B-17s returned to their bases riddled with bullet holes, but if any casualties resulted, they weren't serious enough to scuttle the program. Those incidents raised serious concerns on the American side about whether the Russians truly valued the military alliance and its generous perks.

Cullen spent five months in the country liaising with Soviet commanders, establishing secret bases for U.S. forces to land, and negotiating the minute details of what American personnel would be allowed to do off base versus what they would be specifically prohibited from doing.[10]

But once the flight was done and the attention died down, Cullen was faced with much more mundane tasks connected to his liaison duties with his Soviet hosts. U.S. troops were asking young Russian women out on dates and appearing in public with them, drinking, dancing, and holding hands. This outraged older Russians, who shouted catcalls and complained to Soviet military officials. It fell to Cullen to smooth ruffled feathers. Both sides had agreed that fraternization between Americans and Soviets should be encouraged to promote greater cultural understanding.

Problems arose, however, when American soldiers started bartering their food and clothing or trying to sell items straight off their supply trucks. Cullen's Soviet counterpart, Lieutenant General Alexander R. Perminov, confronted Cullen about the infractions. Cullen had his own list of complaints, which included incidents of Russian jeering and a generally harsh reception by some civilian men, along with insults hurled by Soviet women against any of their own who went out on dates with the visiting Americans.

The time Cullen spent in Russia apparently had the effect of wearing down his sense of mission. He became openly cynical about the merits of Frantic. When one of his Soviet counterparts, Lieutenant Colonel L. A. Neveleff, started berating the American intelligence command as "lacking authority, respect and definite orientation," Cullen made no attempt to defend his countrymen. "Cullen told Neveleff that the Military Mission in Moscow had 'failed to gauge the Russian reaction' properly, and that [Major General] Deane's office did not appreciate the value of intelligence." Cullen berated Frantic operations as "uneconomic and that the only justification for the operations is the bringing together of the two forces in the hopes they will learn to work together."[11]

Voicing complaints about his own commanders' competence to a Soviet officer constituted a tacit offer, in the eyes of the Russians, for cultivation of Cullen as a potential asset. He was disgruntled, talkative, and perhaps a little reckless. And rumor had it that he resented the way his hard work was stolen for self-promotion by the American president's son.

While news arrived of the D-Day landing at Normandy, followed by the American advances along the Western Front, Cullen and the troops of the Eastern Command concluded that their entire operation was little more than an exercise in diplomatic showmanship. Military historian Daniel Bolger asserted, “Cullen’s attitude pervaded the command. The slapdash, sometimes unskilled conglomerate of soldiers assembled for Eastern Command suffered a marked skid in morale. A special report on the morale problem over the summer of 1944 (completed by Eastern Command investigators on 5 October) pointed out the ‘purposeless idleness’ after Frantic II constituted the primary reason for low motivation. The troops knew that their duties were not important, and frustration was a very real feeling among them.”[12]

Cullen had gone from the heights of fame and military glory, celebrated by the president and senior-most echelons of the American military command, to running what he cynically regarded as a largely worthless operation. Having openly shared his cynicism with his Russian counterparts, Cullen helped create the impression that his loyalties were questionable. For someone like Stalin and his top advisers, the American colonel projected the image of someone ripe for the picking.

CHAPTER 5

The Fat Man

STRANGE AS IT MIGHT SEEM, IT WAS OVER THE CLOUDY SKIES OF Japan in August 1945 that the story begins of Globemaster 49-244 and the quest to sneak an atomic team and a Fat Man–sized cargo into Europe. This is where big piloting egos intersected with fuel problems and an obsession with nuclear secrecy to set the conditions for disastrous events to come.

It's amazing how many smart people fail the most basic of trivia questions, such as: *Who was the second man to walk on the moon?* Edwin "Buzz" Aldrin could have learned a lot from the experience of Charles Sweeney, who drifted into historical obscurity as one of those second-person head-scratchers whose identity befuddles the best of trivia experts. Lots of people, especially baby boomers, know that Paul W. Tibbets was the pilot of the *Enola Gay* and dropped the first atomic bomb deployed in war, known as Little Boy, over Hiroshima, Japan in August 1945. Sweeney was in charge of the far more historically significant second bombing, over Nagasaki, a mere three days later. The plutonium Fat Man was more than twice the size and offered about 150% higher blast yield than Tibbets's Little Boy.[1] Nevertheless, the Fat Man killed far fewer people,[2] partly because the pilot badly missed his target for reasons to be explained below. The Fat Man still is largely credited with having ended World War II by definitively forcing Japan to its knees. This one-two punch of atomic bombs was planned from the top, but it couldn't have yielded its war-ending success without the courageous exploits of Sweeney and his team on August 9, 1945.

The largely successful deployment of the Fat Man would render the technology behind Little Boy instantly obsolete. For years to come, the Fat Man's outer shell and plutonium core would become the model by which the United States constructed its nuclear arsenal. And thanks to one of the most devastating espionage coups in human history, the Soviet Union would, within four years, have its own nearly identical Fat Man to play with. The Soviets duplicated virtually every aspect of the shell and nuclear core because of the design plans stolen by the likes of Klaus Fuchs and Theodore "Ted" Hall,[3] which they handed over to the Soviets to assist in the Communist cause and, they hoped, achieve global atomic balance to ensure the United States didn't hold a monopoly on this devastatingly powerful weapon.

The Fat Man was at the center of all the major history to follow in terms of Cold War intrigue and the global nuclear arms race. Everyone seemed to want a piece of it. Alliances and friendships were destroyed over it. The Fat Man, deployed only once in combat, nevertheless succeeded in blowing the world apart after Nagasaki. Even the team of ace pilots Tibbets assembled to train as America's sole atomic attack force found itself riddled with division over the Fat Man and who would get the credit (or blame) for the way it was piloted to its destination.

To this day, it remains unclear who was actually in command of the Silverplate B-29, dubbed *Bockscar,* at the moment it delivered the bomb to Nagasaki. Sweeney was unquestionably the pilot and titular commander, but it was his command authority that came into serious doubt in the skies over Japan well before the Fat Man reached its destination. He would continue to argue until his death over the circumstances of that flight. Lieutenant Colonel James Hopkins, one of the key figures in the Globemaster 49-244 disappearance, served as the focal point of Sweeney's ire and all-too-evident insecurity.

There's something about being a pilot in the heat of war that brings out the best, but often the worst as well, in some people. The glory that comes with, say, surviving a spray of antiaircraft fire in the sky and keeping calm enough to deliver a bomb on target has a way of inflating the ego to irrational levels. Pilots get cocky. The tales of derring-do that get passed around the barracks and mess halls only serve to inflate those egos even more. The competition only gets worse when an elite team is assembled like the one that Tibbets formed in late 1944 to train for what was then an unspecified, top secret mission designed to force Japan's surrender. The atomic bomb didn't technically exist at the time. No one on the team other than Tibbets knew what was being planned in Los Alamos, New Mexico. But they knew that their mission would be of utmost importance in achieving the Allies' war aims.

The very term "Silverplate" was a code word that Tibbets was able to use whenever he needed anything that bureaucrats further up the chain were reluctant to provide. All Tibbets had to do was utter the word "Silverplate" and all doors were open to him and the equally ranked Navy officer assigned to assist him, Commander Frederick Ashworth. Tibbets was charged with overseeing all aspects of the piloting, crewing, and delivery vehicles for the atomic missions. Ashworth was in charge of the bombs themselves. According to Tibbets, even people who had no knowledge of his mission at the Pentagon were nevertheless instructed to honor whatever demands were expressed in conjunction with the Silverplate code word.[4] Tibbets and Ashworth invoked the code word to get better housing and other services for their elite group, not to mention choice real estate on North Tinian for their tightly restricted base.

Members of the 509th Composite Group conveyed an air of privilege and standoffishness that irked other service members on the island who felt they were taking far greater risks and making bigger sacrifices for the war effort than those snooty guys in their country club secret northern enclave. Tensions grew especially sharp when questions arose about the North Tinian pilots' mission, and the reply was a dismissive, terse recital about that information being on a need-to-know basis—*and you don't need to know*. Besides, the pilots chosen for this mission were the best of the best, which meant they didn't just bring talent to the game but also colossal egos.

The need-to-know restriction caused no small number of headaches for Tibbets, who was placed in the awkward position of having to tell his superior officers that they weren't allowed to know what he was up to. "My first hassle was with Brig. Gen. John Davies, commander of the 313th bombardment wing, which was already operating on Tinian when we got there. He had not been let in on the atomic secret and resented the fact that I declined to answer his questions about our mission," Tibbets recalled after the war. Davies insisted that, because his crews had more experience flying against the Japanese, Tibbets's pilots should be required to sit in on briefings where Davies's men would explain how these bombing missions should be done. Tibbets complied and brought three of his crews to a briefing session, during which the invitees completely trounced their briefers when it came to knowledge of the planes, geography, and conditions under which they would be operating.

That afternoon, Davies summoned Tibbets, complaining, "Damn it, they're demoralizing my whole school. They know more about airplanes and navigation and everything else than my instructors know."

Another general balked when Tibbets submitted a request for materiel. When the general refused, Tibbets took the matter to LeMay. In no time, Tibbets had what he had requested.[5]

The term "Silverplate" wasn't just a code word. It also referred to the unique features of a B-29 Superfortress modified to accommodate the Fat Man's weight and dimensions. Everything about the Silverplate B-29 was secret, so much so that no personnel outside the team assembled on North Tinian were allowed to view it. They weren't even allowed to watch the planes take off for fear that someone would notice the dramatically expanded bomb bay door on the plane's belly. The Fat Man itself was so large and heavy, it couldn't be loaded into the bomb bay in the normal fashion. Instead, the plane had to be backed over a trench-like loading bay equipped with a hydraulic lift. Before the actual bomb arrived on Tinian, practice Fat Man shells loaded with 10,000 pounds of TNT were eased into the loading pit using a heavy-duty cart, then the hydraulic lift would raise it into the Silverplate B-29's bomb bay.

All the secrecy wasn't just to keep the Silverplate bomb bay door away from prying eyes but also to prevent exposure of the nonnuclear Fat Man pumpkin bombs the pilots were practicing with. It certainly didn't help reduce outside curiosity when Silverplate B-29s painted with screwy names, like *Strange Cargo*, *Top Secret*, *Up an Atom*, and *Some Punkins*, lined up on the runway for takeoff.

Once during the final weeks of the war, Davies reached his limit of patience. Curious and frustrated with all this supersecret crap happening inside his own base and unbriefed on why all of these special privileges were going to junior officers and their crew assigned to a singular unit, he decided to drive over and demand answers. Davies hopped in a jeep one day and approached the North Tinian entrance, demanding access to a Silverplate B-29. The guard stopped him and demanded to see his credentials. After a cursory review, the guard told him, "I'm sorry, sir. The general does not have a pass. However, I have a gun and have orders to use it." Tibbets, asked afterward whether the guard would have actually shot the general, replied, "Absolutely."[6]

Tibbets had reviewed scores of personnel records and senior-officer recommendations before selecting eighteen pilots for their initial training at Wendover Army Air Force Base in Utah. There, he not only tested their ability to command their crews but also to maneuver their specially designed B-29s to accomplish aerial feats never before performed or even deemed necessary in combat. Because no one in the history of aerial warfare had ever deployed bombs of the size and blast yield that they would be expected to drop over Japan.

Tibbets couldn't tell them what, specifically, they were training for, but after taking a look at the 10,000-pound behemoth pumpkin bombs that were loaded through their bomb bay doors for practice runs, it became quickly apparent that it was some kind of superbomb. If any doubts remained about the power of this bomb, they were erased when the pilots were required to practice banking into steep 155-degree turns immediately after releasing their Fat Man dummy bombs. The idea was to get as far away as possible to escape the nine-mile-wide blast radius of the bomb they would be releasing. It was during those training sessions that pilots began concocting nicknames for their planes that reflected their own curiosity about the upcoming mission.

The training did nothing to help the pilots harness their own egos. Quite the opposite. The more they came to realize the significance of the bomb they were practicing to drop, the fiercer the competition grew to influence Tibbets's decision on which pilot would be chosen for whatever mission was being planned. The best among those pilots wanted the glory of being chosen, to go down in history as the pilot who ended World War II, to be the first person in the world to drop the most powerful bomb in existence. The Fat Man became the object of their desire. The glory of the moment seemed to blind them to the far bigger implications of having their names attached to a mission that killed tens of thousands of civilians. Tibbets and his boss, then–Major General Curtis LeMay, would spend the rest of their lives denying even a hint of guilt over their roles in the mass noncombatant casualties while trying to justify their actions when confronted by reporters, biographers, or audiences.

For now, at least, the Silverplate pilots wanted little more than to be the one who commanded the Fat Man mission. Sweeney wrote decades later that he believed early in the training that he would be the chosen one, arguing that Tibbets had selected him for the early practice sessions at Wendover in the weeks before the other pilots had arrived. The two got to know each other well in those early days, well enough to cause Tibbets to overlook or outright ignore the fact that Sweeney was only a reserve pilot who had never commanded a combat flight in his career.[7] It's one thing to command in practice bombing sessions over Utah, when the stakes are minimal and the ability to address a crisis carries far less pressure than in a wartime situation. Fuel running low? Just abort the mission and land the plane. Disagreement with the bombardier over the targeting strategy? Just drop the practice bomb and analyze what went wrong later. Flight controls malfunctioning? Just circle back and find the runway a few miles away. Don't worry about that Fat Man in the bomb bay. It's just a dummy.

Of course, in the real world of combat, the pressures on a pilot almost always are intense and require split-second decision-making. Crises with potentially disastrous consequences rarely come one at a time. They come in multiples, often all at once amid a spray of enemy flak and bullets. By the time the 509th Composite Group had moved its training base from Wendover to Tinian Island, the idea of entrusting the world's most powerful and expensive bomb, and command of a mission with history-altering consequences, to a combat-command novice like Sweeney was unthinkable to other Silverplate pilots. Some later recounted that they were privately appalled that Tibbets would entertain the idea of putting Sweeney in charge.[8] But their commitment to the chain of command and respect for Tibbets, coupled with the hope that he would recognize the error in his thinking before it was too late, caused them to keep their objections to themselves. Or at least out of Tibbets's earshot.

Clearly, though, they discussed the matter among themselves and tried to find ways around it, as it soon became apparent to Sweeney once the practice missions moved to Tinian. Months before that, while still practicing at Wendover, a faction of dissidents developed, led by Lieutenant Colonel Tom Classen, commander of the 393rd Bomb Squadron. Classen had selected Hopkins, a longtime protégé who was then a major, as his squadron's second-in-command. Tibbets then selected Hopkins to be the Group Operations Officer for the entire 509th Composite Group, a promotion that included a new rank of lieutenant colonel. Something about these two new commanders irked Sweeney long before the Nagasaki mission and continued to occupy his thoughts long after his retirement in 1976.

Not to put too fine a point on it, he despised Hopkins and clearly didn't think very highly of Classen. At least part of it might be the fact that Classen and Hopkins had a long history together from their early training days at the start of the war all the way through their command of combat squadrons attacking Rommel's forces over North Africa. They were unquestionably seasoned, highly qualified pilots and commanders with stellar records of combat achievement—records that Sweeney lacked as a reservist with no combat-command experience.

Sweeney, in his autobiography *War's End*, exhibited a tendency to rewrite history and facts to suit his own narrative regarding the formation of the 509th and his place in the command structure. He described Classen and Hopkins as newcomers who didn't come onboard for Tibbets's secret operation until sometime after March 1945, long after a core group of pilots, namely, Sweeney, supposedly had already established their credentials and won Tibbets's trust. It was this bond, formed early in the practice sessions at Wendover, that caused Tibbets to choose Sweeney for his prominent role on both the Hiroshima and Nagasaki missions, according to Sweeney's version.[9]

In fact, however, Classen and Hopkins were there from the beginning. Hopkins's personnel records show that he arrived at Wendover in November 1944, spending 144 days there before transferring with the group to Tinian. In an efficiency report filed before the Hiroshima and Nagasaki missions, Tibbets described Hopkins as "a loyal and cooperative officer who performs his duty in an excellent manner and holds the respect of superiors and subordinates." Tibbets checked off a box that described himself as having "intimate daily contact" with Hopkins and affirmed "yes" on a second box that asked, "Particularly desire him?" as Tibbets's group operations officer on Tinian.[10]

When Tibbets promoted Classen to 509th deputy group commander, that opened up the position as commander of the 393rd squadron, and Tibbets named Sweeney to that position. While it was an appropriate promotion for a major hoping to acquire command experience and climb the ranks, it still placed Sweeney squarely under Hopkins's and Classen's command. Whatever happened between them, Sweeney arrived at Tinian with his hackles up. And it appears that Classen and Hopkins, among others, arrived ready to put Sweeney in his place.

As Sweeney described it, there was a period during the midsummer of 1945 when the major had already been named to command the second atomic bombing.[11] Classen had been designated as commander of a third bombing mission if it became necessary. Without warning several days before the Hiroshima mission, Tibbets was summoned to Washington for a meeting with the top Pentagon brass. His air travel through the Pacific and back would entail the danger of encounters with Japanese Zeros or naval craft, meaning there was a possibility he would not return. Classen, as 509th deputy commander, decided he needed a backup plan, just in case. "In the event Paul doesn't return by the sixth [of August, 1945], I'll take the first one and Hoppy [Hopkins] will take the second," Sweeney quoted Classen as telling him in a pre-Hiroshima meeting that included other senior officers, including Hopkins, Group Intelligence Officer Hazen Payette, and Squadron Intelligence Officer Jim Hinchey.

"What the hell were those guys thinking?" Sweeney recalled asking himself. "I had all I could do to stifle a laugh, except they weren't kidding." Writing decades later, his old resentments then surged to the fore. He suggested in his memoir that none of them had the competence or experience to fly such a mission (conveniently failing to note that Sweeney himself had never commanded a flight in combat and was by far the most inexperienced of the three). "Classen taking the bomb? Maybe. But the prospect that Hopkins would take the second mission was beyond comprehension. He had virtually no experience in the whole gamut of specialized maneuvers required to command such a mission, and at best was an adequate pilot."

In fact, Hopkins had trained at Wendover as much as, if not more than, Sweeney himself. His flight records register more than 218 hours of flight training, almost all on B-29s as the command pilot during the Wendover sessions. By the time he transferred to Tinian, Hopkins had logged more than 1,700 hours of flight time as a first pilot, most of which he acquired commanding B-25 bombers over Rommel's forces in North Africa. He was already a decorated flying ace.

Classen was a living legend among those who served under him. His list of service medals for valor in combat included the Distinguished Service Cross along with a citation from President Franklin Delano Roosevelt noting an airborne encounter on February 9, 1943, in the South Pacific.

During this mission, Captain Classen's airplane was attacked by eight enemy Zero fighters. The enemy circled at maximum gun range, executing a series of direct assaults. Two of the enemy fighters were shot down and two more were probably destroyed during the initial phase of the air battle, although one engine of the bomber was silenced, ten guns were damaged beyond usefulness, and all members of the crew wounded.

> Captain Classen, blood streaming through a handkerchief gripped in his teeth, directed his crew in the long-running flight that continued. After attacking for an hour and a half, the fighters finally gave up the chase, leaving two motors of the bomber silenced and a third damaged. By this time, the airplane was flying at an altitude of barely twenty feet above the water. Ordering the removal of all possible gear, Captain Classen, by unshakeable tenacity and consummate skill, was able—after approximately an hour's effort—to gain an altitude of 800 feet.
>
> When a water landing of the disabled airplane was necessitated, he directed preparations with such ability that all of his crew escaped from the wreckage. The group of airmen paddled and drifted in two inflated life rafts through torrid sun and tropical storms for more than 600 miles, until on the sixteenth day they made their way through a difficult coral passage to a group of little-known islands in enemy territory where, upon being recognized as Americans, they received what rest and comforts the war-starved native settlement could offer. More than two months after the encounter with the enemy fighters, the air crew reached an island occupied by friendly per-

> sonnel and were returned to their base. Captain Classen's extraordinary determination and skill contributed greatly to the escape and safe return of his entire crew. The personal courage and zealous devotion to duty displayed by Captain Classen throughout this period have upheld the highest traditions of the military service and reflect great credit upon himself, the Thirteenth Air Force, and the U.S. Army Air Forces.[12]

It seems possible that Classen's previous wartime experiences, particularly concerning his own surprise encounters with Japanese Zeros over the Pacific, motivated his desire to have a backup plan should anything happen to disrupt Tibbets's deployment schedule for the Little Boy and Fat Man missions. But Sweeney interpreted it as a thinly disguised power grab—a coup—as if Classen had suddenly decided he would bypass the entire Army chain of command for the most important bombing mission of the war and take it upon himself to override decisions approved in Washington as to who would pilot the two atomic attacks.

What Sweeney apparently didn't know is that Classen and Commander Ashworth had just returned from a meeting on Guam with Major General LeMay. The general was having qualms about the lack of combat experience among Tibbets and his team members. LeMay was also irked that Tibbets was resisting the general's request to cut short his trip to Washington, Los Alamos, and Wendover, and return to Tinian to prepare for the atomic attack. LeMay wrote that he felt the authority granted to Tibbets for this special mission might have gone to his head. And considering the massive egos involved at every level of the operation, it's also quite possible that LeMay was trying to assert his command authority for fear that other generals, fresh from victory in Europe, were now trying to insert themselves on his turf. LeMay was particularly concerned about intervention by General Lauris Norstad, with whom an epic turf battle was already well underway. Norstad also had a long-standing axe to grind with Tibbets and was using the Tinian operation to settle scores.

Taking advantage of Tibbets's absence, LeMay summoned Classen and Ashworth to Guam,[13] after which Classen returned to Tinian to deliver the news to Sweeney that a change in plans might be afoot if Tibbets failed to return in time for the mission. It appears from the context of

LeMay's meeting with Classen that it was the general's decision to have the backup plan that Classen later recounted to Sweeney.

For the purposes of attacking Japan and winning the war, this episode represents little more than a blip on the radar screen, but it helps provide focus that, for future atomic missions involving the Fat Man, Hopkins was clearly on LeMay's radar screen as the person who could reliably be called upon to take piloting command on short notice. (The backup plan proved unnecessary. Tibbets returned with time to spare.)

On the same day that the Nagasaki mission was launched, Classen was dispatched by Tibbets to Wendover to pick up another atomic bomb and deliver it back to Tinian, where Classen would command a third bombing mission in case Japan failed to surrender. (Some of the Tinian pilots speculated that, in fact, Tibbets was trying to get rid of Classen for conspiring with LeMay to subvert his authority.) Regardless of the reasons, there was never any question of Classen's abilities as a pilot to conduct the third atomic mission. Yet Sweeney, decades later, felt it necessary to attach the word "maybe" to Classen's qualifications.

Tibbets himself would become so outraged over Sweeney's selective version of history in *War's End* that he revised his own book, *Return of the Enola Gay*, to insert a full chapter outlining all of the ways Sweeney had botched the Nagasaki mission. The revised, third edition of Tibbets's book was published in 1998, one year after Sweeney published *War's End*. He excoriated Sweeney, as detailed below.

All this commotion could easily be dismissed as the postwar clashing of big pilot egos, but in this case, there was the added element of the Fat Man, to date the world's most destructive weapon. Clearly, the competition was beyond fierce to be the pilot who dropped the Big One and ended the war once and for all. For all the fanfare surrounding Tibbets, Little Boy went down in history as little more than an attention-getter. The Japanese military command registered its determination to continue fighting even after the extent of Little Boy's devastation horrified the world.

The Fat Man was, in the mind of these American bomber commanders, the trophy bomb to drop. It was huge, unwieldy, and required incredible piloting skill to deploy without exposing the plane and crew to the shockwave and blast of radiation as the B-29 banked and accelerated to escape the blast radius. In their minds, it was the glory attached to the mission that these pilots sought. It's not clear from any of their postwar recollections that they contemplated before the mission the mass casualties that the bomb would inflict. Theirs was the headlong, sole pursuit of the title as the first pilot to drop the atomic Fat Man in war. Sweeney's mission nearly ended in disaster.

What, exactly, happened to make this complicated but straightforward Fat Man mission over Japan go so badly awry after Tibbets's Little Boy mission went without a hitch? It started even before Sweeney's plane, *Bockscar*, lifted off the Tinian runway. The first sign of trouble was when he and Tibbets convened a meeting with the pilots of the various B-29s that would accompany the August 9 mission. Two planes would provide scouting services for alternate bombing sites in case Sweeney's primary target, Kokura, was obscured by clouds or otherwise inaccessible. There were two additional B-29s designated to escort *Bockscar* and provide technical support. *The Great Artiste*, Sweeney's normal plane, had already been outfitted with technical instruments for the Fat Man mission, which is why Sweeney had to switch over to *Bockscar*. The third Silverplate B-29, *Big Stink*, piloted by Hopkins, was loaded with heavy photographic equipment and a small group of invited observers from Britain.

A spirited discussion developed during their preflight briefing when Sweeney proposed making a visual rendezvous with the two support planes before their final bombing approach. The other pilots deemed such a rendezvous impossible because of expected heavy cloud cover over Japan caused by an incoming typhoon. Sweeney backed down. After the preflight meeting, Sweeney said he pulled Hopkins aside, hoping to review procedures for a fixed-point rendezvous over Yakushima. They talked privately, so there is no independent account of this encounter other than the recollections Sweeney provided. Sweeney described Hopkins as aggravated, defensive about his superior rank, and intent on using the mission to burnish his own record in hopes of one day reaching the rank of general. Perhaps Hopkins was even a little jealous that he wasn't chosen to command the mission, Sweeney speculated.

Sweeney turned to Hopkins to explain his preferred rendezvous procedures, which, he wrote, prompted Hopkins to snap at Sweeney, "Look, major, I know all about that. I know how to make a rendezvous. You don't have to tell me how to make a rendezvous."[14] (Whether this is an accurate description of what happened remained under dispute for years, especially after Sweeney was caught exaggerating other events in an attempt to demean his colleagues or boost his own command profile, as Tibbets and others recounted.)

If the Hopkins-Sweeney encounter did happen the way Sweeney described, then it was a signal that the major's command was already under challenge even before the mission had started. Even Tibbets started questioning Sweeney's command authority when the major was faced with another big challenge before the planes had taken off. Sweeney was originally scheduled to fly the mission in his normal plane, *The Great Artiste*, but the last-minute switch to *Bockscar* meant he would have to carry out the mission using a quirky plane he had little experience flying.

Each of the Silverplate B-29s was equipped with fuel tanks on both wings plus more than 600 gallons in two reserve tanks behind the bomb bay. Those latter tanks were used not only to extend the plane's range but also to provide balance. The weight of the extra fuel helped offset the enormous weight of a 10,300-pound Fat Man. In the case of *Bockscar*, however, a balky solenoid transfer switch was a big cause of concern for Sweeney. The problem had developed the previous day during a flight, but the normal crew of *Bockscar* had deemed it a nonproblem because the glitchy solenoid eventually kicked in. Rather than take the plane out of commission to fix the solenoid, they found easy ways to make it work without causing a big fuss.[15] In Sweeney's mind, the unreliability of the solenoid effectively made the extra fuel inaccessible, nothing more than a 600-pound weight that had no other use other than to put extra strain on fuel consumption.

Sweeney openly expressed his anxiety to Tibbets and suggested switching to another plane. Since the mission start time was imminent and there was a limited window of opportunity before the mission would have to be scrubbed because of bad weather, Tibbets wrote that he told Sweeney effectively to suck it up and make it work. Sweeney started the mission hesitantly, already having serious doubts about his chances of success, especially if he were to run low on fuel and be unable to access the 600 gallons in reserve. Adding to his nervousness was the fact that, unlike Little Boy's aerial-arming capability, the Fat Man had to be armed—that is, made ready to explode—before takeoff. Any malfunction that led to a sudden aborted takeoff, or, worse, a crash, risked blowing up the entire island and killing America's chances of averting a ground war in Japan. The pressure on Sweeney was intense.

Tibbets finally intervened regarding the question of Sweeney's rendezvous plan over Yakushima. He told Sweeney in no uncertain terms that, given his fuel constraints, he was to perform a single circle to establish a rendezvous opportunity. If either or both of the support planes didn't make it in time, Sweeney was to perform the bombing without them or proceed to one of the alternate targets.

As the planes were preparing for takeoff, Hopkins discovered that the civilian technician assigned to operate the photographic equipment on his plane had failed to strap on a parachute pack as required by Army regulations. And Hopkins was an absolute stickler for regulations. He ordered the technician off the plane to go retrieve his parachute. During the technician's absence, the rest of the planes started taking off, and when Hopkins's turn came in the flight line, he took off, too, leaving the technician back on the base. This meant there was no one to operate the photographic equipment, which was essential for documenting the size of the blast and its effectiveness. Another member of the crew had to learn how to operate the equipment while the plane was in midair.

The mission appeared to be unraveling even before it got underway. Amid all the heavy cloud cover over Yakushima, Hopkins's plane got separated from the others. Perhaps it was pilot incompetence, as Sweeney suggested. Or perhaps it was due to the extraordinarily challenging conditions posed by an incoming typhoon. But the Hopkins problem failed to explain all of the faulty command decisions that followed in his absence.

Sweeney's bombardier couldn't establish a visual sighting of the target as required before dropping the bomb. So Sweeney ignored Tibbets's orders and kept circling in hopes that the clouds would break. Sweeney, fully aware of the importance the command in Washington placed on the photographic proof of America's new destructive device, also kept circling in hopes that Hopkins would find them. It turned out that Hopkins also was circling nearby, but the pilots couldn't see each other because of the clouds. The pilots were under strict orders not to communicate by radio for fear that the Japanese might intercept the communications and try to shoot the planes down. Hopkins decided to violate the radio silence order and spoke into his microphone, saying, "Has Sweeney aborted?" The transmission, broadcast around the Pacific, arrived slightly garbled when overhead by the Pacific command. They received it as a statement—"Sweeney aborted"—instead of a question. The command ordered rescue ships and the emergency landing site on Okinawa to stand down from their alert status. Should any of the pilots be shot down or otherwise forced to ditch in the ocean, there would be no one to come to the rescue.

Sweeney's command authority came under additional question when he and his chief atomic weapons specialist, Ashworth, a Navy pilot of superior rank, engaged in a heated discussion (one account termed it a shouting match) over whether to stop circling or continue waiting for Hopkins's plane to appear. Adding to the uncertainty about the chain of command was the fact that Ashworth, serving as weaponeer and the personal designee of the overall mission commander, General Leslie Groves, had final say over the target sighting and whether sufficient conditions existed to drop the bomb. Effectively, then, *Bockscar* had two commanders: one in control of the plane and the other in control of the bomb.[16] The crew now was witnessing Ashworth's open challenge of Sweeney's command—similar to what had occurred previously among the pilots behind closed doors after Ashworth and Classen had returned from their meeting with LeMay.

They argued to the point that Sweeney ultimately declared, after about forty minutes of circling, that it was time to head to the target site, Kokura. Besides, Japanese antiaircraft batteries on the ground were now firing on the plane. Things only got worse from there. The plane risked running out of fuel. It reached the point that Sweeney, assuming he couldn't access the 600 gallons of reserve fuel, could be forced to abort the mission and dump the Fat Man into the Pacific in order to return safely to base.

Bockscar was forced again to circle repeatedly over Kokura as the bombardier, Captain Kermit Beahan, tried to gain a visual sighting of the target. But the view was obscured by smoke from a firebombing raid ordered by LeMay the day before, and the target had to be abandoned. In the confusion as Sweeney turned his plane toward the final alternative site, Nagasaki, he lost sight of the one plane still accompanying him, *The Great Artiste*, flown by Fred Bock. Sweeney spoke into his microphone to ask his crew, "Where's Bock?" but he had inadvertently hit a switch with his elbow that broadcast his query out to the entire Pacific command. Hopkins heard it and responded, "Chuck, is that you? Where the hell are you?"

These snippets made clear to anyone listening that Sweeney's mission had devolved into chaos.

With fuel tanks now at the point where Sweeney was having to contemplate ditching his plane, the pressure mounted on him to find a target quickly or dump his Fat Man, developed at a price tag of $2 billion, into the Pacific. Either way, he had to lighten his load by getting rid of the bomb because the extra weight was causing the engines to guzzle inordinate amounts of fuel.

Bockscar wound up, of course, reaching Nagasaki and dropping the bomb, albeit embarrassingly off target by 1,800 feet and, lucky for the Japanese, yielding far fewer casualties than it would have if Sweeney's crew had been more accurate. Hopkins caught up with the other two planes and managed to capture dramatic photos and film of the explosion—even without a trained civilian photo specialist aboard. Sweeney was barely able to make an emergency landing on Okinawa despite the airfield's commanders, convinced the mission had been aborted, having stood down from its readiness status to receive the plane. The control tower wasn't answering Sweeney's radio calls, so the only way he was able to clear the runway for landing—flying on fumes—was by shooting off every signal flare his aircraft had onboard. By the time the three planes made it back to Tinian, there were no senior officials or crowds from the 509th to greet them.

Days later, General LeMay met privately with Tibbets and Sweeney. As Tibbets recalled, the general made clear his displeasure with Sweeney's command of the mission, saying something to the effect of, "You fucked up, didn't you, Chuck?"[17] That conversation never made it into Sweeney's autobiography.

His book did, however, try to make the case that it was Hopkins, combined with a series of unfortunate events, that fucked up the mission. By nearly all firsthand accounts, Hopkins made several errors in judgment that made it harder to complete the mission and ensure the planes and their crews made it back safely. His violation of the radio silence order led to the Pacific command's misinterpretation that the mission had been aborted, which prompted the withdrawal of rescue ships and submarines while causing the Okinawa airfield control tower to stand down.

Had Hopkins been more cooperative in working with Sweeney ahead of the flight to establish a fixed rendezvous point, the delays probably would have been avoided. And the quality of photos and film recordings of the explosion certainly would have been far higher had Hopkins not been so inflexible regarding the parachute rules and takeoff time. But as many who knew him later attested, including Sweeney, Hopkins was an absolute, by-the-book stickler for rules and discipline—the break in radio silence notwithstanding.

Those traits, while perceived by Sweeney as a detriment to the Nagasaki mission's success, appear later to have influenced LeMay and the senior Air Force command to put Hopkins on a fast track for promotion. When the war was over, Sweeney was nudged quickly into obscurity. Tibbets was put on a public speaking tour but subsequently excluded from the atomic bomb command. Hopkins emerged as the only pilot among the eighteen who had served on Tinian to be absorbed into LeMay's executive staff when the general took over the Strategic Air Command. If Hopkins truly was the incompetent lightweight described by Sweeney, how was it that he emerged as a leader designated to establish the first atomic strike force on foreign soil and, potentially, go head-to-head with the Soviets?

The historical record cannot be disputed. Sweeney wound up serving in the Massachusetts Air National Guard as a part-time general. He was shunned and discredited by Tibbets, Ashworth, and a host of other officers who witnessed the disintegration of his command authority at the moment it mattered most. Tibbets was asked years later would he have chosen Sweeney for the mission if given a second chance. He replied, "Absolutely not."[18]

Hopkins would continue through the rest of the 1940s and early 1950s training to drop the newest and far more powerful Fat Man nuclear bombs while piloting the newest bombers in the American fleet. In September 1950, Major General August W. Kissner, the Strategic Air Command Chief of Staff, recommended Hopkins be promoted to full colonel, saying Hopkins had "not only demonstrated his ability to lead men, but also proved to be one of the outstanding squadron commanders with the Strategic Air Command."[19]

The week before Globemaster 49-244 disappeared, Hopkins was approved for promotion to full colonel.[20]

CHAPTER 6

Atomic Crossroads

NOT EVEN SIX MONTHS HAD PASSED SINCE THE HIROSHIMA AND Nagasaki bombings, but the Truman administration was already sold on the idea of bigger and better bombs that could yield far greater blast power with mushroom clouds reaching into the stratosphere. For all the supposed qualms that atomic scientists like Robert Oppenheimer and Niels Bohr registered about the bomb and its devastating impact on humanity, there seemed to be plenty of atomic physicists and chemists who were more than happy to oblige the administration's quest for more, bigger, deadlier.

The war was over. Japan was a charred shambles. Europe was rebuilding at a painstakingly slow pace. Russia was in economic ruins. Yet the assessment from Harry S. Truman's National Security Council was that the Soviets were up to no good. No matter what the United States and Britain did to keep their nuclear knowledge secret, it was clear that Moscow was working hard to develop its own bomb, aided in large part by German scientists captured at the end of the war and now forced to put their knowledge to work for their new Soviet masters. The administration had yet to discover that the Manhattan Project was riddled with moles who were supplying the Soviets with priceless intelligence to shorten the research and development time needed to produce a working bomb.

The only option for the United States to ensure it maintained unchallengeable atomic superiority was to take the technology to new and far more destructive levels with development of a hydrogen bomb ten times more powerful than what was unleashed on Nagasaki. In the meantime, the administration decided to organize—in the name of science, of course—two atomic explosions in the South Pacific that would take place with Soviet representatives watching so they could appreciate—in the name of science, of course—the enormity of America's nuclear advantage and relay it home to Joseph Stalin himself.

General LeMay phoned Paul Tibbets in January 1946 with orders to fly to Washington for an important briefing. The plan, LeMay told Tibbets, was dubbed Operation Crossroads, a joint exercise involving the Army and Navy using the remote Bikini Atoll in the Marshall Islands to conduct experimental explosions. The first bomb, code-named Able, would be dropped from a Silverplate B-29. The second, Baker, would be exploded from ninety feet below the ocean's surface ringed by the Bikini Atoll. The same Army Air Forces unit responsible for the atomic attacks on Hiroshima and Nagasaki, the 509th Composite Group, would be in charge of the airborne portion of Crossroads.

Tibbets was still nominally in charge of the 509th, although he and the Nagasaki co-commander, Major Charles Sweeney, had largely been steered away from the South Pacific and placed on an extended speaking tour around the United States. Tibbets was still smarting over the botched Nagasaki run and the embarrassing inaccuracy of the bomb drop. In the days following the attack, he paid a visit to Nagasaki and sat at the very waterfront "in an area that was meant to be the target but that actually escaped serious damage when the bomb missed its mark."[1]

He was a stickler for precision, and anyone who failed to meet his exacting standards risked becoming the target of his derision. He would have no shortage of such targets as the Crossroads mission unfolded.

The assumption from the beginning was that Tibbets would be chosen for the Able test. So certain were the press officers of the choice of Tibbets to command the air operation that they informed reporters in advance that the *Enola Gay*, named after Tibbets's mother, would be the Silverplate B-29 to drop the bomb. *Time* magazine reported: "On A-day the *Enola Gay*, the B-29 that dropped the atom bomb on Hiroshima, will take off from Kwajalein, 250 miles from Bikini. As it makes three trial runs over the orange-colored USS *Nevada*, takes readings of wind drift and adjusts the bomb sights, a loudspeaker will alert the whole area. Ten or more miles from the target, the operational ships will keep up steam in case the wind shifts. Aboard, some 40,000 men will lie down on the decks with their feet toward the blast and their eyes covered against blinding."[2]

But something went astray in the planning. Tibbets's longtime friend and trusted bombardier, Kermit Beahan, was not on the crew list released to *Time* for publication. Instead, it listed Major Harold Wood, identified as "a grocery clerk of Bordentown, N.J.," as the bombardier.

Tibbets then received the news that he, too, would be excluded. Not one of the selected pilots and crew from Tinian would fly, despite their unique experience taking off and maneuvering using 10,000-pound, non-nuclear practice bombs to get a feel for the quirky atmospheric conditions in the South Pacific. Those chosen hadn't even been present for the training at Wendover. Their bombardiers hadn't trained nearly enough to master the complexities of the Norden bomb-sighting system that would guide the plane to the target and determine the precise release time to ensure a direct hit. They were neophytes handling the world's most dangerous technology, which needed to be in the hands of experienced professionals.

But Tibbets himself was running into the buzzsaw of War Department bureaucracy coupled with petty jealousies that had built up from his previous encounters at the war front with other officers who coveted his assignments. It appeared at one point that not even LeMay could protect him from competing senior officers determined to take the famed *Enola Gay* pilot down a few notches.

The military command back then was no less prone than it is today to infighting and overt maneuvering by officers to win the favor and promotion endorsement of decision-makers higher up the chain. Those with a clear record of battlefield experience won the attention of senior commanders by pointing to the results they had demonstrably delivered. Those assigned to desk jobs, who had rank but far less battlefield experience, had to rely on glad-handing and the much closer daily contact they maintained in offices and hallways with the senior commanders to win consideration for promotion. It was a constant tug-of-war among colonels and lieutenant colonels to see who would be next in line for advancement. The sponsorship of an influential general made all the difference in the world.

Sadly, if one of those desk commanders ordered up a daring mission that achieved results, it was the desk commander who tended to get the nod of approval instead of the pilots like Tibbets, Classen, and Hopkins, who were taking all the risks. No matter how unjust that equation might have seemed, it was the way the system tended to work. It was also one of the main impediments to the system working at maximum efficiency. The influence of inexperienced leaders trying to throw their weight around was what sometimes got men killed and led to embarrassing failures of crucial missions.

Tibbets had two main rivals who nipped at his heels repeatedly during his rise through the ranks. One was then-Colonel Lauris "Larry" Norstad, a politically well-connected desk commander with whom he had tangled during their deployment in North Africa. Tibbets was the experienced pro, having successfully led squadrons on scores of attacks against German installations. Norstad at that time had never commanded a flight in war, and the only advantage he had over Tibbets was rank, senior-command access, and dashing good looks.

The two had come to loggerheads years earlier when Norstad ordered a North Africa bombing raid against a German port installation from an altitude of only 6,000 feet, within point-blank range of German antiaircraft guns. Tibbets warned emphatically, with clenched fists, that it would turn into a slaughter for the American airmen. Tibbets issued a challenge, telling Norstad that he would agree to the mission if Tibbets were allowed to fly the lead plane—with Norstad as his copilot. An embarrassed Norstad backed down but held a grudge for years to come and seemed determined to make Tibbets pay a price for having challenged his authority.[3]

When the summer of 1945 rolled around and plans were solidified for the secret atomic missions over Japan, Tibbets locked horns with another career rival, then-Colonel William "Butch" Blanchard. As Tibbets recalled it, Blanchard had sensed upon receiving hints about the new secret mega-bomb that the weapon had the potential to bring Japan to its knees and end the war. Blanchard tried hard to wrestle command of the 509th from Tibbets so he could become the hero. He failed, but only after Tibbets took Blanchard on a practice flight using a dummy Fat Man pumpkin bomb. Blanchard, white-knuckled, sat in the jump seat behind the pilot as their B-29 entered the steep-dive, 155-degree sharp roll required to escape the bomb blast.[4]

Nevertheless, Blanchard persisted. When Operation Crossroads rolled around in 1946, Blanchard, who had hitched his star to the commander of the Able air drop, Brigadier General Roger M. Ramey, intervened to prevent Tibbets from being named the lead pilot—even after Tibbets and his crew had won a targeting competition designed to determine who was the most qualified pilot to command the mission.[5] That was how one of the most famous pilots to emerge from World War II wound up being sidelined during the most high-profile postwar atomic test. It was one of the clearest demonstrations of the role that blind ego can play in high-level military decision-making, and how power-hungry officers will repeatedly risk failure of the mission and the lives of the men under their command in order to flex their muscles and burnish their chest medals.

As a historical side note, Blanchard would leapfrog over Tibbets to become commander of the 509th during the Cold War and, ultimately, a four-star general and Air Force Vice Chief of Staff. Norstad, a protégé of future Air Force Chief of Staff General Hoyt Vandenberg, also would wind up with a fourth star. Norstad grew so confident of the protection he would receive from Vandenberg, who was the nephew of a powerful U.S. senator, that in 1945 he took to sending almost daily letters to LeMay lecturing his then-equal officer on proper conduct and the boundaries for issuing public statements. LeMay seemed to tolerate it, accepting as other senior commanders did that Norstad wasn't worth the trouble (or risk) of a dressing-down.[6] This was the way things worked in the postwar U.S. military, where everyone was scrambling to find a powerful sponsor as a means of protecting turf and constructing an air of importance under conditions in which the military was rapidly losing its sense of mission.

Without a war to fight, why did America need so many colonels and generals? Without a war to fight, why did the military still need all these billion-dollar budget appropriations? Sometimes it seemed that the main job of all those generals and colonels was to justify their own jobs and the money required to keep them employed.

LeMay made clear that he couldn't care less about all these political machinations. He had no problem outlining a clear mission and establishing his own well-justified sense of purpose. The war was over, but a potentially more formidable adversary lurked on the horizon in the Soviet Union. The job fell to LeMay to ensure that the United States maintained unchallenged global military superiority through atomic weaponry. After Hiroshima and Nagasaki, Crossroads was to be the next major step in a demonstration to the world that America must be respected and feared. Yet, for all his power, LeMay was unable or unwilling to exercise his influence when it came to ensuring Tibbets commanded the air drop over the Bikini Atoll.

The extent of Blanchard's intervention became clear to Tibbets as the colonel was sitting in a toilet stall when Blanchard entered an officers' latrine, in mid-conversation, talking to another officer about how "he's already had enough publicity."[7] Tibbets knew they were talking about him. It was not long before he received the word that another crew, with no training or experience handling a Fat Man, would take over the Crossroads drop.

While Tibbets was being shoved aside, another of his Tinian subcommanders, Lieutenant Colonel Hopkins, began emerging as one of the golden boys under Blanchard's protection. Hopkins found himself thrust before the news media as the military's expert assigned to explain what the test was all about. One of his interviews, broadcast across the country, was with ABC Radio, and Hopkins could barely hide his gung-ho enthusiasm.

"Hello, ABC. This is Lee Van Atta reporting from Air Forces atomic headquarters at Kwajalein in the Marshall Islands," the tinny-voiced correspondent began his broadcast. "With me today is Lieutenant Colonel James Hopkins, 27-year-old senior pilot from Palestine, Texas, and operations officer of the 509th Composite Bombardment Group, the embryonic atomic Air Force. He's here to give you a word picture of what's taking place at Kwajalein during the tense hours just before the takeoff of the Bikini-bound atom armada. Colonel Hopkins, who observed his sixth anniversary in the Air Forces just two days ago, is a relative old-timer in the atom field. He was chief of operations of the Superfortress unit that made some real estate transactions at Hiroshima and Nagasaki, and he has been intimately associated with the mighty B-29s since their start of all-out operations in the early part of 1944."

Van Atta continued, turning to his guest, "Jim, how will Able Day run chronologically from where you sit in assault-force operations?"

Hopkins's hick East Texas drawl kicked in, oddly contrasting with his authoritative techno-speak: "Well, Lee, the first word will come about 24 hours before H-Hour, when we will get a tentative alert from Task Force Headquarters at Bikini. This will give us time to top off all planes scheduled to make the mission and to give a final, consolidated briefing to the crews."

"And just when does the definite word come?" Van Atta asked, as if reading directly from a list of questions provided by the Pentagon.

"We shall be fairly certain about 10 o'clock the night before," Hopkins stated, conveying as much command authority and official-sounding diction as he could muster. "That's when General [William E.] Kepner, the deputy commander for air, will signal us that the mission is definitely on. But the last word will reach us about 5:30 on Able Day morning. It'll be a one-word flash reading, simply: 'Execute.'"

"And what are you figuring on as atom-bomb release time?" Van Atta asked.

"I think it's almost certain the bomb will drop between 8:30 and 10 a.m. our time, which is about 3 o'clock the preceding day in San Francisco."

"Well, Jim, what's the trickiest part of the operations plan?"

"Without any doubt, Lee, everything depends on the coordination procedure, which, in all modesty, is something approaching the miracle of timing. We've never attempted something with such a precision timetable. And when I say this operation has been reduced to a matter of split seconds making this a success or failure, I mean just split seconds. You see, to get all the information we are charged with procuring, and getting it safely, every plane has to be at a certain point at a given time-fix. Everything hinges on what the bomb carrier itself does. And I'm pretty much responsible for making sure our air-attack unit is where it belongs when it belongs there."

In other words, Hopkins, as operations officer, was taking personal responsibility for the success or failure of pilot Major Woodrow P. Swancutt, copilot Captain William C. Harrison, navigator bombardier Major Harold Wood, and navigator Major William B. Adams.

"Will they be where they belong?" the interviewer asked.

"They better be."

Van Atta asked about observer and photography planes in the operation.

"Yep. There's four of them, Lee. The communications ships and two C-54s, which will carry picked members of the various evaluation boards and about 30 top Air Force officers who will probably, one day, have air atomic force commands," Hopkins responded.[8]

The young lieutenant colonel's prediction turned out to be the understatement of the century. Swancutt ultimately rose to the rank of major general. Wood enjoyed a twenty-four-year military career that took him around the world in various commands as a lieutenant colonel and included undercover intelligence work in Europe.[9] Harrison rose to the rank of Air Force colonel and retired in 1971 working under the commander in chief of the U.S. Pacific Command. Admiral John S. McCain II, father of then–Vietnam prisoner of war John S. McCain III, presided at his retirement ceremony in Hawaii.[10]

The fact that those men were chosen for this flight was a testament to the skills they no doubt had displayed in previous service to the Army Air Forces. But the ability to drop, say, a 500-pound conventional bomb on target over Germany or a 2,000-pound incendiary explosive over a Japanese city does not even slightly compare with the complexities of dropping a 10,300-pound Fat Man atomic bomb on target over a South Pacific atoll from six miles up, as Tibbets was quick to explain to anyone who would listen. The political forces at play, however, proved too formidable for his protests to persuade commanders to reconsider. The goal was less focused on the accuracy and precision that Tibbets sought, and more focused on ensuring that Tibbets was *not* the one commanding the mission. If Blanchard couldn't be the one to drop the bomb, at least he would see to it that Tibbets wouldn't either.

What happened next, on July 1, 1946, was a catastrophic embarrassment for all involved, most certainly including Hopkins as operations officer. With two Soviet scientists and a Russian journalist as observers among the 42,000 people gathered to watch, the pilot, navigator, and bombardier missed their target by about a third of a mile. Around 100 obsolete Navy ships had been arrayed as if to form a bull's-eye target, a pattern that Tibbets told LeMay would help gauge the accuracy of the bombing, as well as better calculate the effects of the blast as it rippled outward. The bomb, dropped from an altitude of nearly six miles, was so far off target it missed all of the ships but one. The main target ship, the

USS *Nevada*, suffered bent gun turrets and other damage, but gunpowder bags planted in its turrets were left unexploded, and other items left on deck survived untouched.[11]

Observers who were gathered on a ship about eight miles away from Ground Zero braced themselves for the ear-splitting sound of an explosion and the concussive blast of air to follow. But nothing happened. A mushroom cloud was visible in the distance, but it didn't yield the awesome spectacle designed to impress the world with America's military might. Reporters broadcasting live from the ship tried to make the most out of the audio, but they couldn't explain the disappointing absence of a big blast.

The atomic bomb "had grown a little less awful as a result of Bikini. Its apparently infinite power was finite after all," *Time* reported. One of the Soviet observers, Professor Simon Alexandrov, reportedly shrugged and dubbed the distant mushroom cloud as "not so much." The international news media heaped derision on the blast as typical American bombast.

"ABLE operations went smoothly except that the test weapon was dropped between 1,500 and 2,000 feet (457 and 610 meters) off target," stated a classified report on Crossroads compiled by the Defense Department afterward and kept secret for the following four decades.[12] The target was missed by significantly less than Major Charles Sweeney's bomb drop on Nagasaki the year before, but it was still abysmally off the target. Given the fact that there was no enemy shooting at the plane, atmospheric conditions were fully known, and the target was clearly visible from the sky, the bomb should have hit squarely on its mark.

The first aerial bombardment since Nagasaki, designed to impress the Soviets with America's awesome military might, wound up looking more like a dud. The Soviets left thoroughly unimpressed, choosing not to wait for Baker, the second, underwater explosion. Tibbets attributed the disaster to the political decision to shove him aside in favor of pilots and crew who were far too inexperienced to operate the delicate technology aboard their B-29.

Instead of projecting an image of unchallengeable American military strength, the Crossroads display convinced the Kremlin that the United States might be more of a paper tiger. Newly emboldened, Moscow would demonstrate over the following two years how little fear or respect this unimpressive atomic demonstration generated. The Soviet Bloc opted not to demobilize its million-plus troops along the European front. Rather, they dug in. Moscow installed pro-Communist leaders in the neighboring states of Bulgaria and Romania in 1946, followed by Poland in 1947, then Hungary and Czechoslovakia in 1948.

Weeks after the Able test on Bikini, the Strategic Air Command began demonstration flights of military aircraft to Europe in an open signal to Moscow. "Although the flight of the six B-29s to Europe could not have been interpreted as a direct threat to Russia, the implications were obvious," says an official Strategic Air Command history. "The B-29 was widely recognized as the aircraft capable of dropping an atomic bomb, and the appearance of B-29s in Europe would cause speculation that they might be stationed there permanently."[13]

Instead of cowering in fear or loudly complaining, the Soviet Bloc responded with its own display of open defiance, shooting down two U.S. Air Transport Command C-47 cargo planes over Yugoslavia. Soviet warplanes and missile installations escalated the shootdown campaign in subsequent months against American and British military aircraft. Then, in 1948, Stalin boldly ordered the complete encirclement of Berlin with his military forces, cutting off all ground access by the United States and Britain. And, in 1949, Russia exploded its own atomic bomb.

Had the Russian delegation stayed for the Baker test at Bikini, they would have been treated to a far more spectacular display of atomic destruction, which displaced an estimated two million tons of water and sand,[14] and sent a radioactive aerosol surging across the surrounding region. The blast created an eighty-four-foot tidal wave that swallowed the ships arrayed around the blast site. The radioactive shower that followed rendered many, if not most, of the test ships unsalvageable.

The news media and assorted commentators, including the scientists who developed the bomb, used the test as proof of the frivolity and inhumanity of atomic weaponry. LeMay made exactly the opposite argument: that the United States needed to double down on its research and production of bigger, more powerful nuclear weapons. He was so shocked at the dismal results from the Able air drop that he ordered Tibbets to exit the

Kwajalein staging site and head back to Washington early. "I don't want you on this island when all those newspaper people get back from the lagoon and start asking questions," Tibbets quoted LeMay as saying.[15]

Tibbets, hardly an objective observer but nonetheless clearly qualified to opine on the Able test result, labeled it a "fiasco." He wrote that the main reason there wasn't more outrage generated by the failure was "because there wasn't much investigative news reporting in those days. Although they knew that the bomb had missed its mark by a wide margin, the reporters didn't ask embarrassing questions, and the Air Force managed to leave them with the impression that the whole thing was a success."

One congressman present, Edouard Izac, commented, "It was one keen disappointment, I'll say." *The New York Times* covered it with a front-page headline saying, "Blast Force Less Than Expected."[16]

That was only in the initial phase of reporting among journalists who had to perform their work under the watchful eye of their military minders. Months passed with no official word on what, if anything, was gleaned from the explosions. Scientists, including Robert Oppenheimer and Niels Bohr, were openly skeptical about the worth of any scientific data gathered from the blasts. As a few nonclassified results trickled out to the public, there was a growing conviction that the air drop was a dud. Several publications, including *Time* and *The Economist*, declared the test much ado about nothing.

In the various memoirs and interviews that followed Crossroads, LeMay was always very careful not to criticize the results publicly. Part of the reason was professional courtesy and respect: General Roger Ramey was the director of the Able test and had declared it "a complete and unqualified success"—something it clearly was not. For LeMay to criticize the lax training and appalling results of Crossroads, he would implicitly be attacking a close colleague still in active service. The result nonetheless opened LeMay's eyes to the dangers created by the massive demobilization that had occurred immediately after World War II ended. He remained largely silent for the next three years, while slowly boiling inside at everything he saw going wrong, as his memoirs would later document.

The Army Air Forces had decided to warehouse or destroy hundreds of the planes that had previously executed LeMay's bombing strategy to win the war. All of the human expertise that LeMay and others had so painstakingly assembled was now demobilized. At its peak toward the end of World War II, the Air Forces had 273 combat groups. By mid-1946, that number was down to fifty, with even more shrinkage planned. Even worse, the most fundamental element of preparedness—a basic war plan outlining the potential scenarios by which the United States would have to defend itself—also had been scrapped.

Under General George Kenney's guidance as the first chief of the newly created Strategic Air Command, the nation's nuclear delivery force had been allowed to crumble in disarray. "When the war ended we were in the process of tearing the Air Force down," LeMay recalled. "When we would disband an outfit, those that wanted out were sent to a processing station that got them out of the service. Those that wanted to stay in were usually ordered to a base somewhere close to their homes. . . . The whole force was ill-manned. We didn't have the people we needed, and there were a lot of people we didn't need and couldn't use. . . . Then I took a look at the war plan; there was no war plan."[17]

Kenney "was an absentee commander in chief, a commander who could more often be found giving speeches than dissecting the thorny requirements of building an atomic-bombing force. This would be evident during Operation Crossroads."[18]

The lesson for LeMay and other commanders of the nation's atomic attack force was that the program was too crucial and too complex to leave in the hands of neophytes and political game players. The program could not afford to rely on the small number of elite pilots, bombardiers, and navigators who formed the core group on Tinian. For the atomic program to be adequately prepared for the next global challenge—a potential nuclear confrontation with the Soviet Union—scores of atomic crews would need to be trained to the same level as Tibbets and his squadron. And they would need to conduct their training not just in the predictable skies over domestic bases such as Wendover, but also under the same atmospheric and geographic conditions as their would-be target was located. It would take the men on those planes far out of their comfort zone and require that they spend weeks or even months deployed at far-off locations in

Alaska, Morocco, Britain, or Iceland. There would be massive logistical and diplomatic hurdles to be overcome so that atomic-capable Silverplate B-29s could ply the skies wherever LeMay deemed it necessary.

But never again would the embarrassment over the Bikini Atoll make LeMay's command the butt of jokes and derision in Moscow. The element of fear had to be restored.

CHAPTER 7

Atom Bomb Baby

Got a doll baby, I love her so
Nothing else like her anywhere you go
Man she's anything but calm
A regular pint-sized atom bomb

Atom bomb baby little atom bomb
I want her in my wigwam
She's just the way I want her to be
A million times hotter than TNT

"ATOM BOMB BABY," THE FIVE STARS, 1957

FOR REVA JOY HURWITZ, ESCAPING THE SMALL-TOWN, HICK CONfines of Laramie, Wyoming was the ticket to a new life, the only available route to true liberation and career fulfillment. The Hurwitzes were one of only three Jewish families in a rural town with zero synagogues. Laramie residents seemed more curious than anything about the Hurwitzes' presence. Her parents found assimilation to be the quickest route to prosperity as they made their home in Laramie. But Reva wanted more. Her first taste of freedom came at age 19, after graduation from high school, when she said goodbye to her family and embarked on the long bus journey that would land her in the big city of Austin, Texas.

The Lone Star State capital itself wasn't quite that big, but with around 50,000 residents by the mid-1930s, it was twice as big as Laramie, which apparently was good enough for Reva. The University of Texas was like a city unto itself, swarming with students from vastly different backgrounds and outlooks, with minds far more open to new ideas and possibilities than those back in Laramie, where young people's imaginations of their future lives tended to be limited to cattle breeding, horse riding, and mineral mining. Reva, known for her boisterous sociability, no longer had to construct her party conversations around small-town gossip. Even the limestone terrain of Austin, where noisy grackles held daily conventions atop leafy pecan and oak trees on campus, and a big, clear-water river split the town in half, was as different as it could get from the scrubby, hardscrabble hills of Laramie. Austin was a worldly place of big ideas and political points of view far astray from the single-minded cowboy conservativism of rural Wyoming. Austin even had its own Communist Party, with a list of candidates it supported for statewide election and a platform that included such audacious notions as desegregation, abolishing poll taxes, and enforcing equal opportunity for Negroes and Mexicans.[1]

A conservative Lithuanian immigrant family like Reva's needed to think twice in Laramie about engaging in a conversation with customers in their sporting goods store about the dangers to Jews posed by Hitler and Stalin. You adapted in order to get along. Exchange Christmas gifts, like everyone else. Some folks in Laramie weren't so open to people with ways of living and worshiping beyond the boundaries of traditional Christian norms, as demonstrated decades later when a college student named Matthew Shepard was fatally beaten, tortured, and left comatose on the road leading out of town, tied to a split-rail fence, for the crime of being gay.

It was clear from Reva's actions and letters home that she planned to get out of Laramie and never look back.

By her final year at the University of Texas, Reva was immersed in professional training as a journalist and ready to ply her trade at whatever newspaper was willing to hire her. Alas, journalism was a man's job, and unless she was willing to take an assignment running copy or covering women's stuff like bridge clubs or gardening techniques, meaningful work wasn't going to come easily. Taking advantage of local contacts back home, she was able to land a job in Cheyenne, writing for the *Wyoming*

Eagle. Still, the work was far from the glamorous world of reporting the Big Story that she might have imagined during her journalism studies in Austin.

Then came Pearl Harbor, and suddenly the nation was on high alert. News was breaking out everywhere, even in tiny Cheyenne. Like local governments across the country, Cheyenne's leaders faced a federal mandate to schedule full blackouts and other preparedness drills, just in case the Japanese or Germans penetrated thousands of miles of ocean, bypassed the nation's coastal defense batteries, and flew hundreds more miles overland to achieve their one true goal in the drive for global conquest: a surprise attack on Cheyenne, population 22,450.

Of course, America's enemies couldn't care less about Cheyenne and its preparedness drills, but the town's leaders rallied with wartime zeal, doing their patriotic part to keep the nation safe. Reva made the most of it as a young reporter paying her dues, writing in the *Eagle* after one orchestrated blackout:

> Consider yourself bombed to death last night! Cheyenne's first surprise blackout under the newly adopted air raid signals proved unsuccessful, marked by confusion and discrepancies. Despite wide-spread publicity by newspapers and instructions by some air raid wardens a great part of the general public seemed ignorant or misinformed about the signals. And in some instances wardens themselves seemed confused and unable to cope with their duties. The caution period, marked by the first signal, was almost generally mistaken for the blackout, and traffic was stopped, lights turned off, and many pedestrians found shelter. Most violations in the downtown district during this period were caused when storeowners on their way to turn off lights were erroneously stopped by wardens. The next signal, notice of the actual "air raid" caused a blaze of lights—taken for the all-clear. The evidence indicates that in the first month after Pearl Harbor many Wyoming people were afraid of air raids, but after that, fear diminished rapidly. Nothing short of a few bombs could have revived the early alarm.[2]

Her flair for writing and unquenchable sense of humor were obvious. No, this scintillating account was not going to win her a Pulitzer or a correspondent's job at *The New York Times*, but it was one step in her slow climb toward something more rewarding and exciting than selling baseball mitts at the family store back in Laramie. As her parents managed their Midwest Trunk and Sporting Goods Store, next door to the Woolworth's on South Second Street, they continued amping up the pressure for Reva to find a man, get married, settle down, and get down to a woman's business of making babies and building a family. She wanted something different, at least for now. Her travels to Austin had awakened the curly-haired, fair-skinned redhead to greater possibilities. She wanted action, especially after reading the letters her brother David sent home from the war front in Germany. The occasional ego rush of a front-page byline in the *Eagle* was great, but Reva clearly wanted to see and cover the world. She carried herself as if convinced that being a woman could be turned into an asset, rather than a liability, in a profession wholly dominated by self-important men hovering over typewritten copy, wearing nerdy black-rimmed glasses, white shirts, and boring black ties.

There were only so many stories Reva could write enthusiastically about war preparations in a region of the country that might well have been the safest place on the planet in terms of risk of foreign attack. And safety certainly wasn't what she was looking for anyway. After two years of beat reporting in Cheyenne, waiting for the war to end, Reva started sending out her résumé to explore as many far-flung options as she could find. One of those options was the American National Red Cross in Washington, D.C. Much to her surprise in early 1945, she got a response by mail that the organization was interested in talking to her about a position as an assistant communications officer with potential for an overseas posting. Reva wasted no time responding with enthusiasm.

The combination of her press experience, writing talents, spunk, quick wit, and intellect clearly bowled over her job interviewers in Washington. She not only got the job but switched to the fast track of promotion and consideration for an overseas posting in a junior management position. It just so happened that the government had selected the Red Cross as the lead civilian organization to head up a community-building liaison effort in the Marshall Islands, a tiny Pacific island chain that included a series of sandy beaches bathed in the emerald blue waters of the Bikini Atoll. The Americans had claimed territorial control over the islands after forcing the Japanese into retreat. Reva's first assignment was to travel to Seattle, where she boarded a military transport ship, the Matsonia, and set sail on January 6, 1945, to Honolulu to take up duty in the Red Cross offices as an assistant communications director covering Hawaii and the South Pacific. Since the war was still raging, the names of Reva and the other 25 Red Cross women onboard were listed as secret on the passenger manifest.[3] From there, her job was to establish working relations with the Army and Navy to arrange travel to the remote island of Kwajalein, where tens of thousands of soldiers and sailors were consolidating control and preparing for future, postwar military operations.

Reva found herself in surroundings that couldn't have been more starkly opposite those of her upbringing in landlocked Laramie. Palm trees swayed in the gentle Pacific breeze. The beach was just a few blocks' walk from her one-bedroom Honolulu apartment. Her letters home were flecked with casual references to exotic places like Kwajalein and Bikini, as if her parents would know without looking on a map what she was talking about. A girl who might previously have regarded a bus trip to Austin as high adventure was suddenly talking about overnight airplane flights to far-off tropical ports of call.[4]

Her letters home from Kwajalein referred repeatedly to "the Commodore," a fatherly figure who appeared to have taken her into his home and expressed unmistakable fondness for her. He was Commodore Ben H. Wyatt, the governor of the Kwajalein Atoll and commander of the island's Naval Air Base. Reva found herself rarely having to cook meals at home because of the nightly invitations she received for dinner with the Commodore and his distinguished friends and visitors, or with the dozens of military officers she met at various gatherings. Her weekends in Honolulu were filled with beach excursions and sailing trips. She joked in letters about the effect all these free meals were having on her figure, especially her bra size. The more it grew, the more attention she seemed to receive from would-be suitors even if, by Reva's own assessment, she was not what anyone would describe as a beauty. Her brothers grew so envious of her new lifestyle that they began querying her about the possibility of moving there themselves, according to their exchanges of letters.[5]

On idyllic Bikini in 1946, hundreds of unsuspecting indigenous villagers happily inhabiting the atoll warmly greeted the first flotilla of visitors dressed in American military uniforms as sailors and soldiers came ashore in their Navy landing craft. Natives in their outrigger canoes escorted the military boats to shore, where a feast of fish and seafood awaited to celebrate the arrival of their new friends. They even agreed to sit on the beach for long periods to serve as backdrops as a film crew recorded an American military officer—the Commodore himself—delivering rehearsed remarks about the need to evacuate the island in the name of something called atomic progress.

The Bikini chief, Kilon Bauno, told an interviewer he didn't know what any of this meant at the time. The filming required multiple takes because the military officer speaking to them kept flubbing his lines and misplacing his emphasis on key words, which meant the villagers kept having to smile and mimic joy and enthusiasm as they slowly came to grasp the full meaning of what the officer was saying: They would soon have to leave their beloved homes and lifestyle forever.

"We really didn't know what was going on," Bauno stated in the 1988 American Experience documentary *Radio Bikini*. "We were very confused. They were taking many pictures of us. But at that time I didn't even know what a camera was." Speaking of the multiple takes by the film crew, he added, "I couldn't understand why they had to do everything so many times."

"Crossroads, scene 25 take 1!" a crew member says as the key grip closes with a loud slap in the television documentary. Commodore Wyatt speaks to an interpreter, saying, "Well now then James will you tell them that the United States Government now wants to turn this great destructive force [nuclear weaponry] into something *beneficial* for mankind? [another grip-slap signals a second take] something good for *mankind*? [another slap] something *good* for mankind."

"All right. Is that all right? All right?" Wyatt asks the film crew.

"OK cut it!" the film director shouts.[6]

"It is difficult for me to express how sad I was as we were leaving," Bauno stated afterward. "We looked back and saw them burning all of our houses. They burned everything. Even the outriggers we had to leave behind. As we left, a great sadness came over us. We were so sad that nobody ate anything as they moved us from Bikini to the Island of Rongerik."

The person whose job it was to liaise with the natives before the filming was none other than Reva Joy Hurwitz. She wrote cheery letters home about her work evacuating inhabitants, spicing sentences with references to Honolulu, Hilo, Kwajalein, Rongerik, and Bikini. The closer the date got to the explosions of Operation Crossroads, the more her letters home referred to flights to remote islands and encounters not only with natives but also generals, admirals, members of Congress, and visiting journalists.

"Left early Sunday morning, six, damn it, by PBM [a pontoon-equipped twin-engine military plane] for Rongerik, where we went ashore in life rafts and started gathering up the first lot of natives," she wrote to her parents on June 6, 1946. "That is a mangy island, not enough rainfall to produce good coconut trees or any papayas."[7] Then she headed back to Kwajalein, where she met up with Mutual Radio correspondent Don Bell, an apparent suitor. She helped write scripts for several broadcasters, then met with the Commodore, who bizarrely asked her to trim his hair. Dinner that night was aboard a naval tanker with a captain who had survived the Bataan Death March. Then back to Kwajalein.

Her letters were replete with such whirlwind activities. She lost count of all the men vying for her attention and, presumably, affection. The demands on her time from various generals, the Commodore, and journalists caused her to be yanked from one place to another to the point that, sometimes, she didn't even have time to go to the bathroom.[8] Much worse, since Kwajalein was a military base for 40,000 men and only 22 women, the available facilities for women to relieve themselves were scarce. She grew so desperate for relief during one such whirlwind series of meetings that she insisted on breaking away and finding a colonel who would loan her his jeep. She drove away in search of a bathroom, only to be stopped by military police and accused of theft. All she wanted to do, she explained, was go to the bathroom!

In spite of her surroundings and all the fun and excitement she was experiencing, things happening in the world beyond seemed increasingly messy and depressing, particularly as news emanated from Germany of discoveries made by Allied soldiers at the concentration camps they had liberated. Her brother David, an Army officer on deployment in Germany, had fallen in love with a woman and announced his plan to marry her. Reva expressed her outrage to her parents and older brother, Garvin, particularly after learning that the woman had expressed misgivings about giving birth to a Jew.

But then, Reva had her own misgivings about children in general. She wrote home to her older brother, Garvin, "Ya know, Bud, overly conscious as I am about my religion, I have moments and days of wandering [*sic*] what the future holds for me. I like my work, but that isn't enough (on account of how I'd like some brats,) but I just don't know about bringing any children, and especially Jewish children into this world."

There was a description in one letter of military preparations for an oncoming "tidal wave" that required her to visit one island and evacuate families on behalf of the Red Cross. The tidal wave, it turns out, was the one that was expected days later when the second, underwater Crossroads nuclear bomb exploded. The blast turned out to be far more impressive than the first, sending an estimated two million tons of water and sand into the air and creating an eighty-foot tidal wave.

The constant demands on Reva led to some bizarre displays. She wrote that Bell, the Mutual Radio correspondent, openly pouted after another correspondent walked over and gave her a big kiss on the cheek. The Commodore would pout and punish her if she stayed out too late, once imposing a punishment of a 5:00 p.m. curfew just because she was forced to walk home from the dock where her boat had dropped her off from the dinner with the Bataan Death March captain. She'd had to walk because crews were loading airplane fuel on the dock and didn't want motor vehicles to risk giving off a spark that could set the whole place ablaze. The Commodore didn't want to hear excuses. At age 30, she was grounded like a child.

Army generals were constantly demanding that she serve as hostess for their big receptions. More correspondents vied for her affections, even to the point of offering her reporting jobs once she returned to the mainland. During the downtime while awaiting the start of Operation Crossroads, several journalists interviewed Reva and wrote glowing profiles of her, which hit the newswires and were published in scores of daily papers around the country along with her photo. She had become a celebrity. One profile asserted that she was the first white woman to set foot on Kwajalein. Another joked about how soldiers deployed for Crossroads had stripped naked to swim at the beach since no women were on the island. But when Reva's plane flew over them for a landing, she got a free show.

She got so familiar with airplane cockpits, after repeatedly being invited for tours by pilots, that she became able to identify every dial, button, and switch on the console. "I'm getting so sophisticated it's hard to pretend naivete when the crew invited you to ride up front with the pilots. Not that I don't enjoy riding up there, it's much smoother, you get a better view and can walk around and smoke, but they all point out everything to you, and expect you to say you've never seen anything like that or know anything about the gadgets, and someday I'll open my big mouth, and in a very bored voice, admit it's all old stuff to me," she wrote seven months into her stay.

After more than a year into her posting, Operation Crossroads was only a few weeks from happening in August 1946. Reva's narrative started to change. She was winding down her stay and counting the days before she was to leave. Buried in all her talk about island hopping and evacuations, she started inserting vague references to a colonel who was in charge of the photographic unit for Crossroads. She first described meeting him at some kind of press function. A subsequent letter, written in all-capital letters and clearly pounded out on a telex teletype machine with a bad ribbon, got into more detail. It was the same letter that described Don Bell as pouting over her lack of attention, followed by the description of borrowing an officer's jeep so she could go find a bathroom.

After returning, she narrated in the present tense, "[I] go back into the club and meet all the correspondents. I'm the only girl here by the Commodore's orders, and if you talk to one guy another gets mad. Try to talk to Bell for a few minutes and all the while, the chief public relations officer here is glaring at me because he doesn't like Bell because I do. The *Star* editor comes in every two minutes insisting we go in a corner and discuss me taking a job on his paper. The correspondent from *Time* magazine, from *The Washington Post*, from A.P. all have big messages. Finally Don Bell and I leave for a few minutes, come back and have lunch, he departs for the states. The editor of the Honolulu paper starts in on a job offer. In the meantime, various and sundry famous correspondents, including William L. Laurence of *The New York Times*, comes up. I try to be gracious to everyone, and other characters keep jarring you, and saying they don't like the company I'm in. Everyone here hates everyone else."[9]

It was a whirlwind, for sure. She tried to get away and find a place just to lie down for a while, "but [it's] the phone again, and it's the head of the Army Air photo unit saying he has to discuss the flight tomorrow to Bikini, could he come over for a minute. . . . He likes the color of my eyes. But that's the way you accomplish things here apparently."[10]

What she described was unquestionably a flirtatious come-on by the only Army Air Forces colonel in charge of the only photo unit assigned to Operation Crossroads. And the colonel was none other than Paul Thomas Cullen, although Reva didn't reference him by name at the time. It was unclear what she meant by "that's the way you accomplish things here apparently," but it appeared to be her own acceptance that engaging, if not encouraging, flirtatious behavior among the men she encountered was the way to get ahead.

In the same letter, she finished the narrative with a subsequent meeting with Don Bell. "Ah well, the bubble burst as Don Bell bluntly told me today I wasn't good looking but no one that had ever met me would forget me, and the moral of that I can't quite fathom."

She signed her letter, "Your addlepated daughter, Funny Face (according to the air photo officer)," adding on a second line, "Jeepers, why am I so ugly." And finally, she jokingly handwrote: "Do you think I have a beautiful character?"

By early August 1946, Reva had finished her work on Kwajalein, returned to Honolulu to pack up her belongings, and relocated to a hotel in San Francisco while awaiting her next assignment. On August 7, she wrote in unusual detail about that still-unnamed colonel. "The colonel who took me flying over Bikini the Monday after the second [atomic explosion] in an air photo plane, and what a trip that was. Did I tell you about it? He is head of all aerial photography for the Army and was a bomber pilot in the war for a while, then took over aerial photography and trained Elliot [*sic*] Roosevelt, who he thinks is a rat." She then described the flight and buzzing the islands at twenty-five feet. "Scared the natives," she wrote.[11]

The letter is one of the only documents describing the bitterness Cullen felt about commanding, and then being commanded by, the son of the president of the United States.

"Anyway he, the colonel, left Kwaj two hours before I did in his plane. Almost flew back with him, but it wasn't legal, so didn't. And who should turn up at the airport here [in San Francisco], all slicked up, and with the general's car and driver, but he. Which after a bucket seat plane ride, no sleep, was very comforting. After much arguing, he allowed me to carry mine own purse in the car, two minutes before he came I had been wrestling with duffle bags and suitcases."

Cullen had found a way to greet her at the San Francisco airport in an official car. His interest in her was now clearly far beyond any professional realm, but Reva made no mention of the fact that Cullen was a married man. She described a driving trip they took to the mountains before he left. She lamented not being able to fly with him as a stowaway "but inasmuch as there was still work for me here and he wouldn't look so well in Leavenworth [federal prison], decided to be cautious."[12]

This dynamic was about as weird as it gets. Reva was a journalist by training. When stripped of all the nuance, the profession boils down to this: Journalists (this author included) are paid, professional gossips. Our goal is to find the news, get the story, and be the first to tell it to others. Reva was striking up a love affair with someone with access to some of the military's most cherished secrets. It's possible that Cullen kept those secrets compartmentalized in his brain and exercised the strictest discipline in what he shared with Reva, even in their most intimate pillow-talk moments.

When he had to travel on secret assignments, perhaps he made up a story or simply told her, "I can't tell you," whenever she asked where he was going. But nothing so far in Cullen's behavior indicates he was keeping his mouth shut, as his comments about Elliott Roosevelt affirm. Nor was he prioritizing his service to the United States over his cultivation of this new love affair. He was using his position to impress Reva and elevate their relationship to a higher, more romantic level. For a married officer, it was a blatant violation of the military code of honor.

Reva was clearly aware that they were skating way over the edges of military regulations, but she appeared not to fully appreciate what those rules might be, or whether there was some other reason to be discreet. The reference to Leavenworth was an unmistakable reference to the federal military prison there.

Reva opened an August 19, 1946, letter home by quoting the philosophical meanderings of *The Times*'s Bill Laurence. Then she decided to fill her parents in on more details about the flight she took over the still-classified wreckage left after Crossroads.

"I went to Bikini on July 29th in an Army C-54 photographic plane. We flew over Bikini about five hours taking official pictures of the lagoon, the oil streaks and particularly the [Japanese battleship] Nagato starting to sink and some submarines being beached." Those vessels had been positioned in bull's-eye formation for targeting in the Crossroads explosions. Because the plane flew at 12,000 to get to the atoll, she'd had to wear a fur-lined jacket and a pair of flight coveralls. Reva "didn't speak any more than necessary inasmuch as I was a stowaway. When the fellows asked me what I was doing there, I was everything from a female scientist to a civil service technician." She wondered whether the crew members might have compared notes and discovered "what a liar I must be."[13]

She wrote that she flew with the Commodore's permission, which might not have been adequate to circumvent strict rules requiring security clearance to board an overflight over a restricted zone like the Bikini Atoll. The real authority fell on Cullen, who, she made clear, had to lie to get her onboard. "The colonel is head of the army air forces photographic unit, and he was piloting the plane, but inasmuch as I didn't have orders, and wasn't up on official business, [Cullen] didn't want any more people than necessary to find out about it."

Didn't want anyone to know that he had violated security by taking an uncleared passenger on his flight? Or didn't want anyone to know that he was actively courting a woman eighteen years younger, using taxpayer dollars and equipment to woo her? Or that he was actively courting a woman eighteen years his junior *while married to his current wife of sixteen years*?

There were lots of reasons to lie, lots of reasons to conceal the truth. Colonel Paul Thomas Cullen was exhibiting character and leadership traits that, had his superiors been aware of them at the time, would certainly have scuttled his career faster than the *Nagato* sank in the Crossroad explosions.

On what appears to be the first anniversary of the victory over Japan, Reva wrote home from San Francisco: "Happy V-J Day," then described how everyone around her was celebrating the anniversary with partying while she drew the assignment to stay in the office in case anything urgent came up. She was searching for jobs and had obtained a nice recommendation from the Commodore. Then she described the misery of a close friend who was engaged to be married, only to be told by her fiancé he didn't love her. Then Reva lamented not being home to dance with her father on V-J Day. "Have done very little dancing the last four months. Somehow, the places I went were full of conversation with very little music. With the exception of one party, think I have done no dancing until I got back here, and then only once. My colonel doesn't care much for dancing. Which is unfortunate inasmuch as he is six foot one, and I'm sure we would have made a charming sight."[14]

Maybe Cullen just wasn't a dancer. Or maybe he didn't want to be seen dancing in the embrace of a woman his fellow officers knew was not his wife.

CHAPTER 8

Learning How to Lie

THE AMERICAN PEOPLE HAD COME TO BELIEVE IN THE POSTWAR era that they not only lived in the most powerful country on the planet but also the most honorable one. The torch upheld in perpetuity by the Statue of Liberty over New York Harbor symbolized the light and truth that only democracy could bring to the world. The American ideal was one of honor, integrity, and valor in the face of fascist dictatorship. Americans came to trust their government because, after all, it had brought the nation and world through its most daunting test against two powerful aggressors on opposite sides of the planet. The nation understood the need for secrecy when it came to developing the atomic weaponry that won the war. But secrecy and deceit were two different things.

Until this point in American history, the military had very little reason to lie to the public because wartime circumstances gave leaders clearer options: Bad things happen in war, and leaders knew that Americans could handle the truth, warts and all. If German submarines had attacked a flotilla of U.S. ships, the Navy would admit it up front, and the news headlines would reflect the ugly truth. But in a postwar era riddled with espionage and the need for heightened secrecy potentially to save lives and avoid a nuclear war, deception became a far more convenient alternative to admitting inconvenient truths. The "Roswell Incident" might well have been the starting point down that slippery slope of mounting one big lie on top of another. Lieutenant Colonel James I. Hopkins was a witness to its inception.

Americans by the late 1940s had come to expect, for the sake of national security, that their government would hide important projects and information from the people, but they also believed the government and military wouldn't blatantly lie to them. If a scientist in a white coat or a general stood before the cameras and stated with conviction that, say, the radiation emitted from multiple atomic tests would dissipate harmlessly in the atmosphere and not pose a danger to humans, well, that was good enough. The white coat meant authority. Scientific integrity. Honesty.

So residents of the Southwest donned their sunglasses and sat outside in lawn chairs to watch the mushroom clouds rising over a test site in Nevada. Even reporters, those professional cynics whose jobs required them to question everything and demand proof before reporting it as fact, trusted the government when officials told them a pair of darkened goggles were good enough to protect them from the atomic flash over Nevada or at the site of the Operation Crossroads explosions.

People just couldn't fathom the idea that their government would lie to them. In the atomic age, the government—and especially the military—decided at some point after the war that the truth was simply too dangerous for Americans to know. Officials learned how to lie like never before, and once they got started, they found it too difficult to stop. The radio, ubiquitous in all American homes, was supplemented by television as the means for the government to relay its version of the truth to a mass audience.

Near Roswell Army Air Field (soon to be known as Walker Air Force Base) around July 8, 1947, the military demonstrated its mastery of the deceptive arts, and the news media and public fell for it. Over the preceding month, Americans in thirty-two states had reported scores of sightings of "flying saucers" in the sky. Two pilots of a United Airlines passenger plane over Oregon reported seeing several. Another pilot said he clocked a flying saucer at a speed of 1,200 miles per hour. The reports became so voluminous that scientists stepped forward to help the government explain the unexplainable. A scientist at California Institute of Technology asserted that the flying disks were government experiments in the "transmutation of atomic energy." That prompted a quick denial from the U.S. Atomic Energy Commission, followed by a statement from Army Air Forces spokesman Captain Tom Brown, saying the Air Forces were "completely mystified" by the reports. "This is definitely not an Air Forces experiment. We absolutely do not know what these flying discs are. In fact, we wish we did, but we're just as mystified as everyone else."[1]

Military intelligence agencies were assigned to investigate. Various new explanations surged forth. One held that the flying objects were the result of Soviet experiments in rocketry. "If some foreign power is sending flying discs over the United States, it is our responsibility to know about it and take proper action," an Army Air Forces spokesman told United Press (later renamed United Press International).[2] The reports were so voluminous and widespread that officials could no longer laugh it off as the fantasies of cranks and lunatics. Even a judge in Washington State and the Lieutenant Governor of Idaho reported having seen flying saucers. One explanation surfaced that the sightings were perhaps the result of a new jet plane developed by the Army Air Forces that traveled so high and so fast that observers on the ground mistook it for a flying saucer.

Hundreds of such articles appeared in newspapers around the country. The reports circulated to the point that experts speculated about the possibility of some kind of mass hallucination. Editorial cartoonists poked fun at the sightings. Readers sent in letters to the editor addressed "To the Flying Saucers." A radio station took out an advertisement declaring that its top-rated disc jockey was the "Unseen Pilot of the Flying Saucers." A Long Island, California, car dealership joked in an advertisement about the "delivery of 100 new interplanetary space cars from Mars. First come, first served."

Then New Mexico rancher W. W. Brazel decided to step forward to tell his own story. He was doing the rounds on the ranchland he managed near Roswell and discovered remnants of something that clearly had fallen from the sky. Brazel insisted the remnants bore no resemblance to a weather balloon and consisted of a lot of rubber, sticks, and tin foil. He notified the local sheriff, who contacted officers at Roswell Army Air Field. The commander of the 509th Bomb Group, Colonel Butch Blanchard, took possession of the items and examined them alongside Hopkins and a small group of other officers. Blanchard contacted his boss, General Roger Ramey, commander of the Eighth Air Force Division. Later, they authorized Warren Haught, a lieutenant serving as the base public relations officer, to tell The Associated Press that "the many rumors regarding the flying disk became a reality."[3]

Haught's statement circled the globe, appearing at first to provide the first-ever government confirmation that evidence of alien visitation had been discovered on Earth. The *Roswell Daily Record* published a front-page story in early July 1947 headlined: "RAAF Captures Flying Saucer on Ranch in Roswell Region."

The report spawned a rash of new sightings and wild speculation unlike anything the nation had previously witnessed. Government and military spokesmen offered varying explanations, only to prompt others to deny what the previous ones had said. The military officials who actually knew what was going on were bound by their security clearance from telling the world what they knew. They determined that it was better to let the government mislead the public than to risk revealing what was really happening.

The Roswell incident wouldn't be relevant to the focus of this book except for a few key elements: First, the 509th Bomb Wing was the Army Air Forces unit assigned to investigate the Brazel case even though, at first glance, alleged alien sightings appeared to have absolutely nothing to do with the nation's premier atomic attack force. Second, one of the top officers at Roswell assigned to the case and who witnessed the recovered items as they were inspected inside a secure facility was Hopkins, one of Roswell's senior commanders who was soon to join General Curtis LeMay's staff at the Strategic Air Command. Third, the Brazel case ultimately turned out to involve a military program to determine the extent, if any, of Soviet atomic weapons activity. Fourth, just as in the case of the disappearance of Globemaster 49-244 in the Atlantic, the military lied to the public about the items recovered in the Roswell incident and their significance.

The nation's military leadership seemed no longer comfortable hiding behind the veil of secrecy that had once been sufficient during wartime to keep inquiring minds among the populace from investigating further. More and more Americans were demanding to know what their government was up to, and because there was no active war to justify the levels of secrecy that had existed in the past, the government began relying more and more on the art of the half-truth. From the Roswell incident forward, Americans began questioning openly, and with strong justification, whether they were getting the real story from their government about strange events happening in the world.

The jumble of sightings around the country became increasingly complicated when hoaxers and conspiracy mongers conflated different sightings and the timing of events to make it appear that all of them were associated with the Roswell incident. The various sightings actually occurred between 1947 and 1950 and involved various pieces of equipment and experimental materials. Apparently included in some of these experiments were anthropomorphic dummies, also known as crash test dummies, which became mangled after crashing to the ground after being lifted aloft in test balloons.[4] Civilians who came across the dummies reported them as space aliens. Once those stories began circulating, they took on a life of their own. There was no stopping them.

The sightings coincided with two important developments involving stratospheric aerospace research. One was the initiation of near-Mach-speed jet flight under the direction of famed test pilot Chuck Yeager. The name of his plane, developed toward the end of World War II, was X-1. Yeager's test flights began in 1947, around the time people first started reporting sightings of objects zipping across the sky at speeds never before witnessed. Another development was from the chemical company DuPont, which under government contract was trying to develop a material light enough to float through the upper atmosphere like a balloon but tougher than the materials previously used for weather balloons. DuPont developed the material now known as Mylar—a shiny, metallic-looking material that also would have turned heads if sighted floating through the jet stream while reflecting the sun's brilliant white light.

Government officials scrambled to come up with some kind of plausible explanation to satisfy public curiosity while avoiding any revelations of the actual truth that highly classified, top secret experiments were underway at Roswell and Alamogordo Army Air Forces bases, as well as the White Sands proving ground. Some of those experiments involved the kinds of missile technology that later led to the creation of nuclear warheads. But the primary missions at the time were twofold. One was to develop a form of early-warning radar to help the military detect potential incursions from Soviet aircraft. Another was to float balloons at exceedingly high altitudes over the Soviet Union containing sensitive sound- and vibration-detection devices that could alert U.S. commanders to any Soviet test explosions that could reveal Moscow's development of an atomic bomb.

Some of these experiments were conducted under the highly classified title of Project Mogul. "In short, Project Mogul sought to develop a technique capable of recording the sound of a nuclear detonation within the Soviet Union. The idea was to place acoustic sensors on balloons that operated at a steady state within the stratosphere. Mogul flights were conducted at Alamogordo Air Field in New Mexico between summer 1947 and spring 1949. Mogul was a highly compartmentalized project, meaning that only a few people with a 'need to know' were involved."

"Apparently, it was better from the Air Force's perspective that there was a crashed 'alien' spacecraft out there than to tell the truth," Roger Launius, former curator of space history at the Smithsonian's National Air and Space Museum in Washington, told *Smithsonian* magazine. "A flying saucer was easier to admit than Project Mogul."[5]

Mogul had two primary research and development goals. First was the acoustic-sensor project, developed with the assistance of Columbia University. The second was to find a way to suspend a balloon at high altitudes using equipment that regulated its positioning and height. The College of Engineering at New York University worked in 1946 with Watson Laboratories to come up with a design that aimed to keep a balloon at a constant altitude, with a variance of only 500 meters sustained over a 48-hour period. "The few military members involved included personnel from the Army Signal Corps who were already involved in developing ground acoustic instrumentation. MOGUL was so sensitive that the codename itself was classified and the majority of the participants were unaware of MOGUL's real purpose—to listen to (i.e., detect) the sound of a nuclear detonation originating in the far-off regions of the Soviet Union."[6]

Revealing the true nature of either of these missions to the general public no doubt would have created a far worse sense of panic than allowing fanciful rumors to circulate about space aliens. But even that latter option carried significant risks of public panic, especially given the bizarre reaction of radio listeners in 1938 to the broadcast of H. G. Wells's *The*

War of the Worlds. So the government came up with the simplest explanation possible: The "disks" and tin foil and other debris were nothing more than remnants of weather balloons. Decades would pass before the government would officially attempt to clear the air.

An exhaustive 232-page report titled "The Roswell Report: Case Closed," published by the U.S. Air Force in 1994, sought to put the matter to rest.[7] By that point, the general public had largely moved on, save for the stragglers on the fringes who refused to accept any explanation short of confirmation that "we are not alone." Project Mogul actually occurred between 1947 and 1950, and involved more than 100 balloon flights. The balloon debris that Brazel discovered was from the fourth launch.

The "Case Closed" report sought to clear the air first by openly acknowledging that the government deliberately tried to mislead the public:

> On July 10, 1947, a newspaper article appeared in the Alamogordo Daily News displaying for the press the devices, neoprene balloons, and corner reflectors which had been misidentified as the "flying disc" two days earlier at Roswell AAF (Army Air Field). The photographs and accompanying article quoted Maj Wilbur D. Pritchard, a Watson Laboratory Project Officer (not assigned to MOGUL) stationed at Alamogordo AAF· This article appeared to have been an attempt to deflect attention from the Top Secret MOGUL project by publicly displaying a portion of the equipment and offering misleading information. If there was a "cover story" involved in this incident, it is this article, not the actions or statements of Ramey. The article in the Alamogordo Daily News stated that the balloons and radar targets had been used for the last fifteen months for the training of long-range radar personnel and the gathering of meteorological data.

Part of the problem, author and Air Force Captain James McAndrew explained, was that the people going before reporters in 1947 probably didn't have the clearance or access to the highly compartmentalized information regarding Project Mogul to provide a plausible explanation that didn't stretch the truth to the breaking point. They appear to have improvised because they didn't know what all of this debris was about. They clearly believed the weather balloon explanation was the easiest route to success.

> To complicate the situation, events described here took place nearly 50 years ago and were highly classified. This Top Secret project appeared to have utilized the concept of compartmentalization very well. Interviews with individuals and review of documents of organizations revealed that the ultimate objective of the work, or even the name of the project, in many instances was not known. It was unlikely, therefore, that personnel from Roswell AAF, even though they possessed the appropriate clearances, would have known about project MOGUL.[8]

Those going in front of the news media, in other words, didn't know that the U.S. government was aware its monopoly on atomic weaponry was expiring and that the Soviets were almost certainly developing their own test bomb. Project Mogul was designed to detect the seismic and atmospheric shock waves emitted from such an explosion to help alert the United States to the Soviet Union's emergence as an atomic superpower.

The Soviets knew what they were up to. The American government knew what they were up to. The only ones still left in the dark were the American people, who were rapidly losing faith in the truthfulness of what their own government was telling them. And since the news media was at least partially complicit in conveying the misleading information being put forth for public consumption, American distrust in the news media found its roots in these very early days of the Cold War—a distrust that cascaded into a crisis for the news industry several decades later.

The Roswell incident also sparked a new era that cultivated society's worst conspiratorial instincts. Since neither the government nor the news media could be trusted, people took it upon themselves to gather evidence and selectively compile it for presentation to other like-minded conspiracy theorists. An industry was born. Hollywood in the 1950s found a receptive audience for fictitious films about alien invasions. But then film documentaries circulated in selected theaters around the nation purporting to lift the veil of fiction and tell the true story of alien visits to Earth. Central among those films was *The Roswell Incident*, with a heavily skewed timeline that combined events from widely different years and locations but depicting them as happening all at once on the ranch north of Roswell. The 1956 film *UFO* was among the first of the genre, with a promotional poster depicting a frightened pilot grimacing at something he sees in the distance. The headline claims to tell "the truth about flying saucers!" The opening lines of the film set the tone for what is to come:

> Many times in the history of our civilization the introduction of a new thought has brought skepticism, even ridicule. Despite this, there always has remained the duty and inalienable right to tell the people the truth. The Motion Picture you are about to see is true. It is not fiction. Much of the information in it has never been told. You will see it here for the first time.

What Hopkins witnessed in 1947 on the day the debris was brought to the Roswell base is unknown. He never talked to his family about what he saw, only that he was there for the inspection as one of the base's senior commanders.[9] Hopkins carried his secrets into the Atlantic Ocean on March 23, 1951, in an incident that, once again, underscored the public's justification for treating the words of the government and military with skepticism, if not scorn.

Just as the Roswell incident was rooted in the government's efforts to hide its secret attempt to monitor Soviet atomic developments, official accounts of the disappearance of Globemaster 49-244 were rooted in the government's bid to hide the transfer to Britain of atomic attack forces in preparation for war. Just as wild conspiracy theories developed over the Roswell incident, similar theories exploded among family members deprived of the truth after 49-244 went down.

CHAPTER 9

Birth of the Cold War

THE END OF THE WAR MARKED NOT MERELY A TIME OF DRAMATic change on the military front but also on the political front. Franklin D. Roosevelt's death cleared the way for Harry S. Truman to take power in the White House and forge a bold new political path for himself. In Britain, the prime minister who had guided his nation through what he once labeled Europe's "darkest hour," Winston Churchill, recognized the limits of Britons' tolerance for constant demands for self-sacrifice and war-footing wariness. They, like their American counterparts, wanted to restore some semblance of their prewar lives. Churchill was the right person in British voters' minds to ensure the nation's survival in war, but his conservative, cautious bent wasn't what they were looking for to engineer the nation's reconstruction. They wanted someone to rethink the entire model upon which British society was built. So, with the smoldering embers of war barely extinguished in Europe, Britons chose the exact opposite direction from Churchill's brand, electing a Parliament majority that installed socialist Clement Attlee as the new prime minister.

The decision might have been right for Britain in terms of addressing its urgent needs for reconstruction, economic revival, and wholesale health care reforms, but it sent precisely the wrong message to Moscow about the limits of British tolerance for Soviet adventurism. Not only was Stalin refusing to demobilize his military forces on the Eastern Front, he was also dispatching Communist foot soldiers across Europe to enlist sympathetic socialists in a mass struggle to snuff out capitalism and reshape the subcontinent's politics. Moscow's goal was to create a more fertile ground for Communism to flourish. Attlee's rise to power could not have pleased Stalin more, especially since it meant that his nemesis, Churchill, would face exile to the political wilderness.

On top of all this, the American atomic threat now seemed dramatically diminished following the dismal Air Force performance at the Bikini Atoll. The opportunity for Stalin to sow mayhem on multiple fronts in Europe was never stronger. The threat from Hitler was extinguished. The ability—or willingness—of Western powers to restrain him was minimal. Europeans were tired of war and in no mood to keep their military forces mobilized when there was no visible security threat on the horizon. Gloom-and-doom warnings by the likes of Churchill that the Soviets posed a new existential threat failed to resonate among an optimistic populace buoyed by the outbreak of peace. The Supreme Allied Commander in Europe, General Dwight Eisenhower, also seemed not to fully grasp the seriousness of Churchill's warnings, even when it was obvious that the ongoing Soviet military mobilization was designed to help Stalin swallow more and more territory into his Communist empire.

Eisenhower was doing his best to demilitarize and democratize Europe and organize a more peaceful way for the various competing powers to settle their differences. Troubling as the ongoing Soviet military mobilization must have been, Eisenhower displayed no interest in saying or doing anything to antagonize Stalin. The lesson other generals gleaned from Truman's silencing of Generals George Patton and Douglas MacArthur served notice for the senior military leadership in America to shut up, stay out of politics, and do as they were told.

General LeMay was a keen observer of all that was unfolding around him. He knew better than to spout off about political matters, but he also knew better than to let down his guard. His private letters and memoirs made clear he absolutely shared Patton's distrust of Stalin and supported Churchill's desire to come up with more effective military mechanisms to contain the Soviet leader's adventurism. But while in uniform, LeMay was careful to keep his views out of the public sphere.

In addition to writing his multivolume memoirs after leaving office, Churchill used his time in self-exile to compose one of the most controversial and perhaps prophetic essays outlining the dangers to global security posed by the expansionist Communist leadership of the Soviet Union. His remarks became known as the Iron Curtain speech, and he chose to deliver them in Truman's home state of Missouri, at Westminster College in Fulton.

Formally titled "The Sinews of Peace," Churchill's foreboding speech seemed more focused on the viscera of a third world war. He reminded his audience that he spoke only for himself, since he held no formal governmental role and was beholden to no political interest. After cursory remarks praising the American contribution to a more secure world, particularly because of its monopoly on atomic weaponry, Churchill turned his focus toward the dark side: the existence of "some Communist or neo-Fascist State" that might already have attained an atomic capability. There was no mistaking in anyone's mind, especially with Churchill's references to people living under tyranny and oppression, that he was referring to the Soviet Union and Joseph Stalin.

When it came to upholding and defending the values of democracy and liberty, Churchill said, "Let us preach what we practice, let us practice what we preach." With that, the former British prime minister got to the point:

> A shadow has fallen upon the scenes so lately lighted by the Allied victory. Nobody knows what Soviet Russia and its Communist international organization intends to do in the immediate future, or what are the limits, if any, to their expansive and proselytizing tendencies. I have a strong admiration and regard for the valiant Russian people and for my wartime comrade, Marshal Stalin. There is deep sympathy and goodwill in Britain—and I doubt not here also towards the peoples of all the Russians and a resolve to persevere through many differences and rebuffs in establishing lasting friendships. We understand the Russian need to be secure on her western frontiers by the removal of all possibility of German aggression. We welcome Russia to her rightful place among the leading nations of the world. We welcome her flag upon the seas. Above all, we welcome constant, frequent, and growing contacts between the Russian people and our own people on both sides of the Atlantic. It is my duty, however, for I am sure you would wish me to state the facts as

> I see them to you, to place before you certain facts about the present position in Europe.[1]

He warned that the menace of oppressive, coercive Communism stands in the way:

> From Stettin in the Baltic to Trieste in the Adriatic, an iron curtain has descended across the Continent. Behind that line lie all the capitals of the ancient states of Central and Eastern Europe. Warsaw, Berlin, Prague, Vienna, Budapest, Belgrade, Bucharest, and Sofia, all these famous cities and the populations around them lie in what I must call the Soviet sphere, and all are subject in one form or another, not only to Soviet influence but to a very high and, in many cases, increasing measure of control from Moscow.

Those words would alter the lexicon of America's leadership for the next four decades. The term "Iron Curtain" would fill the speeches of Democratic and Republican politicians, all of whom would scramble desperately to convince their constituents that they were the true upholders of anti-Communist values. Churchill's words would push Americans to such political extremes that the likes of Senator Joe McCarthy could rise to national infamy as he vied to be known as the one true person dedicated to exposing the extent of Communist infiltration of the U.S. government. The sad part is that McCarthy's histrionics distracted the public from the fact that Communist collaborators actually had infiltrated the most secretive lair of the government and its military and intelligence apparatus.

But Churchill, to his credit, said what he meant and meant what he said. The only problem was that he was largely regarded as a spent force in world politics. Britons were tired of his bluster and blather. Americans loved the authoritative sound of his wisdom, but they didn't quite know what he wanted them to do. So they got on with their lives. The one person who truly took Churchill's words to heart was none other than Joseph Stalin.

Back in Britain, the big question was whether Attlee could be trusted to hold the line and whether he had Churchill's same chess-like ability to outmaneuver the opponent in Moscow—that is, if Attlee even agreed that Stalin should be regarded as the opponent. Churchill regarded Attlee as a friend, but he was nonetheless mercilessly critical of the socialist who replaced him at 10 Downing. "He is a modest man with much to be modest about," Churchill once quipped. "He is a sheep in sheep's clothing."[2]

Attlee had a reputation for being uninterested in foreign affairs, which might have been fine for a domestic constituency almost totally absorbed with rebuilding and getting the nation back to work. He had trouble getting his American and Soviet counterparts to take him seriously at the Potsdam Conference of July 1945, when the three nations effectively carved up Europe into spheres of influence and established the geographic framework by which the Cold War and other tensions would soon unfold.

"Many political observers questioned whether he was capable of responding to the formidable challenges of postwar foreign policy."[3] Granted, Churchill's was an extremely hard act for any British politician to follow. It wasn't just his eloquence but his bold self-confidence and bulldog demeanor. Where Churchill would fight and argue to avoid ceding an inch of turf to his Soviet counterpart, Attlee seemed not to care enough to continue the fight. Raymond Smit and John Zametica argue, however, that this image was incorrect. Instead of placing emphasis on meeting Stalin's ground forces with like numbers of British, West European, and American troops to fight a war they probably could not win, Attlee correctly recognized that the West's advantage was in air power, and it was air power that would neutralize any military incursions Stalin chose to make.

It was an argument with which LeMay would have wholeheartedly agreed.

It is unclear how Stalin interpreted Attlee's rise to power, but the Soviet leader clearly remained undaunted and undeterred with the change of leadership in Britain. If he ever truly entertained the idea of a massive military swarm to overtake Western Europe once Hitler was vanquished, Stalin appears to have recalculated after the advent of the atomic bomb. His actions in the five years following the war's end suggest that the Soviet leader did decide to exercise a measure of restraint: Instead of swallowing Europe whole, he opted to chew up Eastern Europe in smaller bites, making sure that no action was so over-the-top outrageous as to provoke a

Western military response, yet was big enough to satiate his own desire to spread Communism throughout the land and guarantee his own legacy as a modern-day Russian conqueror.

Long before Churchill had vacated 10 Downing, he and Roosevelt had come to the conclusion that Stalin was unhinged and never to be trusted.[4] Both leaders conveyed that sentiment to their successors, as well as to the ambassadors their governments dispatched to deal with Stalin on a more regular basis. At his first opportunity, Truman named Eisenhower's chief of staff, General Walter Bedell Smith, as his ambassador. On April 4, 1946, Smith arrived at the Kremlin for a late-night meeting with the Soviet premier to present his credentials and to convey a sternly worded message about future Soviet adventurism. The meeting occurred less than a month after Churchill had delivered his Iron Curtain speech in Fulton.

The following day, Smith sent a top secret telegram via the State Department describing how the meeting went. Publicly, Truman and Stalin were doing everything possible to convey an image of solidarity in the quest for global peace. But Smith's six-page, single-spaced telegram—extraordinarily long for any diplomatic cable—made clear how seriously and rapidly relations were deteriorating between the two sides. The tensions were far, far worse in 1946 than most Americans were led to believe. Smith's telegram remained top secret until it was declassified in 1975. He arrived at the Kremlin hoping to have a private audience with Stalin, but Foreign Minister Vyacheslav Molotov also decided to attend. It was two against one.

"Because I thought that the conversation might become stormy, I went alone. Mr. Molotov was with Stalin," Smith's telegram began. He said the conference, lasting a little more than two hours, had "opened on a very restrained note." But as it progressed, the tone grew markedly sharper and less cordial. Stalin's interpreter read aloud a letter Truman had sent to Stalin posing the question that Truman said Americans most wanted to know the answer to: "What does the Soviet Union want, and how far is Russia going to go?"

No one was trying to deny Russia its legitimate right to security and prosperity, including access to raw materials available in other countries. But "the methods used by the Soviet Union caused grave apprehension, and gave the general impression in America that the Soviet Government did not mean what it said." No one was contemplating "aggressive action against the Soviet Union," nor did any foreseeable situation in global affairs seem to merit the use of aggressive action, Smith said. If Stalin needed proof, he need look no further than "the speed with which we were demobilizing our vast military strength."

He told Stalin that the United States had gone more than halfway in efforts to cooperate in the quest for peace. Then his tone grew more ominous: "We appreciate and admire the strength of the Soviet Union, but at the same time we are fully conscious of our own strength." Americans were beginning to doubt the Soviet Union's commitment to world peace, he added. President Truman hoped those doubts were unfounded, "but it would be misinterpreting the character of the United States to assume that because we are basically peaceful and deeply interested in world security, we are either divided, weak, or unwilling to face our responsibilities. If the people of the United States were ever to become convinced that we are faced with a wave of progressive aggression on the part of any powerful nation or group of nations, we would react exactly as we have in the past."

Smith noted that both nations were still in the process of assessing their postwar military needs, and that the United States was basing its assessment largely on how the Soviet Union behaved. If each nation had reason to believe the other was sincere in the desire for peace, whatever current tensions they were encountering could be resolved easily. "On the other hand, if both nations remain apprehensive and suspicious of each other, we may both find ourselves embarked upon an expensive policy of rearmament and the [maintenance] of large military establishments which we wish to avoid."

Smith's message could hardly have been more clear: *Don't mess with us.*

When Smith was finished delivering his message, Stalin responded with "counter-charges directed against our own actions and policies. The sequence and length of his argument made it obvious that the United States' comments had been anticipated," the ambassador wrote. The United States and Britain, Stalin noted correctly, were meddling in the affairs of Iran in hopes of securing access to that nation's vast oil reserves. The United States and Britain were putting obstacles in the way of Soviet access to oil concessions. It was only after making those points did Stalin acknowledge that Soviet troops were still occupying Iran even though the war had ended ten months earlier. (Stalin promised to withdraw them by a May 5, 1946, deadline.)

In spite of reporting in the American press suggesting otherwise, Smith quoted Stalin as saying, "The USSR had no intentions of taking over the Balkan nations, nor would this be an easy matter as the Balkan nations were determined to maintain their national integrity."

Stalin was still smarting from Churchill's Iron Curtain speech in Missouri. "He spoke very strongly about Mr. Churchill's speech in Fulton which he interpreted as an unfriendly act and an unwarranted attack on himself and the USSR."

Churchill's speech was just the latest in a string of actions that "could indicate nothing but a definite alignment of Great Britain and the United States against the USSR," Smith quoted Stalin as saying. Smith said he countered that, whatever Stalin's notions were of the West ganging up on Russia, the Soviet leader need only look at the actions that provoked this response: "the fate of Latvia, Lithuania, Estonia, the present situation in the Balkan States and in the Near East. . . . It seemed to us that what the USSR meant by a friendly government was a government which was under the complete control of Moscow, and not one which was capable of self-determination."[5]

These are pretty bold and courageous words for any American to say in front of a dictator who thought nothing of slaughtering hundreds of thousands of his own people during the purges starting in 1929 and might not have been too worried about the consequences of arranging the shocking disappearance of this lone American diplomat sitting before him.

Stalin zeroed in on Churchill as the primary threat to the USSR, blaming him for an effort to instigate war and counterrevolution in Russia in 1919 "and lately he has been at it again." Smith quoted Stalin directly in the following passage: "Russia . . . is not stupid, and we can recognize our friends from our potential enemies."

If ever there were a moment to pinpoint as the birth of the Cold War, it was this. Smith did his best to dial back the tensions and believed he had succeeded after assuring the Soviet dictator that his goals of securing supplies of Iranian oil and shipping lanes through the Straits of Bosporus would be assured if the United States had anything to do with it. But Smith left the meeting more convinced than ever that Stalin was intent on expanding his Communist empire, one way or another.

Smith's fears and Churchill's stark warnings were borne out in the not-too-distant future. By the end of World War II, Russia was already militarily occupying Iran, Bulgaria, Romania, Poland, and Eastern Germany. Ukraine had been swallowed whole, and U.S. newspaper maps of Russia no longer bothered to recognize the border, Kiev as the Ukrainian capital, or any other geographic distinction between Russia and Ukraine. Under heavy Soviet military pressure, Communist leaders were installed in Bulgaria and Romania. Yugoslavia and Albania followed with their own conversion to Communist governance. In 1947, Poland was set to hold democratic elections for parliament as agreed upon by Stalin, Roosevelt, and Churchill at Yalta. The vote raised the distinct possibility that non-Communists would win the election, as they did in Hungary in 1945, and break their nation free of Soviet dominance. The Communist-dominated election commission purged more than 400,000 Poles from the electoral registry. Mass arrests culled around 80,000 members of the Polish People's Party.[6] Others were killed. Nearly 100 candidates were deemed ineligible to run for office. Of the remaining candidates, Stalin invited sixteen to Moscow, whereupon he ordered them arrested.[7]

It didn't take long for American conservatives to latch on to the Soviet threat as a way to strong-arm the Truman White House into adopting their agenda. A competition began between the Republican and Democratic parties to determine who could stake a claim as the most anti-Communist. In Waterville, Maine, state Superior Court Justice John E. Swift issued a challenge to both parties, calling for a national referendum demanding that Stalin "withdraw his forces from every inch of ground in Europe and Asia where free and unfettered elections disclose that his presence defies the people's will." Swift, a conservative Democrat who also was the Supreme Knight of the Knights of Columbus, assumed such a referendum would pass. He outlined the next step: If Stalin didn't heed the U.S. demand, American forces would "demolish every Communist military establishment and every Communist soldier in groups large enough to prolong the Russian menace that now hangs so heavily over the hearts and minds of mankind."[8]

Swift was proposing nothing short of all-out war against the million Soviet troops still under arms in Eastern Europe. Rather than distance himself from the kinds of talk that could only lead to another war and, inevitably, use of U.S. atomic bombs, Truman embraced Swift's anti-Communist crusade. He responded that America's "goal must be to drive out of our American life every movement which aims to promote within our borders any form of totalitarianism or any subversive movement."[9]

Stalin seemed simultaneously consumed and incensed by such rhetoric yet not even slightly intimidated by it, as his behavior in subsequent years would prove. In Hungary, the non-Communist, democratically elected government survived intact for nearly three years. But a Communist installed as head of the nation's secret police embarked on a persistent campaign of arrests that steadily drained the parliament of its non-Communist majority. By 1948, Hungary's parliament was dominated by a Communist majority that remained in power for the next four decades. In Czechoslovakia, elections in 1948 were rigged so that only Communist candidates could run for office. No surprise to anyone anywhere, the Communists won.

Whatever assurances Stalin had given Truman, Roosevelt, Churchill, and Attlee at their meetings preparatory to the end of World War II, he had found a way to expand Soviet dominance across Eastern Europe without taking any semblance of military action that the West could deem provocative enough to justify a military response. The takeover occurred so slowly, so gradually—and often tinted with the patina of democracy and honoring the people's will—that it was more or less a fait accompli before the American and British populations woke up to what was happening. They had spent the years prior to 1948 shrugging off the warnings of old-guard politicians like Churchill, or outspoken military leaders like General George Patton, as alarmist, Red Scare baiters.

LeMay was intensely aware of his sensitive position and was in no mood to follow the career-destroying path Patton so expertly blazed by being so politically outspoken. That doesn't mean LeMay didn't share those views. Even after taking command of the Strategic Air Command, LeMay kept his views to himself and focused on carrying out Truman's orders to prepare the Air Force for any eventuality and any challenge.

"The Cold War that the United States and SAC had to fight was a new kind of war that most Americans could not grasp. Yes, it was clear the Soviet Union under Joseph Stalin was bellicose and dangerous. And the Soviets proved their expansionist intentions again and again throughout Eastern Europe and later Asia, Africa, and even the Americas, the seriousness of which world leaders, led by Winston Churchill, tried to explain." The big question in the minds of political and military leaders like LeMay who grasped the seriousness of what was happening was whether the American people understood the stakes. "But civilians wondered—if the United States was truly at war with the Soviet Union, if the Soviets were really that great a threat, then why did everything appear to be so normal?"[10]

American public opinion shifted seismically when Stalin decided in the spring of 1948 to impose draconian inspections on all incoming cargo and ground traffic into West Berlin. By June, the blockade had tightened to the point that Stalin was even cutting off electricity to West Berlin. A State Department review, which was passed on to President Truman, termed Americans' reaction as overwhelmingly in support of a forceful response. The vast majority "of press and radio commentators remain united in support of the official U.S. position—that we shall not be 'coerced' out of Berlin."

National commentators' sentiment favored a negotiated settlement that didn't violate American principles or national interests, the review stated, noting that *The Detroit News* and *Omaha World-Herald* were among the newspapers warning against the resort to war. It wasn't worth the risk. In the case of the Omaha newspaper, that position was important, given that it was the paper that soon would be delivered to General LeMay's doorstep every morning. Other newspapers, the review said, warned that any solution resembling surrender "would only result in future aggression elsewhere."[11]

In an April 1948 Gallup poll, 85% of respondents said America should stay in Berlin. Only 8% favored pulling out. Truman selected LeMay to plan and carry out the Berlin Airlift, and LeMay performed the task with such a high level of success that it virtually guaranteed his subsequent promotion to head the Strategic Air Command.

The overall picture during this period was just about as bleak as it could get in terms of East-West tensions. The West and Stalin were at an impasse. Stalin refused to see the military-enforced spread of Soviet Communism across Eastern Europe as anything but a virtuous embrace of Marxist doctrine by the masses. He could not, or would not, see the existence of a million Soviet troops under arms, or the unquestionable involvement of Soviet troops and pilots in the subsequent Korean War, as a military threat. But the more Western leaders talked of the need to counter Soviet expansionism, the more Stalin spoke with outrage at those trying to stoke the flames of military confrontation.

By early 1949, state-controlled radio in the Soviet Union consistently reflected a message that Stalin was the lonely voice seeking peace, drowned out by the shouts of "warmongers" in the West. Stalin was portrayed as pulling out all the stops and bending over backward to "remove all obstacles to building up a lasting peace," said a summary of CIA-monitored radio broadcasts from Soviet-occupied Germany. "Those who reject (Stalin's) fair offer will reveal themselves as warmongers. They will, however, notice that the authority of the Soviet Union and of Stalin in particular, as principal defender of world peace, will have gained even more respect."[12] Other pro-Soviet broadcasts reported that "newspapers were virtually torn out of the hands of the news vendors" in Berlin to read about Stalin's valiant effort to preserve peace.

It was "the unwillingness of the capitalist world to cooperate as the obstacle to peaceful coexistence of the Communist and capitalist systems," stated a February 1951 Central Intelligence Agency memorandum to Truman in a summary of an interview Stalin had given to the official newspaper *Pravda*. "Now he asserts that peace can be maintained if the people take the cause into their own hands and carry it through to the end. War can become inevitable if the deception practices by the (Western) warmongers is successful. This constitutes a notice to the Soviet people and others that war is a possibility."[13]

Apparently comfortable with the knowledge of Truman's views toward Stalin, the CIA writer of the memorandum to Truman waxed political in the final paragraph summarizing the *Pravda* interview, writing, "The standard Soviet 'big lie' for public consumption is continued in Stalin's claim that peaceful orientation has prevailed in the USSR since 1945 and his description of the Korean War as a defense against American aggression."

The two sides were talking past each other instead of communicating. Stalin was preparing the ground on the propaganda front to convince the world that he wouldn't be the one to start another world war. The United States was trying to make the case that peace was the furthest thing from Stalin's mind and that he planned to extend the reach of Communism as far as he could by forceful, though nonmilitary, means. If that didn't work, well, Stalin would have no hesitation to provoke war.

The drumbeat was growing louder and more pronounced. And it was in the middle of the growing recriminations between the two sides that General LeMay, with Truman's blessing, began making preparations to move America's atomic attack forces into place in Europe.

CHAPTER 10

Mr. and Mrs. and Mrs. Cullen

THE AMERICAN PUBLIC HAS LONG HAD A FASCINATION WITH spying, built around the fiction that agencies like the CIA maintain a force of action figures—Jason Bourne, James Bond, or Ethan Hunt of *Mission: Impossible*—who possess miraculous intellectual and physical skills to penetrate enemy lairs, defeat armies of opponents, decipher the codes to impenetrable safes, grab the coveted device or computer chip that contains the desired intelligence, then defeat more armies before escaping and delivering the intelligence back to the good guys. Case closed. Good guys win. World saved.

The popular version of spy craft is that the spying entity devises ingenious ways to exploit vulnerabilities and recruit or, perhaps, blackmail a knowledgeable person into flipping over to the other side and serving as a spy for them. Or saboteur. Whatever the spying agency wants. If the flipped person ever wavers in his or her commitment, the spying agency always retains the threat of exposing the person's treason or exposing whatever it was that made the person vulnerable to blackmail or enticement in the first place. In the early 1950s, the U.S. and British governments believed that homosexuality, marital infidelity, or prior associations with socialism were among the ways the Soviets used blackmail to flip officials to Moscow's side.

Either way, the enemy spying agency tends to command obedience because the person's fear-driven desire to avoid exposure is greater than the fear of punishment for the crime of treason. In the real world, spying by flipping a white-whale source rarely happens. Instead, successful intelligence gathering involves the painstaking, piece-by-piece process of collecting a little tidbit of information here, comparing it with another tidbit over there, discerning patterns from disparate events, and coming up with a convincing scenario worthy of taking bolder action. The 2011 operation that killed Osama bin Laden in Abbottabad, Pakistan, for example, wasn't the result of a single al-Qaeda source flipping or a single *aha!* bit of information gleaned from waterboarding that led the Navy's SEAL Team 6 to his doorstep. Rather, it was the result of an entire decade of piece-by-piece intelligence gathering.

The tedious part of intelligence gathering involves the simple art of listening, much of which these days involves electronic eavesdropping, which the U.S. government does by vacuuming up trillions of gigabytes of information from phone calls, text messages, internet usage, and other communication forms, then feeding it into supercomputers to discern patterns and practices worthy of deeper investigation. But back in the era of World War II and the early Cold War, intelligence gathering focused almost entirely on secrets passed directly by word of mouth or stolen documents handed over.

During the height of World War II, as millions of American men went off to fight and millions of women went to work in factories to feed the war machine, the U.S. government came to the conclusion that spies for Germany and Japan were on the loose inside America, scooping up intelligence. Maybe they were posing as real-estate agents or taxi drivers. Or maybe they were casual patrons of the neighborhood bar. But they were believed to be skilled in the art of conversation, fully aware that Americans like to talk. Thus came the motto plastered on billboards and posters around the country, "Loose Lips Sink Ships," or the sign picturing a ship sinking under the headline, "Someone talked!"

Toward the end of the Manhattan Project, the pilots and crews of the 509th Composite Group were training with concrete-filled Fat Man practice bombs in the skies over Wendover, Utah. No one in the group knew about the nuclear technology that would ultimately go into the pumpkin bombs they were practicing with, but they all knew that their training was top secret. The group's commander, Colonel Paul Tibbets, decided in December 1944 to surprise his men with a Christmas leave in spite of the urgency surrounding their upcoming mission. Aside from serving as a morale booster, the leave was designed to test security, Tibbets wrote years later. Bus, train, and airline routes out of Utah were peppered with Army Air Forces espionage agents whose undercover job was to strike up casual conversations with the 509th airmen and subject them to a leak test.

"Just as I feared, many had failed to take seriously my warnings about the need for secrecy," Tibbets wrote. There were several examples, but he cited one particular encounter at the Salt Lake City bus station, where a "stranger" sat down next to a 509th airman at the station bar. It didn't take long before the young man had divulged important information not only about the existence of a new, specially configured B-29 bomber (the Silverplate with an expanded bomb bay door to accommodate the gigantic dimensions of a Fat Man) but also where the airman was stationed.

Tibbets placed that airman, along with others caught divulging secret information, under arrest just to get their attention. A day later, he released them with a stern warning not to let it happen again. Word swept through the entire 509th about the repercussions of talking, helping ensure mission security remained tight for the rest of the period leading up to the Hiroshima and Nagasaki bombings.[1]

A year after those bombings, Paul Thomas Cullen arrived in the South Pacific to introduce his photographic intelligence assets to the 509th. The colonel had no history of involvement in any prior 509th operation and, because he had largely operated independently of a larger combat command during the war, he rarely if ever faced the kinds of rigorous security constraints that Tibbets had imposed on men under his command. The importance of Cullen's reconnaissance missions and the level of access he had to the highest echelons of the Army command structure appeared to have placed him beyond reproach. He was unquestionably in the club.

If there were any records pertaining to security or background checks on Cullen, they were burned up along with everything else in his personnel file during a July 12, 1973, fire at the National Personnel Records Center in St. Louis.[2] It destroyed 16 to 18 million personnel files, including Cullen's. If not for newspaper coverage of his wartime feats and multiple crash landings, little would be known about Cullen's military service. But because of his apparent inattention to basic security, Cullen also left behind a trail of activities that pointed to him as the weak point in the leakage of secrets that compromised the mission of those aboard Globemaster 49-244.

The romance he struck up with Reva Hurwitz might not have been the starting point of Paul Cullen's wayward trajectory, but it definitely was the point at which his own relatives and family members of the fifty-two others onboard the Globemaster began asking questions about Cullen's background.

Even his wife, Ruth Cullen, had her doubts about his trustworthiness and loyalty. For her, it all started when the colonel arrived home in 1946 after months of temporary duty organizing the photographic detail for Operation Crossroads. Cullen asked her to take his uniforms to the cleaners, and as was her habit to make sure nothing important got lost in the wash, she said, she checked the pockets of his pants and coats. Out came some affectionately worded little notes addressed to him by Reva.

Ruth confronted Paul about one note, which he attempted to shrug off as the meanderings of an innocent young lady he had mentored during Crossroads. "The little Red Cross girl" was how he referred to her.[3] Paul had mentioned her in his own letters home to Ruth. She was the one, Paul reminded Ruth, who brought him the copy of *The Egg and I*, a book turned into a popular 1947 movie starring Fred MacMurray and Claudette Colbert.

Paul Cullen's reference to the book was meant to convey an image of innocence and assuage any concerns Ruth might have had, but perhaps the plot of *The Egg and I* generated more doubt than relief for Ruth. The story involves a young married couple who move to the countryside to become farmers. Another woman enters the picture and flirts with the husband, creating the drama of suspected marital betrayal that fills the book and film with intriguing plot twists. In Hollywood versions, these comedy films always have happy endings where a simple misunderstanding ultimately is resolved happily for the married couple at the center of the story. In real life, flirtatious episodes very often lead to far more problematic outcomes.

After Crossroads, Paul continued to arrange rendezvous trips to see Reva. How many, and to what extent taxpayer dollars were spent on Army Air Forces flights for the visits, is unclear because Cullen's flight records were destroyed in the archives fire. But it was common in those days for the military to let pilots fly around the country on personal business so they could build up their required flight hours. "In an odd calculation, pilots were encouraged to take an aircraft for any cross-country weekend jaunt—to visit a girlfriend or relative—for the sole purpose of burning up gas," LeMay recalled of that period.[4] Cullen appears to have taken liberal advantage of the prevailing freedoms for pilots to do as they pleased with government aircraft.

"He was a nice-looking man. He obviously was intelligent. He had a goal, he had a purpose. . . . It was just his presence, his persona, that attracted her to him," said Reva's niece, Carolyn Hurwitz, who was born after the Globemaster ditching and never met Paul Cullen. But she did spend a lot of time while growing up talking to Reva about him and hearing the stories of how they fell in love.[5]

Aside from Reva's repeated references to "my colonel" in her letters home, her parents knew very little about the man who clearly was courting their daughter. Reva's brothers were openly skeptical and naturally protective of her, Carolyn Hurwitz said. No one knew what to think of this older guy with a murky background. They knew he had flown with Elliott Roosevelt and held an important command position during Crossroads, but Reva had shared precious few additional details about him in her letters home.

Something strange occurred in the spring of 1947 that forced the family to address the seriousness of Reva and Paul's relationship. The letters in Reva's University of Wyoming archives make only vague references to whatever event occurred, but the references coincide with a trip the couple took to Ciudad Juárez, Mexico on March 22, 1947.[6] There, in front of two witnesses required by Mexican law and before Judge Raul Orozco, Paul Cullen swore to a lie, violated American military and civil law, and exchanged wedding vows with Reva Joy Hurwitz. He claimed on the marriage registry, written in Spanish, that he was "divorciado" when, in fact, he was not.

At that moment, through Acta de Matrimonio Numero 007 2278, Paul Cullen became officially married to two women at the same time.

It is also extremely doubtful, given military travel restrictions in effect at the time, that Cullen had cleared his plans to cross the border for the purpose of getting married, especially since the only records the military had on file at the time indicated he was married to Ruth Cullen, who was still residing in the couple's home in Washington, D.C.

Weeks apparently passed before the couple felt comfortable enough with their marital arrangement to let Reva's family know what had happened. On May 12, 1947, at 11 p.m., Reva's brother David Hurwitz placed a sheet of paper in his typewriter bearing the logo and letterhead of his Midwest Jewelry Store in Laramie. "Dear P.T.," he typed. "I know this has been a long time coming but its length of delay does not take away, in any way the way I feel. First, may you get as much enjoyment from our family as you have brought into it. . . . I hope it won't be too long before my folks can meet you and confirm Deed's judgement." (Deeds was the nickname Reva's family gave her.)

The following sentences in David's letter provide the only written indication in Reva's archive that something was amiss in their early marital situation:

> *You know at the time that I last talked with you, I had said that I wished the circumstance had been different and that some things could be changed. Even having told you that then, I still felt that your answers to me at the time were very sincere and that you would try your best to make the most of a bad situation. To say the least, the speed with which you did it surprised me no little but your actions didn't—it only showed that you were as sincere as I thought then.*[7]

The rest of the letter makes enough references to the couple's elopement—and the fact that no family members were present—as one element of the concern David Hurwitz was expressing. It is also apparent that Paul Cullen had come clean with David about that "bad situation"—that is, his existing marriage to Ruth. The speed with which Paul claimed to have resolved it is what David was referring to.

But what Paul didn't divulge to anyone in Reva's family was that he hadn't, in fact, resolved it at all. For the following year at least, and likely longer, Paul Cullen remained married to two women at the same time.

David wasn't the only family member expressing reservations. Reva's oldest brother and Carolyn Hurwitz's father, Garvin, who went by the nickname Buddy, also had his doubts. "Dad was a really good judge of character. There wasn't a prejudiced bone in his body, but he believed in right and wrong. He followed those tenets," Carolyn recalled. On one hand, Garvin was extremely protective of his sister, but on the other, he wanted to make sure she was happy. "Deeds always gushed about P.T.," Carolyn said. Garvin had to be careful what he said about Paul. At the same time, "He said that he [Cullen] was a cocky man. Or arrogant. Very self-assured. There was something about this situation carrying on with my aunt." Carolyn and two other siblings uniformly quoted their father as dismissing Cullen as a "flyboy."

"Dad mentioned one time to me, after Deeds died, he said there was an issue," Carolyn said. "I can't remember if he said they were married in Mexico."

Paul apparently claimed before a judge in Florida to have submitted divorce papers for processing in Mexico prior to his marriage to Reva, but no such files appear in the public record. Only the marriage record comes up in Mexican database searches. Ruth Cullen testified in court years later that Paul had tricked her into signing a blank power of attorney, which he used one year after his marriage to Reva to initiate divorce proceedings against Ruth before Judge Victor O. Wehle in Tampa, Florida.

It was in Wehle's court that Paul committed yet another lie under oath, claiming that the divorce was consensual and uncontested when, in fact, Ruth Cullen later testified that she had no idea what was happening. What Paul submitted to the judge was a power of attorney that Ruth claimed she had signed without putting on her glasses after receiving his assurances that it was just routine paperwork. Wehle accepted Paul's divorce request without Ruth being present. Ruth not only didn't reside in Florida, she also had no idea what was happening because she was never served divorce papers. Paul Cullen had sent them to the wrong address when he knew fully well what the couple's longtime address was in Washington, Ruth testified, claiming the error was deliberate to prevent her from contesting a divorce she had known nothing about.[8]

An equally strange event occurred in 1948 after Wehle granted the divorce: Paul and Reva traveled to Baltimore, where they were married yet again in an official U.S. ceremony. They moved briefly to Washington, where Paul was stationed at the time, then moved to Louisiana, where he was permanently assigned to a reconnaissance command, and promoted to general, at Barksdale Air Force Base, outside Shreveport, where the nation's airborne nuclear arsenal would be based years later.

Reva slowly assumed the social life of a general's wife. Her name would occasionally pop up in the women's section of the local Shreveport newspaper, either as Reva Cullen or Mrs. Paul T. Cullen. When Paul received word that he was to command the Strategic Air Command base at Mildenhall in the United Kingdom, Reva said she expected to follow behind and make that her new home.

"I have always lived with the General," Reva told the New York *Daily News*, "except when he was away on trips. He had been permanently assigned to England before his death and had arranged for the shipment of our furniture. It is inconceivable that he could have maintained two homes during the period of our marriage—as inconceivable as it would have been for him to do such a thing. I have ample proof that this first wife knew of our marriage," Reva told the *Daily News* reporter.

There are hundreds of pages in General Curtis LeMay's archive files at the Library of Congress consisting of personal correspondence, official messages, and diary entries from the 1947 through 1951 time period. Although they contain mentions of Cullen's appointment to head the Seventh Air Division in Britain, not one sentence in all those pages refers to Cullen's questionable behavior even though, as Colonel Carl T. Hughes later testified before Wehle, Cullen's extramarital activities were becoming so obvious that Hughes felt compelled to sit down and have a stern talk with him about the need to clean up his affairs.[9]

The warning bell had been rung, loud and clear. This wasn't just a question of enforcing proper conduct among the military's senior staff. Paul Cullen was someone with access to some of the Air Force's most highly classified secrets—a person whose knowledge and experience was highly valued by the Soviets. And he was cavorting around the country—even across the border—with reckless abandon.

It didn't sit well with Reva's family. It didn't sit well with Colonel

Hughes. It was a direct violation of U.S. military law. And it posed a massive security risk. Yet Paul T. Cullen was the man chosen by Curtis LeMay to head up the first foreign-based nuclear attack force in American history.

The security measures that Paul Tibbets had put in place, including the use of agents to monitor the outside activities of men under his command, might seem draconian by today's standards. But those were dangerous times, and the threats of espionage and sabotage were real, as LeMay himself underscored repeatedly. Those threats only grew in the postwar era, when it became more clear how extensively Stalin had penetrated and installed spies inside the U.S. government. The United States could not afford to have a general of Cullen's stature circumventing strict security protocols to satisfy his personal romantic pursuits.

Nothing has surfaced anywhere to suggest that Cullen had flipped to become an agent for the Soviets, and no one who knew him suggested any such thing. The real danger was that he was flouting basic security and talking about highly classified missions with people who had no business knowing such plans. For example, he informed both Ruth and Reva about his appointment to command the Seventh Air Division in Britain. Both stated that they were told to pack up and make plans to move to the other side of the Atlantic. There almost certainly was pillow talk between Reva and Paul about all of his aspirations and future prospects. Reva had strong reason to believe from the beginning, for example, that Paul's mission involved atomic weapons, her nieces and nephew stated in interviews.

This scenario was ripe for espionage to flourish. No one needed to be flipped for Soviet spies to get the information they needed, even if they had discovered Cullen's adultery and considered using it to blackmail him. All it took was the kind of situation Tibbets set up for his own agents: Approach the subject in a bar or at an airport, train station, or some other venue, then strike up a conversation. Get the person talking. Let humans do what they do. And with a little patience, a little cultivating, those tidbits of intelligence start coming together. Besides, Reva Hurwitz was only the *known* example of Cullen's reckless infidelity. There might have been other opportunities for the Soviets to have exploited his sexual weaknesses, as they were known to do. [10]

Who knows whether the pillow-talk details stayed secret between Paul and Reva, or whether she discussed little bits of what she knew with other Air Force officers' wives at their various, well-advertised social gatherings in Shreveport? Who knows what Ruth might have discussed with her own family members back in Denver, or friends in Washington? If he disclosed details of his mission to them, whom else did he talk to?

What is certain is that Paul Cullen created hundreds of situations for details of his classified assignment to potentially leak to the outside world. He was, by the standards of the time, not just an irresponsible, lawbreaking philanderer. He was a security nightmare.

CHAPTER 11

Spies Everywhere

THE BITTEREST OF PILLS TO SWALLOW TYPICALLY ARE THOSE IN which humility is the main ingredient. Imagine a proud nation, basking in the hubris of becoming the most powerful one on the planet, being forced to accept with no small measure of embarrassment that it had been outsmarted at every turn. It seemed so obvious in the waning days of World War II that the United States was destined to assume the mantle of global leadership and unchallenged military domination thanks to its renown for simultaneously fighting and defeating two enemies on opposite sides of the globe. America's monopoly over the atomic bomb sealed the deal.

Germany, Japan, and Italy were soundly defeated. Their militaries were defanged and governments dismantled to ensure they would pose no threat to global peace for decades to come. "But it was difficult to discern the roles that allies in the war just past might play in the future. Britain, first among equals on the list of American friends, lay economically prostrate" with its colonial empire rapidly disintegrating. "China, praised during World War II as one of the four great powers of the future, teetered on the brink of civil war. Only the Soviet Union, scarred and scorched by the recent war, had the ability to challenge the United States. Logically, the Russians were the most probable future foe."[1]

America's global dominance really had only one potential challenger, the Soviet Union, whose expansive Communist structure had brought its people nothing but poverty, mass starvation, corruption, and dictatorial oppression. At the war's end, there was speculation that Joseph Stalin deliberately kept more than a million soldiers deployed beyond Russia's borders for fear they would come home with tales from abroad of abundant food, clothing, and luxuries that were nowhere to be found under his corrupt domestic management. In the minds of those devoted to the American way, it seemed so obvious that the capitalist system was far superior to anything Stalin had to offer. How could anyone beyond the clutches of Communism choose to support such a horrifically backward system that offered its followers nothing but pain and suffering in the name of uplifting the masses?

The American power elite badly underestimated the global appeal of Communist propaganda. Thinking people in positions of influence—actors, screenwriters, journalists, union leaders, and midlevel government officials, to name a few—found the Marxist philosophy intriguing enough to dabble in organizational membership. Some starry-eyed individuals in government took their interest to a much deeper level, opting to serve the Communist cause by using their positions of influence to gather intelligence and pass it on to the Soviets. As a 1946 FBI memo characterized it:

> Soviet espionage has one clear cut advantage over that practiced by any other country within the borders of the United States. This advantage centers in the existence of an open and active Communist Party whose members are available for recruitment for any phase of activity desired. . . . In almost every instance, Soviet espionage agents, particularly sub-agents, are recruited from among individuals closely associated with the Communist Party, or at least strongly pro-Communist and pro-Soviet, who in the main are native born Americans or individuals not native born but sufficiently familiar with the American way of life to avoid detection.[2]

The American power elite was so consumed with defeating the Axis powers in World War II that they almost completely failed to anticipate the potentially greater threat of Communism in the postwar period. To some, it simply seemed unfathomable that anyone would choose a life under Stalinist deprivation over the comforts and riches promised under capitalism.

That assumption is precisely how Communist spies managed to infiltrate America's and Britain's most secretive lairs dating as far back as the 1930s. The spy network was so well entrenched that, by the mid-1940s, they had stolen the West's most cherished atomic technology with ease. They helped Stalin's agents uncover and kill spies working on the West's behalf. They declared silent war against America's capitalist system and its atomic monopoly while turning a blind eye to the millions being driven to starvation in Stalin's Russia.[3] By the time the Americans woke up to the unfolding espionage catastrophe, it was far too late. The damage wrought by just a small group of well-placed agents, handled masterfully by their Soviet case officers, was deadly devastating—and irreversible. They had handed the atomic bomb to Moscow.

The context matters in the case of Globemaster 49-244 because of the top secret sensitivity of the mission and the direct challenge that the flight and its passengers, if not its cargo, posed to Stalin's plans for European domination. In instance after instance where comparable missions had been undertaken to hold Stalin's advances in check, the Soviet dictator managed to outsmart his American and British counterparts because they were naive or stupid enough not to understand that their secrets were already Stalin's for the picking.

Several cases in point help drive home the vulnerabilities that confronted the unwitting passengers and crew aboard the Globemaster, perhaps long before they embarked on their ill-fated flight across the Atlantic.

The crucial period of 1950 to 1951, just as the United States began shopping around Europe for nations to host a Strategic Air Command base and an atomic bomb, was when conditions coalesced to reveal the extent of Stalin's espionage penetration in the United States and Britain. Two independent, extensive spy networks were coming unraveled—one involving well-placed British officials loyal to Moscow, and the other involving a network of atomic scientists with Communist sympathies. Washington was only just beginning to realize, to its horror, how badly it had been deceived by some of its most trusted servants and confidants.

From January through July 1950, the partial extent of Communist infiltration was coming clear. Alger Hiss was convicted of perjury. Klaus Fuchs, the former Manhattan Project nuclear scientist now living in Britain, confessed to espionage, followed shortly thereafter by Senator Joseph

McCarthy's famous claim to hold a list of Communists working in the State Department. Then Harry Gold was arrested for espionage. David Greenglass followed, and shortly thereafter Julius and Ethel Rosenberg were arrested for spying on Russia's behalf. North Korea invaded South Korea. It was in May 1951, little more than a month after 49-244 had disappeared, when the so-called Cambridge Five spy ring was exposed. Two of the five Britons in the group were secreted out to spend the rest of their lives in the Soviet Union. Another, Kim Philby, came under such heavy suspicion that he was forced to step down from his senior post in the Secret Intelligence Service, or MI6, Britain's supersecret foreign spying operation.

"There can no longer be any doubt about the widespread and successful Soviet espionage operations against the United States and Great Britain during the 1940s, and that, aside from their own professional skill, Soviet intelligence services could count on the aid of the Communist parties of the target countries," William Crowell, deputy director of the National Security Agency, wrote in 1996 as his agency released the Venona files, an intelligence gold mine of decrypted messages that exposed a vast network of Communist spies feeding information to Moscow. Unfortunately for the West, the Venona discoveries came far too late to mitigate the loss of America's atomic secrets, which ultimately cost the nation its nuclear monopoly.

For spies like Klaus Fuchs and Harold Adrian Russell "Kim" Philby, depriving the United States of that monopoly was entirely the point, and they were perfectly placed to ensure that Stalin was kept fully apprised of American technological achievements with such specificity that he was able to duplicate those same achievements by the end of the 1940s. The Americans and British were clearly unprepared to confront the possibility of Communist spies in their midst largely because they didn't really understand what Communism was.

Philby would be the first to acknowledge the utter unpreparedness of Western agencies to address the threat, writing:

> *In those early days, there was very little secret intelligence to work on. The dearth of current material was not wholly disadvantageous. Very few officers in the service at that time*

> *knew anything about Communism, and our first task was to go back to school to learn the elements of the subject, while keeping abreast with current events through the study of overt material such as the Communist press and monitored broadcasts from Communist countries. What little secret intelligence we got was mostly fake.*[4]

The U.S. government was even further behind the British in coming to grips with the threat, realizing only after World War II that it had virtually no agents or assets inside Russia to supply much-needed intelligence on what Stalin was up to. Stalin, on the other hand, already had devoted years developing a vast and deep network of intelligence inside the U.S. government. It seemed as though no secret, no matter the sensitivity or classification, was beyond his reach. Even the top secret monitoring system established by the U.S. Air Force to detect Soviet atomic developments, including the first Soviet atomic explosion in 1949, was relayed to Moscow because of Philby's key position on the U.S.-British Combined Policy Committee on Atomic Energy.

Philby, working in tandem with his Cambridge Five colleagues Guy Burgess, John Cairncross, Anthony Blunt, and Donald Maclean, was by far the most durable and devastating Cold War foe to challenge the notion of American and British atomic superiority.[5] He did it right under the noses of his own government, as well as the Americans', and endured as a spy even as the noose was tightening around his colleagues. Philby calmly stayed in place as pressures mounted to the point that his colleagues either felt compelled to confess or fled to Moscow just as their duplicity was being discovered.

Just as the United States was working secretly to establish an advance atomic attack force in Britain in 1950 and early 1951—the very mission General Cullen was sent to command—Philby was appointed as the U.K. representative to the Combined Policy Committee on Atomic Energy. The appointment placed him directly at the center of talks between the United States and Britain on how to confront the growing Soviet threat to Europe, a threat that Washington deemed so severe and imminent that it felt compelled to move a rapid atomic attack force into place on British soil starting in March 1951. The team aboard Globemaster 49-244 was to establish the command post for that mission, whose secrecy was by no means assured given how badly the atomic security apparatus had been compromised.

In one of the great ironies of the Cold War, Philby also served as the senior counterespionage officer in the British Secret Intelligence Service, which thus tasked a Soviet superspy with detecting and exposing Soviet spies in the service's ranks. Philby's challenge was to make it appear that he was doing his job defending Britain against infiltration when, in reality, he was the infiltrator. Philby was uniquely suited for this mission. Among the great attributes of a successful spy is a broad spectrum of intellectual and social skills. Those skills become so valuable that everyone around the spy willingly looks the other way when signs of trouble surface because no one dares to endanger the services this trusted person can provide. On top of the skill factor, there's the social aspect. Not only are good spies skillful and able to deliver the top-quality services their employers require, they also prove adept at making friends and worming their way into the emotions of those around them. Again, this talent serves to make would-be accusers reluctant to come forth because the friendship the person provides is so emotionally valuable. Philby was exactly that kind of person.

He was charismatic, a bon vivant who could hold his own at the bar or entertain guests with aplomb, telling jokes and war stories at the dinner table. His colleagues became so enamored and blinded by his charisma, they found it easy to shrug off what they knew to be his Communist sympathies dating back to his student days at Cambridge. His chief advocate and most persistent defender at MI6, Nicholas Elliott, wrote of Philby, "He had an ability to inspire loyalty and affection. He was one of those people who were instinctively liked but more rarely understood. For his friends he sought out the unconventional and the unusual. He did not bore and he did not pontificate."[6]

Philby's family pedigree also helped place him above reproach, as if the blue-blooded stature and trustworthiness of his father, Hillary St. John Bridger Philby, naturally passed on to the son. Even when the myth came crashing down around Philby in 1951 with the defection of his colleagues, Burgess and Maclean, the defenders stepped forth from every quarter to attest to Philby's loyalty, as if he were the one betrayed. Those defenders were not only British but included such well-placed American intelligence officials as James J. Angleton, the CIA's chief of counterintelligence.

During this same time period, Klaus Fuchs was wrapping up his tenure as a senior atomic researcher in the Manhattan Project. Despite ample reason to believe that Fuchs was a spy—or at least worthy of suspicion—he was regarded at Los Alamos as sociable and upstanding. When word circulated that the Manhattan Project had been infiltrated by Communist spies, Fuchs was among the last to be suspected. In the lead-up, as names of suspects or arrestees began circulating among the project scientists, a sense of astonishment set in.

> The revelation that a member of the Manhattan Project was a Soviet spy sent shockwaves through the community of physicists at Los Alamos. Discussing these events shortly after [British physicist and convicted spy Alan] Nunn May's arrest, Else Placzek remarked that her former husband Hans von Halban had worked at the Montreal laboratory, and she had therefore met May. When pressed to describe him, she remarked that: 'He was just a nice, quiet bachelor, very helpful at parties. Just like Klaus here.' Fuchs flushed and became visibly uncomfortable. The others assumed this was just because attention was drawn to him.[7]

The very people their friends held out as symbols of loyalty and professionalism turned out to be turncoats working to undermine the primary mission of the United States and Britain: to deprive Stalin of access to the atomic bomb for fear that he would prove to be an even greater threat to global peace than Hitler. Blinded by their Communist beliefs, the spies couldn't see Stalin for the oppressive, murderous dictator that he was. (Ironically, when their spy ring was finally uncovered and they were forced to take refuge in the Soviet Union, Philby, Burgess, and Maclean balked at the prospect of taking up residence at the center of the supposed Communist utopia they had envisioned. Spying for Moscow was perfectly fine, but *living* in Moscow under Stalin's rule was an entirely different thing, and something to be avoided if at all possible.)

Russian spymasters Alexander Feklisov, Anatoly Yatskov, and Yuri

Modin operated for years right under the noses of their American and British hosts while gently nudging Fuchs, Philby, the Rosenbergs, Harry Gold, and David Greenglass, among many other collaborators, to dig deeper and take ever-greater risks in order to provide the intelligence Moscow so richly desired. Their well-embedded agents happily complied. The superspies on the Russian side were consummate professionals, having been schooled since long before World War II in the disciplines of espionage.

The Soviet intelligence apparatus in the United States consisted of two distinct branches. One operated under the auspices of the Soviet Embassy in Washington and consisted of various operators working under the guise of diplomatic service. The second was entirely independent of the first, was based in New York, reported directly to Moscow, and employed hundreds of Americans as their agents on the ground.[8]

FBI Director J. Edgar Hoover warned as early as 1945 that the Soviet goal was to obtain enough information to produce an atomic bomb by the end of that year. Quoting a Soviet military general in Canada, Hoover said Stalin was "frantic" to obtain the bomb and was planning all-out war against the United States and Britain with the goal of "Sovietization" of the entire world. By November 1945, the FBI was fully aware that employees within the U.S. government were conveying intelligence directly to Soviet agents. In a separate memo, Hoover identified twelve individuals as being involved, including personnel from the CIA forerunner, the Office of Strategic Services, the Army, various federal departments, and even the administrative assistant in the White House to President Franklin D. Roosevelt. Also identified was an Army lieutenant colonel, John H. Reynolds, who had previous experience working with the Soviets during the war.

The fact that Paul T. Cullen worked alongside the Soviets, inside Russia, during the war doesn't mean he became a turncoat. Most indications are that he was a true patriot. However, his disgruntlement with Operation Frantic and his lingering bitterness over his experiences with Elliott Roosevelt raise questions about whether he became a target, like Reynolds, to be flipped to the Soviet side. If Cullen harbored any such secrets, he took them with him upon the demise of Globemaster 49-244.

The Soviets learned how to create a cell structure of informants in ways that allowed two people, both loyal to the Communist cause, to be working alongside each other without one knowing that the other was an agent. All operators were assigned code names that were never shared with other operators. The cell structure ensured that if one agent were captured, ignorance would prevent that person from being able to inform on other associates in the spy ring. Even within the KGB and its wartime precursor, the NGB, spymasters didn't always receive briefings about the most sensitive programs their own colleagues were handling. Compartmentalization was the key not only to the success of the mission but also to preventing capture and compromise. Philby, for example, wrote that in fourteen years, he had only met with his Cambridge Five colleague Donald Maclean twice, and then only briefly. "I had no idea where he lived, how he lived, or indeed anything at all about his circumstances."[9] When it came time for Philby to brief another pro-Soviet spy, Guy Burgess, about developing problems involving the potential exposure of Maclean as a spy in 1951, Philby wrote that he didn't know where to begin because he was so unfamiliar with Maclean's activities. That is precisely how the Soviets designed their cell structure to maximize protections against exposure.

The story of spymaster Feklisov helps explain why the Soviets were so good at espionage and why they were light-years ahead of their American and British counterparts when it came to the objective of stealing atomic secrets. The Allied powers were so singularly focused on defeating Germany and Japan during the war, they effectively punted all considerations of developing an espionage network within the Soviet Union until it was far too late for that intelligence to do any good. Moreover, Stalin had so thoroughly frightened his own people into submission through the use of torture, imprisonment, and collective punishment of family members of defectors, few Soviets dared to come forth as recruits for any Western espionage effort during that period.

The opposite was the case in the United States and Britain. Communism became a kind of evangelistic religion in which zealots sought to proclaim their faith and convert nonbelievers. During the pre–Red Scare era, thousands of people openly expressed their Communist or socialist sympathies. There was no shortage of true believers who were willing to betray their own country for the sake of advancing the cause of Communism. For the Soviets, the task of recruitment was made far easier because of the war against Germany. Many American and British Communists were so intent on defeating Hitler, they willingly offered their services when organizations associated with socialist or Communist causes sought volunteers. Once the war was over and Hitler was defeated, many found the transition to supporting the Soviet cause almost seamless and effortless, especially when it came to the issue of atomic weapons.[10]

Philby was an avowed Communist dating back to his student days at Cambridge and, much to the exasperation of his parents,[11] never renounced those sympathies. Klaus Fuchs was not an openly declared Communist but was firm in his conviction that no nation should be allowed a monopoly over atomic weaponry, and that the bomb technology being developed at Los Alamos needed to be shared with the Soviets to ensure a military balance between the two. In both cases, as with scores of others involving well-placed Communist sympathizers, the Soviets had to do little to win their cooperation. The loyalists volunteered it with levels of enthusiasm that sometimes astonished their Soviet handlers. Feklisov wrote that there were times when he had to urge Fuchs to slow down for fear that he would take too many risks and be caught, or simply burn himself out. Fuchs was such a devotee, such a true believer, that he took ridiculous risks and stole mountains of documents but repeatedly refused Soviet offers of compensation or even gifts.

Feklisov and Philby made clear in their respective memoirs that they were deliberately withholding certain information and being careful not to name certain people in the espionage echelons of Britain and the United States in order to protect them and not to jeopardize Russian national security. Given the numerous gaps and unidentified sources of Soviet intelligence in the American Venona files—volumes of decrypted intercepts of Soviet communications—the likelihood is strong that many high-level operatives in the U.S. government and military were never identified, much less brought to justice.

The treachery hardly ended with Russian spying on the Manhattan Project. The Russians weren't satisfied even after scoring the intelligence coup of the century by stealing the plans and designs to build a Fat Man atomic bomb. With the war having ended only weeks earlier in 1945, a group of Russian children arrived at the U.S. Embassy in Moscow with a hand-carved wooden plaque of the Seal of the United States, which they presented ceremoniously to Ambassador Averell Harriman. He proudly had it installed behind his desk in his office, where it stayed for the next seven years, meaning it was in place during any discussions the ambassador had regarding the deployment of American atomic forces to Britain in 1951. The listening device the Russians had planted inside the seal allowed them to eavesdrop on every conversation the ambassador had in his office.

The eavesdropping device, powered in a way that required no battery so that it would remain active indefinitely, provided the Soviets with a spying technology that advanced them far beyond what the Americans were capable of doing in response.

The penetration of America's most secretive lairs was so thorough, it seemed, that no intelligence was beyond the bounds of Soviet infiltration and detection. It became extremely difficult, if not impossible, to keep secret national security analyses and contingency plans concerning the U.S. intersection with Britain and Russia because the Britons whom Americans trusted with their intelligence were the very people transferring it to their Soviet spymasters. The leakage eventually became so obvious, and the British sources so apparent, that Washington decided it would be best to start excluding the British government and its emissaries from briefings on the most sensitive matters.

This consideration may have been a factor in the secrecy surrounding the flight of Globemaster 49-244 and its mysterious cargo, but not the only one. The British public was kept in the dark about the extent of Strategic Air Command activity in their country, mainly because of the extreme unpopularity of the atomic bombings of Hiroshima and Nagasaki, coupled with the growing unpopularity of the Americans themselves. Attlee's cabinet was keenly aware of the growing public anguish that, in the event of an atomic war between the United States and the Soviet Union, Britain would be the first casualty.[12] The British press helped fuel public horror over atomic weaponry with explicit descriptions from the bombing sites of the vast human suffering and devastation the attacks wrought.[13]

"I don't like those people, and I'm not the only one in this country," a British woman told Feklisov in reference to the Americans as he boarded a flight from London to Glasgow in the late 1940s. The woman had just inquired about a vacant seat on the plane, only to decide to sit somewhere else after detecting an American accent from the man with whom she had engaged in conversation. She wound up sitting next to Feklisov, Moscow's superspy. "They're uncouth and common and behave as if they were in a conquered land. They're always building air bases and want to drag us into a war with Russia!"[14]

The distrust ran both ways. As early as 1946, the British government decided that it no longer wanted to rely solely on the United States for access to research required to develop a nuclear bomb. It decided to establish its own independent research facility at a secret site in Harwell, north of London. The government hired Fuchs to assist in its program, apparently unaware of his involvement in the Soviet spy ring that compromised the Manhattan Project at Los Alamos. Fuchs was at the time feeling the net of FBI surveillance tightening around him. The scientist gladly accepted the appointment at Harwell. At the same time, the U.S. Congress, fearing that America's enemies might try to steal U.S. atomic secrets, passed the McMahon Act, which blocked the sharing of American nuclear technology with any other country. The law meant the British government could no longer have access to the research it had helped fund and its scientists helped advance at Los Alamos.[15] The Americans no longer trusted the Brits (and with good reason, as we have seen), and British trust in the Americans was rapidly waning.

Against that backdrop, the odds of Britain being able, on its own terms, to openly host an American atomic attack force on its soil were becoming slim to nil. If any such arrangement were to be seriously contemplated, it had to be treated as a top secret, highly sensitive diplomatic discussion. (The fact that references to Britain, the United Kingdom, and the sites of proposed bases were redacted from official documents declassified decades later underscored the ongoing sensitivity of this subject. Many of those redactions remain in place today despite the release of documents that make clear which nation is being referred to regarding discussions of atomic basing.) In 2024, this author requested access to a nonclassified, innocuous-seeming 1951 document in the U.S. Air Force archives titled "US/United Kingdom Agreements on Joint Use Facilities." The Air Force archivist responded that the document could not be released "due to classification and/or control markings."

As the United States and Britain were working out the atomic basing issue, the FBI in New York was finally tuning in to the possibility that a Russian spy network based in Washington or New York was actively recruiting American Communists and using them to purloin atomic secrets. Feklisov, based in New York, found it almost impossible to move about the city without being tailed by American agents. He knew his phone calls were monitored and had to resort to using pay phones on the street to make important calls. No matter how often he employed evasion tactics, the American agents were on to him, making it impossible to arrange rendezvous with his informants. The KGB in Moscow grew increasingly concerned, mainly because Feklisov had no diplomatic cover and, therefore, no claim to diplomatic immunity if he was caught. The decision came down from Moscow that Feklisov would have to leave the United States, perhaps for good.[16] His next assignment: London, where he would be tasked with handling Fuchs directly.

American assumptions of loyalty and trustworthiness among allies and fellow Americans seem, in retrospect, naive at best. But that's only because the world now knows what was happening back then. When it was going on, no one knew the full extent of Communist infiltration, which is why the spy network was able to continue to the point of inflicting catastrophic damage. Some, including Fuchs and Philby, argued that their espionage was justified by the dangers posed by America's monopoly on atomic military technology. The balance of world power required that the Soviet Union be brought to nuclear parity with the United States, they and other sympathizers believed. So, blind to the potential consequences, they took it upon themselves to make it happen. And the Soviets, despite their already advanced research into developing their own atomic bomb, were more than happy to accept the help of their enthusiastic Communist friends in the West.

Against that backdrop, the Strategic Air Command launched its mission to install an atomic attack force in Britain, believing that both sides shared the understanding of the deadly repercussions should any word of the mission leak out.

Feklisov, having monitored every aspect of the atomic bomb's design and development through his network of agents in the United States, was now perfectly placed to monitor the next steps in General LeMay's quest to maintain the element of surprise and rapid action against any Soviet incursion into Western Europe. While LeMay worked on the military command's plot to install nuclear forces on British shores, Feklisov found himself transferred from his base in New York to his new home in Britain, at almost the exact time that Fuchs was transferred there to continue his atomic research. It was from London that they would watch—for them, in horror—as the pro-Soviet spy network in the United States came crashing down with the arrests of Harry Gold, David Greenglass, and Julius and Ethel Rosenberg. Philby, meanwhile, maintained his key diplomatic position as the British intelligence liaison with the United States, where the spy was kept apprised of transatlantic developments on the atomic front.

These spy stories are fascinating, no doubt, and for subsequent decades provided endless material for novels and films. Graham Greene and Ian Fleming virtually owed their careers to this early Cold War period of spy-versus-spy intrigue. But lost in all the drama was the outlandish treachery behind a supposed World War II ally, Russia, secretly infiltrating the United States' most sensitive projects while outwardly projecting the image of cooperation. Philby's intelligence alone appears to have cost the lives of agents working on the West's behalf and, given his perfect placement to receive details of the mission and provide the Soviets with short-notice data about its schedule and precise route, may very well have played in the disappearance of Globemaster 49-244.

In any event, as Philby and Feklisov made clear in their memoirs, others were feeding information to the Soviets who were never discovered. And given the laxity of security under LeMay's command, it remains possible the culprit (if there was one) was working right under his nose.

CHAPTER 12

"Survival of the Free World Is at Stake"

WHEN CURTIS LEMAY RETURNED FROM EUROPE AFTER SUCcessfully managing the Berlin Airlift, his new assignment seemed perfect for a man who had just witnessed up close the extent to which Joseph Stalin was willing to unleash callous barbarity in order to achieve a geopolitical objective. LeMay needed no convincing about the dangers posed by Stalin's leadership and the expansion of his Communist horizons. The general didn't need to await orders from President Truman to know that it was time for America to prepare itself for another war. And since LeMay's new job in 1948 was to head up the Strategic Air Command, he now had the atomic tools at his disposal to back up any choice Truman might make to send Stalin into retreat.

Nonetheless, when LeMay surveyed the U.S. Air Force bases under his command, he was utterly shocked at what he found. Postwar America saw no need for all the hardware and piloting expertise that had been such a source of pride for him in the final months of the Pacific campaign. "When I came back from Europe in 1948 . . . we were in the process of tearing the Air Force down." Experienced pilots and crew members who no longer wished to serve were ushered into civilian life. Those who still wanted to serve, regardless of talent or lack thereof, "were usually ordered to a base somewhere close to their homes," which might have been convenient for the service members but hardly fit with LeMay's plans to train and prepare them as a cohesive force capable of overcoming a formidable Soviet foe. Just about everything LeMay saw dismayed him, including a lot of unmotivated service members who weren't needed and a lot of bases that were ill-equipped or merely serving as storage spaces for bombers that had nowhere else to go. Everything was out of place. Warehouses contained supplies that had nothing to do with the planes parked outside, meaning they were useless when it came to providing much-needed spare parts. Some planes didn't even have guns on them, he said.

Perhaps most shocking of all, LeMay lamented, "I took a look at the war plan. There was no war plan."[1]

LeMay started with a housecleaning of his favorite attack force, the Roswell-based 509th Composite Group, an elite force that had fallen into disarray after having carried out the atomic bombings of Hiroshima and Nagasaki. Even by the time of Operation Crossroads in the summer of 1946, it was apparent that training levels had gone woefully astray—as made clear by the appalling Able test demonstration at the Bikini Atoll. The degradation of the SAC's bomber force continued to the point that, in 1948, LeMay found group commanders who were not even certified to fly their own planes.

"With the atomic weapon, we could not afford this kind of unpreparedness again," he recalled. What he wanted and demanded was a fighting force so formidable that its mere existence served as a deterrent to the enemy. "So I got guys who knew something about doing this, and we got busy and did it."

Rather than broadcast how underprepared the United States was in the event of a Soviet assault on Western Europe, LeMay tried to send a subtle but effective message to Stalin about the risks of testing American resolve. At the recommendation of British Foreign Secretary Ernest Bevin, LeMay sent two squadrons of B-29s to West Germany, including Silverplates, meaning they had the notably expanded bomb bay doors that signaled instantly to the Soviets that these were nuclear capable. "Nuclear weapons carried no threat without the ability to deliver them. To give the atomic deterrent some public muscle, in mid-July the United States, with great fanfare, announced that 60 'atomic-capable' B-29 Superfortresses, part of the newly-formed Strategic Air Command (SAC), were being transferred to bases in Great Britain, within striking distance of the Soviet Union."[2] The B-29s carried only conventional weapons, though the Russians were kept guessing about what was inside.[3]

Even after Stalin's Berlin blockade, a Soviet-engineered coup in Czechoslovakia and Moscow's support for the Communist sweep of mainland China, LeMay said he never thought war was imminent before 1950. But that didn't stop him from planning for it—with the president's approval. After embarking on an aggressive recruitment program to put the Air Force's best officers in place, LeMay launched an even more aggressive training program to recertify pilots, bring ground crews up to grade, and instill a war-readiness mindset among all under his command. It took months to get the job done. Once he was satisfied that he had at least one division's worth of qualified personnel, he began the process in late 1950 of creating a new Seventh Air Division—the first atomic attack division to be based on foreign soil. The next task was finding a place to put it. Given a host of logistical and diplomatic complications, the decision came down that the new division would be based at British military airfields north of London.

Brigadier General Paul T. Cullen got the nod to be the Seventh Division's first commander, though it's not clear whether this was LeMay's decision or was imposed on him by someone with greater influence in the command chain. (There are several indications in LeMay's diaries that he had preferred someone else.)

As LeMay was busy upgrading the performance of his 509th Composite Group pilots and crews at Roswell's Walker Air Force Base, the U.S. Air Force named General Hunter Harris, Jr., to command the Roswell-based 509th Bomb Wing, Eighth Air Force. Geographically, Roswell was a short distance from his previous job as commander of the Armed Forces Special Weapons Project at Sandia, New Mexico, where he was focused on development of the next generations of nuclear weaponry. Harris performed an unusual inspection of 49-244 shortly before the plane took off on its final mission.

The Seventh Air Division's formation and deployment was the culmination of months of planning after President Truman and the National Security Council had reviewed an exhaustive amount of classified intelligence regarding Soviet military activities in Eastern Europe and Joseph Stalin's intentions for the expansion of global Communism. The result of this review was a document known as NSC-68, a voluminous study of

Soviet intentions that served as a clarion call for LeMay to get his atomic attack forces in place and ready to strike at a moment's notice.

The document signaled the Security Council's approval of previous Defense and State Department analyses concluding that Stalin was on an unmistakable trajectory toward direct military conflict with the United States, and that the United States could not afford to let down its guard. By the time the document was written, in April 1950, Russia had already exploded its first atomic bomb. The threat of war using "thermonuclear weapons," as NSC-68 termed it, was no longer in the theoretical realm. It was real.[4]

Russian power and influence—imposed by military might, coups, and subversion of democratic processes to install Communist puppet governments—had to be forced into "gradual retraction" as the first objective outlined in NSC-68. This meant restoring Russia to its traditional boundaries and returning Soviet satellite countries to full independence from Moscow. Internally, Russia had to be compelled to grant its own people the right of self-determination. People beyond the bounds of Russian military influence had to be decoupled from belief that their destinies were sealed. They did not have to accept subservience to Moscow and Communism. They could resist, and the United States needed to be there to help them.

The final objective was a bit more amorphous: "To create situations which will compel the Soviet Government to recognize the practical undesirability of acting on the basis of its present concepts and the necessity of behaving in accordance with precepts of international conduct, as set forth in the purposes and principles of the U.N. Charter." It is anyone's guess how the writers planned to "create situations," but the strong hint in this language was that undercover intelligence and covert military operations would play a heavy role. The patterns and practices of the SAC in the following months bore all the hallmarks of covert military operations, some of which remain classified even today.

Next came the element that most directly involved the Strategic Air Command. The United States needed to "develop a level of military readiness which can be maintained as long as necessary as a deterrent to Soviet aggression, as indispensable support to our political attitude toward the

USSR, as a source of encouragement to nations resisting Soviet political aggression, and as an adequate basis for immediate military commitments *and for rapid mobilization should war prove unavoidable*" (italics added).[5]

The nation also needed to shore up its defenses "against dangers of sabotage, subversion, and espionage."

It would be essential to "maximize our economic potential" to boost financial reserves in case of a sudden need to draw upon them to finance a war and assist other nations trying to break free of Soviet domination.

Finally, the American public would need to be kept apprised of the threats to national security in order to ensure a state of readiness. A series of favorable newspaper and magazine interviews in subsequent months precisely fit the public relations road map outlined in NSC-68.

The United States was the leader of the free world, like it or not, the document stated. The option remained for America to withdraw into isolationism, but doing so would almost certainly lead to further Soviet expansion. The president could defer action for a later time, but that also would leave the door open to an ongoing expansion of Soviet global influence. The free world was looking to the United States for leadership and the opportunity to join the fight. "Without such a cooperative effort, led by the United States, we will have to make gradual withdrawals under pressure until we discover one day that we have sacrificed positions of vital interest." Reversing the trend of Soviet expansionism necessarily entailed a steep financial cost, but, "It is imperative that this trend be reversed by a much more rapid and concerted build-up of the actual strength of both the United States and the other nations of the free world."

The entire document took on a tone of urgency, warning of dire consequences if the president failed to act. "The whole success of the proposed program hangs ultimately on recognition by this Government, the American people, and all free peoples, that the cold war is in fact a real war in which the survival of the free world is at stake."

Truman faced an epic conundrum. Only five years after the end of World War II, the world's memory remained fresh regarding the horrors inflicted upon the Japanese during the atomic bombings of Hiroshima and Nagasaki. The United States was then, and remains today, the only nation in history to have used atomic bombs in war. Truman had made clear that he would not hesitate to do it again if pressed, but his standing orders conveyed to LeMay were that atomic weapons would not be deployed unless America was attacked first.

The fact that Stalin retained more than a million troops in Eastern Europe and was imposing draconian rule over Soviet satellite states was proof enough that he would do what was necessary to advance his own goals. The people of the world "yearn for relief from the anxiety arising from the risk of atomic war," NSC-68 stated, yet "any substantial further extension of the area under the domination of the Kremlin would raise the possibility that no coalition adequate to confront the Kremlin with greater strength could be assembled. . . . The issues that face us are momentous, involving the fulfillment or destruction not only of this Republic but of civilization itself."

The Soviet Union had to be stopped from continuing to expand its borders into Europe. The years 1950 and 1951 were the turning point when every national security apparatus of the U.S. government geared up to meet the Soviet threat head-on.

The United States did have the option to stand down and try to reduce tensions through diplomatic means, but could the Soviet Union be trusted to do likewise? The Soviet and Communist systems simply couldn't accommodate the notion of standing down. "The fundamental design of those who control the Soviet Union and the international communist movement is to retain and solidify their absolute power, first in the Soviet Union and second in the areas now under their control. In the minds of the Soviet leaders, however, achievement of this design requires the dynamic extension of their authority and the ultimate elimination of any effective opposition to their authority," NSC-68 said.

The design of the Communist system required "the complete subversion or forcible destruction of the machinery of government and structure of society in the countries of the non-Soviet world and their replacement by an apparatus and structure subservient to and controlled from the Kremlin." Moscow could not be trusted, as exemplified by Stalin's radical misinterpretation of the Yalta and Potsdam accords, which divided the world into spheres of postwar influence between the United States, Soviet Union, and Britain, as giving Stalin a right to keep his forces deployed and solidify control over Soviet satellite states—not to mention his attempt to impose a total blockade on West Berlin.

Moscow would not stop with Bulgaria, Romania, Czechoslovakia, Albania, or Poland. The Soviets were backing insurgents in Greece and applying heavy pressure on the government of Turkey. The Communist Party in Italy and France was growing strong enough to potentially prevail in elections. Communist doctrine required expansion, by force if necessary, to achieve global domination. And the only entity capable of blocking Stalin was America.

The U.S. goal was to accomplish this by any and all available *peaceful* means. But if war became necessary, America's atomic forces had to be ready. Moscow's overwhelming number of conventional forces were ready immediately "to overrun Western Europe," as well as the Near and Middle East, to consolidate Communist gains in the Far East and, most crucially for LeMay, "to launch air attacks against the British Isles and air and sea attacks against the lines of communications of the Western Powers in the Atlantic and the Pacific," NSC-68 said.

The United Kingdom was deemed a primary target for elimination "as an effective base of operations for allied forces." The Soviets had learned from Hitler's mistakes on D-Day, the Pentagon believed, and would attack Britain preemptively to block any opportunity for a Normandy-style invasion to retake Western Europe.

It is precisely because of this assessment that LeMay began planning creation of the Seventh Air Division and working out the mechanics of deploying atomic weaponry—or at least the disassembled components of Fat Man bombs—to Britain.

Starting in late 1950, the Joint Chiefs of Staff approved a plan, supported by Truman, to begin transferring nonnuclear atomic bomb components to Britain. Truman allowed the transfers to begin knowing that the Atomic Energy Commission was being kept uninformed of the decision until it was too late for the commission to protest. Truman also allowed the Department of Defense to begin taking control of the fissile cores for atomic weapons, again without AEC approval. The rationale was that the Atomic Energy Act of 1946 stated, "The President may from time to time direct the Commission to deliver such quantities of fissionable materials or weapons to the armed forces for such use as he deems necessary in the interest of national defense."

Globemaster 49-244 is parked at Lakenheath Royal Air Force Base, England, in January 1951, three months before its ill-fated flight over the Atlantic.

Aero UK.

Tail section of 49-244 during loading at Walker Air Force Base, New Mexico, in early 1951. *CriticalPast.*

Loading through the belly of 49-244 using a hydraulic lift.
rgo could move simultaneously via ramps through the plane's clamshell doors beneath the cockpit.
CriticalPast.

General Paul T. Cullen's official Air Force military portrait. *U.S. Air Force.*

Sailors watch as mus
cloud rises over U.S.
ship during the first
Operation Cros
atomic tests, in
Colonel Paul T. C
Lieutenant Colonel Ja
Hopkins, and Reva H
played
National Archiv
Records Administ
(N

Left to right) British Prime Minister Winston Churchill, U.S. President Harry Truman, and Soviet
emier Joseph Stalin meet in Potsdam, Germany, on July 25, 1945, before the start of the Cold War.
U.S. Army Signal Corps, Harry S. Truman Library & Museum.

Then-Colonel Paul T. Cullen (right) demonstrates high-speed aerial reconnaissance cameras to Army Air Forces Major General Roger Ramey.
U.S. Air Force.

U.S. airmen offload two massive aerial reconnaissance cameras from an American spy plane. *National Archives and Records Administration (NARA).*

Then-Colonel Paul T. Cullen makes history, parking his unarmed F-5 aerial reconnaissance plane in Poltava, Ukraine, after a solo "shuttle" flight from England on May 26, 1944. It was the first flight of a U.S. military plane to Soviet territory. *Army Air Forces photo.*

Air Force film processors examine photos as they come off a printing pre
after which they would be assembled onto maps to guide pilots on bombing r
National Archives and Records Administration (NARA).

KB-29 aerial refueling plane (left) is connected by a hose to a B-29 Superfortress. The new technology dramatically extended the flight range of America's bomber fleet.
National Archives and Records Administration (NARA).

Commodore Ben Wyatt stages one of several takes of an explanation he gave to inhabitants the Bikini Atoll explaining why they would have to permanently leave their homeland for the sake of atomic science. Film crews and journalists were coordinated by Reva Hurwitz (not pictured).
National Archives and Records Administration (NARA).

Lieutenant Colonel James I. Hopkins, veteran of the Nagas atomic bombing mission, sits cockpit of his plane, likely a F on an unspecified date. *U.S. Air Force photo courtesy of son James K. Hopkins.*

Reva Hurwitz basks in the South Pacific sun during her 1945–46 stint as a Red Cross liaison to the U.S. military in Hawaii, Kwajalein, and Bikini Atoll. *Reva Joy Hurwitz Cullen archive, American Heritage Center/ University of Wyoming.*

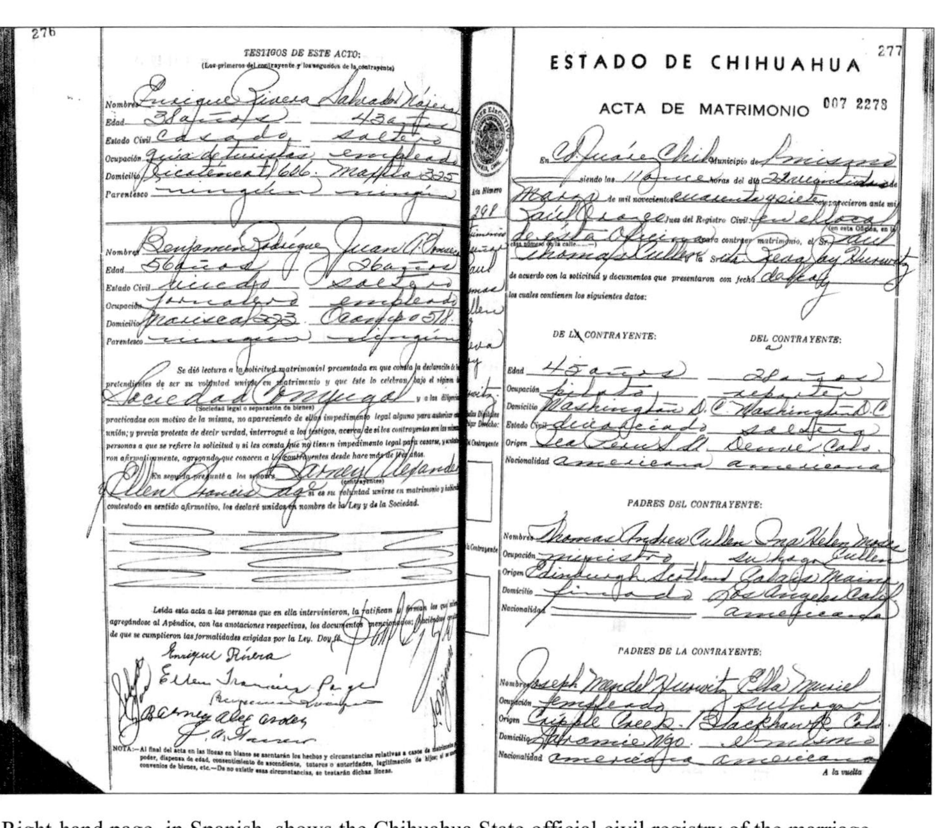

276

TESTIGOS DE ESTE ACTO:
(Los primeros del contrayente y los segundos de la contrayente)

Nombre Enrique Rivera
Edad 38 años / 43 años
Estado Civil casado / soltero
Ocupación guía de turistas / empleado
Domicilio
Parentesco ninguno / ninguno

Nombre Benjamín Rodríguez
Edad 56 años / 26 años
Estado Civil
Ocupación
Domicilio
Parentesco ninguno / ninguno

Se dió lectura a la solicitud matrimonial presentada en que consta la declaración de los pretendientes de ser su voluntad unirse en matrimonio y que éste lo celebran bajo el régimen de Sociedad Conyugal (Sociedad legal o separación de bienes) y a las diligencias practicadas con motivo de la misma, no apareciendo de ellas impedimento legal alguno para autorizar esta unión; y previa protesta de decir verdad, interrogué a los testigos, acerca de si los contrayentes son las mismas personas a que se refiere la solicitud y si les consta que no tienen impedimento legal para casarse, y contestaron afirmativamente, agregando que conocen a los contrayentes desde hace más de [illegible] años.

En seguida pregunté a los señores Barney Alejandro (contrayentes) Ellen Francis Page si es su voluntad unirse en matrimonio y habiendo contestado en sentido afirmativo, los declaré unidos en nombre de la Ley y de la Sociedad.

Leída esta acta a las personas que en ella intervinieron, la ratifican y firman los que quisieron, agregándose al Apéndice, con las anotaciones respectivas, los documentos mencionados; haciéndose constar de que se cumplieron las formalidades exigidas por la Ley. Doy fe.

Enrique Rivera
Ellen Francis Page
Barney Alejandro

NOTA.—Al final del acta en las líneas en blanco se asentarán los hechos y circunstancias relativas a casos de matrimonio por poder, dispensa de edad, consentimiento de ascendiente, tutores o autoridades, legitimación de hijos; y se consignarán convenios de bienes, etc.—De no existir esas circunstancias, se testarán dichas líneas.

Acta Número 298

277

ESTADO DE CHIHUAHUA

ACTA DE MATRIMONIO 007 2278

En Cd. Juárez, Chih. Municipio de [illegible] siendo las 11 once horas del día 22 veintidós de marzo de mil novecientos cuarenta y siete comparecieron ante mí [illegible] Juez del Registro Civil en el local de esta Oficina (en esta Oficina, en la casa número de la calle) para contraer matrimonio, el Sr. Paul Thomas Cullen la Srita. Reva Joy Hurwitz de acuerdo con la solicitud y documentos que presentaron con fecha de hoy los cuales contienen los siguientes datos:

	DEL CONTRAYENTE:	DE LA CONTRAYENTE:
Edad	45 años	28 años
Ocupación	piloto	reportera
Domicilio	Washington D.C.	Washington D.C.
Estado Civil	divorciado	soltera
Origen	[illegible]	Denver Colo.
Nacionalidad	americana	americana

PADRES DEL CONTRAYENTE:

Nombre	Thomas Andrew Cullen	Ina Helen [illegible]
Ocupación	ministro	su hogar
Origen	Edinburgh Scotland	[illegible] Maine
Domicilio	finado	Los Angeles Calif.
Nacionalidad		americana

PADRES DE LA CONTRAYENTE:

Nombre	Joseph Mendel Hurwitz	Ella Muriel
Ocupación	empleado	su hogar
Origen	Cripple Creek	Blackhawk Colo.
Domicilio	Laramie Wyo.	el mismo
Nacionalidad	americana	americana

A la vuelta

Right-hand page, in Spanish, shows the Chihuahua State official civil registry of the marriage between Paul Thomas Cullen and Reva Joy Hurwitz on March 22, 1947, in Ciudad Juárez. Cullen lists his marital status as "divorciado."

México, Chihuahua, Registro Civil, 1861–1997, via FamilySearch.com.

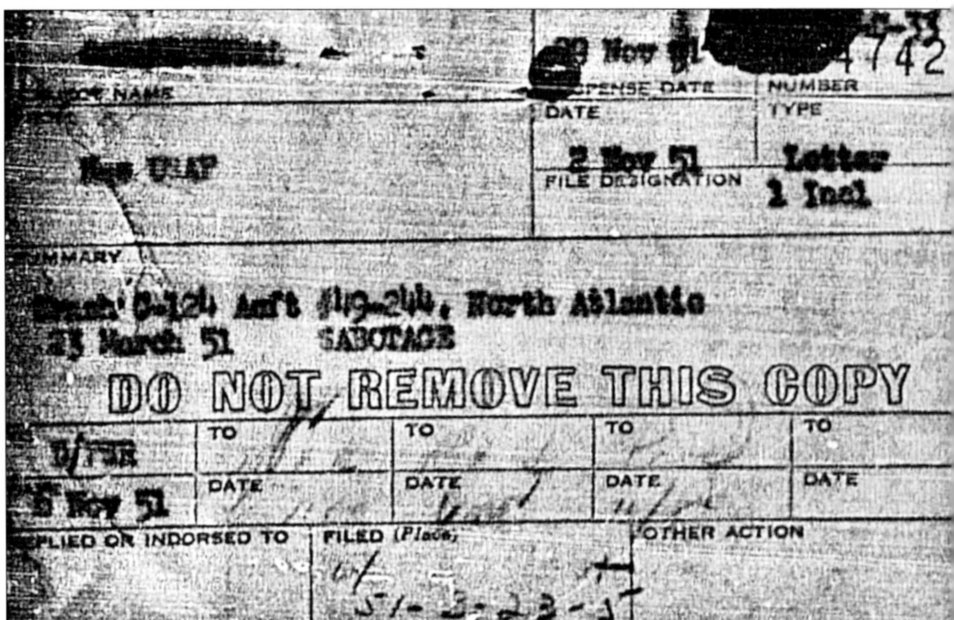

4742

NAME

SUSPENSE DATE | NUMBER

DATE | TYPE

2 Nov 51 | Letter

FILE DESIGNATION | 1 Incl

SUMMARY

C-124 Acft #49-244, North Atlantic

23 March 51 SABOTAGE

DO NOT REMOVE THIS COPY

TO | TO | TO | TO

DATE | DATE | DATE | DATE

Nov 51

REPLIED OR INDORSED TO | FILED (Place) | OTHER ACTION

51-3-23-3

November 2, 1951, investigation document listing the "crash" of 49-244 on March 23, 1951, along with the subject header of the probe: "SABOTAGE."
Department of the Air Force Historical Records Agency.

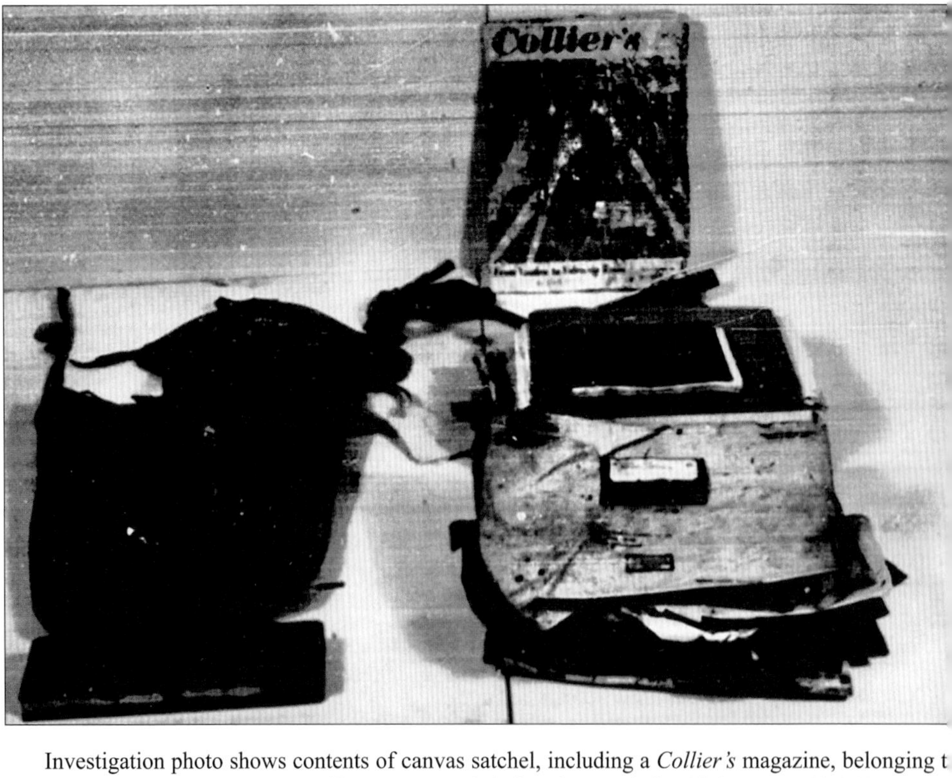

Investigation photo shows contents of canvas satchel, including a *Collier's* magazine, belonging t
Captain Lawrence Rafferty, recovered during the search for Globemaster 49-244.
Department of the Air Force Historical Records Agency.

(2) Bomb carrying aircraft will avoid overflying densely populated areas while enroute to the bomb release point.

5. <u>Emergency Procedures</u>

a. Landing at unscheduled base

(1) If the aircraft is forced to make an unscheduled landing with a bomb aboard, the following procedures will apply:

(a) Bomb Commander will post a guard on the aircraft (only one (1) guard required for a M107 bomb).

(b) He will notify the Commanding Officer, 509th Bomb Wing Prov, by the most expeditious means available of any assistance required.

b. <u>Jettison or Bail Out</u>

(1) In event that an emergency arises whereby it is necessary to jettison the bomb or for the crew to abandon the aircraft, the designated radio ground station will be notified immediately, giving nature of the emergency and position of the aircraft. If it is impossible to contact the designated radio ground station, any other aircraft or relay agency will be contacted and requested to relay the information to the designated radio ground station.

RFT

Bomber pilot emergency procedures for bailout or jettisoning over Europe during Operation Evening Star when carrying an M107 nonnuclear Fat Man. *Department of the Air Force Historical Records Agency.*

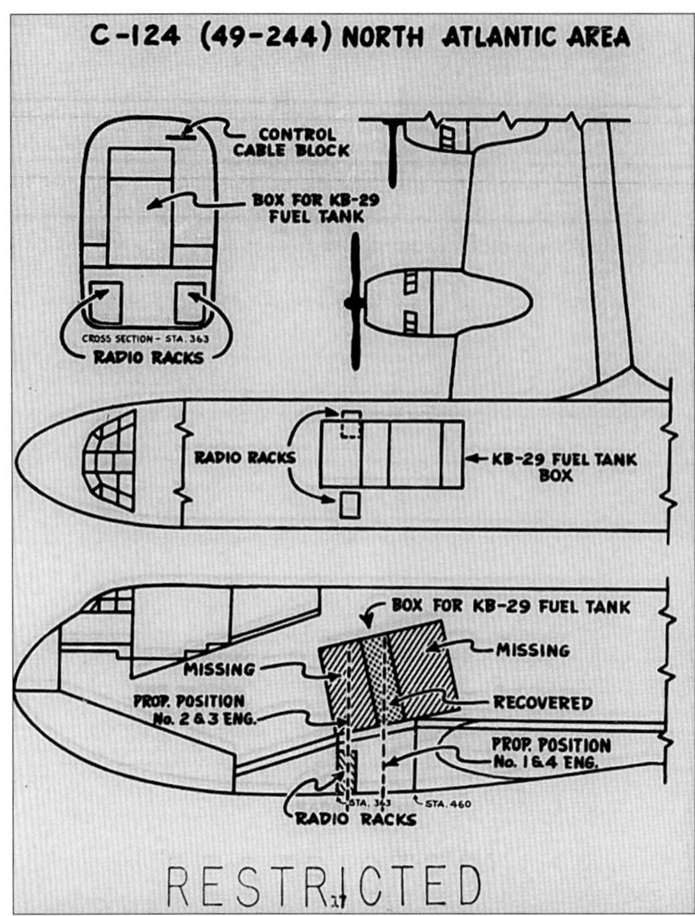

Schematic of ramp loadir
for one of the two KB-29
tanks listed aboard 49-24
Investigators failed to prc
convincingly that part of
the propeller assembly
was responsible for loss
of communications and
flight controls.
Department of the Air Fo
Historical Records Agenc

SECRET

20-53W at 242030Z. At 242042Z, he sighted another flare and many flashlights sending SOS. One crew member reports he saw a large life raft with four to six men waving. USS Muir was in the immediate vicinity and proceeded to area reaching there at approximately 242350Z. USS Muir reported negative results. Search continuing with six B-29 aircraft two SB-29's, three SB-17's, one C-47, one C-54, three RAF

One of scores of messages sent by U.S. Air Force and Navy vessels affirming the times and locatic where Globemaster survivors were sighted hours after the plane ditched before dawn on March 23, 1 *Department of the Air Force Historical Records Agency.*

Cullen is worried. When 300 miles west of Ireland, Globemaster alters course for no apparent reason. We are going dark.

Have to be careful. We are under surveillance. Pieces of wreckage will be found but are not of the Globemaster. A terrible drama has been enacted on this liner.

A handwritten note found in a sealed can on a beach near Renvyle by Irish farmer John Faherty purports to warn of subterfuge and surveillance ahead of the Globemaster's ditching. *National Archives of Ireland.*

THE GENERALS' WIVES REFUSE TO FADE AW

They Just Couldn't Believe Their Mates Could Want Divorce

By JESS STEARN

A LOT of people go along for years, seemingly happily married, and then all of a sudden the thing blows up in their faces. The two cases to be discussed today concern a couple of medium-aged generals who traded in their old partners-for-life for younger copies.

Offhand, there seems no ready explanation for the change of heart. Each wife was loyal, sincere, loving, and did not give up without a struggle. Indeed, though one of the Generals is dead, and the other is planning to remarry, the struggles go on.

Mrs. Edna Hudelson of Los Angeles can't quite reconcile herself to letting go of Maj. Gen. Daniel Hudelson, Korean combat veteran, her mate of 28 years, who came home one day and announced he wanted a divorce to marry a blonde widow.

The General Breaks Through

The Three Cullo

New York *Daily News* two-page story, published November 30, 1952, on generals who betrayed the wives who stayed with them throughout the war. Paul T. Cullen and his wives, Ruth and Reva, are pictured on the right-hand page. *Daily News.*

Another conundrum for Washington was on the political side. Leaders had to measure their words so as not to frighten the world into thinking that war against Russia was imminent while, at the same time, reassuring European leaders that the United States stood ready at any moment to respond to Soviet aggression. Then there was the tricky question of whether to issue a public declaration of Truman's internal policy that the United States would not be the first to launch a nuclear strike but rather would do so only in retaliation against a Russian first strike. The writers of NSC-68 recognized the conundrum but determined the risks would outweigh the advantages of making a no-first-strike public declaration.

Such a declaration "would be interpreted by the U.S.S.R. as an admission of great weakness and by our allies as a clear indication that we intended to abandon them. . . . Unless we are prepared to abandon our objectives, we cannot make such a declaration in good faith until we are confident that we will be in a position to attain our objectives without war, or, in the event of war, without recourse to the use of atomic weapons for strategic or tactical purposes."

Although LeMay was careful never to state a position publicly on the matter, "he strongly disagreed with the policy that promised the Soviets that the U.S. would never use nuclear weapons first. He believed the entire purpose of having a nuclear arsenal was its threatened use, not its actual use. And by promising not to use it, what was the sense in even having it?"[6]

Another complication was the spread of Communist sympathies among the populations and political leadership of various West European nations. The United States expended no small amount of effort through the Marshall Plan to use economic aid to cultivate the spread of democratic ideals across Europe and the rest of the world after World War II, which necessarily meant the promotion of freedom of thought, religion, and pursuit of economic opportunity (capitalism, in other words). The problem with freedom of thought is that it allowed for people to choose for themselves which system they liked more: one that promoted pursuit of riches at the expense of the poor, or one that strictly regulated the accumulation of individual wealth for the sake of egalitarian empowerment.

Russia aggressively marketed socialism after the war and found a surprisingly strong embrace across Europe. Its appeal in America was far less pronounced, possibly because Stalin's model seemed so antithetical to democracy. Besides, the photographic images coming from the Soviet Bloc rarely seemed to depict smiling people having a good time. American news stories emphasized forced labor, long lines for food and clothing, and a general sense of misery. In postwar Gallup polls, Americans regarded the Soviets as prevailing on the Cold War propaganda front, but when it came to quality of life, almost no one believed Russians were better off. A high percentage—68%—of Americans said they were familiar with Churchill's Iron Curtain speech calling for resistance to Soviet expansion. When asked whether they agreed with Churchill's call for a U.S.-British alliance against the Soviets, only 18% supported the idea of the two nations sticking together, and only 4% favored forming an alliance with Britain.[7]

People just didn't see what all the fuss was about.

And yet, Americans seemed enamored with the idea of using the nation's atomic power if war appeared inevitable. In an August 1949 poll, 70% of respondents favored a first use of atomic weapons. By February 1950, that had dropped to 66%, which is still a surprisingly high rate of support. In succeeding years, as Cold War tensions mounted and the threat of atomic war grew more real, American support for a first strike plummeted.[8]

In Europe, there were even greater degrees of ambivalence. The United States couldn't be seen interfering in elections and trying to influence whatever democratic choices the people of Europe made for themselves. America could only lead by example, and the example of atomic bombs exploding over Japan and the Bikini Atoll didn't exactly convey to Europeans the idea of capitalism's loving embrace. So not only did Stalin enjoy an overwhelming advantage in troop numbers on the ground, he also had a high potential to recruit Europeans as political foot soldiers in the rejection of capitalist principles.

Politically speaking, the worst move the United States could make by the time NSC-68 was produced would have been to advertise any plans to place atomic bombs and attack forces on European soil. It had to be done in absolute secrecy, even if it meant limiting the amount of information Washington shared with its closest ally, Britain. If Britons were willing to contemplate socialist leadership under Clement Attlee, the rest of Europe couldn't be far behind. Which meant that any leakage of U.S. plans to deploy atomic attack forces—much less its contemplation of a preemptive nuclear attack on Russia—risked a mass anti-American backlash that could only drive more and more Europeans into Stalin's welcoming arms.

The calculus couldn't have been more tricky. "Domestic Communist agitation buffeted both Italy and France. Moscow had pressured neighboring Finland into a nonaggression pact. Norway feared it might be next." Moscow boasted of its ability, should it choose, to overrun all of Germany in a matter of days and sweep through the rest of Western Europe shortly afterward. "Even adventurous politicians of American imperialism would not now risk starting a war," the Soviet newspaper *Tägliche Rundschau* warned, "because they know they would then have against them the people of Europe who want peace. American imperialists would not venture it in the clear knowledge that the forces of democracy are stronger today than the forces of imperialism."[9]

The Truman administration couldn't even be certain of strong American support should war become unavoidable. Ahead of the 1948 presidential election, Progressive Party candidate Henry A. Wallace decided to challenge Truman's election bid from the far left. His Communist sympathies were obvious to all. His proposal to defuse the Berlin crisis won the support of Stalin himself. Wallace challenged Truman by arguing that the president had strayed too far from Roosevelt's aggressive pro-labor program, and that he had put global peace at risk by needlessly antagonizing Stalin. Left-leaning voters flocked to support Wallace in sufficient numbers that the Democratic Party leadership began to worry whether Truman could survive the progressive onslaught with strength enough to fight a brutal general election. Organized labor, long a reliable vote for the Democrats, also strongly supported Wallace.

The writers of NSC-68 openly worried that America was being subverted from inside, using democracy itself to destroy the capitalist system. NSC-68 warned:

> It is quite clear from Soviet theory and practice that the Kremlin seeks to bring the free world under its communion by the methods of the cold war. The preferred technique is to subvert by infiltration and intimidation. Every institution of our society is an instrument

> which it is sought to stultify and turn against our purposes. Those that touch most closely our material and moral strength are obviously the prime targets, labor unions, civic enterprises, schools, churches, and all media for influencing opinion. The doubts and diversities that in terms of our values are part of the merit of a free system, the weaknesses and the problems that are peculiar to it, the rights and privileges that free men enjoy, and the disorganization and destruction left in the wake of the last attack on our freedoms [by Germany and Japan], all are but opportunities for the Kremlin to do its evil work.[10]

The document repeatedly raised the prospect of war breaking out sometime in 1950 in part because of a rigorous analysis of various political and economic factors, but also to warn the administration that crucial military decisions needed to be made now, not later. Stalin's age and failing health—an issue that even the Soviet leader himself had acknowledged—raised questions of looming instability in Russia and the prospect of a military coup. Any kind of instability, but especially the coup potential, raised even higher the chances of a military move against Europe or the rash deployment of Moscow's growing atomic arsenal.

On the economic front, the Soviets were lagging far behind the United States in terms of manufacturing capacity, oil production, agricultural output, and the production of metals, such as iron and aluminum, that kept the population fed, clothed, housed, employed, and adequately transported. Washington had nothing to fear in comparison with Moscow, but the less the centrally planned system was able to satisfy public demand, the more it stoked domestic upheaval and, therefore, global tensions.

Desperate Soviet leaders didn't make for stable decision-makers when it came to averting war. All of these were considerations Truman needed to keep in mind when calculating his next steps in preparation for war, NSC-68 argued.

The document was quick, moreover, to caution that America's strategically dominant position was by no means a cause for complacency. The nation's military was woefully understaffed compared to the Soviets. The pace of Moscow's atomic bomb production might not bring it to parity with the United States anytime soon, but it was enough to pose a serious threat. Assuming a bomb failure rate of 40% to 60%, a Russian arsenal of 200 atomic bombs would still be enough to bring America's fighting ability to a standstill along with its industrial production capacity. And Russia was already believed to be engaged in an aggressive race to produce a thermonuclear hydrogen bomb.

Russia was ahead of the United States in the development of jet bombers and fighters. It was also believed to be developing a ballistic missile capacity to deliver its nuclear weapons to faraway shores. An all-out U.S. atomic attack on the USSR no doubt would deal a serious blow to Russia's war-fighting capabilities but, "It is doubted whether such a blow, even if it resulted in the complete destruction of the contemplated target systems, would cause the USSR to sue for terms or [prevent] Soviet forces from occupying Western Europe against such ground resistance as could presently be mobilized." There were simply too many Soviet troops on the ground to stop them with a post-invasion atomic assault.

The Kremlin maintained the element of surprise, and the temptation to demonstrate its atomic capabilities "might well act, therefore, not as a deterrent but as an incitement to war."

The options presented by the National Security Council were almost all bleak regarding the prospects of success. The downsides seemed to outweigh the advantages no matter which course the president might choose to take. In the end, the council recommended a blend of a crash military buildup, redoubled strategic alliances and strong economic assistance to Europe in hopes of bolstering democratic institutions, and building the kinds of goodwill that would make Europeans think twice before considering the option of Communism or even neutrality.

The only way to forestall a rapid Soviet sweep of Western Europe, given the paltry size of U.S. and Allied ground forces at the time, was to make sure the United States maintained total air supremacy—and always with the threat of a nuclear option. This was Curtis LeMay's call to action, his call to deploy an atomic attack force on European soil.

Although the Air Force was rapidly developing jet warplane technology and boosting the flight capabilities of its advanced propeller-driven bomber fleet, by 1951, the Silverplate B-29 remained the most reliable and available option should the United States choose to deploy atomic bombs overseas. The only problem was that the planes were too slow. A Soviet attempt to sweep militarily across Europe could be expected to advance far faster than a U.S.-based fleet of bombers could cross the Atlantic. The Soviets would already be entrenched and in control before an atomic response could be launched.

The only solution was to have an atomic attack force ready to strike at any moment from European soil. The only country willing to secretly discuss such an idea—but not necessarily accept—was Britain. And its leaders were in no mood to have that discussion take place publicly, or to risk having it leaked, for fear of antagonizing Stalin and infuriating the British people.

The U.S. military, and LeMay as chief of the nation's sole nuclear force, had to find a way to deploy personnel and weaponry to Britain as quietly and efficiently as possible. That's how Paul T. Cullen and James I. Hopkins found themselves among the fifty-three men crossing the Atlantic aboard Globemaster 49-244.

CHAPTER 13

"We Are Now in a State of War"

WHAT IF THIS WERE ALL JUST ONE BIG MISUNDERSTANDING? Let's say the Globemaster flight wasn't part of some bigger atomic plan. It was just a big, dumb ol' cargo plane full of regular guys on unrelated, short-term deployments to Britain who all just happened to be on the same flight. The cargo really was, as the manifest said, a bunch of assorted items like surgical sponges and spare parts and two empty KB-29 tanks. In fact, there was one exchange of letters in early 1951 in which Major General Samuel E. Anderson, commander of the Eighth Air Division in Europe, advised General LeMay of the need for more KB-29 planes and tanks to supplement the existing force in Britain because of breakdowns and inadequate supplies of equipment. Anderson even proposed using the C-124 flight that would be used to transport Cullen and his team to Britain as a cargo flight to transport supplemental KB-29 tanks.[1] Maybe those really were just KB-29 tanks on the plane. Nothing to see here folks. The plane had a mechanical malfunction and went down. These things happen.

And that's true, these things have happened throughout the course of modern military history. The list is long of general officers, including admirals, killed in accidental plane crashes. And Globemasters had a terrible record of mishaps, most of which occurred on takeoff or due to navigation errors.

But none of the crash casualties came close to resembling the personnel and factors present in the flight of Globemaster 49-244.

The idea of assigning a general officer to cross the Atlantic aboard a cargo flight, serving essentially as an escort for KB-29 tanks, was unheard of prior to the final flight of 49-244. Just as rare was the idea of sending a team of SAC specialists on such a flight, given that their only jobs were the maintenance, loading, and airborne deployment of atomic weapons. All that expertise crammed onto one plane? This Globemaster flight was, indeed, a rarity in every way.

Try as the Air Force did to hide the SAC affiliation of those onboard and portray the passengers as being on random, routine assignments unrelated to atomic attack preparedness, there is no denying that this is what they were selected for. Nearly all aboard 49-244 were attached to the 509th Bomb Wing. General LeMay left no question about his preference for the 509th Bomb Wing (previously the 509th Composite Group) as his go-to unit should the call come for an atomic attack. When he took over the Strategic Air Command in 1948 and quickly discovered how badly prepared the rest of the command was for any kind of military confrontation, he called in the 509th as the unit he knew he could rely upon to stand ready for any eventuality.

"We started with the 509th. That was the outfit which dropped the atomic bombs on Japan. . . . It was in better shape than any of the others. So it was more to the point to get the 509th up to snuff: wouldn't require such a repair job." That was the moment, in 1948, when Lieutenant Colonel James Hopkins got the order to depart from the bizarre space alien episode of Roswell and join the elite of the elite working under LeMay at Offutt in Nebraska. From that point through 1951, the mindset of LeMay and the rest of the Air Force leadership changed from an attitude of cautious relaxation to a conviction that war with Russia could break out at any moment. In fact, the Air Force's top generals had come to the conclusion that the two sides already were at war.

The Soviet explosion of an atomic test bomb in 1949 dramatically changed the Cold War equation. The entire top echelon of the U.S. military command was badly shaken and began scrambling for options to prepare for a Soviet atomic attack, and to fight back with overwhelming force. Until that point, the U.S. military had based its calculations that America would prevail in a hot war on the assumption that the Soviets couldn't compete with America's exclusive possession of atomic weaponry.

American military leaders were thrown into near panic over the news of Stalin's new weapon. Experts had long forecast 1951 or 1952 as the year the Soviets would attain a nuclear capability, with years more in the future to weaponize it. The fact that it had occurred in 1949, only four years behind the United States, meant that all the previous models for containing the Communist threat were now obsolete. The generals needed a new plan, and they needed it now.

"I would like to tell you how severely it affects the Strategic Air Command mission," LeMay stated at a top secret meeting of Air Force commanders convened in Puerto Rico four months after the Soviet test explosion was detected. "Today we have military superiority over the Soviet Union due to our possession of a stockpile of atomic bombs and our capability of delivering them. If war were to occur this year or even next year, I believe that we could probably do our job and guarantee ultimate victory for this country and do it at acceptable cost."

But given the newest intelligence estimate of Soviet bomb production, all bets would be off by mid-1952. "When that date, 1952, arrives and it is already pretty close at hand, the whole military picture will change," LeMay told his fellow generals. "You will no longer have military superiority as we know it today. The enemy, even though possessing fewer bombs than we may have, will have enough either to destroy our striking force or the major cities of this country or both."[2] LeMay was known for his economy with words. He avoided bluster, preferring to let the facts speak for themselves. The words he chose were designed to convey a sense of urgency, not crisis and panic.

He cautiously presented what he believed to be the most viable and effective option: a preemptive first strike.

There had been minimal talk in public about any such prospect, and whenever hawkish political leaders dared to raise the idea openly, critics and prominent personalities like General Eisenhower were quick to denounce them as extremists and warmongers. Following Eisenhower's lead, other generals measured their words carefully when giving speeches or talking to the press. In private, however, they could barely contain their worries over a Soviet atomic threat—or their enthusiasm to smack down Stalin before he had a chance to exercise his new nuclear option.

Speaking on the second day of the April 25 to 27, 1950, Commanders Conference, LeMay was blunt in his assessment of what needed to happen.

"If our estimate of Soviet stockpile figures is approximately correct, then when 1952 arrives, destruction of the enemy industry as presently planned is not enough. It certainly would be an empty victory for us to succeed in destroying their industrial capacity if, at the same time, this country were destroyed or even seriously damaged," LeMay told the generals. He proceeded to outline the case for the "tremendous military advantage" afforded by a preemptive first strike designed to decimate Stalin's war-making powers before he had the chance to use his atomic weaponry. "In other words, unless we take steps now that are not presently programmed, we are pretty apt to lose the next war. In my mind, we now face a basic change in our concept. We must not only plan to destroy the enemy industrial power but we must be capable at the same time of destroying his force *before* it destroys us."[3]

It was time to throw out the old planning models that guided the conduct of previous wars. "The Strategic Air Command cannot carry out its mission after absorbing a Soviet attack of this size. After 1952, the use of European bases as primary launching sites for the atomic attack will be questionable if not impractical," LeMay warned. He compared the conditions to the situation Europe faced in 1940 as Hitler's army rampaged across Europe, and a lack of preparation by Allied forces handed Germany an easy route to conquest. Since intelligence experts had so badly underestimated Soviet atomic capabilities, LeMay openly questioned whether they could be trusted to gauge if and when Stalin might launch a war. The present situation required establishing a national early warning intelligence system to limit the Soviets' ability to launch a surprise attack.[4]

"Second," he added, "place the Air Force on a war footing without further delay. Third, provide funds in such quantities as may be needed to ensure that the striking force will be operational as a long-range intercontinental force not later than July of 1952."

"And, fourth," LeMay added ominously, "re-examine present policies which imply that we must absorb the first atomic blow"[5] before hitting the Soviets.

The meeting was designed as a spitballing session. Attendees were instructed to dress comfortably in sport shirts and casual pants instead of uniforms. They were encouraged to speak frankly, "to let our hair down" in the words of the top Air Force commander, General Hoyt S. Vandenberg, and have no fear of repercussions for suggesting extreme solutions. The comments exchanged among them, however, suggested that once Vandenberg and other top generals had spoken in support of a preemptive strike, not a single general felt compelled to challenge them openly. Groupthink dangerously carried the day, and LeMay unleashed a wave of commentary embracing his call for a preemptive attack, with Vandenberg leading the charge.

"Stop them before they start," Major General William Kepner chimed in.

"I think we in the military ought to do something about educating the people that we do not have to take the first blow," said Brigadier General Sydney D. Grubbs, Jr., boldly venturing a direct criticism of Eisenhower for telling an audience "that the people of this country wouldn't stand for delivering the first blow." Grubbs contended that Americans would, in fact, be fine with the idea of a preemptive atomic assault.[6]

Lieutenant General Ennis C. Whitehead pronounced a recommendation of a specific date to launch a preemptive attack, and "that our entire effort be programmed and our mission be changed where necessary that we may attain the combat power required to win the next war; and that we select 1 July 1952 as D-Day."

That prompted Air Force Commanding General George C. Kenney, who had previously remained silent, to state, "I would like to endorse what General Whitehead has said 100%. I think we are at war and I think we ought to realize it. The only things we are doing is being on the defensive and slowly retreating. We have to make up our minds that some day we have to go on the offensive. I agree with General Whitehead that that date is probably around July 1, 1952."[7]

Their enthusiasm took LeMay aback. "I didn't mean by that statement that we should go out and attack Russia tomorrow. I do mean that there are many ways of determining when you are going to be invaded" and acting to negate the threat rather than standing idly to absorb the first attack. But he also agreed with Whitehead and offered an unusually stark assessment of the pressure he was under, given the end of the U.S. atomic monopoly: "I think I am well aware that the survival of the United States depends on the success or failure of my command."

This is where the plan was conceived to preplace atomic bombs and attack forces in the United Kingdom—a plan that would coalesce in Globemaster 49-244's disastrous flight over the Atlantic. The transcripts of the Puerto Rico proceedings were so sensitive that they remained classified for the following five decades.

The conference opened with a frank, albeit dismal assessment by the Air Force director of intelligence, Major General Charles P. Cabell, of where the United States and its European allies stood in relation to the Soviet military threat. The overwhelming advantage Stalin had in combat-ready troop numbers virtually guaranteed that he could achieve a swift victory in the takeover of Western Europe. The big unanswered question was where and how Stalin might choose to use his atomic bombs, the production of which was forecast to reach nearly 100[8] by mid-1952 but could rapidly double to 200 by 1954. If Stalin opted for a full-blown aerial assault on industrial centers in the United States, even with a limited number of bombs, he could cripple the U.S. ability to mobilize and come to the aid of Europe.

Adding to Cabell's bleak outlook was the paltry state of U.S. air defenses. Soviet Tu-4 bombers would stand a good chance of penetrating American airspace and successfully delivering their bombs without significant challenge, Cabell warned. Covert smuggling of nuclear components by submarine or merchant ships for assembly within the United States meant the Soviets could also achieve their objective without necessarily using aircraft.[9] The blow to American morale would be devastating, and the chances would skyrocket that the United Kingdom could declare its neutrality or appeasement in order to avoid antagonizing Stalin as his forces bore down on British shores.

The United States would be on its own, and unless it had preplaced atomic weapons in Britain for a counterattack, that country would be lost to the cause of freedom.

Cabell asserted that the United States was the only nation standing between the Soviet Union and total world domination, which meant that Stalin should be expected to treat the United States as its number one target:

> Possession of atomic bombs, and the means to deliver them provide the Soviets with a capability to attack the United States directly and

> effectively. This is the first time in United States history that it has been subject to direct and effective attack. It must be expected that this capability will make the Soviet Union more fanatic and aggressive in pursuit of its objectives and, indeed, there are many signs of growing cockiness on their part.[10]

In one of the conference's rare moments of acknowledgment of a dissenting point of view, Cabell told the group that the CIA's assessment of Soviet objectives and strategies differed significantly from his own. The CIA argued that Marxist doctrine rejected the use of military force because it would run contrary to the notion of a grassroots popular uprising in support of Communism. The global defeat of the capitalist system could only be accomplished from the ground up, "through subversion and revolution rather than conquest," Cabell said of the CIA assessment. He strongly disagreed, arguing that Stalin's version of Marxism viewed revolution and subversion as "adjuncts," and that "the Soviet Union is now preparing for a military show-down with the United States." The goal, from Stalin's point of view, was to spread Communism by any means necessary, including brute force.

He outlined five scenarios that could lead to a Soviet victory in a nuclear war. First was for Stalin to launch a surprise first strike; second was the eruption of war because of a miscalculation; third was the employment of "piecemeal acts of aggression" that could steadily whittle away at American resolve to retaliate; fourth was a gradual loss of faith in the United States by the rest of the non-Communist world to the point that America's former allies declared neutrality; and fifth was the decay of American military advantage to the point that it would be forced to negotiate and compromise with the Soviet Union for the sake of its own security.

Cabell noted that the United States was so desperate for useful intelligence that it had resorted to interviewing returning Japanese and German prisoners of war after their release from Soviet camps for possible clues. Stalin was aware that the Americans were stepping up their intelligence efforts and began clamping down wherever he could on potential leaks. Even Soviet satellite states were imposing tight restraints on the presence of American diplomats, thus limiting their ability to gather intelligence from the fringes. Cullen's aerial reconnaissance crews became the primary means by which the United States would attain the precise coordinates for the seventy sites targeted in the initial atomic attack plan.

There was general agreement among the commanders that the Soviets were currently carrying out the third scenario outlined by Cabell, prodding the United States with a series of provocations that fell just short of qualifying as acts of war but certainly couldn't be dismissed as inconsequential. Just two weeks before they convened their conference in Puerto Rico, Soviet fighters shot down a U.S. Navy PB4Y-2 Privateer bomber in international airspace over the Baltic Sea near Libau (Liepāja), Latvia. All ten service members aboard disappeared and were presumed killed. The Navy publicly described the Privateer flight as a routine patrol and meteorological mission, code language for what it really was: a reconnaissance or intelligence-gathering flight. Such flights often were designed to prompt the Soviets to activate their antiaircraft defenses and radio signals so American planes could figure out how to jam them.

"As we see it now, it was certainly a probing," Cabell said of the Soviet hostile action. "We think it was probably deliberately done as a probing to see what our reaction would be. I think that they felt that they did not risk a war by virtue of their shooting down that aircraft."[11]

The circumstances surrounding the Privateer attack would wind up bearing an eerie similarity to those of the Globemaster incident a few months later. Empty life rafts would be found in the water. Wreckage would be recovered. But there would be no trace whatsoever of the men who were aboard. Unconfirmed reports would later circulate, generating substantial government attention, that survivors of the Privateer flight were seen inside a Soviet prison facility.[12]

The absence of a forceful U.S. response to the Privateer downing—it amounted to a strongly worded diplomatic protest—certainly emboldened the Soviets to test the waters further, such as downing other military planes over Europe and using MiG jet fighters to shoot down American bombers over Korea. The Soviets may have felt bold enough to intercept 49-244 because they were convinced the Americans would do nothing in retaliation.

LeMay opened the second day of the Puerto Rico conference with a warning that an even more dismal assessment than Cabell's was coming:

"You will not exactly enjoy this morning."[13] He walked the commanders through the present state of Air Force preparedness and manpower. Of the Strategic Air Command's 512 bombers, only half were configured to carry an atomic bomb. The bombers he favored for use in an atomic attack were the Silverplate B-29s, mainly because they had already proven themselves capable in wartime to deliver their goods, but also because newer B-50 and B-36 models were riddled with glitches and not ready for reliable deployment.[14] The problem with B-29s, however, was that they were no match for a MiG-15 (as the war in Korea would soon prove).

America's fleet of reconnaissance aircraft, which were crucial to the objective of penetrating Soviet airspace and coming back with photos of key military and industrial sites for future targeting purposes, consisted of only sixty-two RB-29s (reconnaissance B-29s). There were only 104 fighters, a far-too-inadequate number to provide the necessary escorts for bombing and reconnaissance runs. In total, LeMay had a paltry 784 bombers, tankers, reconnaissance aircraft, and fighters to protect all 3.1 million square miles of U.S. territory, including Alaska, along with the United Kingdom and Western Europe. He recounted for the group an earlier plan, Exercise Dualism, that "involves a rapid movement of a number of Groups out of the country to the U.K."

None of this information made it into the public sphere, especially that the rapid deployment would include five "A-Bomb Assembly Teams" heading to Britain and another going to Alaska."[15]

LeMay let his deputy, Brigadier General John B. Montgomery, explain the next part of the battle plan. Montgomery laid out the numbers of B-29s and B-50s carrying atomic bombs that would be deployed to each of the three British bases that had runways long enough to accommodate them. Montgomery then told the group that a total of 123 industrial areas would be targeted for attack, and he was quick to note that "several of the targets lie outside the areas of the Soviet Union proper." The plan called for planes departing from the United Kingdom to drop atomic bombs on thirty-two targets on the European front of the Soviet Bloc. On the first day alone, seventy atomic bombs would be dropped, approaching from the north over Scandinavia to Leningrad and from the south overflying France, Italy, and Greece to attack various locations, including Moscow.

"Notice that the whole attack goes off in about four hours from the time borders are penetrated," General Montgomery stated coldly as he pointed to a detailed map. The timing automatically precluded launching the assault from American shores, which would take far longer than four hours to reach the Soviet border. All this hinged on the viability of the U.K. bases, which he noted could be decimated by Soviet attacks even before American bombers were able to take off. "If the United Kingdom bases remain tenable, it is planned to strike the 123 cities in a period of 30 to 40 days."

British leaders had already registered their concerns repeatedly about any plan that called for launching atomic attacks from their soil exactly because of the likelihood that it would make the United Kingdom a priority target for Soviet preemptive attack. This was why Prime Minister Attlee's government was so adamant about reaching an accord stipulating that his government must agree beforehand to any use of the atomic bomb. Their objections would be registered in meeting after meeting between the two sides for the following two years. It wasn't that they objected to the planned use of atomic weaponry. In fact, they sought greater emphasis on its use.[16] They were just squeamish about launching such an attack from British shores.

Montgomery walked the generals through specific details of the attack plan, including the current state of readiness—or lack thereof—of the British bases hosting American attackers. Buried deep in his presentation was this short warning: "Sabotage is a problem. Ground troops are needed for protection" at the British bases.[17] That meant the United States might be seeking permission to deploy thousands of American ground troops on British soil, posing yet another highly potential irritant between the two sides. Opinion polls indicated that, although Britons were grateful for all the help America provided in World War II, they did not support an increase of the U.S. troop presence there.

LeMay interrupted to emphasize "that unless we have adequate air defense over the advanced bases, we stand a very good chance of losing the entire striking force. I am inclined to think that the air defense over the forward area is going to be a lot more important to us, at least for the next year, than air defense here at home."[18]

One of the more pernicious problems was the need to conduct all of these preparations without the benefit of full British acceptance of the American military's plans. There was not yet an agreement to place atomic weapons on British soil because political leaders had yet to agree on the wording of an accord outlining when and how the weapons would be used. The British side demanded veto power over any proposed atomic attack. The United States insisted on full autonomy over any such decision. Whatever the two sides finally agreed upon, it was kept secret at the time and remains secret even today.

For LeMay, this posed a conundrum. "Our plan depends on these bases being pre-stocked and pre-manned. Several of these bases have only recently been finally assigned to us by an agreement with Britain and this has prevented us from working out detailed plans for their use. In fact, it has prevented us from inspecting facilities." The British hadn't even signed off on the numbers of American personnel to be allowed at each of the bases. "If we have an emergency in the immediate future, these deficiencies would delay and confuse SAC in carrying out its mission," he warned.[19]

It was the closest the generals would come to outlining the need for an atomic deployment without full British acquiescence. That is, they might have to smuggle the bomb onto the new SAC bases there.

After the commanders' conference concluded, General Kenney sent a letter to General Vandenberg[20] formalizing the generals' consensus at the conference that the political leadership should embrace the idea of a preemptive strike. For all the talk of "cold war" between the United States and Russia, Kenney believed that the current status already constituted a hot war, and it was time to treat it as such. "I believe that something can be done to bring it home to the people of this country and to their representatives in Congress [who believe] that we are not actually at war. By all previous definitions, we are now in a state of war with Russia. Whether we call it a cold war or apply any other term, we are not winning."[21]

Kenney wrote his letter on April 29, 1950, two months before the war began in Korea and eleven months before Globemaster 49-244 was ordered to Britain with Cullen, the newly appointed Seventh Air Division commander, onboard. The letter helps explain why Kenney regarded atomic deployments to the United Kingdom as crucial to defeating the Soviet menace.

In the following two years, Kenney wrote, Russia would produce "as many as 300 atomic bombs; and I believe that in our planning we must deal with possibilities." Soviet production of the Tu-4, their carbon-copy version of the B-29, was forecast to reach 1,200 by 1952, but Kenney estimated it would take little extra effort to boost that production to 1,600 if the Soviet leadership deemed it necessary. The stakes were too high to gamble that Stalin's production capacity was, as some estimates forecast, much lower. "Remember that we underestimated Japanese air and naval strength prior to World War II and as a consequence had a much harder job on our hands than we had anticipated. If we underestimate the next time, the consequences will be far more serious."

If compared one-on-one, the United States had roughly the same number of Army troops under arms, about 1.5 million, as did the combined Moscow-backed forces along Europe's Eastern Front. The problems with that equation were multifold. For one, the U.S. Army's ten divisions contained only one division that was ready for combat.[22] The Soviet army had never been demobilized from World War II, and multiple divisions were already deployed at or close to any future war front in Eastern Europe. They also had other satellite nations' forces to draw upon if needed. There simply was no match between the ground forces of the two sides on the European front.

The increasingly nervous anti-Soviet nations of Western Europe shared a dilemma that only the United States was in a position to help them resolve. They could devote heavy resources to rebuilding their ground forces and rearming to prepare for a Soviet invasion, but that would mean diverting precious funding from their equally urgent need to rebuild from the devastation of the war. The problem was particularly acute in the United Kingdom, as negotiator Sir Oliver Franks noted during talks with U.S. military commanders and Truman administration officials in July 1952. "The elemental fact was economic," said a top secret memo summarizing the British position at the talks. There was only so much money to go around, and spending it on the levels of defense that the Americans wanted meant denying the British people the huge public investment they demanded to rebuild after the war. "These dual objectives had placed very great demands on British resources, demands which were greater than the resources available."[23] By the time he made that statement, the July 1, 1952, "D-Day" date predicted in the Puerto Rico Commanders Conference had come and gone without direct confrontation between U.S. and

Soviet forces. The British side asked for a reassessment of the actual threat and the most economically effective means to confront it.

British leaders were far from alone in calculating the political consequences of prioritizing defense over postwar economic development. A failure to take care of the latter meant risking domestic unrest and political upheaval—a prospect that Stalin could only exploit to expand his Communist influence. But a failure to build up their ground forces only left Western forces more vulnerable to a Soviet military sweep. Even as the U.S. administration recognized the urgency of protecting Europe from the Communist threat, President Truman insisted that the Pentagon leadership cut back its budget to something more closely resembling peacetime levels. The American people had their domestic needs, too.

For the commanders to prevail in their argument for a policy that didn't rule out a preemptive strike, they had to impress upon the civilian leadership in the White House and on Capitol Hill that Stalin meant business, and the Soviet threat constituted a clear and present danger.

The atomic response turned out to make the best economic sense. It was cheaper and required far fewer military resources than other options emphasizing massive troop deployments. But NSC-68 and one of its offshoots, Operation Offtackle, made clear that an atomic response could only serve to interrupt a Soviet takeover of Western Europe by punishing Stalin *after the fact* with the devastation of his own capital and industrial centers. The plan acknowledged that little could be done to dislodge Soviet troops once they had entrenched across the subcontinent.

In later years, LeMay would tell interviewers that he never openly called for a preemptive strike the way Kenney did. But behind closed doors, LeMay was vocally adamant that the United States reject a no-first-strike policy. Keep all options on the table and, by all means, keep the Soviets guessing about what measures the United States was prepared to take. He also argued for reducing the bureaucratic procedures currently required should an atomic strike be required.

At the time, the Atomic Energy Commission held sole control over the bomb, meaning LeMay could not deploy atomic weaponry without first attaining AEC permission. The bombs were stored at Sandia in New Mexico, Kirtland Air Force Base in New Mexico, Camp Campbell in Kentucky just north of Oak Ridge, Tennessee, and Camp Hood (later named Fort Hood) under Atomic Energy Commission control.[24] To remove the bombs, LeMay would have to complete paperwork, attain removal permission, then load the bombs aboard B-29s, fly those aircraft to Limestone, Maine or Gander, Newfoundland for refueling, then make the jump over to Britain for another refueling if KB-29 aerial-refueling aircraft were unavailable, then begin the atomic attack on Russia. The entire procedure would take days, a period in which Soviet troops would be consolidating their control of Western Europe and, likely, preparing to attack Britain itself.

"The military services didn't own a single one," LeMay told an interviewer about the atomic arsenal. "These bombs were too horrible and too dangerous to entrust to the military. They were under lock and key of the Atomic Energy Commission. I didn't have them, and that worried me a little bit to start with. So I finally sent somebody to see the guy [at Camp Hood] who had the key. We were guarding them. Our troops guarded them, but we didn't own them."

LeMay sent an emissary to negotiate an unofficial understanding that, in the event of a catastrophic enemy attack that wiped out the civilian command in Washington, an atomic counterattack would be necessary without awaiting civilian approval. "I felt that under certain conditions—say we woke up some morning and there wasn't any Washington or something—I was going to take the bombs. I got no static from this man. I never had to do it or anything, but we had an understanding."[25]

There is no publicly available record indicating that LeMay attained presidential approval for this "understanding" that he, and he alone, could claim the power to launch an atomic attack. His rationale was by no means flawed if he strictly limited himself to taking action in the absence of any civilian authority to make such a decision. But it also showed LeMay's willingness to take matters into his own hands if he felt the civilians were failing to recognize the dangers or were too slow to take action when faced with an urgent situation. If the person at Camp Hood with whom he shared this "understanding" had a similar mindset, LeMay's chances of obtaining atomic bomb components to smuggle into Britain were significantly increased.

"There was, definitely, a time when we could have destroyed all of Russia (I mean by that, all of Russia's capability to wage war) without losing a man to their defenses," LeMay recalled in 1965. Russia's atomic program by 1950 to 1951 was still in its infancy. Their defensive capacity to fend off an atomic strike was low. "As for their offensive capacity: not one bomb or missile, in that day, could have hit the United States." So it would have been possible, LeMay believed, for America to impose a nonnegotiable "blueprint" that gave the Soviets, say, five or six months to withdraw from their Eastern Europe satellite countries and "effect a complete change of conduct," after which Moscow would behave itself or suffer the brunt of American atomic might. The capability of the United States to do such a thing was there, LeMay wrote, but whether it *should* have been done was always a question for the civilian leadership to decide.

Did LeMay believe restraint was in order? Hell no. Communist encroachment had to be confronted, not tolerated or accommodated. "I can't get over the notion that when you stand up and act like a man, you win respect. . . . It's when you fall back, shaking with apprehension, that you're apt to get into trouble." It wasn't that SAC commanders were pushing for war, "but we knew for a fact that it would be possible to curtail enemy expansion if we challenged them in that way. Some of us thought it might be better to do so then, than to wait until later."[26]

LeMay wrote those words in 1965, years before the Commanders Conference and Kenney's correspondence were declassified.

The SAC commander proposed in a December 12, 1949, letter to Vandenberg that LeMay receive explicit authority to launch a preemptive atomic strike if such an action were deemed essential to fend off an imminent Soviet attack. "Our readiness in this regard will depend materially upon our ability to avoid or absorb the effects of enemy attempts to immobilize our atomic striking force before it can be committed to combat."[27]

LeMay wasn't as concerned about the Air Force's ability to deliver one punishing blow after another to Soviet positions inside and outside Russia as he was concerned about infiltration and sabotage. He knew the Soviets had spent years building up a secret team of loyalists who would gladly betray their country to advance the cause of Communism. He was convinced that operatives were embedded within the U.S. military, including his own command, and that they could be expected to flex their muscles at whatever moment Moscow deemed necessary.

LeMay repeatedly expressed his concerns that sabotage, not Soviet assault capabilities on American shores, remained a top impediment to the success of any SAC-led operation. He even acknowledged in correspondence with Vandenberg that he believed the Strategic Air Command itself to have been infiltrated, although he didn't offer specifics. Because of the potential for sabotage, LeMay wrote, "No matter how much active defense we provide for ourselves, it is unlikely that we can prevent the Soviets from attaining a measure of success in any attacks against our striking force."[28]

To get ahead of Soviet aggressors and any would-be saboteurs within his own ranks, the solution LeMay pushed for, and that Vandenberg clearly agreed with, was a first-strike, preventive option. *Take them out before they have a chance to take us out.* It's in that context that LeMay began positioning his forces so that the civilian leadership would be able to exercise the option should it so desire. That's where the 509th, and particularly Lieutenant Colonel Hopkins—the only certified nuclear command pilot who had actually participated in a wartime atomic bombing—came into play as the general's preferred option to prepare for any preemptive attack.

But he felt back in 1949 that "too small a portion of our striking force has sufficient range to enable us to strike promptly from this country without deploying to forward bases." Thus began LeMay's effort to put an atomic strike force in place somewhere in Europe. The political support he needed for any such plan came from NSC-68 because it represented not just the view of the military command but also the assessment of the intelligence community and Truman's own top national security advisers. All agreed that it would be essential to place a nuclear strike force in Europe, preferably Britain, well in advance of the outbreak of hostilities.

Like Kenney, LeMay wanted everyone under his command to treat the Soviets not as a threat—that is, a potential danger to be addressed somewhere down the road—but as a real aggressor that already was engaged in military action against the allies.

Heading into 1950, the global security situation was rapidly deteriorating, described by LeMay as "a loose, slippery, fragile pile of broken crockery." He wanted the men under his command to change their mindset from one of preparing for war to understanding, "*We are at war now.* So that, if actually we did go to war the very next morning or even that night, we would stumble through no period in which preliminary motions would be wasted."

A constant practice-bombing routine was designed to create a form of muscle memory, so automatic in its execution that it wouldn't require thought, "whereby a man, if he was assigned a target at Moscow, could bomb Moscow hundreds of times, merely by using his training aid. So when the time came, it would be just another of those training missions, far as he was concerned."[29]

CHAPTER 14

Fuel Tanks, or Fat Man Suitcases?

THE FINAL FLIGHT OF GLOBEMASTER 49-244 ACTUALLY BEGAN more than a week before a single passenger boarded at Walker Air Force Base in New Mexico. Long before the overseas portion of the mission could begin, the C-124's pilots and crew had a very specific assignment involving a diversion to Tinker Air Force Base in Oklahoma. There, they were to load two large cargo items that, to the casual observer, wouldn't seem to have anything to do with the flight of an elite Strategic Air Command team to Britain. Those cargo items were two KB-29 fuel tanks, which were little-known pieces of equipment that the Air Force, at General Curtis LeMay's insistence, had developed to ensure a Silverplate B-29 Superfortress bomber could travel nonstop to any point on the planet, ostensibly with the goal of delivering a Fat Man nuclear bomb to whatever target LeMay or the president had chosen.[1] In 1949, the *Lucky Lady II*, a B-29 Superfortress, became the first plane in history to circumnavigate the globe nonstop, a feat made possible only because of the KB-29 aerial-refueling system.

At the time that 49-244 began its final flight in March 1951, LeMay had in mind only one potential target for his Europe-based fleet of B-29s, and that target was the Soviet Union. The B-29s he had already stationed at Mildenhall and Lakenheath Royal Air Force Bases in Britain had a range of more than 5,500 miles, making them capable of a round-trip bombing run to Moscow or most other points in the western Soviet Union without ever needing to refuel. But there were other strategic sites deeper within Russia

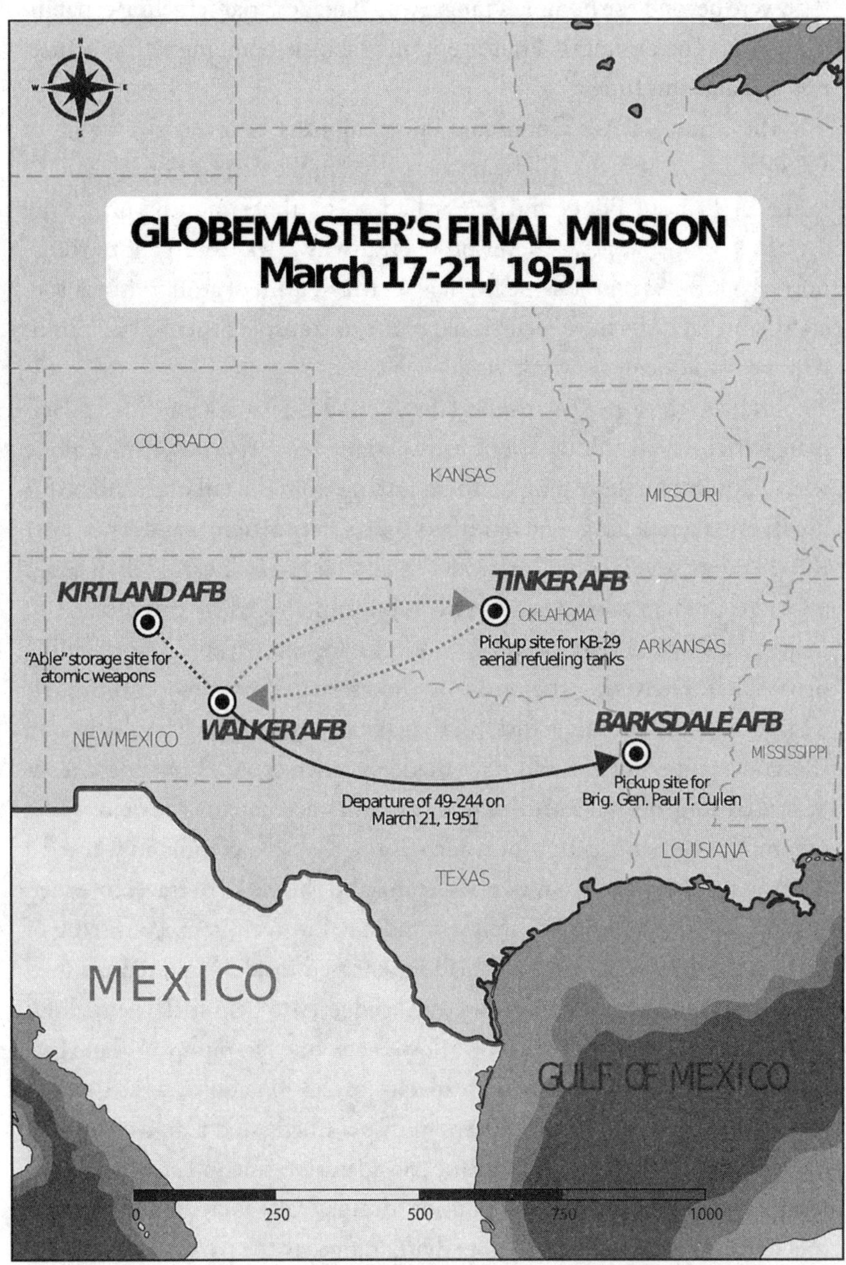

During the week before the fatal flight, Globemaster 49-244 traveled round-trip from Walker Air Force Base, New Mexico, to Tinker Air Force Base, Oklahoma, to pick up KB-29 tanks. Walker is south of the atomic storage facility at Kirtland Air Force Base, New Mexico. The plane departed for Barksdale Air Force Base on March 21, 1951. *Nick Waligorski.*

that were beyond the bomber's range, which made aerial-refueling capabilities a must. The Operation Frantic option of shuttle-bombing was, of course, not available this time.

The Strategic Air Command spent months between the flight of *Lucky Lady II* and the Globemaster's final flight prepositioning KB-29 tanks in Britain. Pilots and crews had spent those months practicing aerial-refueling. So it was never quite clear why it was so urgent to transport two KB-29s on the same flight as LeMay's team of atomic attack specialists. In fact, the most well-suited plane to transport two KB-29 tanks, whether full or empty, would have been the B-29 itself.

Dubbed the KB-29M, the aerial-refueling B-29 was a modified Silverplate with bomb bay doors specifically designed to carry those tanks, along with a 200-foot, telescoping fuel arm jutting from the tail of the plane for use in midair refueling. The modified B-29's sole mission was to transport KB-29 tanks, and it could carry out the task far less awkwardly than could a C-124 Globemaster. Besides, two KB-29s delivered by cargo plane to Mildenhall would have been of no use to anyone without the refueling plane itself. Delivering the tanks by themselves constituted nothing but a cargo mission. Placing a forty-man team of atomic attack specialists on the same cargo flight would have made as much sense as putting a team of skilled surgeons on a semi-tractor trailer to accompany the delivery of, say, an X-ray machine. But for some reason, the SAC command wanted a brigadier general, the atomic attack team, and the tanks to travel together.

The KB-29 tank was a pretty mundane, low-tech item, consisting of little more than a giant rubber bladder encased inside a squared-off shell made of aluminum. There was internal gadgetry to help suck the fuel out of the bladder. A filler cap on top allowed crewmen to pump airplane fuel into the tank until it reached a capacity of 2,300 gallons, which would bring the cargo weight to 13,800 pounds per filled tank. Cargo weight on a Silverplate B-29 was an important consideration since a Fat Man bomb, weighing in at a hefty 10,300 pounds, dramatically increased the plane's fuel consumption and reduced its flying range, as the participants on the Nagasaki raid discovered to their anguish.

At the bottom of the KB-29 tank was a connection for a thick telescoping hose, at the end of which was an aerial guidance device that allowed crew members using a cable to move the end of the hose up, down, left, or right while aiming at the fuel receiver on an airborne B-29. In theory, a nuclear-armed B-29 could stay aloft indefinitely circling the skies near a target while awaiting orders to drop the bomb. The ability to have the bomb already airborne meant saving crucial hours, thereby ensuring the quickest-possible deployment and the maximum level of surprise for the enemy. In the case of any potential strike against a Soviet target, the key wasn't in the existence of a KB-29 tank; it was the existence of B-29 in flight carrying a Fat Man nuclear bomb.

One of the most interesting features of the KB-29 was that it was designed to fit into the same expanded bomb bay doors that distinguished the Silverplate B-29 from the standard B-29 Superfortresses that helped turn the war in the Allies' favor over Europe and Japan. For years after the war, the Silverplate B-29s retained a special classified status, specifically to protect the dimensions of those bomb bay doors. If an outsider knew the dimensions of the doors, that person could deduce the dimensions of the bomb itself—critical information that the U.S. military was unwilling to give up, even after it knew that the Soviets were building their own bomb.

The problem for the Pentagon was that, whenever a crew was needed to perform a task as mundane as checking the air pressure in a Silverplate B-29's tires, that crew had to be security cleared for access to classified information, a process that was expensive, onerous, and time-consuming.[2] LeMay decided that it was too cumbersome to bring in outsiders for cargo transport and maintenance purposes, so he incorporated his own precleared units to carry out those services, including Globemasters and their crews.

The Fat Man required a stronger hoist and more space for maneuverability to ensure it didn't accidentally bump up against the sides of the bomb bay and inflict potentially catastrophic damage. The far-less fragile KB-29 tank was built slightly bigger to utilize all the extra space the expanded bomb bay opening offered in order to maximize its fuel-carrying capacity. It was so large, in fact, that the tank technically had enough room to fit an actual Fat Man bomb inside with room to spare.

Not that anyone would ever have a reason to do such a thing.

LeMay had lots of good reasons to order the aerial-refueling system to be designed and built in time for its first test run in 1948. Top on his and other commanders' minds was the fact that three B-29s had run out of fuel on separate bombing missions over Manchuria in 1944. They were forced to make emergency landings at the eastern port of Vladivostok, Russia, where Soviet authorities seized the planes and crew. It was hardly the kind of treatment the United States expected of its wartime ally.

The United States had invested $3 billion ($53 billion in 2025 dollars) to design and build the B-29 and had worked hard to protect its secrets. LeMay was more than a little irked that the Soviets had gotten ahold of not one but three of them. The crew members were held for days and then released, but the Soviets refused to release the planes, whose development cost far exceeded that of the entire Manhattan Project.

After the war, LeMay was horrified when the Soviets began flying the Tupolev Tu-4 bomber, an exact replica of the non-Silverplate B-29. The Soviets had dismantled the seized bombers, copied each part (including some notable flaws), then launched their own crash production program, taking advantage of American design expertise and all the financial investments it took to reach that aviation pinnacle. It would hardly be the first time the Soviets had stolen and copied U.S. technology, as their first Fat Man replica nuclear bomb would attest a few years later. It was an ingenious plan on Stalin's part: Let the Americans absorb all the costs and development headaches. The Soviets cut their own development time by years, which led to no small amount of embarrassment by U.S. intelligence officials when Russia exploded its first atomic bomb in 1949.

It was the mere lack of fuel back in 1944 that forced the American pilots to abandon their aircraft and hand over the nation's most cherished airborne fighting machine to a foreign nation that had done nothing to deserve that gift.[3] Another motivating factor for LeMay was the second 1945 atomic bombing mission, over Nagasaki, led by Major Chuck Sweeney aboard the Silverplate B-29 named *Bockscar*. That mission was nearly scuttled, with its Fat Man payload on the verge of being dumped into the Pacific, for a perceived lack of fuel.

LeMay, in his memoirs, made clear his frustrations over the fuel problem. He was more convinced than ever that some kind of reliable airborne-refueling system needed to be a priority project once the war was over. And that's how the KB-29 came into existence.

The KB-29 became an essential piece of equipment as the Strategic Air Command began building up its attack capabilities in Britain and air crews started long-range practice bombings over Europe and the Mediterranean.

But that status doesn't explain why LeMay felt the need to have two empty KB-29 tanks be accompanied by a brigadier general and thirty-nine highly trained atomic warriors. The Strategic Air Command was flush with money. There's no indication in the records that LeMay was under any kind of budgetary pressure to consolidate missions and maximize efficiencies by combining two unrelated missions on a single flight. It was a risky decision for the same reason that U.S. presidents and vice presidents don't fly on the same planes: Accidents happen. You don't risk decapitating the mission by putting so many essential personnel on a single plane.

The decision was doubly bizarre because, hours before Globemaster 49-244 took off from Walker and Barksdale, another Globemaster, tail number 49-240,[4] had taken off on an identical route across the Atlantic, apparently with plenty of cargo and passenger space. There was some as-yet-unexplained reason for this odd configuration.[5]

In the days preceding the flights of 49-240 and 49-244, some odd things started happening with the flight records of the SAC's fleet of C-124 cargo planes. Normally, cargo flights were overseen by the Military Air Transport System, or MATS, which was an entirely separate command. LeMay didn't feel MATS offered sufficient security to handle his highly classified and specialized operations. So he secured permission to create his own cargo command and C-124 fleet, based at Walker Air Force Base under the direction of Brigadier General Hunter Harris, Jr. There was a marked uptick in the number of flights and weight of cargo moving in and out of Walker during March 1951.

But documentation of those flights took on the look and feel of utter fiction—which was not unusual when the cargo was related to atomic weapons. Even in the lead-up to the Hiroshima and Nagasaki bombings, crews were instructed to fudge their cargo information to maintain the secrecy of what they were carrying, as 393rd Bomb Squadron bombardier John L. Downey recounted in his story of transporting the Fat Man bomb from Kirtland Field in New Mexico to Tinian.[6]

In 1951, cargo planes loaded with equipment were taking off and flying nonstop for thousands of miles, only to return to the exact same location with the exact same weight of cargo onboard. Whoever was filling out the manifests either was ordered to concoct stories to hide the true nature of the flight or, less likely, the person just couldn't be bothered to provide accurate documentation.

According to the monthly manifest, on March 7, 1951, Globemaster 49-235 departed Walker carrying classified cargo weighing 23,000 pounds. The plane flew for 2,860 miles nonstop, then landed right back at Walker. The same day, 49-241 flew a distance of 2,990 miles from Walker to Walker carrying classified cargo weighing 35,466 pounds.[7] The same day, 49-236 took off from Walker, flew 8,440 miles nonstop, then landed back at Walker with its classified cargo still on the plane. At least, that's what the flight record stated.[8]

That's just one day's worth of flight records. On March 5, Globemaster 49-246 carried a whopping 100,850 pounds of cargo for 2,198 miles—all from Walker Air Force Base to be delivered right back to Walker. Other manifests were just as bizarre. A C-124 was used to transport 18,742 pounds of cargo, listed as "clothing," on a circuitous route from Fairchild Air Force Base in Washington State to Norton Air Force Base in California, then from Norton to Forbes airfield in Kansas. It then returned to Walker with 600 pounds labeled "ailerons."

Perhaps the most bizarre was the flight of 49-240 on March 19, 1951. It left Walker with 16,770 pounds of cargo labeled KB-29 tanks. It landed at Goose Bay (Gander, Newfoundland), then jumped across the Atlantic to Lakenheath, England, where it offloaded 6,012 pounds of cargo—close to the weight of two KB-29 tanks but also close to the weight of the nuclear core filling for a Fat Man—before flying with 10,788 pounds of cargo (still listed as KB-29 tanks) to Lagens, in the Azores, then proceeding to Kindley Air Force Base in Bermuda, then to Hunter Air Force Base in Georgia, followed by Tinker Air Force Base in Oklahoma, where it offloaded 3,000 pounds. It returned to Walker with 7,780 pounds of the same equipment it had when the entire flight began.

The manifest is rife with such anomalies. Strangely, for the month of March, it lists absolutely no flights whatsoever for 49-244 and only one mission for 49-240, on March 19 to 26 (a 7,800-mile round-trip from Walker to Lakenheath and back to Walker). That flight carried only twenty-eight passengers, meaning it had plenty of room, and there was no need to concentrate Cullen and the rest of the attack team on a single plane.

Globemaster 49-244 made a series of flights inside the United States before crossing the Atlantic around March 21 to 23. But none of them are listed, including the Atlantic trip. Diplomatically speaking, the records are curiously incomplete and inconsistent. Undiplomatically speaking, they are fudged beyond any semblance of reality.

The creative recordkeeping on the flight listings added significant cause for speculation among the family members of the 49-244 victims that the Air Force was trying to hide something nefarious. LeMay was such a stickler for proper accounting that he repeatedly admonished officers at SAC bases to report profits and losses of slot machines in their officers' clubs. He wanted to know all kinds of details about housing quality and parking spaces. If bombardiers were several feet, or thousands of feet, off their mark on practice bombings, he wanted an accounting of it. But when it came to accurate reporting of cargo movements involving classified equipment and missions, the lack of specificity simply didn't fit LeMay's command profile. He would not have tolerated it. That is, unless he or those under his command had ordered it to hide the true nature of the equipment they were moving.

The person who decides where to place any given cargo item on a C-124 is the loadmaster. His job is to calculate the weight and size of each item and balance those weights along with fuel distribution and all the other ancillary items that are included on the flight, including passengers, crew, luggage, supplies, and emergency gear. The idea is to ensure the greatest-possible balance between the wings, both fore and aft as well as side to side.

When 49-244 made its first stop at Tinker Air Force Base on March 16, 1951, the cavernous, three-level cargo bay was empty. The loadmaster, Corporal Jack Crow, determined that the best configuration was to place the two empty KB-29 fuel tanks, one weighing 3,530 pounds and the other weighing 3,300 pounds, as closely as possible to the center point directly between the wings. It's unclear why the two nearly identical tanks varied by 230 pounds in weight. The load-distribution plan apparently required strapping down one tank on the flat, second level of the cargo bay while placing the other tank directly in front of it on the plane's loading ramp, angled so that it rested on an awkward downhill slant. The cargo was inspected, then base traffic manager W. E. Blevins cleared the plane for departure on

March 17, destination Walker, where it sat for the following five days as an additional 10,395 pounds was added to the shipment. The Mark 3 Fat Man bomb dropped on Nagasaki weighed 10,300 pounds.

The next order of business was recording the exact weight of each passenger listed on the manifest before departing Walker. Their weights varied significantly, from the skinniest, Master Sergeant H. C. Williamson, registering a mere 132 pounds, to a hefty 212 pounds for Captain P. B. Adrean. Their accompanying baggage also had to be figured in. Captain W. A. Wagner had the heaviest luggage at 164 pounds, contrasting with the 40 pounds brought by Master Sergeant T. H. VanGilder. The vast differences across the board probably reflected the amount of time each passenger was expected to be deployed on the other side of the pond.

Senior officers were spared the indignities of a weigh-in. When all was said and done, the total weight of the plane upon takeoff, including fuel, cargo, and emergency equipment, plus the weight registered by the crew and passengers along with their baggage, came in at 175,118 pounds. That was about 10,000 pounds below the plane's maximum.

Those weights and distribution points weren't just the few tedious details amid a sea of complicated and confusing factors associated with this flight. They would become the focus of intense scrutiny in the weeks that followed as investigators tried to figure out what went wrong and, perhaps more importantly, why.

Something stored in the cargo hold bothered them.

The evidence gathered afterward, scant as it was, indicated residues of a bomb blast or some other kind of combustion that didn't involve fuel, meaning the KB-29s were not the source of whatever happened. And yet, those Fat Man–sized KB-29s were blown to splinters, and the pieces were among the only items left floating when search and rescue ships arrived on the scene. Almost as if someone didn't want those tanks, or whatever was inside them, to reach their destination in Britain.

CHAPTER 15

Actions and Consequences

THERE WERE TWO MOMENTS IN COLD WAR HISTORY WHEN THE hysteria over atomic weapons reached such a fever pitch that nuclear war became a distinct, imminent possibility. Both instances occurred at a time when the Air Force generals in charge of deploying America's most deadly weapon needed little persuasion to do so on a moment's notice. Curtis LeMay was at the center of both crises.

The world knows all about the 1962 Cuban Missile Crisis, so there's no need to dwell on those details here. The vivid accounts of LeMay's stare-down with President John F. Kennedy in the Oval Office, in which he bluntly recommended an attack on Cuba despite the president's objections, underscored LeMay's philosophy that an aggressive posture—"direct military intervention right now"[1] and get them before they have a chance to get us—was the only way to keep the United States on top in a superpower confrontation.

The discussion between the two got slightly heated when Kennedy tried to find a way to avoid starting World War III. LeMay told the president, "And you have made some pretty strong statements about their being defensive and that we would take action against offensive weapons. I think that a blockade and political talk would be considered by a lot of our friends and neutrals as being a pretty weak response to this. And I'm sure a lot of our own citizens would feel that way, too. In other words, you're in a pretty bad fix at the present time."

"What did you say?" Kennedy responded, alerting to the hint of insubordination from his Air Force chief.

"You're in a pretty bad fix," LeMay said.

"You're in there with me," Kennedy said. Nervous laughter followed.[2]

I was five years old at the time and just two months into kindergarten in Denver. My most vivid memory, like others who were in school at the time, was reacting to the sounds of different alarms that alerted us either to crouch under our desks or to walk (not run) into the classroom's coat room to place our heads between our knees. (The joke of older children was: Put your head between your knees, and kiss your ass goodbye.) Teachers told us about these powerful bombs that threatened to wipe out everything in sight. And I distinctly remember wondering, even at age 5, how stupid it was to hide under our desks or huddle in the coat room, as if coats and desks and knees would somehow protect us from an atomic attack. My conviction that we were all going to die anyway stayed with me through college.

I wasn't yet born for the previous moment when atomic annihilation loomed on the horizon, in 1950. But I'm pretty sure that kids didn't have to do practice drills back then because the threat was largely theoretical. The Soviets had exploded their first atomic bomb only the year before, and though they were rapidly building a bomb arsenal, they were nowhere near posing a real threat to the United States. Nevertheless, public pronouncements by a variety of politicians and officials began carrying the distinct drumbeat of war. The mere fact that Russia had an atomic capability was startling enough to send the nation's military commanders into a frenzy of war planning.

Preemptive war planning.

There wasn't a single issue or event in 1950 to help historians tag it with a capitalized name like Missile Crisis. Rather, it was a culmination of events, analyses, and conclusions that led top decision-makers to believe that full-scale war was about to break out, and if that was the case, the prevailing mentality among military commanders suggested: *We'd better get them before they get us.* It was in that context that Curtis LeMay began his campaign with the other top Air Force generals to promote the concept of launching a surprise, preemptive atomic attack on Russia.

There was no such thing as a consequence-free response to the challenges posed by Stalin and the spread of global Communism. Every potential action presented the likelihood of an opposite and unequal reaction. Acting assertively, as LeMay advocated, dramatically raised the risk of yet another world war at a time when the world was still trying to recover from the previous one. But failing to act assertively in the face of Soviet expansionism carried equally severe risks of plowing a large chunk of the world under Communist tyranny. Failing to confront Stalin as he moved to take over Eastern Europe could only be interpreted in Moscow as an affirmation, a green light to keep on swallowing its neighboring states. LeMay didn't want to be the one who stood by idly as another megalomaniacal dictator rolled his tanks across Europe or used the threat of violence to make leaders acquiesce to Communist-friendly policies.

Using blunt military force—firebombings or atomic weaponry—to halt the spread of a political movement risked alienating millions of non-Communists and driving them into the arms of the enemy. But Stalin kept poking and prodding, doing his best to draw the United States into taking rash action, almost as if he believed that an American atomic attack could actually work to his advantage in persuading the world to adopt peaceful Communism over war-loving capitalism.

The pressures coming to bear on LeMay in 1950 were unlike anything he had experienced in his career. Before he took control of the Strategic Air Command, his job primarily involved executing orders from above and delivering battlefield success. Sometimes those victories were small, but very often, they were huge and involved considerable amounts of death and destruction. They were also expensive. All such considerations of cost and consequence at the time were for generals higher up in the command to weigh alongside their civilian bosses. LeMay's only job in his previous commands was to carry out orders, get the job done.

Now, however, LeMay was the one in command. He had to balance all kinds of political and budgetary pressures along with the ones he brought upon himself as the self-appointed defender of freedom. LeMay truly believed he, and he alone, was all that stood between the West and global Communist domination. Before taking over the Strategic Air Command, he had the latitude to deploy bombs, aircraft, and manpower with somewhat reckless abandon in order to achieve his objectives, as the 1945 firebombing campaign over Japan so richly demonstrated. Now, however, he had to be both a strategist and a policymaker, weighing not only the most direct and efficient route to victory but also the political consequences of that victory.

In 1950, the civilian demands on the military to protect and defend the free world were no less severe, but there was the added dimension of keeping costs down. The top civilian leadership fully understood the threat posed by Stalin and the need to contain it. At the same time that President Truman wanted to expand America's nuclear umbrella to cover Western Europe, Alaska, the Middle East, and Southeast Asia, the president also demanded that the Pentagon accept the constraints of a postwar, dramatically slashed budget. It was time to divert those dollars from tanks, guns, aircraft, and personnel to building highways, dams, sewers, electrification grids, schools, and other critical modern infrastructure at home.

At the same time, the explosion of a Soviet atomic bomb in August 1949 dramatically changed the dimensions of the East-West confrontation. The specter of a Soviet atomic attack on America meant that the Pentagon not only had to refine its attack plans but also come up with a far more formidable defense infrastructure against attack. It fell to LeMay's Strategic Air Command to devise some kind of early alert system to warn of approaching Soviet bombers and give American warplanes a chance to scramble in defense.

Having spent his career playing offense and constantly devising ways to go on the attack, LeMay found himself in the awkward position of hunkering down, as if bracing for a surprise Russian air assault. He despised the very notion of playing defense because it carried with it all of the trappings of fear and weakness while the Red Tide threatened to sweep across Europe, China, and now Korea. It was during the hunkering-down phase when LeMay began exploring the idea of a radar early warning system that involved planting offshore rigs in the Atlantic, equipped with radar scanners, to help advise his forces of approaching Soviet aircraft so he could scramble his planes in response.[3]

There was one aspect of this era that no amount of preparation on LeMay's part—offense or defense—could serve to protect his nation. Communism was perceived to be attacking the United States and Europe from within. It was a political-social battle for hearts and minds, and LeMay found his training and experience utterly useless in combating it. He could see it, but political constraints blocked him from articulating his preferred response.

LeMay and the other commanders had to rely on like-minded politicians on Capitol Hill to carry on the political battle against an unseen, stealthy foe. The vast displays of racial inequality and income disparity in the West created fertile ground for Communism to win sympathetic audiences. So did efforts to suppress organized labor. The horrors of Hiroshima and Nagasaki spurred an antiwar movement that made Communism seem like a viable, downright reasonable alternative. In the newly created nation of Israel, Jews were flocking to found kibbutzim based on Marxist notions of communal living, shared wealth, and group sacrifice. The success of that model served only to attract more followers to the point that, barely a decade later, American hippies would begin founding communes that mimicked the kibbutz lifestyle, albeit with lots of drugs and free love mixed into their utopian sales pitch.

As sympathies grew for a form of political thought that eschewed traditional concepts of capitalism, suspicions abounded that something nefarious was afoot. All of these developments couldn't be happening by mere coincidence. It had to be a plot—a Communist plot.

There was a feeling among American military commanders that the free world was being outflanked, enveloped by Communist forces beyond the U.S. military's control to contain. Commanders embraced a sense of urgency that didn't quite translate into the civilian world, which was problematic when it came to convincing members of Congress that the defense budget needed to go up, not down.

While LeMay pressed his case among his colleagues, he maintained a profile of calm, cool, deliberative leadership in the public eye. It was important not to give any appearance of panic that the press could exploit in headlines. On this point, LeMay and President Truman were in lockstep. It made no sense to feed the frenzy.

Some of LeMay's colleagues didn't get the message. The Navy, recognizing that it was being eclipsed by the Air Force and anxious to make a case for its role in transporting and delivering nuclear weapons, began pushing a more forceful public image of toughness against the Soviet threat. Columnist Drew Pearson, writing about a Truman administration crackdown on generals stepping out of their lane regarding nuclear policy, mentioned the repeated outspokenness of General Orvil Anderson, commandant of the newly created Air War College at Maxwell Air Force Base in Alabama. Pearson asserted that Anderson had sought to "indoctrinate students with the idea of an immediate attack" on the Soviets first before they could hit the United States.[4] Anderson denied he was indoctrinating anyone, but the accusation fit a pattern of outspokenness that rendered his denials moot.

Navy Secretary Francis Matthews spoke before admirals and other dignitaries at the Navy shipyard in Boston about the need for Americans to be "aggressors for peace" and "[to institute] a war to compel cooperation for peace."[5] He was calling for the same kind of preventive atomic strike that LeMay and the other Air Force generals had privately advocated. The only difference was that they did so behind closed doors in a top secret setting. Matthews did it in a very public setting, earning his remarks front-page coverage in *The New York Times*, among other newspapers.

President Truman, already irked by the defiant outspokenness of General Douglas MacArthur in Korea, hit the roof. "I have always been opposed even to the thought of such a war. There is nothing more foolish than to think that war can be stopped by war. You don't 'prevent' anything by war except peace," Truman wrote in his memoirs. "Mr. Matthews, of course, was surrounded by admirals and other high Navy people, and he had not had much experience in dealing with men in that category. He told me he had heard so many of them talk 'preventive war' that he had repeated the phrase without realizing just how far it took him away from my policy. He was very contrite and full of regrets when I talked to him and explained why I could not have members of my administration going around the country advocating a view that was so completely opposed to the official policy of the government.[6]"

Matthews received a rebuke from Truman. General Hoyt Vandenberg fired Anderson from the War College.

The Red Scare came into full bloom in 1950, with Capitol Hill providing the stage for anti-Communist theatrics unlike any the American people had ever witnessed. Americans' loyalty was openly challenged, almost always without justification. Citizens were hauled before the House Un-American Activities Committee to answer whether they were now or had ever been members of the Communist Party. Hollywood actors, directors, and writers had to explain their past connections with Communist sympathizers, which of course had nothing to do with national security (in shocking contrast to the utter lack of congressional interest that would follow the Globemaster 49-244 incident).[7]

Since the Soviets were now an atomic superpower, members of Congress demanded to know how Moscow obtained the technology. The Soviet MiG program prompted questions about how Moscow had obtained knowledge of jet propulsion. The theatrics in Washington prompted even more nervousness in an already worried Europe.

The mere mention of atom bombs seemed to put the Europeans on edge, Truman recalled in his memoir. "The possibility of general war, of course, was much more frightening to the inhabitants of Paris and London—barely recovered as they were from the ravages of the last war—than to a great many Americans who had not been subjected to the destruction of their cities. Europeans generally assumed that a new war would be a battle of atomic weapons, and the slightest mention of atomic bombs was enough to make them jittery."[8] The last thing he needed was a member of his own Cabinet or a bunch of generals ratcheting up the tension with talk of preventive atomic strikes.

LeMay got the message loud and clear. He limited his views to top secret discussions behind closed doors with his most trusted colleagues. But when he knew his words would go no further than the men in that room, he left no doubt where he stood when it came to the merits of preventive action. Time could only work in Stalin's favor.

The press was circling like vultures over new roadkill, just waiting to pounce on the nuclear issue as military confrontations brewed around the world. On the subject of Korea, a reporter asked Truman what his response would be if China intervened on North Korea's behalf. "We will take whatever steps are necessary to meet the military situation, just as we always have," Truman responded at a November 1950 press conference.

"That includes every weapon that we have," Truman added.

The predictable follow-up question came right back at him: "Does that include the atomic bomb?"

"There has always been active consideration of its use," Truman responded. "I don't want to see it used. It is a terrible weapon, and it should not be used on innocent men, women, and children who have nothing whatever to do with this military aggression. That happens when it is used."

His press secretary had to scramble for ways to spin the remark afterward into something more innocuous-sounding, saying, "We will take whatever steps are necessary to meet the military situation, just as we always have."[9]

The exchange alarmed world leaders, including Britain's prime minister, who was due to arrive in Washington a few days afterward to discuss next steps in Korea. Prime Minister Attlee was adamant that the use of atomic weapons in Korea should be taken off the table or, at a minimum, be considered only after close consultation and acquiescence with Britain as codeveloper of the bomb. LeMay kept his concerns to himself, which were not that Truman shouldn't embrace the idea of bold action to win the Korean War but rather that devoting atomic weapons to a relatively small regional war in Asia meant diverting the crucial stockpile that he needed in Europe and the Middle East to confront the real enemy: Russia. So he found himself siding with the British prime minister, albeit for entirely different reasons.

Whatever freedom from oppression LeMay thought he could defend with preparations for an atomic offensive against Russia, Congress was busily imposing its own form of harsh oppression at home against freedom of thought and political affiliation. Which is not to suggest Congress wasn't justified in probing serious breaches of national security. There was no question that the Manhattan Project had been infiltrated and that Communist spies were actively working to compromise America's most cherished secrets.

The British diplomatic spy ring headed by Kim Philby had yet to be exposed by the end of 1950, but strong indications were emerging of betrayal within the British ranks. Of the many potential suspects within the Manhattan Project, Klaus Fuchs was considered an unlikely culprit. The focus turned to big-name researchers, such as J. Robert Oppenheimer, who was hauled before a closed-door HUAC session in June 1949 and grilled by then-Republican-Representative Richard M. Nixon. Nixon previously had taken charge of the so-called Pumpkin Papers case in which journalist Whittaker Chambers testified about his previous Communist Party membership and named State Department officer Alger Hiss as a Communist spy. It was the latter case that gave rise to Senator Joseph McCarthy's anti-Communist crusade. On February 9, 1950, McCarthy waved a piece of paper and declared before a Republican women's committee in Wheeling, West Virginia, "I have here in my hand a list of 205" Communists who, he alleged, had infiltrated the State Department.

Given McCarthy's theatrics, the Red Scare often had the appearance of a domestic political witch hunt bereft of substance. He kept waving his lists and arriving at hearings with a briefcase purportedly full of his secret proof of Communist infiltration. His campaign fizzled because he had no proof of the massive conspiracy he alleged. All of which served to dilute the real, serious spy cases that involved Britain's Cambridge Five and Fuchs, among others. Although the net began closing around Fuchs in 1949, it was in January 1950 that he realized he could no longer deny the substantial evidence against him. He confessed to his British interrogators. (The ringleader of the Cambridge Five, Philby, remained undetected in his job for another year, allowing him to continue feeding Moscow with intelligence about America's nuclear plans and, presumably, the movement of American atomic attack forces to Britain. Philby was forced to resign from British intelligence in July 1951, although he did not admit having been a spy for another ten years afterward.)

The news of British betrayal made LeMay's job doubly difficult. He had to simultaneously trust the British because they would serve as hosts for his new atomic attack force while, at the same time, he had every reason to refuse any semblance of coordination with his U.K. counterparts for fear that any one of them might also be part of the spy ring dominating the news in Washington. When American atomic forces did finally set up bases in Britain, commanders repeatedly issued warnings for personnel not to discuss their activities, to be on the watch for suspect activities, and to be constantly wary of sabotage efforts. No one was to be trusted.

On this, the commanders had the full backing of the Pentagon as well as the Truman administration and Congress. News of Klaus Fuchs's betrayal reverberated like an earthquake in Washington. Politicians were expressing open exasperation with the British government and questioning whether the McMahon Act needed to be tightened, rather than loosened, to ensure no critical atomic energy information made it into enemy hands via the Brits. The Attlee government was growing tense and defensive amid the recriminations.[10] If the British couldn't be trusted, the possibilities escalated that LeMay would be faced with smuggling atomic weaponry onto SAC bases rather than seeking a top secret deal to do it with British acquiescence.

The nation immersed itself in a frenzy of fear over an invisible and, quite possibly, fictitious conspiracy of Communist subterfuge. Stalin couldn't have written a more perfect script to serve his own agenda. Americans were divided from within. The U.S.-British alliance was teetering in mutual distrust. Americans had become so distracted with what they thought was the Communist menace in their midst, they lost sight of the real menace lurking at the edges of Eastern Europe.

At least, that was LeMay's view of the drama unfolding in Washington. It got more complicated when, in September 1950, Senator Patrick McCarran of Nevada introduced a bill to empower the government to fight back against the internal threat. "The McCarran Internal Security Act required all Communists and Communist-sponsored groups to register with the Attorney General, forbade the employment of Communists in defense plants, and gave the government the power to deny passports to them and to order the deportation of any alien who had been a member of the Communist party and, most frightening of all, to detain during a national emergency 'any person as to whom there is reason to believe he might engage in acts of espionage or sabotage.'"[11] President Truman strongly disagreed with the bill, but it passed both houses with strong majorities. When he vetoed it, both houses voted overwhelmingly to override the veto.

Even though Congress recognized an actual threat of military aggression from the newly anointed Soviet atomic superpower, the budget it passed for the same year as the McCarran Act certainly didn't reflect it. As a percentage of gross domestic product, U.S. military spending had fallen from an all-time high of 38.4% in 1945 to 7.2% in 1950. Russia, by contrast, went from around 26% of GDP for defense in 1945 to 29.3% in 1950[12]—the exact opposite direction. Soviet investment in its navy, army, and arms production grew by 60% from 1949 to 1951, dwarfing Stalin's minimal investment in nonmilitary expenditures.[13] While the Western world was demobilizing and focusing its expenditures heavily on domestic priorities, Russia was preparing for a military threat it apparently perceived as being even greater, in terms of expenditures, than the one posed by Hitler's Germany. Or Stalin was preparing for a military conquest even more spectacular than the one Hitler attained.

One of the biggest political assets going for LeMay and the Air Force hawks was the fact that General Hoyt Vandenberg's uncle was, until 1949, one of the most powerful men on Capitol Hill, Senator Arthur Vandenberg, chairman of the Senate Foreign Relations Committee. The uncle had been instrumental during his 21-year Senate career in helping establish the political foundations for his nephew's rise through the ranks. Roosevelt and Truman didn't dare make a decision affecting the Air Force's main objectives without first making sure that General Vandenberg could live with it, if not embrace it. The U.S. Air Force and Army Air Forces command didn't dare make promotion decisions affecting Hoyt Vandenberg's web of influence without ensuring that those decisions wouldn't lead to political pushback from Capitol Hill. Since generals' promotions required Senate confirmation, the Vandenberg team's consent was an unspoken requirement.

The two were well schooled in foreign relations and the role that diplomacy played in attaining military objectives. The goal was to win British acquiescence on the preplacement of atomic bombs on their territory. Not only had the British leadership balked at hosting the bomb or U.S. atomic attack forces, they were also squeamish about the idea of the American administration launching a nuclear war without first gaining British approval. From the British perspective, it was a matter of survival, because the most immediate Soviet response would most likely be aimed at the United Kingdom, not America.

"They feel that if a [nuclear] strike takes off from their territory, there will be one coming back their way," said a memorandum of conversation following top-level meetings between American and British delegations. The memorandum was distributed to the Joint Chiefs of Staff (including General Vandenberg) and Secretary of State Dean Acheson.[14] The meetings were particularly contentious over the question of pre-attack consultations and whether a war could occur against the Soviet Union without needing to use atomic weapons. General Vandenberg was among the most adamant participants insisting that, no, war *without* the option of using atomic weapons was not possible. You don't preclude the use of the nation's most powerful weapon when it's a fight for survival.

The question was whether Attlee's government would agree to the actual placement of atomic weaponry on British shores. Although archives from both governments contain considerable records of conversations and written exchanges on the subject, they could not come to an agreement as 1950 came to a close. LeMay was growing impatient as he began choosing his staff for the Strategic Air Command's new Seventh Air Division, which was to establish basing in Britain in March 1951.

The Strategic Air Command opted not to wait for explicit permission. It began secretly deploying M107 Fat Man practice bombs to Britain for training missions over Europe.[15] The Joint Chiefs proposed in 1951 introducing M107s over Korea as well.[16] Some M107s were filled with 10,000 pounds of concrete for practice sessions over Utah. Others were filled with explosives that packed a big, albeit nonatomic, blast. Although the M107 officially counted as a nuclear component, the conventional explosive or concrete filling of the bombs technically didn't count. Thus, a plane that crashed while carrying an M107—even if the core was kept separate—didn't necessarily have to be reported as an atomic accident (even though the Air Force later reported multiple atomic accidents that didn't involve transporting a nuclear core).

The Joint Chiefs acknowledged that the use of tactical atomic weapons in a regional war like Korea increased the risks that the Soviet Union would expand its involvement in that war (even though Russia already was involved), adding to the potential of a direct U.S.-Soviet military confrontation. But they still deemed it necessary to be prepared should the order come down.

> Subject to your concurrence, the Joint Chiefs of Staff propose to dispatch directives to Commander in Chief Far East, Commanding General, Strategic Air Command, and Commander in Chief, Pacific (copies attached) requiring them to conduct practice atomic strikes in tactical support of ground forces to improve techniques and procedures in case such employment of atomic weapons becomes necessary in the future. Actual atomic weapons, less nuclear

> components, will be used in the operations, except in actual flights over enemy territory, to insure that all procedures, such as assembly, testing, and loading of actual weapons, are thoroughly tested in the field.[17]

The phraseology here needs parsing. "Actual atomic weapons, less nuclear components" is exactly what an M107 was. Thus, the M107 was, by the military's definition, an actual atomic weapon.

At the same time these practice sessions were happening, the Truman administration decided secretly to transfer M107s and other components to Europe and the Pacific. The number of bombs contemplated for deployment varied widely when it came to Britain. At least nine were sent to Guam in case the administration decided they would be needed to deter a North Korean–Soviet rout. If the Manhattan Project was treated as the most secret project ever undertaken by the U.S. government to that point—and it was nevertheless thoroughly compromised by the Soviets—the Pentagon's intention to confront the Communist world with atomic weaponry was broadcast far more openly. It was designed specifically for Stalin to get the message.

But the fact that Britain had been chosen as the basing site for American atomic operations against Russia remained top secret for a very specific reason: The issue of American atomic weaponry on British soil was deemed so domestically sensitive that it threatened to bring down Attlee's government if it were leaked. All mentions of Britain were redacted from official documents related to the atomic deployment.

What neither Attlee's nor the U.S. government contemplated, however, was the willingness of one Winston Churchill to use the issue for political advancement. During an open session of Parliament on February 15, 1951, at the exact time when LeMay was finalizing deployment plans for the Seventh Air Division in the United Kingdom, Churchill decided to challenge Attlee over delays in developing Britain's own atomic bomb. The issue for Churchill was sovereignty and military independence. Relying on American weaponry and personnel meant ongoing subservience to a former colony, something Churchill just couldn't stomach. But it also presented a wedge to go after Attlee politically. Churchill's attack appeared to take Attlee by surprise—not for the fact that the Conservative leader was criticizing him but because he was revealing top secret information in a public forum.

"Another subject of grave complaint," Churchill stated, "is the inability of the Government to produce any atomic bombs of our own in the five and a half years which have passed since the war." This was a particular sore point for Churchill, given the amount of money and expertise Britain contributed to the joint effort to develop the bomb. "When we remember how far we were ahead, and how we were able to deal on equal terms with the United States, it is indeed depressing to feel that we have been outstripped by the Soviets in this field. I take the opportunity of repeating now my request that the document I signed with President Roosevelt in the war should be made public at an early date."

Then Churchill blurted out: "We must not forget that by creating the American atomic base in East Anglia we have made ourselves the target, and perhaps the bull's-eye of a Soviet attack."[18]

Until that moment, there had been much speculation but no official confirmation in any public forum of an American plan to establish atomic basing in Britain. The only plan was to establish a Strategic Air Command outpost that would provide an initial response to a Soviet incursion while U.S.-based forces geared up for a more formidable response. But Churchill's statement put it on the official record that the Americans had an atomic base in East Anglia—that is, Mildenhall and Lakenheath. Those were the very destinations of the fifty-three men aboard Globemaster 49-244.

ATTLEE SCRAMBLED TO STOP CHURCHILL FROM DIVULGING EVEN more secrets. He interrupted Churchill in midsentence to interject: "The right honorable Gentleman really ought not to mislead the country on a matter like this. He knows perfectly well it was by his agreement, and the agreement of the Government of which I was a Member, that the development of the atomic bomb and the making and everything took place across the other side of the Atlantic, and it is utterly untrue to suggest there has been a failure to develop it here. It is entirely wrong of him." By returning Churchill to the argument about delays over British development of the atomic bomb, he deftly steered the discussion *away* from the topic of East Anglia and U.S. atomic forces in Britain.

Churchill stated what many British politicians had feared but had been reluctant to articulate: The presence of American atomic forces would put Britain in the Soviet Union's crosshairs. The statement had another unintended effect of putting U.S. Air Force flights to and from British bases also in Moscow's crosshairs. Stalin now had confirmation from a highly credible (though hated) source that, in fact, the United States was moving forces and weaponry to Britain in preparation for an atomic attack against the Soviet Union.

The British opposition leader was pressing Truman with similar questions, demanding the public release of atomic agreements between Britain, Canada, and the United States. Truman was no less rattled than Attlee over Churchill's antics, writing on February 16, 1951:

> *I hope you won't press me in this matter. It will cause unfortunate repercussions both here and in your country, as well as embarrassment to me and to your government. The reopening of this discussion may ruin my whole defense program both here at home and abroad. Your country's welfare and mine are at stake in that program. I hope you are in good health and enjoying life as much as one can enjoy it in these troubled times.*[19]

Why Churchill was pressing for a public airing of these details isn't clear, but Truman joined Attlee in trying to calm him down—and keep him quiet. Writing again to Churchill on March 24, 1951, he advised:

> *Publication of the Agreement would be misleading unless it were also decided to make public the current status of cooperation and collaboration among the United Kingdom, Canada, and the United States in the field of atomic energy. Indeed, it would be exceedingly difficult, if not impossible, to resist pressures to make known this information once the Agreement were made public. I feel strongly that in present circumstances such a development would be seriously prejudicial to the interests of the United Kingdom and the United States as well as to our Allies under the North Atlantic Treaty.*[20]

Truman's latter letter was dated exactly one day after Globemaster 49-244 had gone missing, the search was in progress, and newspaper headlines were filled with questions about what the flight was all about. The Air Force was doing everything it could to tamp down speculation in the press that the flight was related to an atomic mission and that sabotage might have caused its ditching. And here was the former prime minister of Britain doing his best to turn the entire issue of America's atomic basing effort into a topic of public debate. Fears were rampant that Churchill could bring down the government with his careless remarks. And perhaps that was the whole point: He wanted to be back in power, and Attlee was all that stood in his way.

He was trying hard to reap political capital from simmering British popular resentment to the effort by both governments to beef up American forces there. Wherever the Americans set up camp came restrictions on Britons' freedoms. They weren't allowed to travel in certain areas or take photographs. They weren't allowed to know what the Americans were up to. The irony was that Churchill had actively promoted a direct atomic confrontation with Stalin, believing that only a forceful response would convince him to back down. But now Churchill appeared to be leading a populist campaign to expose what the Americans were up to, much to Attlee's and Truman's horror.

Newspaper columnist Drew Pearson strongly suggested at the time that exactly such an atomic prepositioning operation was being planned. Truman went to great lengths to deny the report, effectively arguing that deployment of disassembled components of the bomb didn't constitute deployment of the bomb itself. It was a conundrum for politicians on both sides of the Atlantic because they simultaneously were seeking to assuage any public concerns that preparations were being made for atomic war while they also wanted Stalin to know in no uncertain terms that he faced nuclear ruin if he pushed the United States too far.

Churchill had managed to convert a vague threat of atomic preparations on European soil into a reality. By identifying East Anglia as the basing site, he gave Moscow all the information it needed to begin focusing its espionage on U.S. flights coming and going from those British bases.

Stalin was already engaging in serious provocations, if not outright acts of war, against the United States in Korea. Would it have been far-fetched for Stalin to do everything in his power to thwart the American plans when it came to Europe?

American military research on Soviet sabotage during this era makes clear that the threat was perceived as real, and the danger imminent. American military bases at the time were not heavily fenced, barbed-wire fortresses guarded by checkpoints and security cameras. In fact, there was no fencing at all surrounding LeMay's nuclear command center in Nebraska, which was arguably among the five most sensitive military bases in the nation. The general performed a hard assessment of the sabotage dangers and decided that it was time to take action. He ordered fences constructed around all SAC facilities and boosted security procedures to the point that any and all visitors to his bases, including soft-drink vending machine attendants, had to produce identification badges and proof of authorization for being there.[21] LeMay had received briefing materials regarding domestic Communist activities warning that sabotage was, first and foremost, the tool of preference Moscow would use to stop any perceived threat from the West, especially if that threat involved a nuclear attack. What LeMay's commanders proposed with the flight of Globemaster 49-244 was the worst-imaginable scenario for the Soviets: the installation of the Strategic Air Command's first-ever overseas atomic base, with an explicit mission to prepare for an attack on Russia. It couldn't get any more threatening than that (as the United States would realize a decade later when the Soviets tried the same thing in Cuba).

Before the Globemaster flight, the Truman administration had been engaged in a spirited debate with the U.S. military command and the Atomic Energy Commission over who should have authority to control and deploy atomic weaponry. In response to the horrors of Hiroshima and Nagasaki, Congress passed the Atomic Energy Act of 1946 to ensure that the nation's atomic arsenal remained under civilian control. It was too powerful a weapon to entrust to generals who, in the heat of a military entanglement, might resort to the bomb's use as the most efficient route to victory. But the generals, LeMay included, offered a powerful counterargument: The threat of a Soviet sweep across Europe was too real and too imminent to waste several days going through the AEC approval process before being allowed to deploy the arsenal overseas. The bomb needed to be ready and fully accessible at a moment's notice. The debate went back and forth for months in 1948 until the two sides reached agreement on a "dual chain of command" that allowed the military to have possession but still required civilian approval before any deployment could occur.[22]

The temporary accord didn't put the matter to rest. The approval process remained too cumbersome and failed to fully grasp the pressing Soviet threat. James Forrestal, the first Secretary of Defense, met with Truman at the White House on July 21, 1948, to present his critique of the current arrangement and to argue for greater flexibility in favor of the National Military Establishment, or NME.

> Forrestal offered four arguments: (1) that a surprise attack could expose the United States to "unreasonable risk of mistake, confusion and failure to act with the necessary speed and precision"; (2) that the military needed to learn in peacetime how to maintain and operate atomic weapons; (3) that giving custody to the NME "will facilitate the storing of the . . . Components in the most favorable strategic locations"; and (4) that delivery of the weapons to the NME "should further the research and development activities in weapon design.[23]

Forrestal felt so strongly about these points that, at one point, he threatened to resign if Truman turned down his appeal.

It was the third point that pertained specifically to the U.S. Air Force's plans for Britain. If Truman would permit the storage of components in strategic locations, proper personnel could begin moving those components into place. If the components were kept separated, as Truman had already argued publicly, they didn't constitute an atomic bomb and, therefore, didn't have to be reported as such to the Air Force's British hosts.

Truman vacillated but ultimately accepted Forrestal's argument. The AEC's nuclear monopoly was broken. By 1950, "even as ardent an advocate of civilian control as Truman recognized that should a major emergency erupt, the military would be able to respond more quickly if the weapons were readily available. And since the transfer orders he issued in 1950 applied only to nonnuclear components, the principle of civilian control remained basically intact. Later would come the question of transferring nuclear components as well."[24] Over succeeding months, the U.S. administration informed Britain that it would no longer accept restrictions agreed in 1943 that required British concurrence on the use of atomic weapons in war. At the same time, it presented a forceful case for the storage of atomic bomb components on British soil. Technically, the United States had the ability to smuggle such components onto the British bases it already controlled, but there was one technicality that would have immediately tipped off the British no matter how well the Americans tried to conceal their activities: The Fat Man was still too bulky to be loaded onto a B-29 without first being lowered into a pit so the belly of the B-29 could be parked over it. Digging such a loading pit and installing the hydraulic lifts necessary to make it work could not have been accomplished without British observation. But since a KB-29 tank also required loading through those trench-like bays, the tanks provided plausible deniability for what the Americans actually were up to.

And with British observation came the pesky problem of compromised secrecy. Stalin had the means, through Philby and others, to know what the Americans were planning. Churchill's remark in Parliament served notice to Moscow that the plans were further advanced than Stalin might have recognized. With the help of Philby, Stalin may have been able to determine exactly when LeMay was deploying his forces and which flights would be carrying the personnel most important to carrying out that mission.

The designated commander of the SAC's new Seventh Air Division, Cullen, was aboard Globemaster 49-244, and Cullen had done an abysmal job of caring for his own security, having told his two wives where he was going and why. Both made no secret of their plans to join him and make a new home in Britain. Could it really have been that difficult for Soviet spies to find out what the Americans were planning?

CHAPTER 16

Rushing to Get Somewhere Fast

IN THE WEEKS PRECEDING THE FLIGHT OF GLOBEMASTER 49-244 across the Atlantic, there was a sudden uptick in activity among LeMay and his senior Strategic Air Command staffers. Starting in December 1950, an event that remained classified even seventy-five years later prompted a rush of high-level meetings. It started with President Harry S. Truman's declaration of a national state of emergency on December 16, 1950, warning that "world conquest by communist imperialism is the goal of the forces of aggression that have been loosed upon the world." Truman's basis for concern was the war in Korea, which U.S.-led United Nations forces were losing. But his declaration went geographically far beyond the conflict on the peninsula.

The tone of crisis was unlike any that Americans had seen in peacetime or during a period when the United States was not under direct attack. The Communist threat "requires that the military, naval, air, and civilian defenses of this country be strengthened as speedily as possible to the end that we may be able to repel any and all threats against our national security and to fulfill our responsibilities in the efforts being made through the United Nations and otherwise to bring about lasting peace."

Truman declared "the existence of a national emergency" and summoned "all citizens to make a united effort for the security and well-being of our beloved country and to place its needs foremost in thought and action that . . . the Nation may be readied for the dangers which threaten us."

He asked farmers, industrial workers, the business community to boost production as they did during World War II. He called again for sacrifices "necessary for the welfare of the Nation."

Truman concluded, "I am confident that we will meet the dangers that confront us with courage and determination, strong in the faith that we can thereby "secure the Blessings of Liberty to ourselves and our Posterity."[1]

The stunning speech led the Sunday *New York Times* front page with a three-line banner headline. Although it fell short of an all-out declaration of war against the Communist world's leading entity, it made clear Truman wanted to put the nation on a war-footing mentality. For the military, and more specifically for LeMay's command, the declaration signaled a green light for the campaign LeMay and other Air Force generals had long advocated to step up the pressure on Joseph Stalin and put him on the defensive. A clear demonstration of America's atomic superiority was the way to get Stalin's attention.

Within two days, LeMay departed Offutt for what his diary described as an "emergency meeting" in Washington. He selected Lieutenant Colonel Hopkins as one of the four officers to accompany him.

The meetings on his schedule included General Vandenberg, the Air Force Chief of Staff, and Air Force Secretary Thomas K. Finletter. A long-standing power struggle between LeMay and General Lauris Norstad came to a head during the visit as they dueled over control of U.S. Air Force assets and bases under expansion in Britain and other European countries. Norstad, who commanded the U.S. Air Force in Europe, insisted he be the one to control those assets and atomic-trained units. LeMay was adamant that, when it came to all things atomic, the SAC commander should have unchallenged authority.

Vandenberg agreed in early January to intervene directly if LeMay and Norstad couldn't work it out. It appeared that Vandenberg was inclined to take LeMay's side, although General Dwight D. Eisenhower, the Supreme Commander of NATO in Europe, appeared to support Norstad.[2] The fact that these turf battles were taking place even as the United States was preparing for all-out atomic war against Russia speaks to the disarray at the top of the U.S. military command. They had yet to establish a clear plan on how to engage America's most powerful enemy. Commanders wanted to frighten Stalin into submission, but a lot of big egos were getting in the way.

At particular issue was the status of bases in the United Kingdom and LeMay's plans to establish a new SAC Seventh Air Division there. The controversy didn't just place LeMay in opposition to Norstad but also to Eisenhower. Before meeting with Vandenberg, LeMay posed his concerns with General Frank Fort Everest, according to LeMay's diary, as recounted by his unidentified assistant:

> *One point of serious discussion between General Everest and General LeMay was the effect on SAC's mission of the newly constituted command in Europe headed by General Eisenhower with General Norstad as Air Commander. General LeMay is seriously worried as to this structure's effect on SAC's primary mission which is to place the bomb on the target. He does not feel that we can do this if the resources are not ours, i.e., if air fields, supply, etc., are under the control of another commander. General LeMay was unable to receive any suitable answer from General Everest on this subject and will further discuss this item at a conference with General Vandenberg and General Norstad on 22 December.*

Ominously, the final sentence of LeMay's diary entry states: "The results of this conference are extremely important to a successful prosecution of the atomic mission by SAC."[3]

The political sensitivities of discussions around atomic weaponry and the United Kingdom were so elevated that documents referring to it remained classified for decades afterward, and even when they were declassified, censors blacked out any mention of the United Kingdom, Britain, the British, and bases located in Britain from some key documents. To this day, some documents within the Library of Congress and National Archives related to the atomic deployment in the United Kingdom remain classified for reasons that remain unclear. Yet other documents make crystal clear what the objective was. Those who decide what the public is or is not allowed to view are not required to explain why or how they determine that a document created seventy-five years ago is so sensitive that it still cannot be declassified.[4]

There are no declassified records, for example, of orders explaining the mission Hopkins and the other members of the atomic attack force were to undertake once they arrived in Britain. The orders simply say he was to deploy for temporary duty, or TDY, as of March 21, 1951. This order came after a decision on January 27, 1951, to send Hopkins's old unit, the 509th Bomb Wing, to the United Kingdom to replace the underperforming Ninety-Seventh Wing.[5] LeMay was specific that he wanted no "loss of effectiveness" of the 509th in this transfer and that the 509th commander should report directly to him despite any instructions the commander should get elsewhere (an apparent reference to Norstad).[6]

Other documents indicate that General Cullen was not LeMay's first choice to lead the newly created Seventh Air Division that would incorporate the 509th and other bomb wings. LeMay had originally pushed for Brigadier General John Paul McConnell to head up the mission.[7] Although there were consultations about reconnaissance with Cullen throughout the period from December 1950 through February 1951, Cullen did not enter the command picture until two or three days before the Globemaster flight was scheduled to depart. The suddenness of this decision could explain why he didn't undergo a more thorough security vetting and suggests that someone other than LeMay stepped in to impose Cullen as the new Seventh Air Division commander. Newspaper and biographical accounts indicate Cullen's links to Norstad and Eisenhower dated back to their days serving in Europe during World War II.

During the Washington trip, LeMay's top-level meetings were consumed with the question of where to put his principal atomic bases in Europe. His counterparts and bosses raised the options of Thule in Greenland, along with others in Spain and Ireland. LeMay was cool to the alternatives for various reasons, such as the distance between Thule and the main Soviet targets, and the trustworthiness of Stalin-friendly Ireland should war erupt. Secretary Finletter contended in his meetings with LeMay that they needed an alternative to Britain and France "in the event of an emergency when the UK and French bases were denied to us"[8] because they had been overrun by Soviet forces.

Finletter then made clear where he stood on the question of which general should be in command of SAC assets and bomb wings in Europe. "He admonished General LeMay to let him know if they tried to take them away from SAC."[9]

The "they" in that diary entry would most likely refer to Norstad, with Eisenhower backing him. It's worth noting that upon taking office as president in 1953, Eisenhower named Norstad as Supreme Allied Commander Europe, a position that effectively made LeMay subservient to him on European atomic deployment matters. Cullen's close links to Elliott Roosevelt and deep involvement on the European front during World War II would have placed him directly in Eisenhower's sphere of influence and attention at a time when LeMay's mission was focused on the Pacific front. There's no archival evidence to prove any such link, but there also is no archival evidence to explain why LeMay's choice of Cullen to command the Seventh Air Division came so abruptly and unenthusiastically.

What is well documented is the rivalry between LeMay and Norstad, which grew even more pronounced as the Cold War deepened and the two engaged in a bizarre public relations battle. LeMay cultivated ties to Hollywood and encouraged pro-SAC films as well as stories in national magazines, while Norstad cut a dashing figure in posed photos accenting his square jaw and swept-back silver hair. Had he not been a general, he could easily have been a model or perhaps a movie star. LeMay, with his slightly chubby cheeks and face frozen in a perpetual frown, simply couldn't compete. He seemed to treat Norstad more as an annoyance than a serious threat to his war plans.

Two days before Christmas 1950, LeMay continued to be consumed with the question of basing for his atomic forces in Europe. The choices for a headquarters were narrowed down to the United Kingdom and Morocco. Instead of directly referring to the storage of atomic weaponry in whichever location was chosen, his diary entries often use more generic terms like "depot."

LeMay's pre-Christmas entry, at a time when other fathers and husbands were focused on gift purchases and holiday preparations, instead demonstrated the general's preparations for war. His December 23 entry concluded: "Will need an aggressive officer to command it, not necessarily a supply man." The entry made clear that Cullen's name still wasn't in the mix for the top job, given that he had minimal combat-command experience and hardly fit the profile of an "aggressive officer." Cullen was a picture-taker, not a bomb-dropper.

The day after Christmas, LeMay resumed his bickering with Norstad over who got to command what in Europe. Norstad continued insisting that, as commander of the Third Air Division in Europe and its support mission for B-29 bombers based in the United Kingdom, he should retain domain over British-based units. The two simply could not agree, meaning that it would require intervention from someone higher up the chain of command to settle the dispute. In the meantime, LeMay continued to press his case for appointing McConnell to command SAC atomic forces in Europe.[10]

It's important to note that, at the same time LeMay was grappling with all of the challenges of preparing for World War III, he also had to contend with the daily challenges and problems of the 60,000 men under his command. One lowly airman at Offutt who felt he had been wronged by his sergeants barged into LeMay's outer offices one day and demanded a personal meeting with LeMay (he didn't get it). There were constant budgeting and housing issues to be decided. LeMay had worked hard to boost staffing and recruitment, but his bases around the country weren't equipped with houses, apartments, and barracks for all the incoming officers, enlisted men, and their families. LeMay took it upon himself to personally fix the problem.

Something of an unidentified intelligence nature prompted the Air Force Chief of Staff to order substantially elevated security measures around LeMay. He and his staff were ordered to carry sidearms with shoulder holsters at all times. All planes on which he flew were to be declared confidential, with their timing and routes kept secret until takeoff. The flights were to undergo preflight security checks, with strict monitoring of all items loaded or unloaded from them. Air police were to be posted outside his aircraft, as well as at his office and home. He and his family were to be tailed by security agents wherever they went, including "unofficial off-base activities, such as sports, dinners and parties. This function will be accomplished in as inconspicuous a manner as possible.[11]"

Clearly, the threat level against LeMay and the SAC was perceived as critical.

Code language began appearing in transcripts of phone conversations, as if to protect confidential information from being detected by third parties. When a caller wanted to refer to a possible atomic deployment in Europe, the person would refer to "that place you just came from," meaning Berlin and the airlift mission. If the reference was to bombs heading to Guam in the Pacific, the caller would use references to that place where the war ended.

Despite this new security obsession, an inordinate amount of the general's time went into the mundane question of whether to install slot machines in the officers' clubs of his various U.S. bases as a way of generating revenue. Slot machines were installed, but in some cases they ran afoul of local and state laws banning such gambling devices. In other instances, the machines weren't generating enough revenue to offset the expenses of the officers' clubs. LeMay issued a threat to impose mandatory membership in the clubs—and mandatory fees—for all officers, regardless of whether they used the clubs. He even threatened to stall or advance their promotions based on whether they joined.

Then came the huge question of racial integration. The Truman administration had issued orders for the U.S. military to embark on a gradual but deliberate effort to integrate its forces at this same time in the Cold War. LeMay, despite his association years later with the racially tinged presidential campaign of Alabama Governor George Wallace, showed no signs of reluctance in carrying out the president's orders. His airmen, however, apparently didn't get the message. Whenever racial tensions rose at his bases, word was delivered directly to LeMay's doorstep, as if other generals, colonels, and lower officers either didn't have the wherewithal to solve the problem or, more likely, LeMay insisted on dealing with it himself.

In one case, a black airman shot a white SAC airman for reasons that were unclear. In another instance, the racial integration of air units being sent to Europe was generating tensions with host countries. The British and Canadian governments were cool to the idea of black airmen being housed on their bases. This prompted a flurry of exchanges as LeMay tried to enforce the integration rules while contending with governments that didn't care what Truman wanted; they wanted to maintain their own traditions of racial separation. The State Department got involved. Letters and internal directives went back and forth referring to the "negro problem."

The issue came to a head in late 1949 and early 1950, exactly as LeMay was ramping up preparations for SAC forces to deploy to Britain temporarily until a basing agreement materialized. LeMay went back and forth on the issue, at times worrying about the local sensitivities in Britain and how integration might affect his bigger plans, while at other times insisting that a presidential directive to integrate his forces was not to be questioned, and host countries would simply have to accept that Negroes would be an integral part of American fighting forces.[12]

LeMay was juggling so many disparate issues at once that it reached almost comic proportions in late 1950. There was a high-level meeting on December 14, 1950, in which he stated that the next six months would be critical in the preparation for war against Russia "and that he felt that Joe [Stalin] would strike when the MDA became effective (or slightly before)." Shortly after that conversation envisioning the start of World War III, he turned to "the colored problem" and ordered General Robin Olds to organize a party at MacDill Air Force Base in Florida.

"Call in some of your NCO both Colored and White and explain the situation and enlist [their] cooperation in this matter and ask the Whites [to] invite some colored people and then make sure they enjoy the party . . . Also enlist all the help you can from Colored officers on station."[13] Two days later, President Truman declared the national emergency in response to the buildup of Communist forces.

In mid-January 1951, LeMay's entourage briefed Secretary Finletter on his latest war plans for Europe. Finletter interrupted one of the briefers and began peppering the group with questions. *Good* questions. Such as: "What would you do if you were the Russians?"; "What is a reasonable estimate of their capability?"; and "Are we going to examine sabotage today?"[14]

The latter question, the lack of attention to which LeMay had worried for months, was clearly on the minds of those higher up the chain. Signs of sabotage were starting to show up in various locations and taking various forms. Foreign metallic particles were showing up in air fuel, which LeMay's diaries declared, without equivocation, as overt sabotage.[15] LeMay knew the signs, since some of the examples he was seeing were almost identical to methods that appeared in the 1944 Office of Strategic Services field manual for sabotage techniques.[16]

LeMay also had to worry about the dangers posed to air crews by exposure to atomic blasts. He received one report in February 1951 that crew members should not look directly into the flash of an atomic explosion without protective eyewear for fear of blindness. Then came the ongoing danger of flying through radiation clouds after an explosion. Pilots were advised to steer their aircraft clear of the blast area and remain upwind of the blast for at least thirty minutes, if not a full hour, after dropping an atomic bomb.[17]

The war preparation challenges, racial problems, and Norstad's constant annoyance were all bearing down on him. On top of all this, the SAC commander also had to play the political game, a job he clearly found onerous but obligatory. Since the Strategic Air Command was headquartered in Nebraska, the state's senior senator, Republican Kenneth Wherry, needed constant updates on the command's status. Maintaining good relations with the senator was crucial to LeMay's overall objectives, especially since Wherry was leading the charge to boost the construction of living quarters at SAC bases around the country—dubbed "Wherry housing."

For LeMay, the relationship was particularly tricky because Wherry had clashed repeatedly with Senator Arthur Vandenberg (General Vandenberg's uncle) on Marshall Plan aid for the reconstruction of Europe. Keeping Vandenberg happy was essential to keeping his boss, General Hoyt Vandenberg, happy. So LeMay, whose patience was paper thin in the best of times, was forced to play the diplomat at the very moment when the general might be ordered to launch an atomic strike on Russia.

Wherry and other Capitol Hill conservatives were organizing a political push to economize on an expected war against Russia by emphasizing air power—atomic bombing—over a costly and unpopular deployment of ground forces. The assumption was that high-profile Air Force generals like LeMay would embrace their effort since it naturally would entail more funding for them. But the generals were in no mood to get involved in congressional politics, especially when the stakes involved nuclear war and potentially running afoul of President Truman's orders to stay away from such discussions.

Wherry phoned LeMay on the afternoon of February 16, 1951, to ask whether the general could come to Washington for a briefing of the House and Senate Armed Services Committees on the situation in Europe. Wherry particularly wanted LeMay to "bring to this committee a picture of what it means to destroy a country through the air. See what I mean?"

LeMay's disinterested reply: "Uh hm."

Wherry tried his best to get a more enthusiastic response, recounting how the Senate committee had heard from Generals George C. Marshall and Omar Bradley, "and these monkeys are committing us to a ground offensive in Western Europe and they are making preparations for a ground warfare. . . . It seems to me that to be masters of the air, we've got to have air strength anyhow. We have to have that to defend the United States of America regardless of what we do in Western Europe. See what I mean?"

LeMay: "Yes, sir. I certainly do."

Wherry was trying to use the prospect of higher appropriations for the Air Force as a way of enticing LeMay into testifying for the House and Senate committees, but the general was clearly cool to the idea. He told Wherry to go through the proper Defense Department channels if he wanted the SAC commander to come.

"Everybody recognizes you as a man that's been through the mill, and I think the bombing of Japan and your experiences of what the destructibility through the air could be, I think it's just the thing that the American people want. . . . You see what I mean?"

"Yes, sir. I do."

Wherry tried repeatedly to get LeMay to be more expansive over the phone, suggesting that air power was the way to wage war in Europe, not through reliance on ground troops. But he kept getting "uh hm" responses. In one of his longer responses, LeMay finally told Wherry that, in his personal opinion, "some troops in Europe" would be necessary. "It's a matter of policy and strategy of how we're going to fight a future war."

After they ended the call, LeMay quickly appealed up the chain to General Vandenberg, pleading for someone to get him "off the hook" so he wouldn't have to testify. His diary entry states: "The answer to this came one hour later and stated that the Gen [LeMay] was on the hook and that the address would be in open session and from the cuff and that Gen Van [Vandenberg] would brief Gen leMay before the talk takes place."

He then received a lengthy briefing paper outlining the positions taken by the defense secretary and top Pentagon chiefs during their own testimony. Vandenberg told the committee that Russia had amassed troops and "large stockpiles of war material close to the borders of Western Europe and that military forces of Russia are ready to advance." Relying on American air power was not enough to stop the Soviets, he added. Deploying ground troops was a matter of military necessity and "not a political decision."

Since the hearings were public, LeMay and the other generals were careful in their responses, refusing to delve into classified matters in open session. They did, however, make clear that air power alone could only delay a Russian ground assault, not prevent it. And once the Soviets broke through, they would not be stoppable without the presence of Western ground forces. "It would be infinitely easier to hold a European beachhead rather than attempt to make an amphibious re-entry in view of the atomic bomb threat" from Russia, LeMay's briefing paper stated.[18]

On February 22, 1951—a month before the departure of Globemaster 49-244—LeMay sat down in his office at Offutt to evaluate his testimony and begin preparations for establishing the new atomic air division in Europe. He phoned General Cullen at his Barksdale base in Louisiana to discuss possible personnel changes. But his diary recorded no commitments on who would command the new Seventh Air Division. In fact, it wasn't even clear where the division would be based, partly because General Norstad continued to get in LeMay's way.

Various exchanges between LeMay, Norstad, and Vandenberg "do not indicate that completely satisfactory assignment of functions has been accomplished as yet but it looks as if SAC will get its AD [air division] hdqts in UK as well as in the North Africa region. The supply functions are still under Norstads control and that is not good."[19]

Meanwhile, LeMay returned to the day-to-day headaches of commanding his airmen. There was a fight in the barracks at Offutt that prompted a private first class identified only as "Johnson" to make a bold phone call directly to LeMay. Then there was a call from a general in Fort Worth to advise LeMay of a bomb drop that was twenty-two miles off target.

Preparations for war and the deployment of atomic attack forces to Europe intensified in March. LeMay began investigating ways to modify the holds of airborne tanker aircraft to expand their ability to carry non-fuel cargo. A visit to the Boeing factory in Seattle yielded bad news that the tanks took up too much space to allow for other bulky, unspecified cargo to be loaded. It wasn't clear why LeMay wanted to put cargo aboard tankers instead of just using regular cargo planes for that task.

At Spokane, Washington, he received a briefing about a shortage of parachutes that was "affecting the combat potential of the organization."[20]

He received a Rand report warning of a 79% loss rate if he contemplated a low-level conventional bombing campaign against Soviet forces. LeMay pushed back against the assessment, saying Rand had given the enemy far too much credit for antiaircraft capabilities that the Soviets had never demonstrated.[21]

LeMay took another trip to Washington on March 4 for briefings at the Pentagon, where he complained that he wasn't able to generate much excitement regarding SAC capabilities. "Gen LeMay does not feel that he is getting the priority that is intended for the Atomic Offensive and either they want to lay the attack down or they do not[.] he needs and is asking for a statement of policy . . . Well Gen. Twining assured him that he did have the priority and the Atomic offensive was the number one project of the air staff."[22]

The diary entries continued on a nearly daily basis from early to mid-March. The preparations for war—an atomic offensive—were intensifying. On March 18 to 19—less than a week before the Globemaster flight—there was a bizarre entry. Then, and only then, was General Cullen informed that he would be the one to command the new Seventh Air Division. One of the most momentous command appointments of this phase in the Cold War entailed giving the chosen person less than a week to prepare, pack up, and go. The appointment was made only after a call between LeMay and General S. E. Atkinson querying whether Cullen might be suitable for the job. Once they agreed, LeMay ordered an aide to summon Cullen "right away and we will get him over there to get started. He can come back later to get his family."[23] It appears LeMay was unaware that Cullen's "family" consisted of two wives and no children.

There was no mention of any discussion with Cullen about the need to keep this appointment secret. After Cullen was notified, his wives would later testify and declare in a newspaper interview that they knew all about what was coming and were told to start their own preparations for the move overseas. Neither wife mentioned any request to keep this matter hush-hush for the sake of security. Whether they informed their friends and family is unclear, but it would be a matter of simple human nature to let people know in advance of a big move overseas rather than just disappear from one day to the next.

Assuming the move was discussed outside Cullen's immediate circle, any question of pre-deployment secrecy was now out the window. Any number of Soviet agents—and LeMay knew they were out there given his own intense focus on security and use of code language in his phone conversations—could have infiltrated the Cullen circle to glean details of what was coming. Of course, there was also Philby placed in a key liaison position in Washington to keep his Soviet handlers informed.

The Globemaster was less than a week away from taking flight with a general onboard who would, if called upon, lead the nation into an unprecedented atomic attack on the only other nuclear superpower in the world. And there was no indication that Cullen had been thoroughly vetted, no indication that his history of deceit and marital infidelity had been investigated, no indication that LeMay had weighed Cullen's trustworthiness and reliability given the mess he had made of his homelife. Cullen's elevation to the job of Seventh Air Division commander appears to have been an afterthought, as if LeMay couldn't get agreement on the other options and settled on Cullen as the least-worst choice.

There's no way of knowing what other conversations might have taken place because LeMay's diary entries in the Library of Congress archives go from nearly daily entries to completely dark for the next six days, almost as if they had been scrubbed.

There is only one entry from March 19 until March 25. During that time, the Globemaster with Cullen and Hopkins aboard along with fifty-one others took flight, along with the plane's strange cargo. Then the flight diverted southward over the Atlantic and disappeared. In terms of the number of people lost, it marked the worst single-plane air disaster in U.S. military history, and yet LeMay's diary entries carry almost no mention of it.

The SAC commander, who typically recorded daily entries of minutiae such as slot machine revenue at officers' clubs, housing shortages, and racial fights among airmen, had nothing to say for six days regarding the most catastrophic loss under his command. He offered no public statements. He sent no immediate letters of condolence or concern to the victims' families.

When his diary entries did pick up again, on March 25, 1951, the Globemaster disaster received the following treatment:

> *The CG* [commanding general] *terminated his short leave at Colorado Springs and was picked up by C-97 aircraft and returned to Offutt. Upon return, a conference between General LeMay, General* [Walter C.] *Sweeney and General* [Thomas S.] *Power was held at the CG's home and a complete discussion of the loss of the C-124 took place. Also discussed was the next day's business for the CG in Washington which was a conference with General Vandenberg and Secretary Finletter on the new base at Thule.*

The following day's entry returned to far less important minutiae, mentioning a discussion with Vandenberg about "the status of airmen's barracks throughout the command and throughout the Air Force with particular view towards utilizing the SAC metal permanent type barracks in lieu of the wood type barracks now being bid for by the U.S. Engineers." But there is almost no further mention of the disappeared brigadier general, the lieutenant colonel who had accompanied him on an emergency trip to Washington, or any others aboard the Globemaster. There is almost no discussion of what event might have caused the plane to veer so wildly off course and ditch in the Atlantic.

LeMay did, however, turn to the question of who should replace Cullen as the Seventh Air Division commander. LeMay nominated the person he had preferred from the beginning, General McConnell, and this time the appointment sailed through. McConnell took up the job slightly more than a month after the Globemaster ditching, and the transition was complete. Aside from brief references in historical logs from the period, it was almost as if the C-124 disaster had never happened.

To get an idea of how bizarre this situation was, consider the amount of space he devoted in his diary to the question of airmen parking their cars on the lawns outside offices at Offutt. On April 17, 1951, while the Globemaster investigation was still in progress and signs of sabotage were surfacing, LeMay's diary devoted paragraph after paragraph to "spring house cleaning" and "wheel marks of cars on almost all lawn areas around buildings other than quarters." LeMay was absolutely focused on the problem, directing a long series of measures to install paved parking and get the base looking spick-and-span. He returned with equal vigor to the same subject on April 18. But there was no mention of the Globemaster follow-up. These entries about lawn maintenance and house cleaning were stamped "Top Secret" and remained classified until 1981.

None of this makes sense today, and it probably didn't make sense to the family members back then. The loss of such a large and important group of officers and airmen on a secret mission could not have simply vanished on LeMay's watch without prompting some kind of reaction from him. Or at least more of a reaction than the amount of attention he devoted to wheel marks left by cars when personnel parked on the lawns at Offutt.

In the days before the Globemaster flight, LeMay and Major General Anderson, commander of the Eighth Air Division, exchanged a series of detailed letters about practice bombing runs related to Operation Evening Star, during which M107 Fat Man dummies were dropped over the Mediterranean between the coasts of Italy and Spain.

It was during this time that a B-29 carrying an M107 disappeared over the Mediterranean with no trace of wreckage and no surfacing of bodies afterward.

"We simply cannot figure out what happened to this plane and crew. It was a bomb carrier and had a M107 aboard. It was in a cell of bomb carriers and when it made its last position report was within 1½ minutes of where it should have been. Ten minutes latter [*sic*], at the IP, the cell commanders tried to contact this crew but was unsuccessful. Nothing has been heard since," Anderson reported to LeMay on March 13, 1951. "The complete absence of any distress signal indicates that something went radically wrong in a matter of seconds but what, we simply do not know."[24]

The wording of Anderson's message was similar to the description provided by Navy search and rescue officers after a Privateer reconnaissance plane went down off the coast of Lithuania one year before. The plane just seemed to disappear. No survivors. No bodies. Only that time, the Soviets acknowledged that one of their MiGs did it.

CHAPTER 17

Point of No Return

GENERAL LEMAY HAD A COUNTERINTUITIVE THEORY ABOUT the best way to carry out a major wartime operation. His fellow American commanders typically favored attacking the enemy on a large scale, using overwhelming force. If the attack was by land, they would soften the target with a barrage of artillery backed by tanks and massive deployment of ground forces. If it was by sea, an entire armada with aircraft carriers and frigates and battleships was the go-to organizational strategy. If by air, then the bomber or bombers in question would be escorted by fighters and other bombers.

The effect, LeMay wrote, was to broadcast to the enemy that something big was coming, as if to tell them, *Dig in and prepare your defenses.* When it came time to lay out the plan of attack for the Hiroshima and Nagasaki missions, LeMay recommended a counterintuitive approach: *Don't broadcast it. Rely on the element of surprise. Attack during the daytime. Send in a single bomber, perhaps with a couple of support planes. Make it look like an innocuous surveillance or weather-monitoring flight.*

When he first suggested such a plan, other commanders were aghast. The Manhattan Project involved more than $1 billion in research and development to produce three atomic bombs—Fat Man, Little Boy, and a reserve pumpkin bomb waiting back in New Mexico. Sending nuclear-armed bombers over the Japanese mainland without a large escort was a far too risky approach, given that these were the single most important aerial missions of the entire war. LeMay's argument, however, won the day. Even though the United States had dropped leaflets warning of bad days ahead, the Japanese did little or nothing to harass the Nagasaki and Hiroshima flights because there didn't seem to be anything particularly special about them, especially in contrast to the massive waves of B-29s that had dropped thousands of napalm firebombs during the preceding months.

This may well have been the guiding philosophy behind Globemaster 49-244's transatlantic flight. The personnel onboard unquestionably were high-value targets all on their own. But if the cargo they were accompanying also deserved that high-value status, it would have made no sense to advertise it to the Soviets by sending a squadron of escort planes. Why not just disguise it as an innocuous, routine cargo flight? Whatever the reasoning, and whatever the cargo onboard, 49-244 prepared to take off from Walker Air Force Base in New Mexico on March 21, 1951, as a solo, unescorted flight full of some of the U.S. Air Force's most valuable personnel.

As if to signal the unusual importance of this flight, a curious thing happened in the hours before its takeoff: The commanding officer of the entire 509th Bomb Wing, Brigadier General Hunter Harris, Jr., decided to personally inspect the cargo already secured aboard the Globemaster. Actually, he didn't bother with the assorted boxes and duffel bags and supplies that were listed as being onboard. His sole focus, apparently, was the ramp and cargo deck immediately behind it, where two KB-29 fuel tanks were housed inside pine cargo crates and lashed securely with steel cables.

The secure status of those crates would become a major point of scrutiny by investigators only two days later as they tried to understand what went wrong aboard the Globemaster. When investigators arrived to ask questions, everyone who had played a role in loading and preparing the plane was scrambling to convey a message that said, effectively: *Hey, I did my due diligence. I'm not the one who fucked up here.*

An April 1951 letter, bearing the letterhead of the Forty-Seventh Air Division at Walker Air Force Base and signed by Lieutenant Colonel George W. Von Arb, placed the following in the record:

> *STATEMENT: Approximately 1130 hours on 21 March 1951, the undersigned accompanied Brigadier General Hunter Harris, Jr. to aircraft C-124, serial number 49-244. Upon*

> *arrival at the aircraft, personal baggage was being loaded in the forward compartment of the aircraft. A crew member was briefing the passengers as to the route and bail out procedures. Although the undersigned did not observe the personal baggage storage in the aircraft, the tie-down of the bomb bay tanks was observed to be stored securely by metal cables and clamps. The forward bomb bay tank was placed at an angle and secured in position on the top part of the ramp. The second bomb bay tank was level with the floor and well forward in the fuselage. The steel cables holding the bomb bay tanks in place were running the length of the bomb bay tanks as well as across the width of the bomb bay tanks. Sufficient space in the fuselage remained for seats to be lowered on one side of the bomb bay tanks for passengers.*[1]

The mere fact that Harris went aboard the Globemaster to conduct inspection duties far below his pay grade merits a closer look at his background. In addition to having commanded the 509th Bomb Wing and having been newly assigned to command the Forty-Seventh Air Division at Walker, Harris had been deputy commander of the Armed Forces Special Weapons Project at Sandia Base[2] in New Mexico, a job that entailed development oversight of the nation's number one special weapon: the atomic bomb. This was a man who had little, if any, reason to spend his time making sure fuel tanks were properly secured on a supposedly routine Globemaster flight. But he had every reason to be onboard performing inspections if the cargo had anything to do with his areas of expertise in atomic weaponry.

A separate portion of the investigation report summarized this same statement and added that Harris and Von Arb were accompanied by yet another senior officer, Lieutenant Colonel Avery J. Ladd, commander of the Second Strategic Support Squadron at Walker. In other words, two lieutenant colonels and a brigadier general found cause to inspect this particular cargo—officially, two wooden crates supposedly containing empty fuel bladders—before it departed for Barksdale en route to the final destination of Mildenhall Royal Air Force Base in Britain.

For some reason, despite the specter of war with Russia and the real war escalating in Korea, the commanding general of the nation's premier nuclear attack force wanted to take time out from his busy schedule to inspect the tie-downs of two mundane crates aboard a cargo plane preparing for what was deemed to be a routine flight to Britain.

Harris's visit to the Globemaster was unusual for all kinds of reasons, but mainly because such an inspection was so far below his pay grade as to deserve ridicule had it gotten around to his colleagues. Just because he held such a high rank didn't mean he had anywhere near the training or qualifications to perform an inspection of cargo tie-downs. Generals don't inspect the space to ensure there's enough sitting room for passengers next to the cargo. That's the job of a low-ranking specialist of airman or sergeant rank. Generals don't inspect cargo crates, just as cargo-transport company chief executives don't personally check tie-downs or door locks on their freight trucks before they hit the road. The chief executive of General Motors doesn't personally check to see that the spare tire of a Chevrolet sedan is properly secured in the trunk before it rolls off the assembly line.

When Colonel Tibbets was preparing for takeoff from Tinian in 1945, he wrote of no such visit by any superior officer to ensure Little Boy was securely hoisted in place above the bomb bay doors of the *Enola Gay*. The top commanders trusted him to do his job and properly oversee the men under him. Major Chuck Sweeney made no mention of any such inspection by a general officer before he embarked on his Fat Man mission over Nagasaki. The generals on Tinian—and there were plenty of them—left it to their subordinates way down the line of command to handle the nitty-gritty details of whether the atomic payload aboard their Silverplate B-29s was properly secured in place.

And yet, General Harris felt that there was something so particularly sensitive with the cargo aboard this Globemaster that he needed to pay a personal visit, accompanied by two colonels, and check the cargo straps for a flight whose manifest listed those items as two empty KB-29 tanks encased in pine crates.

Other cargo that had been loaded onto the plane, or at least listed on the manifest as having been loaded, consisted of a strange assortment of goods: propeller equipment, aircraft spare parts, tools, technical order compliance kits, electrical equipment, and medical supplies. That latter item was one of the more curious ones on the list because it included 8,000 surgical sponges, along with other implements. It's unclear why a British base with presumably unlimited access to medical supplies from Britain would need to have so many items lugged over from the United States on a flight whose purpose clearly had nothing to do with medical resupply. It was also noteworthy that surgical sponges would be among the most buoyant items on the plane, and yet not one of the 8,000 sponges was listed among the items recovered from the Atlantic surface several days later.

During the inspection by Harris, Von Arb, and Ladd, they indeed overheard one of at least two briefings the passengers received before crossing the Atlantic relating to bailout procedures, should such emergency procedures become necessary during the flight. They heard that the plane was equipped with sixty parachutes, more than enough for every man aboard to exit the plane in midair should such an emergency bailout become necessary on the air route up to Limestone, Maine. Once they had landed and disembarked at Limestone, a far more thorough briefing occurred since the rest of the flight would happen over the chilly Atlantic. But before heading up to Limestone, the Globemaster had to make a stop outside Shreveport, Louisiana, where the 311th Reconnaissance Wing had relocated after previous basing at Andrews Field in Maryland and MacDill Army Air Field near Tampa, Florida.

The sole purpose of that stop, at Barksdale Air Force Base—future home of the Air Force nuclear fleet—was to pick up Cullen and a support staff of four, along with their bags. Four passengers from Walker disembarked along with their luggage, meaning that the number of people now preparing to complete the rest of the journey totaled fifty-three, including thirteen crew and forty Strategic Air Command passengers. The aircraft stayed at Barksdale about six hours before departing for Limestone late on the night of March 21. After an uneventful six-hour flight, it arrived at Limestone on the morning of the 22nd.

Upon landing, the pilots asked for an instrument specialist to come aboard to check out an unspecified but apparently minor problem with a latitude-longitude positioning component. But no specialist was available, and since the component wasn't deemed essential to the flight, they decided to deal with the instruments as they were. At no point did any pilots or crew members register concerns about continuing the flight with the

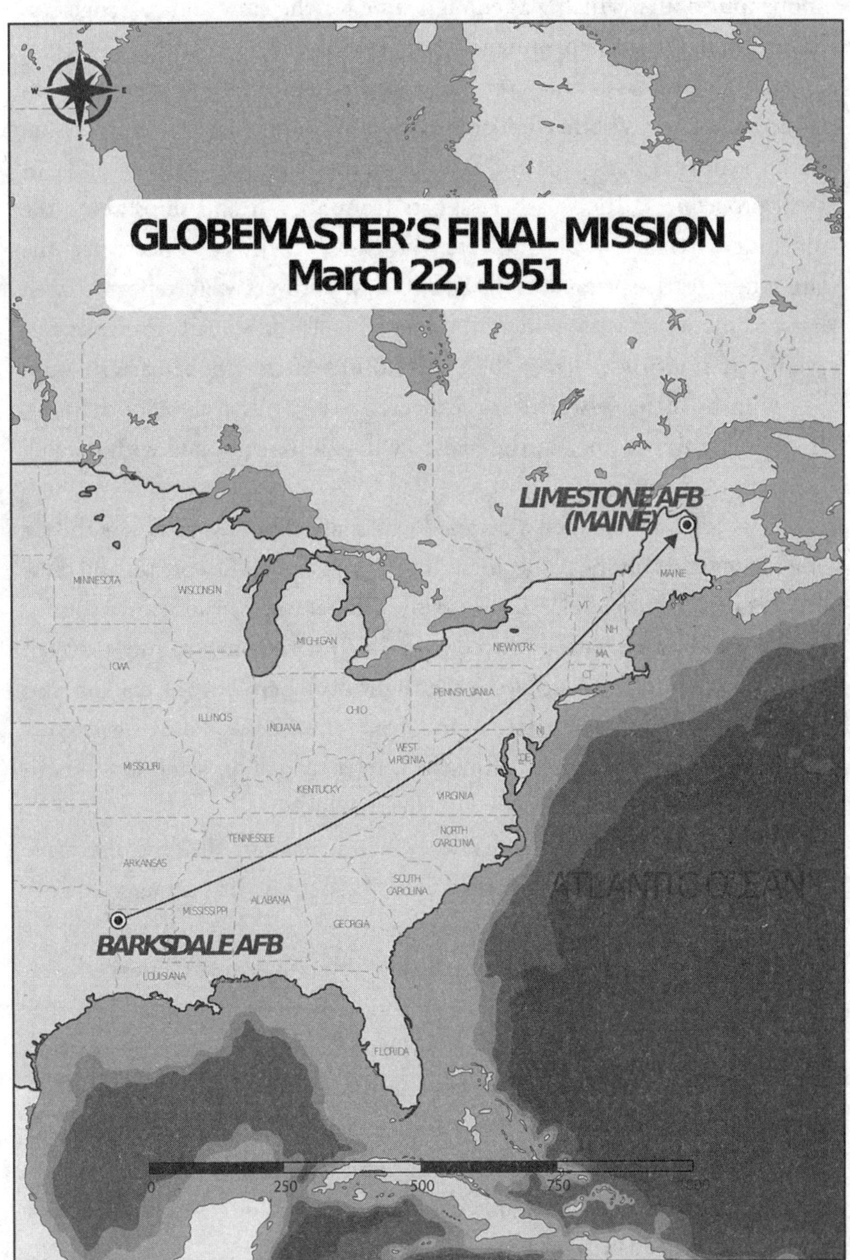

From Barksdale, the Globemaster flew north to Limestone, Maine, for refueling and a safety briefing on bailout and survival procedures. *Nick Waligorski*.

instrument problem going unresolved. The layover in Limestone was only about four hours, which was enough time for the crew and passengers to have a meal, catch a nap, or handle paperwork.

All aboard, including crew, attended a mandatory briefing that included the latest weather updates along with a far more specific session than the ones at Barksdale and Walker on crash landing, bailout, and survival procedures. The weather reports from aircraft and ships along the scheduled Atlantic route indicated nothing worthy of concern for the late-winter/early-spring season. Some snow showers were reported with light to moderate icing potential closer to Iceland. Some turbulence was predicted at altitudes lower than the 9,000 feet the Globemaster would be flying, but otherwise, this was expected to be a relatively smooth flight. If any icing were to occur, the plane's wings were equipped with deicing heaters.

This briefing included a detailed explanation of how to access the six emergency exits on the plane, including two just over the cockpit and crew quarters on the top level. As soon as the Globemaster headed over the Atlantic, standard operating procedure called for the crew to move two of the nine life rafts onboard up to the flight deck between the cockpit and crew quarters. Before departing Limestone, the crew and passengers got a reminder about parachutes before the briefer turned his attention to bailout procedures in the event of a waterborne ditching.

There were nine six-man life rafts onboard, meaning all of the fifty-three onboard would have access to one if needed. They also had enough life vests for all, but, importantly, there were enough cold weather survival suits for only about a third of those onboard. The veterans with experience flying in World War II knew to pay close attention to all of these procedures because rare was the airman who hadn't experienced some serious situation in the past that could have—or did—lead to an emergency bailout. Cullen had been through several hair-raising experiences, including three crash landings.

The plane itself was new, having been delivered only six months prior and having logged only around 300 hours in the air.

The Globemaster pilot, Robert S. Bell, had more than 4,500 hours of flying time in the military, including 237 hours flying fifty-four combat missions. In the three months preceding this flight, he had logged 149 hours as first pilot commanding a C-124. Copilot Emmett E. Collins had logged 4,186 hours of flying time, including 3,609 as first pilot. "Major Bell is a very experienced pilot. I have flown with him on many occasions," Lieutenant Colonel Avery J. Ladd, commander of the SAC Globemaster squadron at Walker Air Force Base, would later testify when asked about the level of expertise among the pilots. "Capt. Collins has flown a military mission through China and had a lot of responsibility, and inasmuch as there were VIPs aboard, I don't believe they would take any chances."

The navigator, Captain Francis N. Davies, was on the crew when Ladd himself was selected as pilot for Lieutenant General Roger Ramey, at the time the director of operations for the Air Force. Davies had 4,553 total hours of flying time, including 1,203 in combat and 254 aboard C-124s. Davies's navigation experience included nighttime and daytime crossings of both the North Atlantic and Pacific.

Their hours included plenty of time handling adverse, even severe, weather conditions. The rest of the crew (as well as passengers) had their own airborne wartime tales to tell. In the event the plane had to ditch, chances were extremely good that they would be in experienced hands, both in the air ahead of the landing and in the water afterward. Competent leaders abounded, ensuring those who made it through any unforeseen crisis would take charge and do their best to ensure the survival of as many men as possible.

The Limestone survival briefing also included instructions on how to operate the three Gibson Girl emergency hand-crank radios aboard the plane. All were advised to ensure the Gibson Girls, tucked away in canvas floatation packs, were included in any bailout, given the radios' crucial role in helping search craft locate survivors. The radios were dubbed "Gibson Girls" because of the curvy design that allowed the user to hold the heavy device firmly between the knees while operating the charging crank at the top. The radios had a wire antenna extension that was to be attached to a balloon sent aloft using a small canister of helium included in the canvas pack. The bright yellow radio wasn't for voice communication; it sent out an automatic SOS signal only by Morse code, which could be picked up by any receiver within a 200-mile radius.

The entire time the crew and passengers were inside a base facility receiving their briefings, both at Barksdale and Limestone, guards were posted outside of the Globemaster. Why? Because even though these were supposed to be inside secure facilities, the Air Force was constantly on the alert for sabotage—specifically by the Soviets.

The Airman's Handbook, originally published in 1949 and updated annually through the mid-1950s, left no question why tight security was essential:

> The American people count heavily on the ability of the Air Force to strike hard and fast when needed. This readiness for devastating attack on our enemies has been the keystone of our national defense and a powerful factor in maintaining the uncertain peace of the world since World War II. For this reason, our Air Force is the number one target of the Communist enemy. He is seeking by every means at his disposal to weaken it and to render it a less potent factor in the defense of the free world.[3]

Under the boldfaced heading "Necessity for Security," the manual warned that the Russians would spare no effort to sabotage operations or use espionage to infiltrate the nation's defenses for the sake of blocking the American agenda and advancing the Communist cause. "What, then, can the United States do to protect information and material vital to our national defense program? What can we do to prevent our secrets from being stolen and exploited? The answer lies in security—a security based on our desire to protect our way of life—and in each individual's personal responsibility to keep the United States secure."[4]

Any airman who knowingly aids the enemy in its attempt to commit sabotage or glean secrets through espionage risked life imprisonment or death, the manual warned. But crucial security data could be lost through "carelessness and ignorance," it added. It was up to all individuals "to be cognizant of the dangers of infiltration by potential enemies into activities of the U.S. Air Force and cooperate aggressively in the protection of the defense potential against acts of espionage and sabotage."

The Air Force regarded the threat as a clear and present danger that required the utmost, constant vigilance by all involved in the force's missions. That mandate was particularly emphasized when it came to operations of the Strategic Air Command and, in particular, the 509th Bomb

Wing, given its sole mission as the preeminent atomic attack force. By 1951, Moscow had made abundantly clear the priority it placed on stealing America's nuclear secrets and sabotaging anything the United States might do to prevent the Soviet Union from gaining atomic parity, if not superiority.

Add that to all the baggage and cargo loaded onto Globemaster 49-244, and it might have seemed as if the weight of the world was borne upon the shoulders of the fifty-three passengers and crew as their transatlantic flight eased off the tarmac and into the air above Limestone. The enlisted men found themselves sharing knee space with two oversize pine boxes that stood as tall as any of them and, lengthwise, seemed big enough to house an Italian sports car. The officers, including Cullen and Hopkins, received VIP seating on the upper deck. VIP treatment didn't really mean much. They still had to endure the flight in uncomfortable canvas seats held in place by metal pull-down racks. The only difference might have been greater leg room and less-encumbered access to the latrines at the back end of the plane. But no one would dare call this luxury.

For those among the crew and passengers unbriefed about the full significance behind this mission, it still couldn't have escaped their notice that a brigadier general and two lieutenant colonels had come aboard to inspect those two massive cargo crates during their safety briefing. Nor could it possibly escape their notice that yet another brigadier general had boarded for the rest of the ride during their stop at Barksdale. That was a lot of top-level brass for what was billed as a simple personnel transport and cargo run.

During pilot Bell's predeparture check of the manifest and weights of humans, baggage, cargo, equipment, and fuel aboard, he had neglected to note that the ground crew had topped off the plane's tanks with an additional 2,300 gallons of fuel at Limestone. Though it added an estimated 13,800 pounds[5] to the overall takeoff weight, the extra fuel also ensured the plane could not only cross the Atlantic but could keep going for several hours beyond.

Bell was no doubt aware of the added fuel weight, but he had simply neglected to note it on the preflight clearance form at Limestone. But even accounting for the extra weight of the fuel, there were more than 10,000 pounds of unused cargo weight to spare before reaching the Globemaster's maximum limit. It was a bookkeeping mistake more than anything, although from a safety standpoint, the weight distribution did matter when calculating fuel consumption during the flight and estimating how far the plane could travel as the fuel burn-off lightened the load and, consequently, boosted the flight's longevity.

Once airborne, the Globemaster set a course to overfly Gander, Newfoundland, which had been listed as the final stopover point on the original flight plan before Bell opted to make the transatlantic jump straight from Limestone instead. His commander would later testify that the decision to stop at Limestone, made before the plane departed from Barksdale, was entirely the pilot's choice and fully within his purview as the flight commander. The plane radioed a routine check-in upon overflying Gander on an easterly track, then banked to a slightly more northerly track to take advantage of the shorter Great Circle pathway toward the Irish coast. Four hours and twelve minutes into the flight, the plane made another radio check-in, most likely via a weather ship on the surface, about 650 miles due south of Greenland. So far, everything was going exactly according to the flight plan with no abnormalities to report. The weather was clear. Temperatures at 9,000 feet were in the range of 10 degrees below zero, and northerly winds were listed as an insignificant factor.

A report of icing on the wings of 49-240, following the same flight pattern on March 19 to 20, did not appear to be consequential. These Globemasters were equipped with heaters in the wings to prevent ice buildup.

After another 450 miles, or six hours and twelve minutes into the flight, the plane made another position check by radio with a weather ship down below. Again, all was going according to plan with nothing of importance to report. The radio check at this moment was significant, however, because navigator Davies had scrawled on the flight plan he had filed at Limestone that, at six hours and five minutes into the flight, Globemaster 49-244 would reach its "POINT OF NO RETURN."[6] It's not clear whether the navigator's calculation was based on the erroneous listing by Bell of the fuel level being identical to what it was when the plane left Walker instead of noting that there were 2,300 additional gallons onboard, potentially advancing the plane's actual point of no return to a location much closer to the Irish coastline.

It didn't really matter. There was fuel to spare—at least six hours of it—

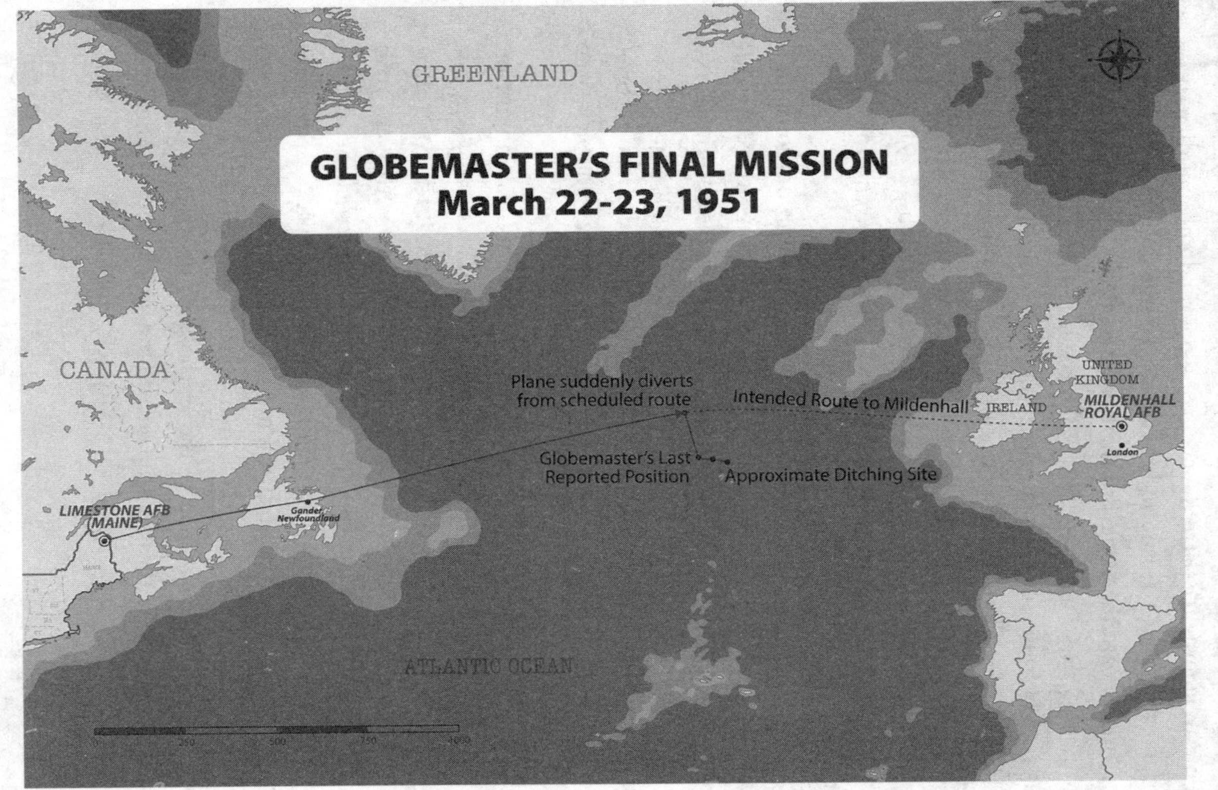

The Globemaster departed Limestone at 4:20 p.m. GMT on March 22, 1951, overflying Gander, Newfoundland. In the early hours of March 23, the plane ceased communications and diverted nearly 300 miles to the south before ditching. *Nick Waligorski.*

when the plane made yet another radio check with a weather ship below a little more than eight hours into the flight. These check-ins were scheduled to follow an identifiable pattern—occurring not randomly but directly on the hour, every hour—as one additional way of signaling that all systems were normal aboard the plane. But then another check-in happened at thirteen minutes *before* the hour—at 0047 Greenwich Mean Time (GMT).

Instead of following the same arc it had been traveling toward Shannon, Ireland, the Globemaster's position indicated a startling diversion. It had suddenly turned sharply to the south and had already traveled 152 miles in that direction,[7] though it apparently was still flying at 9,000 feet. The plane's position report offered no other details or even hints about why it had diverted.

Even if the plane had lost all access to radio communications—unlikely given its ability to broadcast its off-kilter position—the crew still had access to any one of three Gibson Girl hand-cranked transmitters. No radio contact of any kind was made after this point from the plane. However, once the plane had gone down, a B-29 search plane did report a brief interception of an SOS signal broadcast at a 500 kilohertz frequency—the frequency of a Gibson Girl.

Lieutenant Colonel Ladd tried to explain in an official inquiry on April 4, 1951, that the final check-in, thirteen minutes early, was not necessarily unusual since the plane was probably right at the controller-handover point, where it would cease communications with New York flight control and initiate control from the tower at Prestwick, Scotland.

Informed by an officer at the inquiry that the plane had already made the control tower switch, and that Prestwick was already handling the Globemaster, Ladd expressed surprise in a transcribed question-and-answer exchange. The 152-mile diversion to the south wasn't specified by the questioner, but the context of the follow-up questions suggested this was the point where Ladd believed the plane had started to seek refuge from whatever crisis had befallen it.

Q: "Apparently he had already switched [to Prestwick]."

A: "I thought he was working New York but Prestwick was [just] monitoring him."

Q: "Would it indicate to you a report and a switch in destination?"
A: "No sir, not necessarily."
Q: "Your feeling is that something unusual happened rapid?"
A: "That is the only thin[g] I can think of."[8]

The questioner didn't follow up for specifics on what might have happened.

Before the plane diverted, it was well past the midway point in its journey. In the darkness to the west lay 1,177 miles of empty ocean between the Globemaster and Gander. The tip of Greenland was 743 miles to the northwest, while Reykjavík, Iceland stood 753 miles to the northeast. The coast of Ireland was due east at 780 miles, and the final destination, Mildenhall Royal Air Force Base, was still 1,120 miles away. Almost due south was Lagens Field in the Azores, about 1,090 miles away. These distances would have been known to the navigator at the time and no doubt would have been communicated to the pilots so they could be fully aware at any given moment of their options should any emergency develop that required them to seek the fastest-possible landing. Given the distances to these various landmasses, the obvious choice in a crisis would be to choose the ones closest to the plane's position—not Lagens, the second-farthest one.

Obviously, something major did happen at that point. In the seven decades that have transpired since that crucial moment no one has been able to explain publicly what it was, but something big caused the plane to take a sharp turn to the south and keep on going in total radio silence, save for that final position check. Given the tailwinds pushing the plane toward the east-northeast, the worst choices in an emergency would have been to turn back against the wind or try to make the coast of Greenland, even if it was the closest point.

The two most logical options would be to take advantage of the tailwinds and proceed to the Irish coast or head northward to Reykjavik. Making a southward beeline toward Lagens would have taken hours more flying time than simply seeking refuge in Ireland or Iceland. The plane would have had to fight against a significant side wind of up to forty-five miles per hour. Nevertheless, Ladd told the inquiry board that it appeared the pilot might have made the choice of Lagens anyway. Again, no one knew for sure because there were no radio communications to help them piece together this puzzle.

For all they knew, some other force might have been jamming communications and directing the plane in a new direction. In fact, the trajectory would not have taken it straight toward Lagens but rather hundreds of miles to the east of the Azores. It continued on that southern trajectory for another 120 miles, meaning it had traveled about 270 miles off course before ditching. At least some of those onboard, no doubt mindful of the briefing they had received at Limestone on emergency procedures, launched into action. They either donned their parachutes and began bailing out of the plane in midair while deploying life rafts ahead of them, or they rode it out with the plane all the way to what was almost certainly a bone-crushingly hard landing on the water, swiftly exiting the gigantic Globemaster before it began sinking. Given what happened in the hours afterward, it appears the latter scenario was the more likely one.

This is the precise point in our story when things get very murky and even more complicated, with lots of people offering up speculation about what happened, including some Air Force personnel making statements to the news media that later proved to be outright lies. Whatever happened on the plane, neither the pilots nor the radioman appeared to have completed any communication with ships on the ocean surface to explain the nature of their emergency. No Mayday signal or radio messaging is listed in the investigation record.

It was the utter *lack* of communication that made it so difficult afterward for investigators to pinpoint what was going on as the plane lunged wildly off course while following a distinct trajectory and altitude that made it appear that the plane was still under control. It didn't nose-dive into the water but glided to a landing, investigators wrote. There was no report in the investigation files of an explosion or fire aboard; no report of turbulence, lightning strike, or bad weather; no report of engine failure or equipment malfunction.

The lies that Air Force personnel told the news media made it into print and onto both Associated Press and United Press newswires, perhaps deliberately creating the public image of a routine transatlantic flight that ended in a sudden, unsurvivable midair disaster. The word "routine" continues to appear in some online accounts today, even though there was nothing routine about the Globemaster's mission. The passengers onboard were on a secret mission accompanying cargo that couldn't be explained by the existing manifests. Whatever happened onboard, it was entirely survivable as made clear by the fact that survivors were later spotted. It was the Air Force's incompetent, delayed reaction that helped ensure no one made it to safety, and that not one body of the people who had been on the plane would ever be found.

They had truly reached the point of no return.

CHAPTER 18

Ditched

It's anyone's guess what terror and suffering actually befell the survivors after 49-244 ditched in the frigid North Atlantic and they struggled to stay alive. Some, though it's not clear how many, scrambled aboard life rafts as dawn broke over the water on March 23, 1951.[1] Sightings by search planes of orange objects in the water strongly suggested the presence of life vests. No one can know the fears and doubts that screamed in their heads, the limbs shredded by jagged metal or skulls cracked by the impact, the unfathomable obstacles that Mother Nature must have thrown at them, and whether some other force—not of nature but of human military origins—might have pushed them ever closer to a disastrous end at their moment of maximum vulnerability. If the old World War II slang word "fubar" applied anywhere, it was here, soaking wet and cold in the middle of a vast ocean. Truly fucked up beyond all recognition.

The longitude and latitude estimates sent out to search ships and aircraft of where the plane went down probably seemed precise for that era, but by today's standards, they were vague to the point of being useless. The geocoordinates listed for the search area formed a big rectangle that, from the farthest northern edge to the southernmost point, and from the farthest eastern edge to the westernmost point, measured roughly 40,000 square miles of open Atlantic Ocean. That's an area about equal to the entire state of Kentucky.

Even though the U.S. and British navies launched their largest-ever search operation involving dozens of planes, ships, and submarines to locate 49-244, the amount of water they had to cover remained almost impossibly immense. The raft (or rafts) they were looking for were no bigger than a Chevy station wagon. There were no satellites to scan from high above, no heat-registering technology to locate warm bodies, no infrared scopes to help searchers see at night.

The technology that existed at the time was ancient compared to today's geolocation tools, which a teenager holding an iPhone could master in no time to zero in on a lost toy drone stuck on a rooftop or car parked on, say, a remote Montana farm. Back then, the idea of high-resolution overhead photos was still very much in the early developmental stages and more focused on sensitive land-based sites in Russia than vast, empty expanses of the Atlantic. There were no GPS tracking devices or ability to triangulate signals from cell phone towers to pinpoint a lost person's location. In the case of a plane ditching in the deepest section of the Atlantic, the ability of the sea to swallow up everything on its surface, without leaving many traces, was huge. The chances of survival were beyond bleak, which could explain why the Globemaster's headquarters at Walker Air Force Base began preparing a casualty list containing all passengers and crew within hours of the plane being reported missing.

Whatever caused the Globemaster to attempt a waterborne landing remains unknown to this day, though there is plenty of circumstantial evidence to feed a variety of scenarios. What is certain is that the men aboard were bracing for absolute disaster in the seconds before the plane's first impact with the water. Of all the personnel onboard, the only person known to have piloted a disabled plane to a survivable landing multiple times—on hard earth rather than water, no less—was General Cullen. No evidence has surfaced to indicate he was present in the cockpit or advising the pilots of 49-244 ahead of the ditching.

Nobody knows what occurred in the cockpit, or who among the many experienced pilots onboard was offering advice. Nor is it clear whether the plane survived the impact intact or immediately broke into pieces and sank. Investigation documents concluded, based on the wreckage recovered, that the aircraft eased onto the water surface fully intact but probably broke up shortly afterward.[2]

One of the unusual features of the C-124 was that it was built with tubular crawl spaces running through both wings to enable crew members

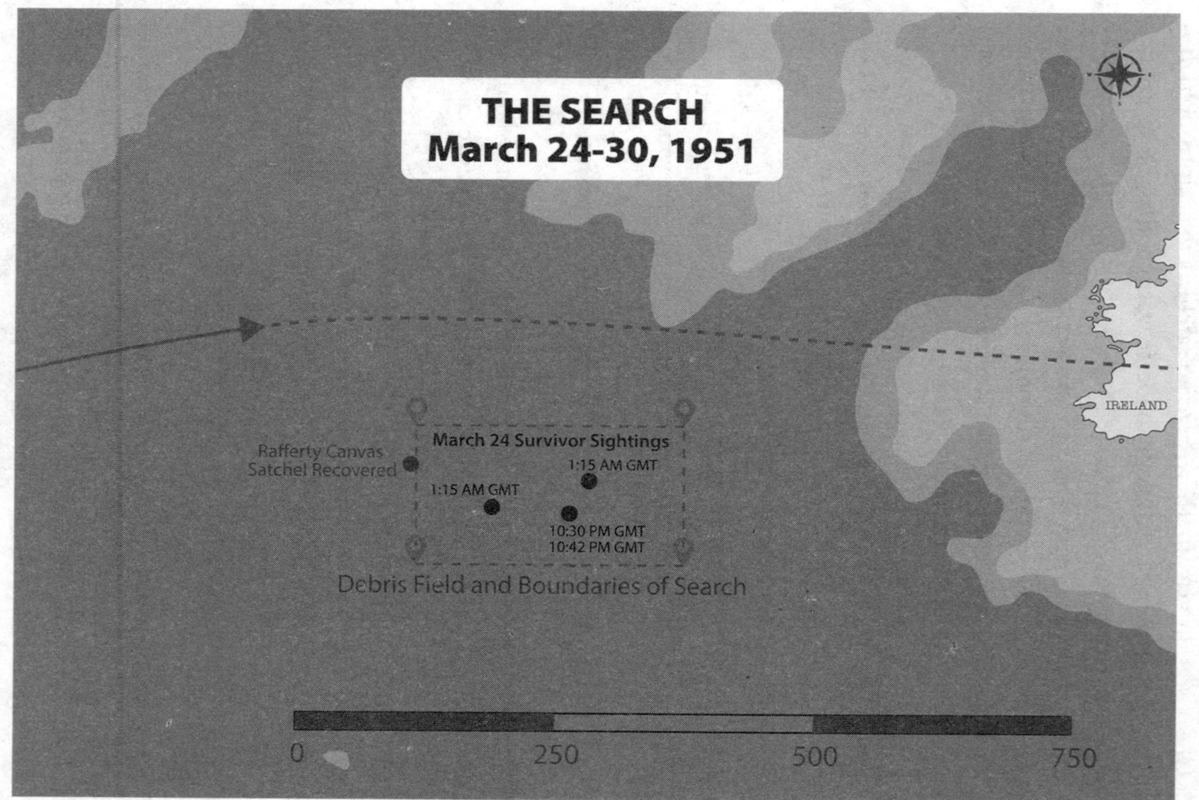

The 40,000-square-mile search zone in the North Atlantic was about the size of Kentucky. During the search, an SOS call was intercepted, and aircraft reported four separate sightings of survivors. *Nick Waligorski*.

to access the engines in midair. If necessary, the pilot had the ability to shut down an engine during flight so a crew member could crawl through the tube and perform basic maintenance on the engine, such as replace its spark plugs.

If the wings stayed intact during the ditching, those air-filled tubes likely would have provided enough buoyancy to keep the fuselage afloat long enough for the survivors to launch all nine of the plane's six-person life rafts and exit safely. There were fifty-five yellow-orange life vests onboard, more than enough for everyone, although the plane had only enough survival suits for the thirteen crew members plus a few lucky others. Whoever got ahold of those and had time to don them had a far greater chance of survival than the many who didn't.

Imagine an aircraft bigger than the largest semi-tractor trailer rig smashing into the water at a speed of no less than 100 miles per hour. Human nature being what it is, the passengers were likely jolted physically and terrified psychologically. Even the most battle-hardened among them would have been hard-pressed to stifle a sense of panic, especially as frigid water began gushing in through cracks in the fuselage. The plane had a clam-shell double-door opening in the front, just below the cockpit. It was hardly watertight, and even if it survived the impact in closed position, the gaps in its opening would have sped the intake of seawater, hastening the sinking. The impact with water almost certainly killed some of those onboard as the massive plane crashed into the undulating, five- to eight-foot sea swells.[3] The water probably didn't trickle in but rather blasted through in what felt like ice-cold plumes. The shock would have rendered even the most hardy among the fifty-three onboard woozy and disoriented, if not briefly unconscious.

The survivors would have had to regain their senses, remember where they were and what had just happened, then summon the courage to scramble through the rushing water, bodies, and wreckage to locate and deploy the life rafts they needed in order to stay alive. But then they would have had to search for any emergency hatches that hadn't been so badly damaged by the impact to render them too jammed to open. Once they found a workable hatch, they would have had to push the raft out, then inflate it while simultaneously evacuating all who were conscious and capable of exiting on their own.

In the triage of the moment, survivors would have had to weigh saving a badly injured colleague versus the risk of both of them going down with the ship. These are the awful, split-second decisions people have to make in disasters at sea.

Under such conditions, people don't behave rationally. Theirs would not have been an orderly exit where each man waited patiently in line for his turn to exit. No, it would have been a mad scramble, with some clawing and scratching and fighting to clamber over others to get out of the plane as fast as they could. Whoever was in charge, barking commands and trying to instill a sense of order, would instead have encountered abject panic and unbridled chaos. No implied threat of future disciplinary action for insubordination would have stopped a drowning, frantic airman from pushing aside a major, colonel, or brigadier general in order to reach the emergency hatch as quickly as possible: *Fuck the command structure. Fuck honor and duty. It's every man for himself.*

Assuming the wings and upper part of the Globemaster's fuselage remained nominally intact during the hard water landing, the amount of air trapped inside would have provided enough buoyancy for the plane to remain afloat for perhaps a minute or two, maybe longer, but not much. Even with the buoyancy provided by the tubes in the wings, the weight of four massive Pratt & Whitney R-4360-20WA engines would have counteracted the ability to stay afloat. Neither the engines nor the wings were likely to have stayed attached to the fuselage for very long—if they survived at all after the impact with the water. With thousands of gallons of cold salt water gushing in, the three-story fuselage would have been a horror show. Sparks from the plane's electrical system and live wires slashing through the air would have added to the danger and chaos.

As the plane began to sink, the uppermost deck where the pilots and crew were located would likely have been the least-damaged air pocket for survivors to congregate and exit the plane. It had two exit hatches. Among the recovered pieces of wreckage was a two-foot by two-foot pillow, the kind of item usually available in the crew bunking quarters located behind the cockpit and navigation station. For the pillow to have made it into the floating wreckage, it would have almost certainly escaped from an opening or hatch in the upper deck.[4]

What is unquestionable from wreckage recovered days later is that a fire broke out, consuming anything combustible in its path, perhaps ignited by the plane's remaining reserves of gasoline and oil. So imagine what it must have been like for the survivors as they struggled to regain their senses from the initial crash, seeing everything on the plane collapse and burn around them, perhaps being horrified by the sight of their bloodied, dead colleagues floating next to them, and then having to jump into the frigid Atlantic water in hopes that a life raft was waiting outside. The word "terror" doesn't come close to describing what they must have felt.

Those who made it onto life rafts could do nothing but watch as the Globemaster and its strange cargo sank before their eyes, carrying to their watery graves the dead, the unconscious, and the injured who were too immobilized to escape quickly enough. Once the plane had disappeared, the survivors had nothing left to rely upon but their comrades and their inflatable rafts, floating on an immense expanse of dark, empty ocean. The sense of hopelessness and survivor's guilt had to have been overwhelming.

The sea is a tireless, relentless foe. It will work patiently for thousands of years to cut a path through solid rock. It swallows coastlines one mouthful at a time. The sea's only mission in life is to make anything in its path give up and give in.

This assumes that the sea was the only foe in the survivors' path. The record suggests that perhaps another—human—foe also was present.

The survivors were soaking wet from the moment they climbed aboard, badly shaken by the ditching ordeal and whatever air disaster that preceded it. Many if not all were probably injured, perhaps with compound bone fractures or head injuries. Seasickness, debilitating as it certainly is, would have been the least of their problems. The water temperature was estimated by rescuers to be a numbness-inducing 51 degrees, and the air a crisp 46 degrees. Their misery no doubt worked overtime to extinguish any faint hopes they had of surviving.

That said, there were several factors working in their favor. For one, the weather upon ditching was described in a preflight weather briefing as moderate. Weather ships reported wave swells of only around five to eight feet. There were no looming storms in that area, though a cold front had carried rain and wind over the waters to the distant north.[5] The survivors no doubt were shivering uncontrollably. Though extremely uncomfortable, they would have found it survivable.

Given the hours that passed from the moment the plane veered from its scheduled route and traveled southward for nearly 300 miles, the crew and passengers would have had plenty of time to prepare for the ditching. During that time, they most likely would have donned life jackets. They had more than enough time to prepare the life rafts. Had they chosen to bail out before the ditching, there were sixty parachutes and fifty-five harnesses.

The Globemaster had three portable Gibson Girl hand-winding radios to send out emergency signals, although it's unclear how many of those radios actually made it onto the life rafts. The survivors had access to a "very pistol," otherwise known as a flare gun, plus sixty-five rounds of flares. There were three five-gallon water cans, five cases of food rations, and four 2.5-gallon jugs for water or coffee.[6] It was enough to keep all aboard alive for days, if not weeks, depending on how supplies were rationed. Even if a big wave—unlikely given the calm seas at the time—managed to flip a raft, it would not deflate. All they had to do was hang on and work together to flip it upright and climb back aboard. There was even a reserve pump and repair kit onboard each raft to cover leaks and keep it afloat.

In other words, they had access to everything they would need to survive indefinitely on life rafts. Even if the weather turned rough and the waves did their best to overturn the rafts, the survivors needed only to cling tight and stay together. Those with survival suits had the best chance of staying dry and warm, but even those who wore only their flight suits and flotation vests still had a decent chance of survival.

For at least nineteen hours after the plane went down, they did exactly that: They survived. At least some of them beat the odds. However, given the water and air temperatures, the survival rate for the North Atlantic was 40% to 60%, and the chances dropped with every passing hour.[7]

The prevailing Atlantic current, fed by springtime winds from Canada and the United States to the west, pushed the rafts and wreckage from the plane steadily eastward. Without any propulsion other than waves and wind, the survivors and wreckage appear to have drifted 140 or more miles in the span of two days, according to search-craft records. Given the trajectory and speed, they (or their bodies) would have washed ashore somewhere on the coastline of Ireland, Cornwall, or Southern England within a week or two. At worst, they would skirt the British coastline and wind up drifting across the English Channel to the coast of France or Belgium. The supplies they had access to would have kept them alive for that journey. Even without a drop of water from their five-gallon cans or from their two-gallon jugs, they had excellent chances to collect rainwater and make it to shore, albeit bedraggled and heavily traumatized. There was ample cause for hope.

By the time the Atlantic had swallowed the Globemaster and its contents, the sun was rising from the east. Each ray of light would have helped warm the shivering souls who had scrambled for survival aboard the rafts, growing even warmer as the sun rose higher in the sky. Whatever feelings of hopelessness and dread that overtook the survivors in the predawn crisis hours would likely have been replaced by a gradually uplifting mood.

But nothing could have lifted their spirits more than the low rumble of a distant plane whose sound signature was easily identifiable to the airmen: a lone B-29 following a pattern that made clear it was on a search mission. As the plane flew closer, the survivors fired off flares, according to search-craft records. The pilot or crew spotted them and radioed back to the plane's base—Royal Air Force Base Mildenhall, the Globemaster's intended destination—that they had located survivors and sighted life rafts.

The B-29 pilot radioed that he was reaching his limit on fuel and needed to return to base. But if the pilot followed procedures, he probably overflew the survivors and dipped his wings repeatedly to signal that they had been sighted and their location registered. It would have signaled that help was on the way. The plane banked, then returned to Mildenhall. The search-plane pilot reportedly was Captain Harold Muller, coincidentally a close friend from the same squadron as one of the fifty-three who had been onboard the Globemaster, Captain Walter A. Wagner.[8] In all likelihood, Muller had no idea that his buddy was among the men he saw.

Whatever assurance the survivors might have gotten from the B-29, long hours of cold discomfort lay ahead. At least they knew that their latitude and longitude was now logged and reported back to base. Their only job now was to cling to their rafts, keep their Mae Wests lashed snugly, and stay as warm as possible until a rescue craft could reach them.

If those were the hopeful thoughts going through the men's minds, they were horribly deluded.

CHAPTER 19

The Search Begins

WHILE THE SURVIVORS FLOATED ON THE RELATIVELY CALM but cold Atlantic surface, they had no way of knowing what, if anything, was being done by the Air Force command to organize their rescue. All they could fall back on were the procedures recited in their preflight briefing at Limestone,[1] plus the practices honed from years of experience during World War II when other planes were lost at sea.

It would have been unthinkable, from their perspective, for the U.S. military to leave its men behind, especially when the personnel aboard this flight were of such high value. So whatever doubts might have been swirling in their heads, they in all likelihood tried to remain calm and reassure one another that help was coming. The most reasonable assumption for anyone on the life rafts would be that the B-29 search plane had radioed the coordinates back to his base and that another search plane would soon be scrambled to pick up where the first plane's search had ended—that is, the coordinates where the survivors from Globemaster 49-244 were last seen,[2] not necessarily where they drifted after the search plane banked away to return to base.

It didn't quite work out that way. Long hours passed before another craft would arrive anywhere close to their coordinates. The only way to determine how many hours passed is by deciphering the time stamps placed on the classified communications that traveled across the Atlantic to alert ships within a few hundred miles to drop everything and head toward the ditching site. Unfortunately, those time stamps introduce just as much confusion as clarity about who arrived where and when.

The earliest all-points emergency alert came from Washington with a time stamp of 3:07 a.m. Greenwich Mean Time on March 24 (the actual time stamp said "240307Z," with Z standing for Zulu, the military's shorthand for GMT). Specifying the coordinates of 50 degrees, 23 minutes north and 22 degrees, 20 minutes west, it said an unidentified observer "sighted what appeared to be wreckage and parachutes with one man rafts."[3] Aircraft in the area would continue to patrol, it added.

Almost exactly nineteen hours passed before the U.S. Third Air Division in London broadcast a restricted message to U.S. Air Force headquarters in Washington (it was sent in all-capital letters with multiple typographic errors):

> Redline for Twining from Johnson. 1. Intensive search continues for survivors of C-124 with US UK air and surface craft participating. Search under control of 9th Air Rescue Squadron assisted by US Navy, USAF, RAF *[Royal Air Force]*, Royal Navy, and merchant shipping. All shipping, civil air lines, etc., alerted for search measures. Full utilization being made of all aircraft in area. 2. Our recapitulation of air search activites follows: 30 B-29; 1 SB-29; 2 SB-17; 3 British aircraft; 1 PB4Y; and four (4) MSurface vessels in searchrarea as of now. 3. Sighting of aircraft by civil air lines from Shannon reported false by ARS controller. He also reported no positive results as of 1500Z. 4. At 0400Z B-29 nbr 1256 received radar scope return 50-20N 22-20W, started cirnc *[circling]* at 500', noticed derbis *[debris]* on water and white bojects *[objects]* that appears like chutes. Also object resembling aircraft wing. This sighting was lost at 0430Z. Aircraft descended to 100 feet and with landing lights on sighted life raft, right side up, with blue tarpaulin (note: life raft possible capsized.) This aircraft remained in area until daylight then lost sighting. Night was clear and sea calm. 5. At daylight B-29, nbr 5512, sighted debris in same area. Debris covered area of 20 miles. Sea very calm, no positive identification of debris. 6. At 1356Z another B-29, nbr 4539, reported sighting small orange colored object at 50-00N 19-00W. Same aircraft re-

> ported at 241512Z, two (2) more objects at 50-30N 19-38W and orange colored objects also sighted at 50-27N 18-38W. Unable to give positive identification. List sight while circling. 7. Two (2) surface vessels dispatched to above areas. Negative results at 241700Z. 8. Search continuing. CGTAD.[4]

Translated into civilian language, there was a massive mobilization of U.S. and British military aircraft and naval vessels, along with merchant ships, to comb the suspected crash zone. A commercial airliner reported having seen the Globemaster, but the Air Force deemed the sighting unreliable. (Some newspaper reports stated that the passenger ship *Queen Mary* had either diverted to assist or had offered to do so if needed.) At all times, airplane and sea-level searchers reported the weather as clear with calm seas,[5] which is important because of untruthful reports that would later come from the U.S. Air Force about bad weather being a contributing factor in the disappearance. Swells were reported roughly seventy-five feet apart with heights of only five feet from peak to trough. For the Atlantic on the trailing end of the Gulf Stream, it doesn't get much smoother than that.

And yet military spokesmen began circulating stories of heavy fog, rain, and high winds, almost as if they were trying to prepare the public with a ready-made excuse for disappointing news to come. A front-page Associated Press story in *The New York Times* on March 24 cited a Royal Air Force officer as saying "that seas were running high and that there were strong winds in the area. Gale warnings had been posted along the British coast."[6] Not a single search vessel at the scene reported any such weather conditions.

The same Associated Press story quoted Major Horace A. Stephenson, commander of the U.S. rescue mission out of Shannon, Ireland, as simultaneously discounting and confirming reports indicating there were survivors. He said he was waiting for the B-29 to return to base "to find out from the airman that he definitely saw what he reported he saw." Yet Stephenson added: "Further wreckage and flares have been sighted sixty miles from the spot where the first wreckage was sighted," which he clarified to mean that additional flares were spotted sixty miles to the *east*, closer to the Irish coast, than the previous sighting. The prevailing tides were moving all remnants of the plane and contents to the east at a steady clip.

At 4 a.m. Zulu (GMT) on March 24, or roughly 24 hours since the Globemaster last reported its position, a B-29 search plane reported sighting debris and white objects that might have been parachutes. But by 4:30 a.m., that sighting was lost. The plane's pilot dropped to 100 feet above the water surface, then turned on his landing lights, after which he spotted a life raft covered by a blue tarp. The advisory raised the possibility that it wasn't a blue tarp but rather that the raft might have been capsized, meaning that the raft's blue underbelly was exposed, making it appear to be a tarp. Debris was spread across twenty miles, the advisory added.[7]

Nine hours later, another B-29 returned to the same area and reported seeing unidentified orange-colored objects across a 26.7-mile stretch from north to south. Unfortunately, the plane was heading away from a site, about thirty-six miles to the west of where the previous B-29 reported positive sightings of survivors.

As the search was getting underway, Private First Class Keith Amsden was with his unit training as a B-29 gunner at Roswell's Walker Air Force Base—the same base where the Globemaster flight had originated. Amsden's brother, Robert, was one of the two engineers crewing the Globemaster flight, and when it went missing, Robert should have been among the first of all the family members to hear about it since the base commanders had already been alerted. Instead, Keith said he heard on the 11 o'clock news the night of March 23 that a Globemaster was missing over the Atlantic. Keith said he knew instantly that it was his brother's plane. The next morning, he received permission to take leave, then phoned his parents. He said his father, a career military man with experience in both world wars, knew fully well that if a plane went missing over the middle of the Atlantic, there was a good chance Robert had not survived.

Upon hearing the news, "my father had a heart attack, if that'll tell you anything," Keith recalled. He spent days hopping flights and taking buses to get home from New Mexico to the Albany area of New York. The Air Force, he said, even "bumped a full-bird colonel" off one flight to open a seat to help Keith get home. By the time he reached New York, the news reports had become spotty and inconsistent. One day, the family's hopes were buoyed with reports of survivors. The next day's reports cited only wreckage recovered but offered no additional sightings of survivors.

The field of debris was immense. Whatever force that took the plane apart splintered nearly all pieces of wreckage to the point that the vast majority were smaller than one square foot. The largest piece was a nine-foot by three-foot panel apparently from a KB-29 fuel tank encasement.

Around 8:45 p.m. Zulu on March 24, now a day and a half after the Globemaster radioed its last position report, came another advisory from the Third Air Division general command in London, stating in all-capital letters (typos included):

> Latest development on C-124 search. Identification tags and schorched repeat schorched pouch with papers belonging to Captain Lawrence E. Rafferty, AO-696483, found by weather ship Charlie at 50-45N 24-03W at approximately 1914Z. Captain Rafferty's name was on passenger list received at this headquarters. Search craft being diverted to that area. This is first positive identification establishing location of possible survivors and wreckage.[8]

Use of "positive identification" was only to distinguish it from the original search plane's visual sighting of men in rafts amid wreckage. That plane technically had no specific detail to affirm that the raft-borne personnel he spotted were from Globemaster 49-244. (As if there might be raft-borne survivors from some other flight bobbing about in the waves at that same time.)

Press accounts presented nowhere near such specific details, although they did report early hope of locating survivors, only to quote military officials as downplaying the possibility that anyone would be found alive. The press reports grew increasingly bleak as the days passed even though the navies and air forces of Britain and Ireland had joined the United States in the search. By March 25, the same area would be combed by twenty-four American B-29s along with various other British aircraft. The U.S. Navy even added the aircraft carrier *Coral Sea* to the search along with two destroyers and three other military ships, but their arrival was far too late to do any good. The British Navy dispatched the submarine *Thule*, along with other craft.

Rafferty's briefcase, which was more like a canvas satchel, was located on the far western edge of the expansive debris field. The B-29 search plane that had reported a life raft with a blue tarp was sweeping the far eastern edge of the debris field. The distance between those two sightings was 227 miles. All of the debris was clearly drifting east-northeast, toward the southwestern tip of Cornwall or the central coast of France. If survivors had managed to stay afloat and alive that long, the current would have taken them on the same eastward path.

There is no evidence that searchers combed the shores of Cornwall or France for additional clues, although a curious incident on the southern coast of Ireland would later raise questions about the origins of the ditching. More on that later.

Hopes of finding survivors were buoyed when the U.S. air command in London sent out another advisory before dawn on March 25, two days after the ditching: "Message received from USS General Muir at 250220Z indicates he is in contact with B-29 aircraft which reported spotting several floats with yellow sodium flares. Aircraft states he actually observedneeveral [observed several] survivors waving from one float. D.R. [dead reckoning] position 50-00N 20-53W. General Muir position 50-16N 21-09W."[9]

If those coordinates were correct, the *Muir* would appear to have been more than 950 miles to the east of the search zone, in the English Channel. Far more likely, a glitch in the transmission had caused a number to be dropped from the latter coordinate, meaning the *Muir* was actually 50 degrees, 16 minutes latitude and either 21 degrees, 9 minutes west longitude or 18 degrees, 9 minutes west—much closer to the actual ditching site. That later proved to be the case. The *Muir* was, in fact, very close to the position where the survivors were last spotted.

The Third Air Division reported, "B29 search acft rptd sighting white and yellow flares" at 50 degrees, 0 minutes north by 20 degrees, 53 minutes west at 8:20 p.m. Zulu on the 24th. "At 242042Z he sighted another flare and many flashlights sending SOS. One crew member reports he saw a large life raft with four (4) to six (6) men waving."[10] Wherever the *Muir* and weathership *Charlie* (also identified as the U.S. Coast Guard cutter *Casco*) were, there could have been no ambiguity about their need to reach the destination as quickly as possible where the survivors were spotted.

At 11:50 p.m. Zulu on the 24th, the *Muir* reached the reported site of the survivors. "USS *Muir* reports negative results," the Third Air Division reported. The *Charlie*, the next-closest ship, was still about 127 miles to the west. With a top speed of roughly twenty-five miles per hour, it would have taken the *Charlie* about five hours to reach the same site.

News media reports of the early hours of the search gave the distinct impression that only one vessel, the original B-29, had reported evidence of survivors and that search ships were unable to find anything afterward. That single report is what buoyed hopes of family members that the men were still alive. But it was only one report, and that was all they were left to hang their hopes upon.

In fact, there were at least five separate indications of survivors. There was one B-29 report from 1:15 a.m. Greenwich Mean Time on March 24 reporting a sighting. Four hours earlier, at 9:20 p.m. GMT on March 23, a B-29 search plane had intercepted radio signals broadcast at a frequency of 500 kilocycles (kilohertz). That's the same signal sent by a Gibson Girl emergency transmitter, at least three of which were aboard the Globemaster.

The third, and well-publicized, sighting of survivors occurred at 11:30 p.m. GMT on March 24. Then there was a fourth sighting from the same B-29 at 11:42 p.m. GMT. These latter two were treated as a single sighting even though 12 minutes had elapsed between them. The 1:15 a.m. sighting on the 24th was discounted because the crew member aboard that B-29 said he had seen "wreckage, flares, lights . . . and parachute with one-man life raft." The Globemaster didn't carry one-man rafts, which apparently made the sighting less credible.[11] But, clearly, the crew members aboard the B-29 saw something worthy of attention.

As the search continued and additional ships arrived to help, various versions of the same basic messages about the B-29 sighting went out across the Atlantic for the following seven days. Some confusion was introduced in communications because telex operators from some military branches referred to the plane by its tail number, 49-244, while others referred to it by its radio call sign, 5882. There were times when the message traffic made it appear that not one but two planes were missing in the same area.

The *Coral Sea* diverted course from its Mediterranean destination to join the search, along with various other ships in that carrier group. More planes and ships converged on the search area, combing the debris field for clues but largely coming up empty. The survivors and their rafts just disappeared during the five hours that elapsed between the B-29 sighting and the arrival of the USS *Muir* at the same coordinates.

Given the far lower levels of radio-transmission security at the time for routine, all-points bulletins that would not require sophisticated decryption methods, the chances were high in the early hours of the search that the American, British, and Irish searchers were not the only ones listening in on communications. The coordinates easily could have been intercepted by Soviet vessels cruising in the same vicinity.

By late morning on March 25, the survivors had been floating at sea since sometime after dawn on March 23, or more than two days, with no visual, physical, or radio contact with would-be rescuers other than that single B-29 overflight. But it might be possible that other vessels, more intent on *intercepting* rather than rescuing survivors, were also patrolling the debris field.

It wasn't until 2016, however, that the United States stated for the public record its belief that Soviet ships and submarines also were active in the area. Russian officials, challenged about it during a binational commission meeting to find answers to unresolved missing-in-action cases from previous wars, stated that they had been unable to locate records confirming Soviet ships were active near the ditching site.[12]

An inability or unwillingness to confirm is not a denial. The Russian military officials simply declined to engage on the matter and expressed disinterest in looking further into their files for possible answers.

The earliest reports from both United Press and The Associated Press regurgitated misinformation from ground officials and contained serious errors, such as that search planes were battling "gale-force winds," and that the plane had embarked from Gander, Newfoundland, which it had not.[13] Some of these errors were the result of confusion. Others bore the marks of an early attempt by the Air Force to hide the true nature of the mission and/or the conditions under which the plane disappeared.

Although there were sporadic, infrequent references to Hopkins and three other officers onboard having connections to the Strategic Air Command, reporters appeared to know too little about the officers' backgrounds to draw any links to their involvement with an atomic mission. Cullen was identified in nondescript terms as a brigadier general attached to Barksdale Air Force Base. *The Daily Telegraph* of London reported that he was described as traveling to Britain on "routine temporary duty" (as opposed to his real, permanent assignment heading up a new SAC air division). Several news reports that mentioned the sighting of life rafts said no survivors were seen when it was clear from classified military communications that survivors were seen along with life rafts and flares.

As the weather ship *Charlie* sped toward the site of the wreckage in the hours after the plane's disappearance, Lieutenant Junior Grade Carl R. Newton was working the watch from 3 p.m. to midnight. His log report did not specify the latitude or longitude of the ship, only the ship's compass heading. A previous log entry noted sightings of wreckage in the water, making it clear the ship had reached the debris field. Unusual in Newton's handwritten entry was this: "investigating possible gunfire." He provided no further details.[14]

After days of sporadic and increasingly dismal reports from the search effort, the story began falling off the front pages of American newspapers. At the end of March, the United States announced it was ending the search and sending all vessels back to their original missions. But then, on April 2, a tiny story ran as a brief in some U.S. newspapers announcing that the search had been resumed for reasons U.S. military officials wouldn't specify. By this time, stories about the Korean War and Red Scare were dominating the news, and Americans' attention had quickly turned elsewhere.

Try as Air Force investigators did over the following 12 months to find out why the Globemaster veered so wildly off course, then successfully ditched only to have the survivors be located and subsequently lost, no one could come up with a plausible explanation. Investigations—at least the declassified ones—focused only on the possible causes of the ditching, not the failed search effort for survivors or their fates.

The tiny size of the splintered wood and tattered rubber or plastic items from the plane suggested that some kind of explosion had ripped everything to shreds. A United Press report on March 29 quoted a U.S. Air Force spokesman stating bluntly that the aircraft had been "blown to bits" in a "terrific explosion" that almost certainly killed all aboard.[15] The unnamed spokesman did not explain the discrepancy between his statement and the positive identification by the B-29 pilot on March 24 that he had seen signal flares, life rafts, and survivors.

The spokesman also stated, "In any investigation of this kind, the possibility of sabotage must be taken into account. But it should be stressed that, so far, there is absolutely no evidence to indicate sabotage in the case of the Globemaster."

Actually, there was substantial evidence, but the Air Force wouldn't share it with the general public for another five decades.

Many if not most of the collected pieces carried burn marks that indicated a fire had started either after the plane hit the water or shortly beforehand. Air Force historical archives carry dozens of photos of the charred pieces, which mainly came from the wooden decking on the bottom or middle levels of the three-level cargo plane.

Whatever the cause, it clearly wasn't so violent that it was unsurvivable, as demonstrated by the fact that several of the people onboard were able to deploy life rafts and float away from the wreckage. The fact that they fired flares—which were part of the survival package wrapped into the raft container—when the B-29 search plane approached was a strong indication that the rafts remained intact after deployment, with their stored survival equipment and rations intact. Why their Gibson Girl SOS radios didn't transmit after the initial reception on the evening of March 24 has never been explained.

Among the many curiosities about the way the Air Force handled the release of public information during the crisis were the identities of the passengers and crew aboard the cargo plane. According to the official account released to major news media during the search, only four of the passengers aboard, all officers, were associated with the Strategic Air Command, including Lieutenant Colonel Hopkins.[16] The Air Force did its best to dissociate the vast majority of those onboard with the SAC and its atomic attack mandate. In truth, every single person onboard, including the Globemaster pilots and crew, were assigned to the Strategic Air Command, with all but one attached to the 509th Bomb Wing, LeMay's favored atomic bombing unit.[17]

It's entirely possible in the chaos of the rescue operation that the Air Force spokesman had received only partial details of each passenger's and crew member's service unit affiliation. The far more likely reason was that the U.S. and British governments did not want it publicly known that such a high-profile group attached to America's primary nuclear attack force was being deployed on British soil—and that the mission had ended in disaster.

By March 25, there were fifty planes, five ships, and a British submarine combing the search grid. The Associated Press quoted one of the search pilots as stating, "The sea was calm. There were no whitecaps. There was good visibility. But we saw nothing."[18]

Among the major anomalies and mysteries of the search is the fact that the Globemaster was equipped with fifty-six Mae West flotation vests, along with nine inflatable life rafts and other items that were specifically designed to remain atop the surface of the water no matter what. Keep in mind that the flight manifest also listed 8,000 surgical sponges, each measuring two inches by two inches. The very nature of sponges, whether natural or human-made, involves encasing pockets of air inside absorbent material. When squeezed, then released, liquid is sucked into the air pockets. When an unsqueezed sponge is dropped on water, its tendency is to float because the air pockets haven't been filled with liquid. The sponges should have floated on the surface like 8,000 rubber ducks.

Yet this massive search, which recovered hundreds of tiny pieces of splintered wood, yielded not one single surgical sponge, no buoyant Mae Wests, none of the sighted life rafts, no watertight containers full of survival gear. Even if a massive explosion had occurred aboard the plane, those items or remnants of them would have been the most likely ones to float to the surface and remain there. Even though the tendency of human bodies is to float, especially several days after death when decomposition causes gasses to form that naturally lift the corpse to the surface, not a single body or body part was found. There was, however, evidence of human flesh found on screws attached to a piece of recovered wood. Most of the signs of a typical air disaster of this magnitude were simply not there.

Every time there is an air accident involving injury or loss of life, an Air Force medical examiner was required to fill out a detailed 14-B form for every affected individual listing the name, date of birth, service number, date of accident, date of last physical exam, and other key personal information. Then the examiner was supposed to mark a drawing that shows the front, back, and sides of a body. Wherever the examiner found a sign of injury, the diagram was marked on the part of the body where it was found. It was a tedious but necessary process, so the examiner tried to fill one out for all fifty-three aboard, starting with the pilots and crew. After three of them were completed, a handwritten note in the file stated: "As per my conversation with Maj. McConnell and Maj. Westfall 15 May. It was decided that 14-Bs would not be needed for all 53 personnel aboard this aircraft." It was signed by First Lieutenant W. M. Pelton. Without bodies, the entire process was a waste of time.[19]

Aside from Captain Rafferty's satchel, the only other item of significance found in the wreckage was a nine-foot by three-foot section of a KB-29 fuel tank encasement. The investigation would prompt much discussion and follow-up tests to determine whether the two fuel tanks—that is, residual fuel inside them—were somehow a source of the disaster. That probe proved to be another waste of time because the tanks were new and empty, never having been used to store fuel.

As much time and effort as was devoted to the possible causes of the ditching, very little, if any, dealt with a lessons-learned analysis of the rescue effort and what might have been done differently to get rescue vessels to the scene more quickly. In the crucial hours between the first sighting of survivors and the arrival of additional search aircraft and naval vessels, it is clear that something terrible occurred—something that caused a number of survivors and their life rafts to disappear without a trace.

What that event was, the U.S. military either doesn't know or will not say. Documents of the communications between the search vessels and command centers in Britain and the United States remained under seal for five decades, which prevented reporters or inquisitive members of Congress from looking further into the disaster in hopes of deciphering what happened.

Although LeMay's diary indicates he met behind closed doors to discuss the disaster, he issued no public statements on the matter—not even a word of sympathy for the families' losses. Acknowledging an SAC connection with the flight could only serve to weaken operational security and equate it with an atomic mission and thus fuel public alarm.

The fact that other important news events were happening at the same time helped distract many in the American news media from following up. Meanwhile, Air Force public information officers did a masterful job of discouraging curious reporters from looking into the details. To the American public, it was effectively sold as a routine flight to Britain that went awry. There was nothing more to be written. Just move along, folks.

In the British and Irish press, however, the Globemaster story stayed alive throughout this period, partly because there was less going on domestically to distract reporters but also because of ongoing leaks by various people involved in the investigation from bases in Ireland. A few reporters refused to let a juicy story die. In London, *Daily Express* air reporter Hugh Dundas wrote a column pointing to various suspicious elements of the wreckage and victims, then stated bluntly that he had reason to believe there were atomic materials on the plane.

"I say it was sabotage," Dundas added, according to a United Press report.[20]

Almost exactly at the time that U.S. press reports indicated the search would be resumed, a report distributed by Britain's Press Association wire service quoted an unnamed U.S. Air Force senior officer in Shannon, Ireland as stating that sabotage was being investigated as a possible cause of the plane's ditching.

Suddenly, this supposedly "routine" and nondescript flight by a cargo plane to a base north of London was looking far more sinister than the American news media was being told.

CHAPTER 20

Questions of Sabotage

FOR ALL THE ATTEMPTS BY THE AIR FORCE TO SQUASH NEWS MEdia speculation about sabotage, that very topic became the focus of secret investigations into Globemaster 49-244's disappearance in the following months. In public relations terms, the goal seemed to be aimed at diverting attention from the ditching as quickly as possible while pinning the disaster on some kind of maintenance failure, manufacturing or design flaw, or perhaps even adverse weather conditions.

Exhaustive reports and interviews were conducted along those lines, but investigators found nothing conclusive. Still, they tried hard to make a case for some kind of equipment malfunction as the culprit, because if they allowed the question of sabotage to dominate the investigation, the message sent to the general public would no longer be controllable. Press inquiries would explode. Congress could get involved. The entire probe, slathered with the word "sabotage," would be yanked away from the Air Force's jurisdiction and become the focus of a full-blown criminal probe. There would have to be inquiries into personnel, motives, security leaks, and, perhaps most foreboding, exploring the potential involvement of foreign agents. With the Red Scare already dominating the headlines, the results of any such probe would spell disaster for the SAC and LeMay.

Sabotage would require the FBI and State Department to get involved. And the CIA. If any such probe were to become public knowledge, expectations would rise for the Truman administration to respond to what could only be interpreted as an egregiously hostile attack against America's atomic forces in international airspace. Hawks in Congress, already demanding an atomic preemptive strike against Moscow, would certainly demand retaliation. There would be congressional hearings. And since the entire U.S. Air Force mission to Europe was now focused on addressing and countering the Soviet threat of a ground invasion, all fingers would point to Moscow as the culprit for this outrageous action.

The Air Force quietly ordered a multifaceted investigation into the most likely causes of the disaster. One focused on the competence of the pilot and crew, all of whom had stellar records. Another focused on the airplane's manufacturer, Douglas Aircraft Company. A third was devoted to the four massive Pratt & Whitney engines that powered the Globemaster and its 74,000-pound cargo capacity into the sky. A fourth probe was devoted to possible fuel leaks from the KB-29 tanks in the cargo hold. A fifth explored the potential of a catastrophic midair fire onboard.

And a sixth was stamped with the ominous word "SABOTAGE."[1]

Each of these independent probes presented what seemed like plausible scenarios to explain why the plane might have experienced problems in the air and suddenly diverted to the south. Yet none of those investigations concluded with certainty that this versus that was the cause of the disaster. It remains entirely possible that a horrific combination of factors was behind the ditching, such as a fire caused by an engine failure linked, say, to an unresolved maintenance or manufacturing issue.

Other C-124s in the same production line had experienced catastrophic engine-related failures that resulted in crashes. There might even have been other contributing factors that the investigators never contemplated and, therefore, never looked into. Because the mission was classified, much of the information investigators needed to access in order to reach a proper conclusion might have been unavailable for lack of security clearance. There is no indication in the reports that the investigators were allowed to know the nature of the mission that the fifty-three men were undertaking at the time.

At least one crew member, Robert D. Amsden, told his brother, Keith, that he could not discuss the nature of the mission because it was top secret. Keith, himself an airman serving at the same Walker Air Force Base as his brother, didn't have the clearance to know what Robert's mission was.[2]

Investigators looked into the possibility that someone had entered the plane but left before it had taken off from Limestone. Guards were interviewed. Investigators scoured a list of passengers who had embarked at Walker but disembarked when the plane reached Barksdale,[3] where General Cullen and his aides had boarded. Those probes yielded no useful clues. They even scrutinized those who boarded the plane at various intervals during its various stops for maintenance or security checks—including, oddly, a brigadier general at Walker who took it upon himself to inspect the straps used to lash down the two KB-29 tanks.[4] Why someone of his rank would undertake such a menial task seemed not to have interested the investigators. The investigation report seemed to focus only on the reassurance the general provided that those straps were secure, meaning the KB-29 tanks didn't come loose and somehow contribute to the disaster.

Even as the North Atlantic search was still in its early stages on March 24, 1951, and hopes remained of finding survivors, investigators back at Walker began interrogating associates of the pilots and senior crew members to see if there might be any clues or recollections that might be useful. The questions posed to the witnesses delved into the backgrounds of the pilot and crew members to determine if incompetence or catastrophic errors might have caused the Globemaster to go down. Each was read his rights under the 24th Article of War, was treated as a witness, and was sworn in before giving a deposition.[5]

The witnesses consistently described the pilots, navigator, loadmaster, flight engineers, and other personnel as professionals who were well trained and trustworthy in every regard. To a person, they responded as if flummoxed regarding the possible causes for the Globemaster's ditching.

Top on the list of possibilities was a manufacturing or design flaw. In all the time that General LeMay had flown and commanded missions over Europe and the South Pacific, he seemed willing to accept that a certain percentage of missions would fail simply because the equipment would not hold up under such demanding conditions. As the war began, entire lines of planes had been designed in a rush and forced into mass production with a minimum of preparation time. They were almost destined to fail at a high rate, often taking their crews with them.

There were literally thousands of crucial items that had to work perfectly in order for the planes' crews to survive, regardless of whether they faced a wall of flak, ground fire, or constant midair pestering by German or Japanese fighters along the way. The engines were a complicated combination of housings, bearings, gears, pistons, carburetors, fuel injectors, spark plugs, gaskets, and propellers that all had to work in perfect sync. Any one of those items, perhaps rushed a little too quickly into production without proper inspection to reveal manufacturing cracks or improper welds, could bring down not just one plane but an entire batch from the same production line. Hundreds could, and did, die as a result.

America celebrated the "Rosie the Riveter" women who joined the workforce to help factories churn out all the weapons and machines and uniforms needed for the war effort. But the demands on American assembly plants were so infamously heavy that they couldn't possibly be sustained without severe consequences somewhere down the line. The demands became the theme of a 1946 drama by Arthur Miller, *All My Sons,* about the deaths of service members in World War II caused by a single plant owner's greed and lack of courage to tell the military that he couldn't meet their stepped-up production schedules. The play was based on the true story of Lockland, Ohio–based Curtiss-Wright Corporation and its production of defective P-40 fighter engines that were nevertheless approved by three Army Air Forces officers for installation in military planes urgently needed when the United States entered World War II.[6] The three officers wound up going to prison.

"The Lockland scandal was a prime example of what happened when a huge government-built, spare-no-expense factory tried to turn out an enormous quantity of material with inexperienced management and impossible production schedules while maintaining quality in the face of constant changes in tolerances and specifications."[7] Curtiss-Wright survived the scandal and emerged as one of the nation's largest and most profitable military contractors. Both President Harry Truman and his successor, Dwight Eisenhower, became vociferous skeptics of the powerful financial forces behind the American military manufacturing industry, which Eisenhower famously labeled "the military-industrial complex," whose success and profitability depended on keeping America perpetually on a path toward war.

But the P-40 scandal wasn't the only time that wartime pressures led to disaster. The chemical defoliant Agent Orange, when produced under its inventor's original formula, was so harmless to humans that chemists felt no reluctance to dip their hands directly into vats of the stuff while it was cooking. But the Air Force during the Vietnam War demanded tons and tons of the defoliant on a daily basis to help clear thousands of square miles of jungle in hopes of denying Vietcong fighters their traditional hiding places for guerrilla attacks. To meet those production schedules, Dow Chemical and other producers altered the original formula, boosting temperatures and pressures to yield the chemical mix faster. And in doing so, they introduced dioxin into the mix, exposing thousands of American troops (and Vietnamese) to a powerful cancer-causing toxin.[8]

So it was well worth asking the question when Globemaster 49-244 went down: Was this ditching an isolated case, or did it fit a pattern of defective manufacturing? On May 1, 1951, an inspection of C-124 number 49-236[9] revealed significant deterioration in the engine propeller assemblies on that plane even though it had completed only 500 hours of flying time. On May 23, 1951, exactly two months after the 49-244 North Atlantic disaster, Globemaster 49-232 experienced a serious engine problem caused by a sudden throttle reversal. It crash-landed in a field during a test flight from Wright-Patterson Air Force Base in Ohio, fatally injuring seven onboard while another five survived their injuries. Less than two weeks later, on June 2, 1951, Globemaster 49-250 went down after another catastrophic engine failure during takeoff outside Tucson, Arizona.

The rapid succession of accidents bolstered speculation of a manufacturing flaw when investigators took into account how relatively new these planes were. For example, 49-244 was manufactured only six months earlier and had less than 325 hours of flying time before it departed on its final flight. It was too new to have needed any major overhauls. Even newer still was 49-250, which developed a problem with the No. 3 engine on the plane's left side when pilots attempted to abort takeoff by reversing thrust to help brake the plane. In this case, a propeller broke free under the intense stress of the reversal. It could have been flung in any number of directions, but in this case, it sliced straight through the lower level of the fuselage, severing crucial control cables, hydraulics, and radio instruments.[10]

Investigators tried hard to make a case that this is what happened to 49-244, given the fact that the plane diverted so suddenly and inexplicably. They posited the argument that the pilots lost control because of severed control cables leading to the rudder and flaps, and that the pilots stopped communicating with ground controllers and weather ships because two essential radio-transmission boxes might have been destroyed by a propeller or other part flung from the No. 2 or No. 3 engines, with which the radio-transmission boxes were aligned on the cargo hold's lowest level. "Conclusions: The possible causes of the accident involving C-124A 49-244 are as follows: A propeller failure which resulted in a portion of a propeller being thrown through the fuselage and causing damage which resulted in loss of control of the aircraft and rendering communication equipment inoperative," the investigators stated confidently.[11] They went on to recommend a sixteen-point refitting procedure to fix what they asserted was the cause of the North Atlantic disaster based on what happened in the other cases that actually bore no resemblance to the conditions 49-244 had experienced.

Because the three incidents involving planes 236, 232, and 250 happened in such quick succession, the Air Force grounded all of its C-124A aircraft pending further inspections and modifications to help ensure that vital equipment was removed from the path of a wayward propeller blade.

Their conclusion linking the 49-244 disaster with what happened to 49-250 required a logical leap. A throttle reversal upon takeoff, at one of the most dangerous and stress-inducing portions of a plane's flight, is hardly comparable to stress conditions that a plane cruising in midflight at 9,000 feet would experience. And if a propeller had become dislodged and sliced through the fuselage at the point investigators speculated, the result from the loss of hydraulics and several control cables being severed would have likely been an immediate crash of the plane or a pattern of zigzagging or flying in circles due to loss of rudder and flap controls.

Globemaster 49-244 showed no signs of being out of control. It veered from its scheduled route and flew in a more or less straight line almost due south. A simple wind gust would have thrown the untethered rudder to one side, sending the plane into a circular pattern. Planes that are out of control don't tend to fly in a straight line. And if the plane had lost its ability to communicate by fixed radio due to a destroyed transmission box, a separate investigation noted, the pilots still had the ability to send emergency signals using one of the three Gibson Girl hand-cranked radios onboard.[12] No distress calls were received by surface vessels below or by either the British or American control towers while the plane was in flight.

Whatever happened onboard, it was clear that the plane was experiencing a crisis. Could bad weather have factored in the diversion and ditching? "Crew and passengers attended an overwater flight briefing at Limestone; the crew received the latest weather information at a weather briefing which indicated there was an occluded front off the coast of Newfoundland with scattered snow showers." The front was more than a hundred miles north of the flight path and not expected to affect the plane's course. "No appreciable icing or turbulence was anticipated," the accident investigation said. "The expected flight plan duration was 13 hours and 10 minutes. The aircraft made regular hourly position reports on the hour up to 0000Z on 23 March. The last position reported was 51°30′N and 27°00′W at 0047Z. This indicated the aircraft to be at 9000′ on top of a cloud layer the tops of which were estimated to be 7500′. There was no further word from the aircraft."[13]

Again, investigators tried to establish a scenario in which icing had combined with the loss of a propeller bearing to create enough stress to make a piece of the propeller assembly, called a cuff, become dislodged and fly into the fuselage. "Since the particular design of the Curtiss-Wright propeller blade installed on the aircraft has been known to fail in air carrier operation, it is possible that a failed propeller blade could sever the rudder and/or elevator control cables and throw the aircraft out of control."

Then, returning to weather as a possible contributing factor, the investigation report added that the pilot might have been misinformed about the severity of a system brewing off the Irish coast. "The forecast tended to minimize the severity of the icing and turbulence in the area of bad weather which existed approximately 400 miles to 500 miles off the Irish Coast." But the Strategic Air Command inspector general, Brigadier General John C. McBlaine, determined that "the aircraft had not entered the geographical area in which this adverse weather was located. . . . On the basis of these locations, it has been concluded that weather was not a factor."[14] Nevertheless, reporters briefed at the time of the plane's disappearance were told in no uncertain terms that bad weather had played a role.

Among the issues carefully excluded from all press briefings was the presence of the two KB-29 fuel tanks onboard. That information was classified, along with all details about the construction and design of the tanks, because the last thing LeMay wanted was to give the Soviets clues on how to extend the range of their own atomic bombers (even though the Soviets already had designed their own aerial-refueling systems).

Although the Soviets had successfully copied the B-29 in order to produce the Tu-4, they had been unable to obtain the specifications for the Silverplate B-29—the limited version altered to accommodate the dimensions of a Fat Man bomb. For that reason, the dimensions of the KB-29 tanks remained closely held for fear that the information might help speed a Tu-4 redesign for future atomic attack missions.

For the purposes of the investigation into 49-244's disappearance, though, the KB-29s had to be explored as a possible cause. Investigators were particularly concerned with the possibility of manufacturing defects in the tanks, assembled at a Boeing Airplane Company plant in Wichita, Kansas. Of particular concern was that the tanks had been loaded with fuel ahead of the flight or that residual fuel inside might have exploded.

It turned out that the tanks were brand new and had never been used. An oil-based fuel was used to test the internal rubber-nylon bladders for leaks before shipment, and residual amounts were deliberately left as a preservative for the rubber. The mixture was specifically designed to be nonexplosive, even at high temperatures, the report found.

It is worth noting, however, that remnants of the KB-29s were among the most prominent and voluminous of all the wreckage recovered at the ditching site. Yet no pieces of rubber bladder were recovered even though they would have been at least as buoyant as any other part of the tank structure. The absence of such remnants defies explanation other than the possibility that the bladders were never installed or were removed before the flight, perhaps because the tank shells were being used for some other classified purpose.

The way at least one KB-29 broke apart led to further speculation that it had been sliced through by a detached propeller.

> The two KB-29 bomb bay tanks were loaded in the forward part of the fuselage, the front end of one box being in the [vertical] plane of rotation of the propellers. As previously pointed out, one end of

> the recovered side of the KB-29 bomb bay tank box separated due to forces exerted in an upward direction. Assuming that this piece came from the left side of the front box in the fuselage it appears that a failed No. 3 or No. 4 propeller could have pierced the fuselage and caused the upward separation of the front end of the box. This same propeller failure could have damaged the radio equipment and severed or loosened the rudder and elevator control cables.[15]

Many questions surfaced during the investigation about a non-sabotage, midair explosion having occurred onboard. The probe turned to possible items on the cargo manifest that, under the right conditions, might have spontaneously combusted or somehow played a role in an explosion. The only culprit was a rubber-lined wooden crate in the cargo hold that carried ten gallons of the chemical solvent ethyl acetate. The investigation sought to determine whether it could have been the source of an explosion onboard, but subsequent testing ruled that out as a factor. "No explosion would be possible from this source," the report concluded. In fact, talk of some kind of midair explosion that caused the plane to suddenly veer southward wound up amounting to pure speculation, since no communication from the plane suggested that an explosion had occurred.[16]

But something of an extremely violent nature most certainly blew the plane to bits either just before it hit the water or shortly afterward.

A careful analysis of the direction of the split in wood pieces that formed the flooring of the lower level, plus the point where hinged or fastened pieces broke from their metal attachments convinced investigators that a powerful upward force, coming from the underside of the plane, was responsible for the breakup. It is entirely possible that this upward force was nothing more than the plane crashing down violently against the water surface as the pilots attempted a waterborne landing. That kind of violent collision with the water most certainly would have broken the flooring apart in an upward fashion. But the plane would not have been traveling fast enough, nor would its rate of descent into the water have been fast enough, to splinter the wood into the tiny bits described in the investigation reports. Nor would it explain the charring on pieces of the recovered wreckage.

The speculation that some kind of catastrophic fire had erupted during the flight, causing it to divert and ditch, was put to rest by the investigators' conclusion that the flames that burned the recovered wood pieces had not been on fire very long before the water extinguished them. "A microscopic examination of the ramp section, photographs of which are attached, showed the upper surface to be coated with a protective resin or varnish. This coating is unblistered and substantially intact. The wood underneath shows no sign of thermal decomposition, and the areas that had been coated with anti-skid strips are not discolored." They exposed a sampling of uncharred wood pieces to direct flame from a Bunsen burner to duplicate the charring of other recovered pieces. To duplicate the depth and intensity of the charring required a burn of only ten seconds before the test piece "closely resembled the existing burned section. The latter test is indicative that the undersurface of the ramp section of this investigation was not severely exposed, or if there had been direct flame impingement, it was of short duration."[17]

That test was necessary to dispel any notion that a fire had started at the time of the plane's diversion from its intended flight path. Had such a fire been responsible, it would have had hours to burn the underside of the ramps. Instead, the fire appeared to have burned the wood for less than a minute.

Here is where the mystery gets truly interesting: Investigators discovered the presence of a tubular piece of metal embedded in one piece of recovered wood. A forensic analysis of that piece also turned up a strange chemical combination that couldn't be explained by a single other item known to be equipment on the plane or cargo listed on its manifest. The elements zinc, magnesium, antimony, lead, and vanadium were present in some of the samples tested, which the investigators traced as potentially being linked to metals contained in the KB-29 tanks. But the combination inside pieces of splintered wood was perplexing.

The combination of those distinct elements is found in a number of munitions and munition casings from the World War II period,[18] none of which were listed on the manifest or part of the equipment carried on the cargo plane. One compound was the chemical AN-M36-CI-A, which is a slightly modified version of an explosive used in World War II munitions. The search for a possible source was exhaustive and involved every single item in the plane's equipment inventory, its cargo, and even exterior components, such as the wheels, brakes, hydraulic pumps, hydraulic fluids, the varnish on the floorboards, and the nonskid coating applied to the ramp. Anything that could offer clues, they examined with microscopic, forensic thoroughness—even to the point of sampling seawater to see if it contained that mixture of chemical components.

Investigators took samples of wood, sealants, ramps, varnish, lubrication compounds, and other substances from two other C-124s in that production line to nail down the possible source of the chemicals. Nothing yielded that chemical formulation.[19]

The key findings of that portion of the investigation were these: "This fragment [of metal containing the chemical compound] has not been identified as having been any part of the airplane or its cargo," and "the absence of these deposits at the breaks [in the recovered, splintered wood remnants], under the washer seats, or the underside of this flooring even though there was considerable charring and burning of the flooring itself on this side . . . indicates that these residues were deposited prior to the impact."

Something impacted the plane and embedded in the wood before it hit the water. And whatever it was, the chemical components were similar to those found in the casings of many types of munitions, none of which were carried on the plane.

Another finding involved tests conducted on the plane's "scuff plates," which are used in this context to protect pieces of equipment from damage caused by foot traffic, wheels, or anything else that can cause bangs or dents. Even if a fire were to have broken out on the plane, investigators determined, the scuff plates would not have ignited. But the charring included the scuff plates, "a fact which lends support to the probability of an explosion."

From the Douglas Aircraft Company's point of view, the evidence was insufficient to determine the primary cause of the crash. "There is evidence to the effect that the airplane was on fire while still airborne," it concluded. "There are indications of an explosion, whether or not this occurred in flight could not be determined. All of the following items were burned and/or forced about the inside of the airplane with explosive violence: The tank crate liner of one of both crates. The scuff plates along the interior of the fuselage. Gasoline or the tank bladders or both."

A slightly contradictory set of conclusions was reached by investigators assigned to the case from Norton Air Force Base, home of the Air Force's flight safety directorate in California. They agreed with the Douglas experts that the pieces of the plane's flooring shattered because of "an upward force from under the floor" and that the wood pieces appeared to have burned while floating on the water.

But the Norton investigation was far more definitive in this conclusion: "The aircraft was evidently, more or less, intact when it hit. This is indicated by the small number of pieces recovered, as well as the fact that two inflated aircraft tires carried as part of the cargo were never found." That suggests the fuselage sank as a kind of intact container that carried its contents with it to the sea bottom, a conclusion invalidated by the fact that so much of the plane's interior contents wound up on the water surface. "Also, the debris found was burned by fuel fire from fuel in the wing fuel cells, which indicates that the wing fuel cells were still attached to the fuselage."

Importantly, the Norton findings said, "There is no conclusive proof that anything unusual happened before the aircraft struck the water, nor that it struck the water out of control. There is evidence that a fire occurred on top of the water after the aircraft hit."[20]

What the two investigations, approaching from entirely different points of view, appear to say is that this was a more or less controlled descent, as opposed to a nosedive or other kind of out-of-control crash. The pilots appeared to have decided a waterborne landing, catastrophic as it might be, was the only option under the circumstances to save the lives of as many people onboard as possible.

The findings also consistently refuted the notion that a propeller might have slashed through the fuselage and cut through control cables and radio-transmission boxes. A plane whose control cables have been severed cannot smoothly glide to an intact waterborne landing, no matter how talented the pilots might be. As for the complete silence from the plane after its final check-in at shortly before 1:00 a.m. Greenwich Mean Time on March 23, nothing surfaced in the investigations to come up with a plausible explanation.

An April 10, 1951, "preliminary report" concluded: "The aircraft was properly loaded. The crew and passengers were properly briefed. The crew was qualified to safely operate the aircraft and accomplish the mission. That security of the aircraft was accomplished as directed by higher headquarters. The weather conditions along the intended flight path were reasonable. That there is no known reason or chain of events which might have caused this aircraft to fail to reach its destination."[21]

Commanders ordered a complete security review of every stop the C-124 made as part of the mission, starting with Walker, then Tinker, then Walker again, then Barksdale, then Limestone. When investigators turned to the question of sabotage, they necessarily had to first look at all personnel who might have had access to the interior of the plane before its final takeoff. They examined all procedures for preparing the box-lunch food provided to the passengers and crew. Fuel was tested for possible contamination. All testing yielded negative results of potential foul play.[22]

The investigation only lightly touched upon the location of the plane for the four days after it had returned from Tinker. There was no mention of whether it sat on a side apron or was moved to a hangar. There was no mention of whether the KB-29 tanks remained onboard the entire time or whether they were removed. But the weight of the cargo listed on the manifest broke down as 6,830 pounds for the two tanks. That would leave the weight of the remaining cargo at 9,852 pounds. The medical supplies were listed on the manifest as weighing ninety-three pounds. When asked to account for the total amount of equipment onboard the plane that should now be listed as missing, 1st Lieutenant Billy E. Stewart of the 509th Refueling Squadron certified that the total items were two bomb bay tanks, two 20-ounce claw hammers, twenty-one extension cords, nine buckets, five grease guns, twenty-four high-pressure chucks, ten padlocks, and one instrument bleeder. There was still a lot of weight unaccounted for on a manifest that, as was demonstrated by other classified flight manifests during that month, may well have been a work of fiction.

The April 10 preliminary report tried to explain some other anomalies regarding the weight of the cargo. It correctly listed the weight of the two KB-29 tanks, then added, "In addition, there was 10,395 pounds of medical supplies, prop equipment, spare parts, tools, technical order compliance kits, electric equipment." It listed the total cargo weight as 17,215 pounds plus 4,000 pounds of baggage and fifty-three people onboard. The numbers fluctuated on different manifests and forms, but there was no escaping that the plane sat for four days at Walker, after which it departed with a cargo weight, in addition to the passengers, their baggage, and the two aerial fuel tanks, as being nearly equal to the weight of a Fat Man and its nuclear core.[23]

Manifests of SAC cargo flights from that same period show bizarre patterns that make no sense: KB-29 tanks that were transported thousands of miles, only to be returned to the exact same spot where they were supposedly loaded. Cargo weights bore all the markings of having been concocted for the sake of completing paperwork—or hiding the true nature of the flight.

There are no available cargo manifests that list, for example, the transport of M107 nonatomic Fat Man bombs to Britain even though they definitely were delivered there. Equally bizarre was a diagram submitted with the investigation report for 49-244 purportedly depicting where the KB-29 tanks were loaded and where other cargo and passengers were situated. Upon closer examination of the small type at the bottom of the diagram, it becomes clear that it has nothing to do with 49-244. Rather, it is from a plane labeled 49-133.[24] A separate diagram depicting the loading of 49-244 shows only one KB-29 secured on the ramp.[25]

Although the various investigation reports offered scant details of what went into the probe regarding sabotage, the FBI and Air Force Sabotage and Counterintelligence Brigade most certainly dug in hard on this question. The files released decades later include cover letters from the chief sabotage investigators listing a series of four files that contained their findings, but the files themselves remained classified. The pages in the investigation report that were released, declassified on authorization of a person identified only as Major Figg—the same person who declassified the sabotage investigation cover letters—suddenly switched to a discussion of radioactive waste found off the Azores island chain east of Portugal. The waste was from a barrel that washed up onshore and appeared to have no relationship to the ditching of Globemaster 49-244. But it is still intriguing that the investigators' attention would focus on *radioactive* waste in relation to the ditching of a Globemaster whose cargo officially had no radioactive materials onboard.

If there was nothing of a radioactive nature on the plane to begin with, why take the investigation in that direction?

Perhaps there was more to the flight than the Air Force and its classification experts wanted to acknowledge. The existence of something more extensive on the plane could help explain why the Air Force couldn't get its story straight when it came to simple diagramming of the cargo layout or itemizing consistent flight manifests.

The final page of that sabotage investigation section, concluded in January 1952, lists the findings as "pending" and states: "Closing of this investigation held in abeyance pending development of leads set forth in R/I, Special Agent James G. Hindes, this district office, dated 14 December 1951. Undeveloped leads set forth."[26] A report filed on January 8, 1952, by Charles R. Roos at Bolling Air Force Base clearly references Douglas Aircraft Company's identification of an unusual chemical compound on certain pieces of wreckage. It states: "Specifications of AN-M-50 type bomb with changes, and specification of AN-M-36 type bomb, ascertained. Deviation in chemical composition of AN-M-50 bomb not determined due to non-systematic method of storing old records. Assistance in determining deviation or waiver of chemical composition of bomb would be facilitated by knowing shape and chemical content of fragment."[27]

Investigators were attempting to verify that a slight modification to a four-pound AN-M50 incendiary bomb used against Japan in World War II might have been the source of the unusual chemical found on the wreckage. Several such bombs were produced for various purposes during the war with numbered labels to distinguish their thermal power, magnesium content, and other factors. The smaller bombs ranged from two to eleven pounds, but bigger ones designed by the Germans and British weighed 250 to 4,000 pounds or more.

The tubular, threaded piece of metal embedded in the wood piece found among the Globemaster wreckage bolstered investigators' theory that these components, in fact, were remnants of an exploded bomb. An AN-M36 bomb would differ only slightly from an M50 bomb, containing almost exactly the same percentages of aluminum, zinc, magnesium, and manganese. The M36, unlike the M50, also would contain small amounts of calcium, silicon, copper, and nickel.[28]

The manufacturing description of an AN-M50 bomb specifies the inclusion of a screw-top connector to wed the housing of the bomb to the explosive component.

These bombs were designed to be loaded by the hundreds into B-29 planes, then dropped in almost scattershot fashion over Japanese cities. Once they detonated, they ignited a chemical mixture of highly flammable, gel-like fuel—also known as napalm—that resulted in a conflagration. One Japanese house set afire could quickly start a chain reaction in neighboring houses. If the bombs were dropped by the hundreds, an entire city could be ignited in flames in no time. The bombs were a signature part of Curtis LeMay's strategy to win the war by setting as much of Japan on fire as he could.

Another key factor of the M50 was its portability. At four pounds, it was easily carried by hand and easily concealed. British and American versions of these devices were listed in once-confidential documents from immediately after the war as "sabotage incendiaries (for hand placement)."[29]

CHAPTER 21

A Question of Self-Sabotage

IN ALL OF THE PUBLICLY AVAILABLE PROBES INTO WHAT CAUSED the disappearance of Globemaster 49-244—a fire emergency onboard, a disaster-inducing propeller failure, an explosion, a fuel tank leak, and sabotage—the one thing investigators didn't dare touch upon was perhaps the most glaringly obvious possibility of all: that the crew and passengers aboard the C-124 destroyed the plane themselves. To understand how that outlandish possibility might have played in the plane's fate, it's important to review the background of the secret missions happening at the time.

The plane was heading to Britain at the exact time the SAC was conducting Project Evening Star, a secret series of simulated atomic bomb attacks scheduled to take place over Europe and the Mediterranean Sea throughout March 1951. All but one of the fifty-three men aboard 49-244 were from the four nuclear-trained squadrons of the 509th Bomb Wing conducting Evening Star's simulated attacks.

The idea of self-sabotage might seem preposterous on its face, but Air Force documents outlining procedures during Project Evening Star strongly suggest the Globemaster's mission was an integral part of a much larger plan not only to install an attack-ready atomic force in Britain but to have that force practice repeatedly the exact procedures that would be essential to a successful atomic bombing raid over Moscow. The kinds of expertise required for such a mission went far beyond what was required of the two dozen pilots aboard the Globemaster. By 1951, the Soviet Union not only had its own atomic capability but also had developed sophisticated radar technology to identify incoming planes. Even worse for American pilots, the Soviets had utilized the technological expertise gleaned from their capture of top German engineers and scientists to develop ground-to-air and air-to-air antiaircraft systems, as well as their most potent and deadly weapon: the MiG-15 jet fighter. They were well ahead of their American counterparts in the ability to intercept and shoot down the World War II–era, propeller-driven B-29s, and newer B-50s that were the only aircraft General Curtis LeMay trusted at the time to reliably deliver a Fat Man atomic bomb on target.

The development of radar by both sides in the Cold War proved to be yet another hurdle for the Americans to overcome before executing a preemptive nuclear attack or some kind of atomic response to Soviet aggression in Europe. The introduction of the MiG-15 into the Korean War, coupled with Soviet radar installations to warn of incoming U.S. bomber formations, led to devastating consequences and humiliating defeats for the once-superior U.S. Air Force.

> The Soviets learned by practice and demonstrated their ability to deal with certain classes of threats. From the Soviet point of view, the series of air battles fought in October 1951 by ground-controlled MiG-15s in regimental-size units against daylight B-29 raids with fighter escorts demonstrated an ability to inflict crippling losses against daylight bomber formations. . . . While the behavior of the individual interceptor pilots in Korea was important, even more significant was the Soviet deployment of an operational command and control system for integrated twenty-four-hour air defense.

The installation of twenty-five radar intercept stations along the Yalu River gave the Soviets the ability to locate U.S. bomber formations from seventy miles away, giving them plenty of time to scramble their faster, more nimble jet fighters to bring them down.[1]

The dangers were just as pronounced along the European Iron Curtain, where almost forty British or American aircraft had been lost within the Berlin air corridors from 1945 to 1947.[2] Whatever notions LeMay might have had about total domination of the skies against far less sophisticated Soviet air forces, those assumptions were rapidly disappearing.

A major warning sign of Joseph Stalin's willingness to test American tolerance came in April 1950 when a U.S. Navy PB4Y Privateer spy plane was on patrol over the Baltic Sea. The United States insisted the plane had always stayed in international airspace, but the Soviets asserted the plane had violated Lithuania's sovereign zone. The only way the Soviets could make that determination would have been with radar. MiG-15s scrambled and shot the plane out of the sky.

The Soviets, like the Americans, also had developed sophisticated means of jamming communications between pilots and their ground controllers. So the cat-and-mouse game was on to figure out ways to circumvent radio-signal jamming and to devise codes that would prevent the Soviets from intercepting communications and deciphering the Americans' plans for an atomic attack. The United States began using "ferrets," or planes whose crews were advised to approach Soviet Bloc airspace and provoke an activation of defensive radar and jamming capabilities. Other U.S. aircraft would monitor the Soviet signals to measure their response times and techniques. As was the case for the Privateer, however, dozens of these ferret flights ended tragically.[3]

Then came the difficult calculations of devising an attack route that would fool the Soviets into thinking that American planes were on some other kind of mission or that some other location was the actual target of a U.S. attack. So it couldn't just be a straight practice run between Britain and a Moscow target. Such a route would open the planes up to interception as they overflew Soviet rump states such as Poland and Belarus well before they could reach Moscow. Rather, the plane or planes carrying Fat Man atomic bombs would have to fly extremely long diversionary routes that could take them northward over Denmark and Sweden, or across the Mediterranean and then northward over Turkey.

Such routes meant turning the 1,500-mile direct route between Mildenhall and Moscow into a 3,000- or even 4,500-mile jaunt. A heavily loaded B-29 simply couldn't complete such a journey using the fuel available in its tanks, as Major Chuck Sweeney discovered much to his embarrassment after he completed the bombing raid on Nagasaki. The KB-29 refueling tanker plane thus became an essential component to any plan of attack on Moscow—that is, unless LeMay contemplated sending his pilots and crews on one-way suicide missions.

Refueling in midair required pilots and crews of the tanker plane and receiver B-29 to train repeatedly on the procedure until it became second nature. The tanker planes had to follow their own distinct routes to avoid detection, while the B-29 attack planes had to fly entirely separate routes. They had to practice rendezvous at 20,000 feet in the middle of nowhere, then ensure that the tanker plane was able to maneuver just above and ahead of the receiver plane before extending a boom-like hose that would couple with the receiver plane's grapnel-hook nozzle. They had to be flying at exactly the same speed, which meant mechanics had to precisely tune the engines of the two planes ahead of time to deliver the exact same speed when their tachometers showed specific revolutions per minute.

Flight engineers, mechanics, pilots, navigators, and airborne-refueling specialists all had to be choreographed to perfect synchronization. There could be no repeat of the navigational screwups that nearly scuttled the Nagasaki mission. It was no accident that Lieutenant Colonel Hopkins, a veteran of that screwup, was included in the Evening Star mission. Once the pilots and crews had practiced airborne refueling over the United States until the procedure was as close to automatic and routine as they could get it, they then needed to practice it again and again and again with the B-29s carrying nonatomic, 10,000-pound M107 Fat Man bombs.

Next came the task of practicing this procedure over the skies of Europe, where the stakes were far higher. Not only did the complicated airborne-refueling procedure need to be practiced and perfected, it also had to occur while pilots and crews practiced jamming countermeasures, ground-fire evasion, and interception. In order to conduct these practice sessions in the skies over Europe, the Air Force relied on diplomats and military attachés in roughly a dozen European and North African countries to deftly communicate to their host countries that important training exercises would be occurring within their airspace, that there was no hostile intent, and that any form of military interference could lead to tragic consequences.

Essential in such diplomatic communications was the need not to divulge the secret nature of these exercises for fear of tipping off the Soviets to what was happening—a tricky undertaking considering that several of those countries maintained close ties with Moscow, not to mention political leaders who were sympathetic to Communism. Not only did those countries have to agree not to respond when loud and lumbering American B-29s and B-50s invaded their airspace but also to tolerate sorties by British fighter planes assigned to simulate Soviet interceptors.

That was complicated enough. But there was also a hot war going on in Korea—a war in which Soviet pilots were disguising themselves as North Koreans, taking to the skies in their MiG jet fighters and actively engaging in airborne warfare against American warplanes. The psychological effect on American pilots in their lumbering, slow, and relatively defenseless B-29s was palpable. Former B-29 pilot Earl McGill expressed the fears he and his fellow pilots in Korea felt: "I'll tell you, everybody was scared. On my first mission, we were briefed for heavy MiG interception. I was so scared on that day that I've never been frightened since, even when I flew combat missions in the B-52 [over Vietnam]."[4]

Soviet pilots were prompting similar fears in the skies over Eastern Europe as U.S. and British reconnaissance flights were repeatedly downed by MiG fighters. The threat was real that Moscow, perhaps through espionage or leaks from any of the Soviet-friendly countries in Europe or North Africa that had been alerted to the American exercises, would attempt its own airborne interference. In the case of Operation Evening Star, the intercepts wouldn't involve friendly simulations but rather the real thing. Shootdowns and forced ditchings were entirely possible, procedural documents warned. American generals were fully aware of the dangers and did their best to warn their pilots and crews to expect worst-case hostile encounters.

This was no "cold" war scenario.

Just as the Roosevelt administration, anxious to maintain the secrecy of its atomic bomb development program, managed to hide the entire $1 billion budget for the Manhattan Project inside several obscurely worded budget outlays put before Congress,[5] the Truman administration found ways to hide its preparations for a military buildup in Europe should war become necessary to stop a Soviet invasion. The fiscal 1952 budget contained exactly three lines devoted to the Evening Star military plan, stating simply, "Additional amount to cover special reserve (as required by TS document, subject: Consolidated requirement for project 'Evening Star,' priority 27)—$600,000." The actual expenditures for Evening Star were far higher and were contained in a $296 million budgetary outlay called Project 551, which accounted for sundry items such as overseas pay, rations, fuel, maintenance, and equipment. It wasn't until questioning by House Appropriations subcommittee members that the military let on what the true nature of the program was.

Testifying before a House Appropriations subcommittee in July 1951, then–Air Force Brigadier General Donald Norton Yates offered a three-point outline of the military's objectives in the event of a nuclear war. Although the Soviet Union wasn't specifically mentioned in his remarks, it was the only other nation on the planet at the time capable of engaging in an atomic attack, so the references were implicit. Yates said the first objective was to ensure the United States could absorb the first blows of such an attack and survive to take the war to the enemy. "Our radar and other detection methods must be adequate to locate any enemy approach to our boundaries early enough to permit the launching of aircraft and weapons in time to prevent the delivery of their bombs. Our aircraft and weapons must have sufficient capability to divert or knock out the bombs or other weapons used in such an attack. The air defense system must provide this insurance." He added:

> Second, and certainly equally as important, if we do as we must, in fact, survive or repluse [repulse] an initial attack, is the provision of adequate means to deliver our stockpile of atomic bombs on an enemy, efficiently and effectively knocking out his ability to launch or continue an offensive against this country, destroy as far as possible his industrial and economic potential for waging a war and retard to the maximum extent those forces he may be placing into operation in a land battle. The third task, which certainly cannot be relegated to a secondary position in winning a war, is to assure that our aircraft can obtain and maintain complete air supremacy over a field of battle and carry out without costly interference the important mission of supporting the ground troops of ourself and our allies in their mission of holding against numerically superior ground forces. The accomplishment of these three tasks, requires in turn the accomplishment of subsidiary missions or supporting services such as air transport, intelligence, and communications. The provision of

> superior aircraft and weapons to perform these tasks becomes even more important when we recognize the numerical superiority of our potential adversary.[6]

Project Evening Star was designed and executed precisely to meet the objectives Yates outlined. But by the time Yates was delivering his remarks to Congress, the project was already well underway. Unexplored in the committee hearing was the Strategic Air Command's philosophy under General LeMay's leadership that the United States didn't necessarily need to wait until the Soviets had fired the first shot in order to attack. LeMay believed that an atomic preemptive attack would be feasible and justifiable if it became clear that a Soviet invasion was imminent. Regardless of whether such a strike was preemptive or in response to a Soviet first blow, Project Evening Star bore all the hallmarks of elite Air Force units practicing for an American nuclear attack on the Soviet heartland.

On March 20, 1951, LeMay issued order No. 364 for key personnel to make preparatory trips ahead of the transatlantic Globemaster flight planned the next day. Citing Project Evening Star, he ordered Captain John P. Clark and Master Sergeant James S. Arrington to fly from Offutt to Wright-Patterson Air Force Base in Ohio, authorizing them to be granted a top secret security clearance. The same order dispatched Hopkins and Lieutenant Colonel Kenneth E. Marts from Offutt to Forbes Air Force Base in Kansas for a one-day trip regarding unspecified personnel matters. The same day, he issued order No. 366 dispatching Hopkins, Colonel Kenneth N. Gray, Lieutenant Colonel Edwin A. McKoy, and Major Gordon H. Stoddard to join Brigadier General Paul T. Cullen on a March 21 flight to South Ruislip, outside London, although the officers' actual destination was Mildenhall Royal Air Force Base, sixty miles to the northeast. The entire context of the two orders was Project Evening Star, though it was only mentioned specifically once.[7] Other references to the project simply used its code name, Operations Order 50-51.

The scheduling orders for Evening Star exercises were issued throughout the month of March 1951, but the actual execution dates weren't specified. Hopkins was listed as a pilot on some of those schedules even though he hadn't yet arrived. Evening Star exercises were underway—along with preparations for any potential Soviet sabotage or interference—when Globemaster 49-244 departed Limestone for the final leg of its journey toward Mildenhall.

The air combat simulations began with repeated secret overflights of British air bases so that navigators and other technical crew members could practice jamming British radar stations while utilizing a new diversionary technique called electronic countermeasures. Part of it involved releasing chaff, effectively metallic confetti, to confuse radar monitors on the ground as to the exact location of the "enemy" plane flying overhead.

This was the first step in a plan distributed to participating forces during the previous month "to fly a complete simulated combat mission of the current strike plans." The Soviet Union was not mentioned anywhere in the Air Force's 204-page report on the March training sessions. "This test was conducted in order to provide realistic training in order to determine the capabilities of the 509th Bomb Wing to perform combat missions as directed by the 8th AF Operations Order 50-51. Special emphasis was placed on compliance with all requirements of range, profile, weight, bombing altitude, composition, timing, and navigation. These plans included Special Weapons Loading, M107 drops, and Air to Air Refueling."[8]

The 509th Bomb Wing consisted of the 509th, 719th, 830th, and 393rd Bomb Squadrons—the exact units from which the passenger and crew list of Globemaster 49-244 was drawn. Although the 509th Bomb Wing had numerous weapons in its arsenal, its primary mission was managing the deployment of the atomic bomb under LeMay's Strategic Air Command. The M107 was the code name for the Mark 3 and Mark 4 Fat Man bombs used for practice in case the wing was ordered to launch a real strike. The M107 had the exact size, shape, and look of the atomic version. Its explosive contents were weighed to almost exactly match those of an atomic bomb in order to give loading crews, bombardiers, and pilots a feel for the real thing.[9]

Despite the high lethality of the payload in the Silverplate B-29s carrying Fat Man bombs, the March 1951 mission over Europe didn't appear on its face to be a high-risk exercise. The pilots were well practiced in maneuvering with their bombs and coupling at high altitudes with the KB-29 refueling planes. There was a slightly higher risk involved because an electronic countermeasures plane had to fly slightly in front of the bomber and about 500 feet higher in altitude, releasing chaff and radio jamming signals ahead of the bomb drop to confuse ground radar stations. So the Silverplate pilots and navigators not only had to coordinate high-altitude rendezvous with tanker planes but also with electronic countermeasures escorts.

During one of these procedures on March 9, 1951, something went wrong, and a B-29 from the 329th squadron disappeared in darkness about 41 miles southeast of Huércal de Almería, Spain, and 100 miles northeast of Oran, Algeria.

"This position was established during a VHF transmission with another aircraft flying the same course and mission at an altitude 400 feet lower" at 9:05 p.m. Greenwich Mean Time on March 9. "This was the last transmission from aircraft 45-21840.[10] The mission of the B-29 was not specified in Air Force reporting, but the plane was listed as a B-29MR, a designation that means it was modified according to the Silverplate format to carry a Fat Man payload.

There was no apparent radio transmission advising the accompanying plane of a problem, although strict radio protocols in effect at the time might have limited the pilot's ability to report whatever abnormality his plane was experiencing. It disappeared without a trace, and all subsequent efforts to locate survivors or wreckage were unsuccessful after forty-two sorties and more than 550 hours of combined flight time in the days that followed. All twelve aboard were believed to have been killed. "The entire search was negative with one hundred (100) percent of all search areas covered," an Air Force secret communique reported. The plane, according to records, was carrying an M107.

United Press International termed the plane as carrying out a "routine training flight."[11] The Associated Press labeled it a "navigational flight." As the Air Force was preparing to abandon the search, a "faint" SOS signal prompted a renewed, but unsuccessful, bid to locate possible survivors.

The disappearance was a stark reminder to all participants that the dangers were absolutely real. The 509th Bomb Wing announced that at least one future mission would include fighters from the Thirty-First Fighter Escort Wing, an element to these exercises that had not been announced for previous simulations. In other words, the Air Force believed it needed to protect the bombers from hostile actors.

Secret orders for the March 4, 7, and 9 mission listed flight assignments for 16 B-29MRs—that is, B-29s loaded with one Fat Man M107 each. The orders carried ominous language that hadn't appeared in previous mission instructions but that applied to future flights attached to the operation:

> Abort Procedures: In the event of an emergency at any point on the route wherein it becomes necessary to salvo the bomb, the Aircraft Commander will insure that he is at least ten (10) miles from any land. He will clear the area by radar, and visually if possible, before release. Bombs will not be returned to the bases, nor will they be carried over any landmass except as listed in [the pilots preassigned route]. In the event a bomb fails to release using all means available, the aircraft will be flown to a prescribed alternate airbase, avoiding densely populated areas.[12]

The fact that the M107 planes were ordered to avoid populated areas indicates that these were not concrete-filled practice bombs but something far more dangerous. The mission orders also carried a detailed list of all survival equipment aboard the planes, including exposure suits, parachutes, one-man life rafts, flotation vests, and "morphine syrettes." Next came radio frequencies that were monitored by cooperating countries, including Britain, France, the Netherlands, Portugal, Algeria, Tunisia, and Italy. Then came another stark security warning:

> Because of the probability of interception of all radio transmission it is essential that strict radio security and discipline be exercised. Radio transmissions must be limited to those prescribed herein and those consistent with the safety of personnel and aircraft. In no event will any transmission be made which would disclose the purpose of the mission.

Built into this mission, so that all air crews could get a feel for the dangers of an airborne confrontation with enemy planes, was a plan for various American and British jet fighters and propeller-driven planes to stage interceptions. Such simulated interceptions would occur "during all daylight hours," the orders specified. But that didn't mean uninvited foreign aircraft would necessarily stay away or not attempt to interfere. Because of that very real danger, the orders warned that "no Intelligence estimate of the situation will be assumed for this mission." That is, there could be no predicting how hostile forces might react upon encountering planes in a bombing formation in the skies over Europe and the Mediterranean. Crews were advised to write down:

a) Type, number, and identification of any strange aircraft approaching formation
b) Marine activity in target area.
c) Any sign of interference or jamming on Electronic and communications equipment.
d) What rumors were heard concerning this mission prior to take-off.
e) Were there any attempts made by unauthorized personnel to interrogate crew members prior to this mission.

Under the heading "Measures for Handling Potential Subversives," crews were advised to "seize suspected personnel," "get names of witnesses," and "notify the Bomb Squadron Commanding Officer and the Wing Intelligence Officer."

Importantly, pilots and crews associated with these ongoing missions in March 1951 were then given the most gruesome and dangerous tasks of all, beginning with, "Survival: In the event of 'ditching' in the North [Atlantic] or Mediterranean Sea, the approved ditching procedures will be followed."

SECURITY AND COUNTER-COMPROMISE MEASURES

a) In the event of forced landings or crash landing in neutral territory, the provisions of paragraphs 14d and 34 of Air Force Regulation 205-1 will be adhered to as follows:
    1) If an aircraft carrying classified matter is forced down, stranded or otherwise landed in unfriendly or neutral territory where capture appears immi-

nent, or in any other circumstances where it appears unlikely that any classified material can be properly protected, such material will be destroyed in any manner that will render recognition impossible, **preferably by burning.**

2) If the emergency occurs at sea and no better method of destruction can be found, the **classified material may be sunk** in the sea by the most practicable method.[13]

The descriptions of the wreckage strewn across the North Atlantic ditching site of 49-244 bear many of the fingerprints of the "Security and Counter-Compromise Measures" described in the Project Evening Star orders. Investigators were flummoxed in their attempts to explain why so much of the recovered pieces appeared charred at the same time the wreckage bore all the hallmarks of having been blasted to bits by an explosion. Under the orders in effect at the time, the passengers and crew, clearly having ditched in neutral or unfriendly territory, were under instructions to take assertive action to prevent classified material aboard from being compromised.

The entire flight, including its cargo and passengers, was classified. Survivors and parachute material were spotted north of the wreckage, which suggests that some might have bailed out before the plane hit the water. The lack of thorough burning of the wreckage indicates a fire started just before the plane hit the water, after which it was extinguished by the water itself. The extreme fragmentation of the wreckage suggests an explosion occurred shortly after the survivors bailed. The chemical components found in some pieces of wreckage, along with a tubular fragment that couldn't be traced to anything listed in the plane's equipment or cargo manifest, suggests that an explosive device was set to go off or that a hostile attacking force fired a device in an effort to force the plane down.

The survivors had a duty either way to ensure that the contents of their plane didn't fall into hostile hands "preferably by burning" or "sunk in the sea by the most practicable method."

The Air Force went to great lengths after the plane went down to conceal the linkage of the passengers and crew to a European nuclear mission under the auspices of the Strategic Air Command. They did everything in their power to convince reporters that this was nothing more than a routine transfer of personnel—much as reporters were led to believe that the disappearance of B-29 No. 45-21840 in the Mediterranean only a few days before was nothing but a routine training mission.

The last thing authorities wanted the public to know was that all these flights were part of exercises to simulate a nuclear attack on the Soviet Union, complete with Fat Man bombs whose targets were placed on flight routes to match the 1,504 air miles between Mildenhall and Moscow.

On March 24, 1951, a pilot Hopkins (no first name or rank was specified, although no other senior pilot in the SAC roster had that last name other than Lieutenant Colonel James Hopkins) was scheduled to fly one of those exact routes, according to the posted mission schedule. But he never made it.

Among additional procedures the pilots and crews were required to follow: "Each crew member will be armed in advance of 'station time.' In specialized briefing, all assigned Bomb Commanders, weaponeers and IFI operations will be briefed on Special Weapons procedures and instructions for advance base strike operations and on instructions for couriers of nuclear materials." For the security of this operation, there could be no assumptions that personnel aboard any flight or on the ground had authorization to be there.

"Bomb Commander will ascertain that SAC passes are in the possession of all personnel on his loading list. He will also have a roster showing clearance status of all personnel." The orders also made a sharp distinction between the sensitivity of the armaments procedures undertaken by the 393rd and 715th Bomb Squadrons. Support crews were entrusted with loading of the armaments aboard the planes flown by the 393rd and 715th. "Bomb Commander and IFI operator will be transported to a Bomb Control Point, be identified to the Bomb Monitor through SAC passes and access lists. The Bomb Commander signs for a M107 bomb."

The orders stated explicitly that "Bomb Commanders will insure that all aircraft **atomic equipment** is operational and that an FCT check is performed between M Day and M - 2," or Mission Day and two days prior.[14]

The above quotations (boldface added) are straight from the orders. They make clear the deadly serious nature of what was going on during the month of March 1951 involving American strike forces taking off from British bases. The bombs were simulated but there appears to have been some nuclear element to them. The words "nuclear" and "atomic" were never thrown about casually in military orders, simulation or not. The fact that all crew members were required to be armed during the mission meant there were dangers that extended beyond the simulation element. The fact that bomb commanders were required to check the SAC credentials of every member of the plane and loading crews meant the threat of infiltration or sabotage by spies was real.

The 393rd and 715th received orders, dated March 12, to launch simulated attacks on Navy warships *Indomitable* and *Swiftsure*, which were to be cruising the Mediterranean waters off Palma de Mallorca, Corsica, and Sicily. The code word for the attack aircraft was "Millpond," while the *Indomitable* was code-named "Parkin" and the *Swiftsure* "Laceman." Both ships were assigned to gauge the effectiveness of jamming techniques and report back to the "attacking" aircraft.[15]

Although pilots reported some frustrations with the amount of time it took for the *Indomitable* and *Swiftsure* to report back on the accuracy of the mock attacks, those frustrations were nowhere near as pronounced as they were during an early practice session involving the jamming of British radar stations outside London. Although the American side of the operation was planned and timed with precision, either there was a miscommunication with their British counterparts, or the Brits simply had turned their attention elsewhere.

The jamming operation took place as planned, but the British stations had neglected to turn on their radar that day. There was no way of gauging the effectiveness of the operation "so the mission was wasted for this portion. It has been recommended that better liaison between higher Headquarters and installations to be jammed be maintained, to prevent a recurrence of this situation."[16]

Even worse, from a standpoint of readiness, it meant the British couldn't be relied upon to alert the Americans of any incursions by potentially hostile aircraft because they didn't seem to appreciate the need for round-the-clock radar monitoring. Thus, if a Soviet MiG had penetrated British airspace en route to the North Atlantic, it's entirely possible no one would have noticed.

By the time Globemaster 49-244 diverted sharply from its scheduled route over the North Atlantic, it had switched away from communications with the control tower in Maine and was now relying on the very British controllers behind the lax, failed radar exercise.

Decades later, the United States would directly challenge their Russian counterparts about the presence of Soviet ships and submarines in the area where 49-244 went down. The orders for participants in Project Evening Star made clear that the dangers of hostile naval vessels and aircraft were real. That helps explain why the SAC issued orders for participants to note the "type, number and identification of any strange aircraft approaching formation," "marine activity in target area," and "any sign of interference or jamming on Electronic and communications equipment." Commanders already knew that the Soviets were actively monitoring and potentially interfering with the exercise.

The following is entirely speculative, as is much else regarding the plane's disappearance, but if the passengers and crew of 49-244 believed such dangers of capture existed, the standing orders attached to their mission were to scuttle the plane and ensure nothing of a classified nature remained for the enemy to capture. In the case of 49-244, everything about the flight was classified, including the passengers. There were no records of orders for the survivors to kill themselves if their capture were imminent, but they were absolutely required to scuttle their aircraft to prevent its contents from falling into hostile hands.

The presence of MiG jet fighters along the flight route could help explain why the plane diverted so sharply while maintaining radio silence. Or an intercepting plane could have used the exact type of jamming techniques that the Evening Star participants were practicing at that very time. The pilots might well have been screaming "Mayday" into their headsets, only for nothing but static being received on the other end.

In any event, the plane's orders again were explicit: "Because of the probability of interception of all radio transmission it is essential that strict radio security and discipline be exercised. Radio transmissions must be limited to those prescribed herein and those consistent with the safety of personnel and aircraft. In no event will any transmission be made which would disclose the purpose of the mission."

It is important to keep in perspective the overall context of Operation Evening Star and the Globemaster flight. Air Force commanders and the Truman administration wanted to sharpen the skills of Britain-based atomic attack forces by conducting repeated flights using M107s. But those practice bombs would have been of no use if suddenly faced with an actual Soviet invasion of Europe. Nothing could substitute for having fully operational components of the atomic bomb in place in Britain, ready to deploy at a moment's notice. Putting the real thing in place, ready for use, was the objective from the start. That was the intent expressed in the Commanders Conference of April 1950. Those components weren't going to magically appear at British bases all on their own. They had to be delivered, perhaps even smuggled, to ensure their presence remained secret. The use of M107 Fat Man shells would have helped disguise the arrival of the real thing.

Investigators trying to answer the many questions left behind in the minimal amounts of recoverable wreckage of 49-244 faced one of the most formidable obstacles of all: The highly classified nature of Project Evening Star prevented Air Force officers from discussing details of what they were doing in the skies over Europe. General LeMay uttered not a single word to reporters after suffering the worst single-plane air disaster in his command's history. He conveyed no explanations to the families of the lost airmen and officers. Certainly, the loss of a brigadier general and dozens of others purportedly on a "routine" personnel-transfer flight deserved some kind of statement from the man in charge. There are only two imaginable reasons why: Either LeMay was a heartless bastard who couldn't care less about the men charged with carrying out his orders, or he was constrained by the hyper-classified, very much nonroutine nature of the mission they were on.

The fact that LeMay went behind closed doors after the Globemaster's disappearance to discuss what happened, excluding the senior officer assigned to record his activities for his diary, suggests his priority was secrecy, not sympathy.

Tough as LeMay was, he was not a heartless bastard. Throughout his career, he was always insistent about never requiring his airmen and officers to undertake a mission that he wouldn't undertake himself. He had befriended and socialized with his subordinate officers, including Lieutenant Colonels McKoy and Hopkins.

> LeMay is often seen as the autocratic dictator who listens to no one, barks orders to scurrying subordinates, and enforces his decisions through intimidation or fear. This view epitomizes him as the iron fist on SAC's emblem: my way or no way. Historically though, this is not LeMay. While LeMay was a man of few words that often led to the autocratic assumption by many, he truly did care what his subordinates thought when they could present a valid and cogent argument to him about a better way to do things. Through this, he actively sought to mentor and develop them.[17]

Even among enlisted men, he took the time to help those who made individual requests to him. In July 1945, as the 509th Composite Group was in the final stages of preparing for the atomic attacks on Japan, an airman, Sergeant C. R. Hazelton, sent LeMay a handwritten letter recounting his previous service under LeMay's command in India and with the 49th Bomb Squadron. "I like your tactics," he wrote, asking for the then–major general's help getting a new assignment in one of LeMay's squadrons, adding, "Anything the Gen. can do for me to get me in his command will be appreciated."

The fact that the airman had reached out to such a senior general, skipping over numerous rungs in the command ladder, deeply impressed LeMay. The general wrote a three-paragraph response to Hazelton to say that LeMay had initiated the request and instructed Hazelton on next steps. "Your desire to return to combat duty is highly commendable and it is hoped that you will be back with us soon to carry the battle forward," LeMay responded.[18] His typewritten reply shows none of the formatting and initialing at the bottom that usually indicates a secretary or assistant handled it on LeMay's behalf, which means he might actually have typed it himself.

That hardly fits the profile of a heartless bastard.

In the case of 49-244, the need for secrecy trumped all other considerations. Once the British public knew of the American nuclear training exercises being conducted from their bases, in all likelihood, public outrage would have pressured Prime Minister Clement Attlee to shut the program down. Likewise, if the public in France, Spain, Italy, the Netherlands, Algeria, and Tunisia knew that Fat Man bombs were being transported in the airspace above their heads, public outrage would have put a quick stop to it. And even if Soviet spies had already alerted Moscow to the existence of these exercises, the public embarrassment of Fat Man bombs being waved under Joseph Stalin's nose might well have prompted a diplomatic crisis, if not a direct military confrontation. Given all the complexities, silence was the best possible option.

CHAPTER 22

She-Said, She-Said

MONTHS AFTER ALL THE PRESS ATTENTION, MINIMAL AS IT was, had died down and the Strategic Air Command seemed ready to breathe a sigh of relief that it had escaped greater scrutiny over the Globemaster tragedy, two embarrassing developments helped bring the tragedy back into the headlines. One involved the crash of yet another Globemaster on a secret flight to Alaska. Fortunately for LeMay, the press focus was less on flights and preparedness for an attack on Russia than it was on the dangers posed by continued reliance on a shaky, four-propeller plane with a growing reputation for deadly accidents. The Air Force had ways of using the Alaska crash to divert attention from the atomic aspect of cargo moving around the world and more toward Globemaster deficiencies.

The second embarrassment was one that caught the Air Force entirely unprepared. It was a scandal of gigantic proportions that threatened to besmirch the reputation of someone who had been, up to this point, treated in the news media as a national hero.

General Paul T. Cullen had featured in headlines around the world as the central personality worthy of focus because he was aboard 49-244 when it went down. By overwhelming reporters with background information and biographies of Cullen's pioneering past work in reconnaissance, the Strategic Air Command succeeded in diverting press attention from the more important, atomic mission of the transatlantic flight. Aerial photo reconnaissance was such a novelty and so complicated to explain, it was easy for the Air Force to make it appear as if the flight's mission was little more than a transfer of personnel with the highest-ranking individual aboard moving to a new role as a base commander with a past specialty in taking pictures from the air. Cullen was about as far away from an atomic focus as the SAC could get.

Once the nation's newspapers had published one or several of the voluminous profiles of Cullen supplied by the major wire services, there seemed little more to report about 49-244. The Globemaster's disappearance was history. Amazingly, no one in the news media tried to track down Cullen's family members to get deeper background information to spice up their stories. There were no feature-story openings describing a tearful wife sitting alone in the living room under a dim table lamp next to an ashtray full of smudged-out cigarette butts, flipping through photo albums in disbelief, reminiscing about how *he was just sitting here a few days ago. . . . Everything seemed fine. . . . He was planning to repair the door on our garden shed just as soon as he got home. . . .*

Then the story would carry the requisite transition to the grieving, lonely wife's worries about what would happen next. Would the Air Force take care of her? Would she be able to find a job? Maybe she had given up her own career prospects to play the traditional housewife role of that era. Or who knows, maybe children were in the offing, and now all of those plans for the future were scattered to the winds, not unlike the Globemaster wreckage itself.

Just a little bit more aggressive reporting by the news media could have turned up some great stories. When Captain Lawrence Rafferty climbed aboard the Globemaster in Roswell, for example, he had only recently been called from reserve status. His wife was eight months pregnant at the time. When the plane went down, she faced a future full of uncertainty with her daughter in tow and another child on the way. The baby, born seven weeks after his father's disappearance, wound up being named Larry in his father's honor.[1]

For all the attention paid to Cullen, no one in the news media appears to have made any attempts to track down Mrs. Paul T. Cullen. If they had, the scandal would have broken much sooner, once reporters discovered that two women laid claim to that title.

One was Ruth Gravett Cullen, the general's wife of sixteen years, who had nursed him to health after multiple plane crashes on his various missions. The other was Reva Joy Hurwitz Cullen, the much younger and more active former journalist who had been garnering mentions in the society columns of Louisiana newspapers for her involvement in the various activities of general-officer wives at Barksdale Air Force Base outside Shreveport.

The odd thing about the news media inattention to Reva was that she was very well known to the journalism community, especially at the national level and especially among the correspondents who covered atomic affairs. Recall that only five years earlier, she was the person chosen by the military and Marshall Islands Commodore Ben Wyatt to shepherd scores of newsmen around the base at Kwajalein and help arrange the interviews they needed to keep their editors happy and verify that they weren't wasting their time on beach volleyball and beer-drinking. The friendships Reva developed with some of those newsmen endured for years afterward, including her ongoing letter-writing relationship with William L. Laurence of *The New York Times*.

If anyone in the press corps should have been expected to exploit that resource and phone Reva in search for answers, or even just a good quote or two about what the tragedy meant to her, it would have been Bill Laurence. But he was hardly the only journalist with connections to Reva. She had established close friendships with correspondents from The Associated Press, NBC, *Stars and Stripes*, the Army News Service, Paramount (newsreels), and Mutual Broadcasting. Sam Green, a Paramount news photographer, had offered to take her around the Paramount studios in Hollywood once Operation Crossroads was finished. These were the types of people she established close and enduring ties with. The long nights drinking at the press club led to some deep and introspective conversations about personal conduct and what young people should aspire to later in life.

One such discussion occurred in mid-August 1946, with the older and wiser Bill Laurence apparently weighing in on his philosophies of life, relationships, dating, and adventure. Reva had mentioned it in a previous letter but decided perhaps she needed to clarify in a later one, dated August 19: "When i mentioned Bill Lawrence's [*sic*] philosophy, i didn't mean that either he or I though [thought] that one should live wantonly, or immorally for the remainder of life. Just that you shouldn't waste time. The discussion came up because Lawrence said he wanted to do a lot with the remaining years, spend each minute in a worth while fashion, work hard, see a lot of the world. [International News Service correspondent James L.] Kilgallen was disagreeing, saying to relax, ease up." Kilgallen enjoyed a distinguished journalism career working for The Associated Press and United Press International.

Their discussion of morals and adventure occurred right around the time Reva began encountering a man she referred to in letters as "my colonel." This wound up being the same man, Paul T. Cullen, who would disappear aboard Globemaster 49-244. Yet none of these journalists appeared to have been the least bit inquisitive when Reva's now-husband was all over the headlines, having disappeared in the middle of the Atlantic. It couldn't have been for lack of information about whatever happened to Reva. The letters in her archive made clear she had continued writing to her old friends from Kwajalein long after the journalists had gone home. But this was a story no one seemed to want to touch, perhaps out of respect for their old friend's privacy, or perhaps they sensed that this was a subject better left unreported.

Fewer than seven months after Cullen's plane went down, Reva's name began surfacing in newspaper stories across the country in the most unflattering of ways. Ruth Cullen discovered after all aboard 49-244 were officially pronounced dead that she would not qualify for military survivor's death benefits because another survivor was claiming the same benefit as the general's spouse.

A. Obie Stewart, one of Paul Cullen's old crew members from his World War II reconnaissance missions with Eliott Roosevelt, was now a prominent lawyer in Tampa, Florida. Ruth and Paul had apparently kept in touch with Stewart when Cullen was stationed at MacDill Air Force Base after the war. Stewart, like Ruth, had no reason to believe that anything had changed in the couple's marital status even as Paul's work-related travel required long absences away from home. When the military rejected Ruth's claim for death benefits, she contacted Stewart for lawyerly advice. Stewart investigated, and what he found prompted him to file a lawsuit on Ruth's behalf.

That's when the embarrassing headlines first started popping up across the country. The Associated Press reported from Dade City, Florida, on October 12, 1951: "Ruth G. Cullen, whose husband, Brig. Gen. Paul T. Cullen, was killed in a plane crash in March, charged in circuit court here he obtained a divorce from her without her knowledge and remarried. A. Obie Stewart of Tampa, her attorney, said there was no doubt of identification."[2]

Florida circuit court records have long since been destroyed, so there is no official record of Stewart's actual filing or subsequent testimony or court rulings in the case. Stewart's family and former law firm said they could find no records to explain how the case ultimately was resolved. Paul Cullen's military records were destroyed in a fire, so there's no record of any mention of his marital status or possible disciplinary action taken when questions arose before his death about his marital affairs. Reva Cullen's archives at the University of Wyoming offer only a few clues about any prior knowledge she might have had that he was committing adultery when he began romancing her in the Marshall Islands. But there is enough evidence from press accounts, personal letters, and official filings to make clear that Paul T. Cullen was a bigamist of the first order.

The lawsuit Stewart filed in Florida's Pasco County Circuit Court wound up in the hands of Judge Victor O. Wehle. There was nothing random or happenstance about Wehle's involvement. It turned out that, back in 1948, Paul Cullen had appeared before Wehle and presented documents asserting that he and Ruth had agreed to an uncontested divorce plea. Ruth was not present. Wehle apparently accepted the documents at face value as affirming that both parties wanted to end the marriage. So he granted a divorce.

Paul Cullen apparently had neglected to tell Wehle at the time that he was already married to another woman, Reva.

In October 1951, attorney Stewart appeared alongside Ruth Cullen to claim that she had never consented to the divorce, had not signed any such papers, and had had no idea that the marriage was dissolved until she attempted to file for survivors' benefits. The divorce Wehle had granted was obtained through fraud, Ruth Cullen charged in her filing.[3]

We'll get back to that, but the story gets even weirder. Much weirder. Recall that the romance between Reva Hurwitz and Paul Cullen began sometime in the summer of 1946 as he was overseeing the massive photographic project documenting every split second of the two atomic bomb explosions at the Bikini Atoll. After the atomic tests were finished, Cullen was ordered to return to the continental United States. He routed his return through San Francisco. Lo and behold, it just so happened that Reva's assignment in the South Pacific ended at that exact same time, and though the two briefly toyed with the idea of her flying to San Francisco on Cullen's military plane, they decided it wouldn't be a good idea. In fact, it would be illegal. So she took a commercial flight to San Francisco. Meeting her at the airport in a chauffeured Air Force staff car was then-Colonel Paul T. Cullen. Reva's letters home described how they took a long drive through the mountains west of the City by the Bay and took in other sights.

The letters home that were included in the University of Wyoming archives don't include any mention several months later of a trip to El Paso, Texas, followed by a trip across the border to Ciudad Juárez, Mexico. But the two unquestionably wound up there.

In the official records of the Estado de Chihuahua, across the border from El Paso, is an Acta de Matrimonio, number 007 2278, dated the 22nd of March, 1947. On that day, Civil Register Judge Raul Orozco recorded the marriage of Paul Thomas Cullen, age 45, to Reva Joy Hurwitz, age 28. The groom's profession was listed in Spanish as a pilot living in Washington, DC, which is exactly where Ruth Cullen was listed at the time as living with her husband, then-Colonel Paul T. Cullen.

On the Mexican marriage certificate, Hurwitz, the new bride, was listed as a journalist residing in Denver, Colorado. Cullen's marital status was listed as "divorced"—a lie—while Reva was listed as "single." The bride and groom listed the names and birthplaces of their parents, although Reva mysteriously listed her parents as having been born in Cripple Creek and Black Hawk, Colorado instead of their real birthplaces in Lithuania.[4]

So their marriage, an act of unquestionable bigamy on Paul Cullen's part, was recorded in an official document containing at least three lies. And the list of lies only grew from there.

Recall the May 12, 1947, letter from David Hurwitz, Reva's brother, reflecting the Hurwitz family's belief that Cullen had properly divorced his first wife. Despite the fact that they were married at that point, Reva moved back home to Laramie and lived with her parents. Paul had no doubt convinced Reva and her family that he was off on some important assignment, or that his current basing in Washington or Tampa wouldn't allow for spousal cohabitation. What it certainly wouldn't allow was base cohabitation by two wives.

Whatever the explanation, the arrangement enabled Cullen to carry on two marriages without either wife apparently knowing of the other's existence as a spouse. But the two wives knew of each other's existence as women of interest in Paul Cullen's life. Reva Cullen's niece, Carolyn Hurwitz, described her father, Reva's brother, as someone of exacting moral standards and conservative religious views. She said he had always been protective of his sister and would not have tolerated such a situation had he known that no divorce between Ruth and Paul had occurred.[5]

So now Cullen had embedded the divorce lie with Reva's family. Given the social mores at the time, the Hurwitzes almost certainly would have objected in the most strenuous terms had they known that Reva had married an adulterer and bigamist.

Buried in Reva Cullen's archives is a small collection of letters that she apparently found in Paul Cullen's belongings after he disappeared. Rather than return some of those items to their intended recipient—Ruth Cullen—Reva decided to hold on to them. One is a letter addressed to "Mrs. Paul T. Cullen," dated July 7, 1941. It was from Ruth's father, Joshua Gravett, a pastor at the Galilee Baptist Church in Denver. The address for Ruth was 1523 28th Street S.E., Washington, D.C. The couple moved there from their previous base at Lowry Field, in Denver, after Paul was promoted to lieutenant colonel and assigned to perform top secret reconnaissance missions over North Africa months before the United States had entered World War II. Other letters, dated in early to mid-1941, were addressed to Paul Cullen via the American Legation in Cairo, where he was based. Ruth remained a resident of Washington for the entire time he was deployed overseas and after he had returned.

That it was an empty marriage, bereft of love and passion, was readily apparent from the fact that Paul Cullen's eyes wandered and from remarks Ruth made after his death about the sad state of their marriage. Paul no doubt confided in Reva about his distance with Ruth. People who have extramarital love affairs don't tend to spend time with their lovers pining away about how passionate and loving their relationship was with the spouse back home. Perhaps Paul convinced Reva that the affair was morally okay since Ruth and Paul had not shared a bed in months, if not years. It was a marriage in name only.

But it was still a marriage under the law.

Reva sent letters to her many friends announcing that she was the new Mrs. Paul T. Cullen. She moved to Washington. On January 3, 1948, an old colleague from her Marshall Islands days, Bob Newburgh, sent a handwritten letter to Reva addressed to "Mrs. P.T. Cullen" at her new address, 2962 2nd Street S.E., in Washington, an apartment building just a block away from Bolling Air Force Base and a short distance up the Anacostia River from 1523 28th Street S.E., where Ruth was living. Newburgh wrote, "From the return on your card, guess I better send my heartfelt congratulations and best wishes to the bride and groom and my hopes that you are both very happy."

Another three months elapsed before Paul Cullen filed his first divorce papers in Judge Wehle's court in Tampa. In the lawsuit Ruth Cullen filed in October 1951, she alleged that Paul Cullen had resorted to "trickery and fraud" to obtain the divorce decree. "She said that she never learned about the divorce until after his death: that he never told her about it and continued to support her in their Washington, D.C. residence . . . even living there at times," *The Tampa Tribune* reported.[6]

Paul Cullen's dirty little secret was now front-page news in Florida. But not just anywhere in Florida. It was on the front page of the newspaper of record where MacDill Air Force Base, one of the largest bases in the country, was located. Generals, colonels, majors, and enlisted men were now learning from the local newspaper that one of the most celebrated figures in their most senior ranks was being accused in court of bigamy.

The message it sent to enlisted men was that their commanders were fallible and, perhaps, less deserving of airmen's awe and respect. For junior officers, it would have been a source for endless gossip. For senior officers, it had to be the source of harsh embarrassment. At Offutt, General LeMay and his team offered nothing but utter silence.

And there's no record of reporters anywhere, especially not among the LeMay-friendly staff of the *Omaha World-Herald*, that the question was even asked: How could LeMay entrust the command of the nation's first overseas nuclear attack force to a man who couldn't even demonstrate basic loyalty to his own wife, much less military law?

Once the *Tampa Times* published its first story on the subject, the wire services picked it up and ran with it. Within days, newspapers across the country and even some abroad were reporting on the scandal. As the story circulated, distortions were introduced that skewed the factual details of what actually happened. Some of the distortions were Ruth's fault because she testified that Paul Cullen had filed for divorce from her in Mexico. But in Mexico, there was no record of any divorce filing. It's not clear what led Ruth and her lawyer to allege that in court. It is possible she confused the record for Reva's marriage to Paul, written entirely in Spanish and much of it handwritten with flourishes in hard-to-read cursive, for a divorce filing and assumed the worst.

Either way, Ruth's court filing alleging a fraudulent Mexican divorce in 1947 followed by a fraudulent divorce filing before Judge Wehle in 1948 was what became part of the official record cited by reporters as the story circulated around the country in newspapers like the *Fort Worth Star-Telegram*, the Fort Collins *Coloradoan*, the *Billings Gazette* in Montana, and the *Kenosha News* in Wisconsin.

Much as LeMay and his staff probably wanted this story to die quickly, it simply wouldn't go away. After the first flurry of stories reporting the filing of the lawsuit, the next round involved the opening of the trial and witness testimony. For months, the wire services kept churning out the story of Paul Cullen's lies, deception, adultery, and bigamy. The trial never completely delved into what the general was telling his fellow officers about the state of his marriage, but it's clear from the context of testimony that he was not fully truthful with his commanders about what was going on.

If they had received the slightest hint that Cullen was involved in a bigamous relationship, they wouldn't have just been upset; they would have been obligated by military law to order his arrest and a court-martial.

One of the witnesses called to testify before Judge Wehle was Colonel Carl C. Hughes, who headed the photo reconnaissance unit before Cullen succeeded him. Hughes said he wrote to Cullen warning him to clean up his affairs and "straighten out the mess," according to press accounts.[7]

On the same day as that bombshell testimony on March 26, 1953—two years almost to the day after Paul Cullen disappeared—Ruth Cullen testified that her husband had continued to conduct his homelife with her as if everything were normal, offering not a single hint that he had filed for and been granted a divorce. She said she was tricked into signing a power of attorney, having been assured by her husband that it was a pro forma document.

Ruth Cullen said she had wanted to go grab her reading glasses before signing, but Paul assured her the glasses were unnecessary. The power of attorney was what he submitted to obtain the divorce, claiming he had legal authority to act on Ruth's behalf.[8] Wehle would later publicly state his regrets about not having scrutinized the situation more carefully.

Reva Cullen did not take the witness stand, according to press reports. Her nieces and nephew said that, for years afterward, she discussed all the details of her relationship with Paul and was obsessed with the circumstances of his death, yet she never told them about this ugly phase of courtrooms, lawsuits, and harsh public embarrassment.

The final stage of the trial, in which Wehle was supposed to render his verdict on Ruth's request to nullify the 1948 divorce decree, was recessed until the final week of April 1953 after Ruth reportedly came down with an unspecified illness. For some bizarre reason, all newspaper coverage of the case ceased at that point. There is no newspaper record nor available court document to indicate what Wehle's verdict was, although he appeared to express exasperation with the general's antics as the trial proceeded. His final words before recessing the trial were: "If General Cullen were alive, I certainly would like to talk to him."[9]

All official records of that case have been destroyed. But five months later, in a federal court in Wyoming, the Aetna Casualty & Surety Company had its own questions about who the real Mrs. Paul T. Cullen was. Aetna filed a lawsuit challenging Reva Cullen's claim as the beneficiary of an insurance policy Paul took out in 1937, naming only "Mrs. Paul T. Cullen" as the beneficiary. If the federal court recognized the 1948 divorce filing and Paul Cullen's marriage (either in Mexico or Baltimore) to Reva as legitimate, it would mean that she was, in fact, the rightful beneficiary. A properly divorced Ruth Cullen would have no legal right to call herself Mrs. Paul T. Cullen and, therefore, would have no legal claim to the life insurance policy.

Federal Judge T. Blake Kennedy examined the evidence and ruled that Reva Cullen had no legal claim to the insurance benefits. She was not recognized by the court as Mrs. Paul T. Cullen. Since Reva had already received a payment for the $5,000 benefit, Kennedy ordered her to reimburse Aetna—plus $545.25 in interest.[10] This ruling generated its own new round of press coverage around the country, extending the embarrassment not just for the Air Force but for Reva Cullen herself, who was trying to restart her journalism career and get on with her life.

The ruling was significant because it didn't matter whether the policy was taken out in 1937 or, say, 1947, when the couple wedded for the first time in Mexico. What mattered was the court's interpretation of Paul Cullen's legal actions to obtain a divorce, disestablish Ruth Cullen's status as his wife, and subsequently establish the basis for Reva Cullen to be legally recognized as "Mrs. Paul T. Cullen." The court didn't buy Reva Cullen's argument that Paul had taken the necessary steps under the law to qualify Reva as the sole claimant to the title of his wife. In fact, the court ruled that, as far as the policy was concerned, she had no claim at all to the title.

It was unclear whether the ruling established Ruth Cullen as the policy beneficiary, and there's no record, other than a single New York *Daily News* reference, to indicate that Ruth tried to cash in on the policy after Reva lost the case. But what is absolutely clear is that Paul Cullen married Reva without having taken the proper legal steps to divorce Ruth first. That made him a bigamist in the eyes of the law, and had he survived the final flight of 49-244, he almost certainly would have been subject to court-martial, demotion, and perhaps even imprisonment under military law.

This was the man General Curtis LeMay deemed to have the judgment, mental acuity, and leadership qualities suitable to take control of nuclear forces at the Strategic Air Command's first foreign base, in Britain.

This is the man who, if called upon, would launch an atomic attack against the Soviet Union.

The clues that something was badly wrong with Cullen's entire marital status should have been detected by an observant journalist at *The Tampa Tribune* in August 1951, only five months after his disappearance. *The Tampa Tribune*, like most local newspapers around the country, regularly sent a reporter to the courthouse to collect information about routine legal proceedings such as marriages, divorces, civil judgments, and lawsuits filed over the previous week. On August 19, 1951, the first listing for Pasco County under the sub-headline "Circuit Court Decrees" stated: "Paul T. Cullen vs. Ruth G. Cullen, divorce."[11]

Why would the newspaper be reporting a divorce decree five months *after* Paul T. had been declared dead by the Air Force? Why would the Pasco County Circuit Court only now be registering a divorce that supposedly had been granted by Judge Wehle three years earlier? Someone, somewhere was apparently attempting to establish a record either in anticipation of potential legal trouble ahead or, perhaps, was attempting to correct some judicial oversight. Maybe Wehle's paralegal had failed to record the 1948 divorce and was only now recording it for the record. It was just one of many anomalies in this case that probably will forever remain a mystery.

The press coverage of the Cullen scandal tended to ebb and flow with developments in the two court proceedings, all of which were embarrassing enough for the Pentagon. Perhaps the most embarrassing of all, however, was a two-page spread in the New York *Daily News* on November 30, 1952, under the headline: "The Generals' Wives Refuse to Fade Away." The headline was a play on the words "Old soldiers never die, they just fade away," uttered by General Douglas MacArthur after President Harry S. Truman fired him in 1951 for insubordination. The *Daily News* story highlighted the cases of two generals whose wives stood behind them throughout World War II, only to learn after the war that the generals were in love with other women.

The newspaper introduced its readers first to Mrs. Edna Hudelson of Los Angeles, whose husband, Major General Daniel Hudelson, returned from combat in Korea to dump his wife of twenty-eight years because he "wanted to marry a blonde widow." Back then, the term "blonde" in this context didn't merely connote hair color but also a Marilyn Monroe quality of voluptuous, temptational youth. The Hudelsons were parents of two children when the father was called back into active duty in 1950 to supervise the training of soldiers at Camp Cooke, California to fight in Korea. "Generals, particularly commanders, get lots more social life than corporals or privates. Hudelson was no exception. He met many attractive women, but blue-eyed Patricia Lemoge, wealthy, vivacious widow of an electrical contractor, was the only one to register," the newspaper reported.

Lemoge was forty and had a sixteen-year-old daughter. Edna Hudelson was forty-six. "The age disparity" between the two "was not enough to be a factor. But the widow apparently supplied something that the wife didn't." Lemoge traveled twice to Tokyo during the general's deployment to have a secret rendezvous with him. All seemed normal once the general returned in June 1952, and Edna had no reason to suspect anything was amiss. She went off to play bridge one night, and her husband handed their son a note asking him to tell her goodbye.

At least the general was up front and honest about the affair, his unhappiness in their marriage, and his desire to get a divorce. Then the *Daily News* article transitioned to the sad story of another general's wife, Ruth Gravett Cullen. This story was far more lengthy and sordid, and the reporter provided ample space for Ruth to tell her story in all its awful glory, along with photos of what the newspaper labeled "The Three Cullens." Reva also was given a chance to have her say. The result was a blow-by-blow, she-said, she-said account of how Paul T. Cullen, the hero general who dined with a president, wowed the Soviet dictator, and impressed the senior military brass with his aerial spying prowess, was a skunk when it came to marital loyalty. Ruth claimed to have been hoodwinked.

She told the *Daily News* that she and Paul had been together since he was a second lieutenant. "I rose up through the ranks with him, and he always gave me credit for his rise in the service. I prepared him for all his examinations in the service," Ruth told the *Daily News* reporter. They bounced around from one base assignment to another. They spent three years at Lowry Field in Denver before taking up residence in Southeast Washington, D.C., in 1941. That's when Cullen teamed up with Elliott Roosevelt and began heading out on long, secret missions overseas. She waited and waited and waited.

Paul Cullen's longest stretch at home came in 1943, after he was injured during the crash landing in St. Louis. She joined him at his boyhood home in Huntington Park, California and nursed him back to health. It couldn't have been an easy time, since Paul's entire career was put on hold, meaning he stood no chance of advancing in rank unless and until he returned to active duty. Others at his level were off fighting the war, gaining battlefield promotions, and, like Elliott Roosevelt, leapfrogging over him. He had to get back in the game quickly.

Ruth said that Paul assured her he was devoted to her, even to the point of naming his planes with reference to her, such as *Little Lady Love*, *Leading Lady*, and *Loafin' Lady*. This was years before Paul had met Reva, so there was no chance that the references were to the redheaded girl from Laramie. Ruth said she knew that wartime deployments often lead to flirtatious or romantic encounters, but she decided that whatever happened during the war needed to stay outside their home. *Don't ask, don't tell.* She quoted Paul as telling her reassuringly, "When I'm with you, darling, we will talk about nothing but ourselves, because I love only you."

After Operation Crossroads, he returned home for a brief stay. She went through his pockets to make sure they were empty before she sent his uniforms to the cleaners. In one pocket, he found *The Egg and I* letter—from Reva. At this point, either Ruth retold the story wrong or the reporter misstated the facts, because the *Daily News* account paraphrased Paul as explaining to Ruth that Reva was "the Red Cross girl" that he had met "during the war." (They met a year after the war had ended.)

Ruth didn't buy his story and took it upon herself to investigate. In January 1947, she found out Reva was in New York and arranged for the two to meet at a hotel where Ruth was staying. It was snowing so heavily outside, Ruth even offered to let Reva stay with her. "I really had a feeling of sympathy for her," Ruth told the *Daily News*. She and Paul had a happy marriage, Ruth told Reva. According to Ruth's narrative, Reva didn't respond. As far as Ruth was concerned, the case was closed: *He's my man. Go get your own.*

Two months later, unbeknownst to Ruth, Reva and Paul sneaked off to Mexico to be wedded. From then on, the *Daily News* reported, Paul carried on a marital relationship with both women, maintaining separate households and leading both women to believe theirs was a monogamous, man-and-wife relationship.

Paul received a new command and basing assignment at Barksdale Air Force Base. Reva took up residence there and slowly assumed the social life of a general's wife. Her name would occasionally pop up in the women's section of the local newspaper, either as Reva Cullen or Mrs. Paul T. Cullen. When Paul received word that he was to command the Strategic Air Command base at Mildenhall in the United Kingdom, Reva said she expected to follow behind and make that her new home.

"I have always lived with the General," she told the *Daily News*, "except when he was away on trips. He had been permanently assigned to England before his death and had arranged for the shipment of our furniture. It is inconceivable that he could have maintained two homes during the period of our marriage—as inconceivable as it would have been for him to do such a thing. I have ample proof that this first wife knew of our marriage," Reva told the reporter.

Even as both women cooperated with a reporter who promised to do nothing less than publicize their respective embarrassments over this sordid affair, both women complained to the reporter about the embarrassing publicity brought by the case. Reva was trying to get a new job with the Red Cross, and the coverage wasn't helping persuade prospective employers. Ruth said she had been saddled with all of the expenses of paying the bills for the home she kept in Washington with Paul, and now she was broke. With Paul's estate now in dispute, she had no possibility of using his assets to sustain her meager existence. "It's a matter of fraud as far as I am concerned—absolute fraud," she said.

Ruth claimed to have a substantial body of written evidence dating all the way to the week before his departure over the Atlantic that he still regarded her as his wife. They maintained a joint bank account. He kept up his membership at the Denver church where Ruth's father was the pastor. She said that Paul would insist to their friends that he was devoted to her and asked them to make sure she was taken care of in case anything happened to him, the *Daily News* reported. She received five letters from him the week before he departed for Britain. One letter "seemed to sense the impending tragedy." The final letter was dated only five days before the Atlantic disaster, and it "was definite," Ruth said, that Paul intended for her to "go to England."

It would seem, after Paul's wanton deception and betrayal, that Ruth would bear a significant grudge. But she spoke only in adoring terms. She forgave him for his obvious lapses of loyalty and spoke of their love as an eternal flame that could never be extinguished. Certainly not by a little Red Cross girl.

The final lines of the *Daily News* piece revealed something that no previous newspaper coverage of the court cases had specified: Ruth submitted her own claim to the Aetna insurance policy.[12]

The quest for a financial payout, like their love, was an eternal flame that could not be extinguished.

CHAPTER 23

Shooting the Messenger

THE FRONT-PAGE, TOP-HEADLINE TREATMENT THAT AMERICAN newspapers gave to the Globemaster's disappearance subsided with a level of uniformity that seemed uncharacteristic of America's supposedly aggressive, independent news media. Reporters everywhere have this internal trait—maybe even an obsession—with getting to the bottom of a story that has as many unanswered questions as this one did. Were reporters really that clueless when it came to LeMay's efforts to install atomic attack forces in Britain?

It's entirely possible that the news media was simply distracted by all the other big stories going on at the time: the Red Scare, the Rosenberg trials, the steadily unfolding story of British espionage on behalf of the Soviets, and, of course, the war in Korea. No news organization had the resources to hire a boat and send reporters to explore the waters 600 miles southwest of Ireland in search of clues to explain the Globemaster disaster. Which means the news media was almost entirely reliant on information provided by the U.S. military and, to a lesser extent, by British and Irish authorities.

Reporters for the two main American news agencies, The Associated Press and United Press, stuck close to the wording provided by their U.S. Air Force briefers. If those briefers stated that the plane ran into bad weather, that's what the news agencies reported. And since every major newspaper in the United States relied on those two agencies, including *The New York Times*, the words of U.S. Air Force briefers became the gospel of the day, regardless of how misleading it might have been. The briefers either lied outright or simply repeated what they were ordered to tell reporters. So, for the early days of the search, the American public was told that the plane diverted after encountering stormy weather over the North Atlantic.

Then the American public was told that there were no sightings of survivors. Then the public was told that maybe there were survivors, but the chances of survival were minimal because of storms, rough seas, and huge waves. The search itself was also supposedly hampered by those conditions. Not even slightly true. Weather posed no significant factor in the ability of search ships and planes to conduct their mission in the early days. But as far as the American public was concerned, the search for the Globemaster and any survivors was a lost cause.

The Air Force briefers also were careful not to divulge the mission of Globemaster. Reporters delved lightly into Cullen's background and focused mainly on what had been his new assignment as commander of the newly created Seventh Air Division. No American newspapers delved into the mission itself or the unmistakable trajectory of the Strategic Air Command to prepare for a potential full-scale nuclear attack on the Soviet Union.

Had an aggressive American press bothered to put these puzzle pieces together, the American public and Congress would have had ample cause to demand answers from the Truman administration. But those were different times. The American press, although distrusted and loathed by many generals during World War II, was largely compliant and complicit. Reporters wore military uniforms while covering the war. They submitted their stories for censorship, even after the war was over. *The New York Times* reporter who was aboard a support B-29 on the Nagasaki atomic bombing mission, Reva Hurwitz's friend William L. Laurence, actually turned out to be a paid shill for the very government and military he covered.[1] His exclusive story on the Nagasaki atomic explosion was republished in just about every major newspaper in the country, and those that didn't use his report relied on the Associated Press or United Press account of his reporting.

If anyone would have been plugged in with the commanders and other insiders who knew the true story behind Globemaster 49-244's mission, it would have been Laurence. Aside from his friendship with General Cullen's co-wife, he also knew General LeMay and the other top-level generals in charge of the mission. And yet Laurence stayed away from this story. When the chances of finding survivors dimmed with each passing day, American press interest died out commensurately. No one in the American press seemed to care or demand answers about why the Globemaster diverted so dramatically and ditched in the middle of nowhere. Perhaps the effect of so many plane disappearances during World War II and Korea had numbed the press corps to the significance of the big story staring right at them.

But the British and Irish press didn't have all of the competing stories that served to distract their American colleagues. For sure, they treated stories about the Rosenbergs and Korea with all the prominence they deserved, but the Globemaster story happened in their own backyard. They received the same briefings but were far less inclined to take the word of U.S. Air Force officials as the final answer, and they were far less vulnerable to the self-censorship pressures that appeared to tamp down American reporters' curiosity. British and Irish columnists felt far less restrained in delving into informed speculation about what was behind the Globemaster mystery. In the absence of aggressive reporting from their American colleagues, British and Irish reporters gladly accepted the challenge of putting the puzzle together as best they could.

In the *Daily Express* of London, air transportation reporter Hugh Dundas stated bluntly, "I say it was sabotage."[2] He noted the absence of a distress signal, which could have been activated automatically no matter how pressing any onboard emergency might have been. The French Communist newspaper *L'Humanité*, not typically among the top tier of breaking news organizations, garnered international coverage with its stunning report that the Globemaster "carried gear related to atomic warfare."[3] The sourcing of the French newspaper's report was vague. It cited reports from Shannon, Ireland, where the United States, Britain, and Ireland had established a staging ground for search activities. But given the newspaper's open affiliation with the Communist Party, the potential was elevated that its reporter had received the information from a Moscow-related informant. If so, how would Moscow have known, unless it had somehow gleaned the nature of the flight through espionage? While the French

Communist paper zeroed in quickly on the most obvious question related to this flight, the American news media didn't seem interested in delving too deeply or asking follow-up questions.

"The spokesman at the American air base at Shannon to whom this information was brought hasn't denied it," *L'Humanité* reported, according to United Press. "The American airplane and its passengers—have they been the victims of mysterious cargo?"[4]

Neither Dundas nor the French newspaper claimed to have any special access to inside sources to make their assertions. That's the difference between American and European styles of journalism, with U.S. reporters placing heavy emphasis on filtering out reporters' opinions and publishing only information that can be sourced or independently verified, or both. The European style allows journalists to look closely at the evidence or trajectory of events and decide for themselves, within certain limits, what the information appears to be saying. Dundas simply looked at the context of who was on the Globemaster flight, where it was heading, and the splintered remnants of wreckage to deduce that some form of sabotage was involved.

As for the French newspaper, it appeared to be echoing precisely what Moscow almost certainly already believed but wanted the rest of the world to understand: The United States was putting nuclear forces in place in Europe not out of fear of a Soviet invasion but because Communism was becoming too popular, and the powerful interests behind the capitalist system could not allow the masses to be empowered in alignment with the Soviets. The FBI and CIA had repeatedly linked reporting in *L'Humanité* with the Kremlin's point of view,[5] although the agencies had not explicitly stated that the newspaper served as the voice of Moscow in France. Nevertheless, it was extraordinary that a newspaper with no correspondent on the scene and no apparent access to any information to substantiate its claims felt confident enough to boldly assert an atomic connection to the Globemaster flight.

The Dundas and *L'Humanité* reports were enough to prompt deeper questioning by British and Irish reporters of what others suspected but were reluctant to ask. United Press quoted both the Dundas and French reports in short pieces that made it into print in various U.S. newspapers. But American editors either chose not to assign reporters to follow the story more closely, or their reporters tried but failed to unearth any information significant enough to make it into print. The result was that the American public and Congress had little reason to demand answers. The family members of the fifty-three victims were informed with form letters from the Air Force that the men were killed in a likely explosion. In their grief and amid the disruption of being cut off from a military paycheck and forced to vacate their military housing, few took the time to write their congressmen or the Air Force to demand a more thorough account of what caused the disaster. Even if they had, the entirety of the investigation's findings were classified at the time and remained so for decades to come, so they would have been told nothing additional.

The Dundas and French reports were published only two days after the Globemaster disappeared. On the third day, March 26, 1951, United Press quoted an unnamed U.S. Air Force spokesman as saying the possibility of sabotage could not be ruled out, but the source branded the *L'Humanité* report as "nonsense" and "absolutely false."[6]

Eight days after the plane disappeared, the search was officially abandoned. All the collected wreckage was sent back to the United States for analysis. The rescue staging site at Shannon was dismantled, and the newly created Seventh Air Force Division went about revising its command structure to fill the void left by the loss of its never-to-be commander, Cullen. The bulk of reporters covering the search moved on to other stories. The disaster didn't just fall off the front pages of American newspapers, it disappeared altogether. And that apparently suited the Pentagon just fine, even though the Air Force continued to vigorously pursue answers in secret.

Suddenly, on April 2, the Air Force announced it had resumed the search without stating a reason. Press Association, a British-Irish wire pool that drew from the reporting of various constituent newspapers, began quoting a "high American official" at Shannon Airport as stating:

> He believed the sudden revival of the search for the missing Globemaster was due to the fact that so far most of the material picked up suggested sabotage. He said that it would be necessary to get more conclusive evidence before this theory could be established finally. He also added that certain material had been picked up

> which would not be welcomed in the hands of an outside authority and that although there was no hope of picking up survivors at this stage, the search would go on until that patch of the Atlantic, 600 miles west of Ireland, was combed free of the smallest fragments of debris.[7]

The Press Association story made the rounds in scores of British and Irish daily newspapers, reprinted almost verbatim, with the word "sabotage" appearing prominently in most headlines. American newspapers then picked up the story in brief form deep on their inside pages, only to drop it shortly afterward without attempting independent follow-up.

Whatever the reason for the lack of attention from American newspaper editors, the Air Force command took the Press Association report very seriously. So seriously, in fact, that commanders launched a separate investigation to find out how the story originated—because it revealed the existence of an actual, nascent probe that was meant to stay highly classified.

On August 16, 1951, the Air Force Inspector General's Office of Special Investigations issued a memo, saying:

> Investigation reopened upon receipt of letter from Headquarters OSI, USAF, 6 July 1951, which set forth information that a Reuters News Agency report from Shannon, Ireland, dated 4 April 1951, quoted a high Air Force officer as stating that 'the wreckage found by USAF investigators indicated that the 80-ton troop carrier was destroyed by sabotage.' Public Information Officer, 3rd Air Division, received same information from the London Press Association on 3 April 1951. London Press Association declined to reveal source of allegation on grounds that such disclosure would violate journalistic ethics. Investigation conducted by Colonel OSWALD W. LUNDE Air Attache, U.S. Embassy, Dublin, Ireland, revealed that Mr. ARTHUR QUINLAN, reporter for the Irish Times, admitted that he had written the article. QUINLAN refused to divulge the name of individual from who he had allegedly received the information. American and Irish members of the Shannon staff are of the opinion that QUINLAN made up the story in order to make a headline. The Catering Comptroller at Shannon stated that there

> is not a single senior official at Shannon who has not been hurt at one time or another by QUINLAN's unscrupulous twisting of the news in order to make a headline.[8]

The memo added that all personnel associated with the rescue effort had departed Shannon by the time journalist Arthur Quinlan had filed his story, "However, he stated that his source had indicated that the individual from whom he heard this information was reliable. Mr. QUINLAN further stated that he did not know who the 'high American official' was but it was his opinion that it was someone in transit."

Quinlan refused a request by Colonel Lunde to provide the name of the source. At this point, the investigation of how this information made it into public view got sidetracked as Air Force officials turned to a concerted effort to besmirch Quinlan's reputation in every way they could. Lunde appeared to have led that effort. Paraphrasing Lunde, the inspector general's memo added: "Colonel LUNDE revealed to this office that through confidential discussions with American and Irish members of the Shannon staff, it was learned that Mr. QUINLAN is completely distrusted and despised by every member contacted. Not a single individual at Shannon with whom contacts were made had a good word for Mr. Quinlan." It concluded that no high American official made the statement "and that the press release in question was purely and simply a figment of Mr. Quinlan's imagination in order to sell a story."[9] The inspector general's report remained classified until December 9, 1954, a date so far removed from the accident that virtually everyone linked to the case had moved on.

There was just one problem: Quinlan's story was true and 100% accurate. The debris collected from the North Atlantic site did, in fact, suggest sabotage. The Air Force just didn't want to acknowledge it publicly because of the sensitivity of the matter. In hopes of quelling further inquiry, the Third Air Division headquarters issued a statement, saying: "Identity of the high American air official reported to have made a statement early today at Shannon Airport concerning the missing Globemaster is not known to Headquarters 3rd Air Division. However, his alleged statement does not represent the official opion [opinion] of this headquarters."

Any Air Force personnel who received additional queries were told to state: "An investigation is being conducted and until that has been completed it is not possible to speculate on what happened to the Globemaster."[10]

Quinlan was no hack. His story represented the kinds of responsible and aggressive journalism upheld by American as well as European standards. There was no speculation or conjecture. This was no figment of Quinlan's imagination. He quoted an American official as describing the nature of the debris and what the remnants suggested to investigators as to what happened on the Globemaster. His reporting also reflected that this was not a conclusion, nor was there any attempt to characterize the statement as a final answer. It simply presented that status as it was known at the time.

Attempts by government or military officials to undermine the reputation of a reporter very often are rooted in one of two motives: Either the person involved (possibly Lunde himself) was the source of the information and was trying to cover his tracks by attacking the reporter, or the person was under intense pressure from superiors who were demanding answers that could not be gleaned without forcing the reporter to give up his source. In this case, the result was that Quinlan's reputation was trashed for the crime of *accurately* reporting the existence of an ongoing sabotage investigation.

Whatever damage it might have caused to his career, Quinlan clearly recovered. If he was such an "unscrupulous," headline-hungry reporter, how was it that he managed to wrangle some of the most coveted interviews of any reporter in the world? In 1965, Quinlan was the only reporter to obtain an interview with Argentine Communist revolutionary Ernesto "Che" Guevara during a visit to Limerick.[11] Writing Quinlan's obituary in December 2012, *Irish Examiner* writer Jimmy Woulfe described him as a "master of executing international scoops."[12] Woulfe noted that Quinlan had also obtained rare interviews with Charles Lindbergh after the famed pilot's son was kidnapped and killed. After a source tipped Quinlan off that Air Force One would be stopping over at Shannon Airport after a presidential trip to the Middle East, Quinlan snagged a rare 4 a.m. interview with then-President George H. W. Bush as he perused the aisles of the airport's duty-free shop. In fact, Quinlan interviewed every president from Harry Truman to Bush. He also interviewed Soviet Foreign Minister Andrei Gromyko, among other global figures.

If Quinlan were a reporter to be avoided for his allegedly unscrupulous tactics, how was it that the U.S. president at the time of the Globemaster disappearance, Truman, would have been allowed by his handlers to be interviewed by the Irish reporter?

Quinlan would hardly be the last Irish headache for American investigators. A few weeks after Quinlan's report went out on the Reuters and Press Association wire services, an equally curious incident occurred in the coastal village of Tullybeg, Renvyle, County Galway, on Ireland's southwestern coast. On April 28, 1951, a local farmer, John Faherty, was walking along the beach when he came across a small, battered metal container, apparently a paint can, with its top sealed tight. The container was described as being flecked with rust and its paint slightly chipped. The can was nondescript, carrying no labeling to help identify where it came from. Faherty opened it and found a torn slip of paper inside. Written in blue-black ink, it read:

> *Cullen is worried. When 300 miles west of Ireland, Globemaster alters course for no apparent reason. We are going north. Have to be careful. We are under surveillance. Pieces of wreckage will be found but are not of the G-master. A terrible drama is being enacted on this liner.*

The message bore all the hallmarks of a badly constructed, sick hoax. The cursive writing was smooth, bearing none of the penmanship aberrations that certainly would have occurred on a bumpy Globemaster, even under the smoothest of flying conditions. The Globemaster didn't get its nickname "Old Shaky" for nothing. The author wrote out the first part of the message on one side, then flipped the paper over to finish it. The ink bleeds through one side onto the other.

The wording is neither the language an American would use, nor does it reflect the terminology any Air Force pilot, crew member, or passenger would have used under such circumstances. Military people did not then, nor do they now, refer to their aircraft as a "liner." Civilians unfamiliar with the terminology of air flight most certainly would have used such a word at the time. And for someone on the plane to know what Cullen's thoughts were as the plane was diverting from its scheduled course, that person would have had to be sitting alongside the brigadier general. The author would have had to be a fellow senior officer, meaning an experienced pilot who simply would not refer to any military plane as a "liner." The plane was more than 800 miles west of Ireland, not 300 miles. It did divert 300 miles off course, but it was nowhere near that close to the Irish coast. No informed person onboard would have mistaken the position by 500 miles. The writer penned the message cautiously—"Have to be careful"—as if whoever was surveilling the aircraft could see that he was writing something on a torn strip of paper—an absurdity on its face. The context doesn't make sense. Add to the absurdity the notion that a battered, empty paint can would be sitting around, within ready access, aboard a heavily inspected and meticulously maintained U.S. military aircraft.

The most preposterous aspect of the message comes in its closing lines. How could someone in-flight know that wreckage would be found on the surface—much less know that the wreckage would be found in a place other than where the Globemaster would be heading? Air Force personnel at the time did not refer to the cargo aircraft as a G-master. If they needed to abbreviate it for some reason, C-124 would do it. None of this "liner" stuff was in the Air Force vernacular of the time, nor is it today. But the British and Irish did have a habit of referring to passenger aircraft in the same terms they used for passenger ships, calling them liners.

Faherty nonetheless decided the message was important enough that he took it to the nearby town of Letterfrack and reported it to a police sergeant, Patrick Connelly. A police analysis prepared by Deputy Commissioner Garrett Brennan appeared to dismiss the message as a hoax, noting the firm handwriting and the careful wording. "The message bears no date, time, position by latitude or longtitude [*sic*], or signature, such as might be expected if written by a person with military or technical training," Brennan's analysis said. "The paper is quite dry and crisp, suggesting that it was not long in the container, in which it should have otherwise become damp from condensation caused by changes in temperature." Brennan, emphasizing his skepticism, launched inquiries to determine whether the paint may have been of local origin. He noted that news of the Globemaster's disappearance had received considerable attention in Irish and British newspapers, including prominent display of Cullen's name and photograph.[13]

Connelly traveled to Dublin on leave and used the trip to deliver Brennan's report to the U.S. Embassy Air Force Attaché, Colonel Lunde (the same Lunde who denounced journalist Quinlan). Lunde reportedly traveled to Renvyle and, accompanied by Connelly, interviewed Faherty.[14]

The Air Force Inspector General's Office took the note seriously enough to consult handwriting experts and interview suspects. Two particular individuals were of interest: Navy service member Oriento Anthony Buccigross and Captain William Richardson. Both had boarded the Globemaster at its point of origination in New Mexico but had disembarked when it stopped at Barksdale in Louisiana to pick up Cullen. Buccigross had been on assignment at a U.S. Air Force station in Alaska but was reassigned in August 1951 to a naval station in Seattle. Once tracked down in Seattle, he was ordered to provide a handwriting sample. He was discharged from service one week later and returned to his family home in Barberton, Ohio. It is unclear what became of Captain Richardson.

Under the "sabotage" heading, Special Agent John F. McDonnell wrote on February 21, 1952, from Westover Air Force Base in Massachusetts: "FBI Lab analysis concludes that handwritten note was not the handwriting of two submitted specimens. No definite conclusions reached on additional specimens since known writings were not in the working of questions text."

Even if the FBI couldn't determine the source of the mysterious note found in a can on an Irish beach, authorities still took it seriously enough to send agents on a mission to identify suspects and follow leads. The existence of an active sabotage investigation was undeniable, yet authorities did everything in their power to deny it publicly and destroy the reputation of the Irish reporter who accurately wrote about it. If the mission of 49-244 really was as they claimed—simple transfer of personnel from one or two American bases to a temporary base north of London—then why go to all of this trouble to hide the truth from the public?

The Globemaster flight was of far greater importance to national security than the Air Force wanted to admit. The passengers were joining an in-progress training session to evade radar, frustrate enemy fighter planes, refuel in midair, and drop Fat Man bombs on practice sites over the Mediterranean. Maintaining the secrecy of that mission was priority number one. Apparently, if some journalists had to be dragged through the mud to protect national security, so be it.

CHAPTER 24

Mourning Without Closure

THE HUMAN BRAIN IS REMARKABLE IN ITS ABILITY TO MAKE LOGical leaps and fill gaps in knowledge with assumptions that could or could not turn out to be accurate. We humans aren't suspicious by nature, but we become suspicious when presented repeatedly with examples of treachery, lies, or the deliberate withholding of information. When suspicion takes up residence in the brain, the search for information leads to conjecture. Conjecture establishes the foundation for assumptions to morph into what the brain interprets as "fact." And once the brain begins processing a series of conjecture-based "facts," voilà, a plot is born. Which plot was behind the John F. Kennedy assassination? Some choose the set of facts that lead to the conclusion that it was a CIA plot in retaliation for Kennedy's failure to support the Bay of Pigs invasion in Cuba. Or maybe it was the Mob. Then there was Lee Harvey Oswald's well-documented associations with the Soviet Union. Once the human brain ventures down these rabbit holes, the route back to daylight and sensibility becomes arduous, if not impossible.

While writing this book, I was recruited by ESPN as a senior investigative editor. One of my major projects was to reinvestigate the April 2004 death of former National Football League defensive back Pat Tillman, who walked away from a stellar career and lucrative contract to become an Army Ranger. He was killed in Afghanistan following the ambush of his platoon mates by enemy fighters. The Army initially portrayed Tillman's death as the result of a relentless enemy barrage in which Tillman died while heroically defending his fellow soldiers.

For thirty-five days, that was the story the Army told to the American people and Tillman's family. In fact, however, Tillman was killed by his own platoon mates. The cover-up of the truth sent Tillman's family, particularly his mother, Mary "Dannie" Tillman, down one of those rabbit holes. Hazy memories, incomplete stories, censored documents, and the hiding of the truth behind a wall of top secret classification led Dannie to make her own logical leaps. It didn't take long for her to conclude that her son's death was no accident. It was deliberate, she believed. The government ordered the assassination of her son to generate public support for the flagging war effort in Afghanistan and Iraq. Or perhaps it was because Pat Tillman had criticized the war in Iraq. For most of the next twenty years, she held on to those beliefs and wouldn't listen to anyone who tried to convince her otherwise. It consumed her to the point that friends started avoiding her. Family relationships weakened.

Dannie eventually found her way out of that rabbit hole and came back to the surface of reality. Yes, the Army had lied. Yes, the commanders whose orders set the platoon up for disaster escaped full accountability for decisions that led to Tillman's death.[1] But the bottom line is this: It was an accident, not a government conspiracy to assassinate her son and then cover up the truth. It took an independent investigation and analysis by Pete Blaber, a retired Special Operations lieutenant colonel, who sifted through and made sense of thousands of pages of documents that Dannie had collected, to bring Dannie around.

One thing Dannie Tillman had that the family members of the fifty-three aboard 49-244 never had was closure. She knew her son was dead and was never coming back. All the Globemaster families knew for certain was that their husbands, fathers, or brothers were missing and *presumed* dead. But there were life rafts! Survivors! They might have been captured by the Soviets and carried away to a gulag somewhere.

"You cannot mourn a POW/MIA," Charlotte Busch Mitnik told *Smithsonian* magazine in reference to the Cold War disappearance of her brother, Sam, in 1952. "What you do is you hope and you pray and you worry if they're well, and wonder if they are ever coming home."[2]

The absence of answers, the absence of closure, is what drives surviving family members to assume the worst. It takes them to the darkest places in their imaginations and dumps them there. A 1992 statement by then-President Boris Yeltsin acknowledging that some American airmen were shot down over Soviet airspace, captured, and imprisoned by Stalin during the Cold War[3] only affirmed what many of the 49-244 families already believed: Their loved ones might still be alive and languishing in a godforsaken gulag.

The 49-244 families had no one to help them sift through the documents and explain what really happened. For decades, there were no documents, and the only people capable of explaining it were the same people trying to keep it secret. The government kept so many details classified for so many decades that it became impossible to arrive at any definitive conclusions. Some documents connected to the Globemaster flight remain classified to this day, which in itself suggests that the government still has something to hide. The available documents lead in two divergent directions, one leading to the conclusion that the plane's disappearance was just a series of unfortunate events that led to a tragic accident, and the other suggesting that nefarious forces were at play.

Some members of the so-called survivor community—the surviving family members left behind—have made Olympic-quality leaps and bounds to conclude that the fifty-three crew and passengers all survived and were somehow captured by Soviet naval forces and whisked away to a gulag, where they have lived for the past seventy-five years. Such a conclusion is reached not because the overwhelming balance of information points to it, but because the *absence* of information has caused the believers' brains to fill in the gaps with misinformation, wild assumptions, and conjecture. They know that something strange happened on this flight, but they can't quite arrive at a consistent narrative that explains each of the anomalies. Some have latched on to a story of an explosion that supposedly occurred while the plane was still on course for an on-time U.K. arrival. They also cite a Mayday call allegedly received by the weather ship *Charlie*. The only problem is that none of the classified investigation records reflect any such report or Mayday call.

Keith Amsden said his brother's only job "was to move A-bombs from Point A to Point B." He acknowledged, however, having received no direct information from his brother or anyone else in the squadron that led him to make such a statement. Which is part of the problem with some of the relatives of the victims. They have spent years filling in gaps and guessing when they didn't have access to the full story. The truth is, Robert Amsden did as he was ordered and never discussed the classified parts of his missions, including the cargo of the planes he crewed. Just before the final flight to England, Keith asked Robert why he was going, and the immediate response was that he couldn't talk about it. "As far as I know, everything was classified up until the last night I saw him before he left. That's all he said to me: I'm going to England for seven days," Keith Amsden said.

Almost from the moment his family received news of the ditching, the speculation began about what forces were behind it. "My father said: That plane was sabotaged. And it turned out it was," Keith Amsden said. The U.S. Air Force letters of condolence, all containing identical wording except for the name of the addressee, listed the possibility of an explosion onboard as the cause of the disaster, even though the investigations didn't support any such firm conclusion.

"The form letters were full of lies. Lie after lie after lie," Keith Amsden recalled. At the time I interviewed him in 2024, he was ninety-three. When his brother, Robert, was working as a C-124 engineer, Keith also served at Roswell as a B-29 gunner. When the Globemaster ditched, he was a private first class, but he eventually reached the rank of master sergeant. Keith said he and Robert talked all the time, but whenever Keith tried to ask about Robert's missions, his brother said he couldn't talk about it. Even though the men's father suspected from the start that Russian sabotage had caused the disaster, Keith said he "didn't think anything about it" at the time. Over time, he adopted his father's suspicions and even went several steps beyond regarding the extent of Russian treachery.

Many family members concluded that the Russians were somehow involved, but no one was able to cite a plausible explanation of who, what, when, and how the Russians made it happen. The alleged Mayday call and explosion 300 miles north of where the plane ditched simply doesn't fit with the Russia-did-it scenario. Yet some of the family members still clung to this explanation. There has been infighting among some members of the survivor community. There have even been threats of lawsuits over claims by some that they own the documents that turned up in family members' searches of government and military archives. Government and military archives are public domain.

One of the people who became consumed with speculation was General Cullen's co-widow, Reva Joy Hurwitz Cullen. Unlike the others in the survivor community, however, Reva was someone with significant experience at the intersection of atomic weaponry and military operations. Her experience began before the end of World War II when the American Red Cross sent her to Hawaii to liaise with the U.S. military as it focused naval and air forces on bringing Japan into submission. After the war, she stayed in the South Pacific as a liaison for the Red Cross helping coordinate press coverage of the Operation Crossroads atomic tests. After the tests were finished, she married Cullen, leaving her own professional world to take on the ceremonial duties of a general's wife at Barksdale Air Force Base in Louisiana. If there was anyone outside his professional world whom Cullen would feel comfortable confiding in, it would have been Reva.

Her nieces, Carolyn and Barbara, and nephew Mike all provided consistent, independent descriptions of Cullen as being cocky to the point of reckless. Their father, Garvin, seemed to keep Cullen at arm's length, which they attributed to their difference in military rank. Garvin had been a lieutenant colonel in the Army, and Cullen apparently made clear upon meeting him where Garvin stood in the pecking order. Garvin often dismissed Cullen as a "flyboy," the children said. Cullen was likeable enough, but there was something about him that caused their father, Garvin, to keep his distance.

By Reva's own account in an interview with the New York *Daily News*, Cullen talked about his overseas mission to Britain. He talked enough, her nieces and nephew said, that she knew what the nature of the mission was. She knew enough to know that it involved members of the 509th Bomb Wing and that it was atomic in nature. The one thing that Reva could never understand, they said, was why the Air Force decided to send all of those key personnel together on a single flight.

"It's like the president and vice president. You don't put them on the same plane," Mike Hurwitz said.

Reva spent the years after Cullen's disappearance convinced that the Soviets were involved. She could never accept that he was dead, and since the Air Force never provided convincing explanations of how the survivors could be seen from a search plane, then disappear without a trace, Reva spent the rest of her life believing that Paul Cullen was still alive, her nieces and nephew said. She believed he was being held prisoner by the

Soviet Union. And partially because she believed he was still alive, Reva never remarried.

The lack of answers, added to her own knowledge of the flight and the top secret operations underway, convinced Reva that the government was covering up something big. She thought about it a lot, got herself worked up. Sometimes she would work herself into a frenzy, Mike Hurwitz said. She would get angry. She started drinking. Then came the Valium. Then combinations of the two. The more she talked about Paul and her theories about his imprisonment, the more her friends and family started drifting away. Those closest to her became convinced she needed professional help. Mike said there was an intervention in the late 1960s, and Reva was committed to a state hospital in Evanston, Wyoming. That's not a fact her family is proud of, and they were reluctant to share it for this book. In this context, however, it matters because it underscores the psychological effects the Globemaster incident had on those left behind. It drove some people crazy.

James K. "Jim" Hopkins, the son of Lieutenant Colonel James I. Hopkins, said he spent much of his childhood convinced his father was still alive. He traced that belief back to the arrival of an Easter card in the mail after the plane went down. Colonel Hopkins had popped it into the mail just before the plane departed right before Easter, but because of delivery delays, it didn't arrive until after the plane had disappeared. In the mind of a 10-year-old boy, however, such explanations didn't override the all-consuming hope that his dad had survived, that he was still out there, somewhere.

Keith Amsden, brother of flight engineer Robert Amsden and one of the only contemporaries of that generation still alive, said he believes his brother and all others aboard the plane are still alive and still languishing in a Russian gulag somewhere.

There's a vague, entirely unsubstantiated story circulating among the family members that the Globemaster victims were sighted at a Soviet prison in the years after the plane's disappearance. The story bears a resemblance to secret reports that made it all the way to Gerald Ford's White House by a former Soviet prisoner who heard from another prisoner that some American airmen were being held in the prison where he stayed. Ford's administration spent considerable resources investigating the rumor but determined that if the sightings were true, they would have involved the airmen aboard the Navy Privateer spy plane shot down by the Soviets off the coast of Lithuania in 1950. How Ford's White House made that determination is not clear. The entire investigation was canceled when it was determined that the source was not credible.

But it appears this story morphed over the years and was adopted as the survival affirmation among the family members of 49-244. In Keith Amsden's telling, the source of the story was a major in the U.S. military who was in a Soviet prison but was released, and he allegedly claimed to have talked to survivors of the Globemaster ditching. Not a single document has surfaced publicly to substantiate this story, and yet it has circulated as if true among the survivor community. Amsden said he only began looking into these issues around 2012, when other family members began communicating with each other. It was only the advent of the internet that allowed individuals in the survivor community to perform their own investigations and then begin tracking down others in the community to share notes.

It's not a story Reva Cullen would likely have heard because she didn't know the other family members or the person who claimed to have heard about the prisoners. It was Reva's own, independent analysis, based on her experience covering the military and having been co-married to the general onboard the flight who was being sent to command an atomic attack division in Britain, that led her to believe the same thing that other family members came to believe after decades of silence from the government. And yet, almost from the day the plane went down, Reva told the people around her that she believed the flight had an atomic component and that the Russians were behind the Globemaster's ditching.[4]

Some accounts, clearly immersed in conjecture and outright fiction, have circulated so widely in the news media that they have taken on a life of their own and are treated as fact merely because they've appeared so often in respected outlets. An unfounded narrative continues to circulate around the globe. A Russian website has now taken a fiction-tainted account and embellished it further, helping create such a haze of misinformation that the truth is no longer distinguishable from pure fantasy in many accounts.

One of the reasons I embarked on this book project was to correct the record and help restore the closest version of the truth I could find. But even this account involves some level of assumption and conjecture, properly labeled as such, to fill the gaps in the record.

The thing is, the mysteries of Globemaster 49-244 cannot be reconciled in the vacuum of assumptions about what happened. If the surviving passengers and crew had, in fact, been carted off to a Soviet gulag, for example, that opens up an entirely new set of questions that demand answers: To have had ships or submarines in the area to recover the survivors, the Soviets would have had to know in advance that the plane would be ditching in that exact spot of the Atlantic. How could they know something so specific unless, first of all, they had somehow forcibly guided the plane down to that spot—an overt act of war. And second, how could they know that this, of all American aircraft traversing the Atlantic in those days, was the plane worthy of their military efforts? To know who and/or what was aboard the Globemaster, the Soviets would have had to infiltrate the Strategic Air Command at a high enough level to have obtained the specific flight plan, passenger list, and cargo manifest of the plane. Who would that insider have been? Family members in interviews have been quick to focus their suspicions on Paul Cullen, but when pressed to explain how he might have been involved, they struggled for answers.

If a bomb went off during the flight, as some have speculated, the Globemaster's path afterward would have been unpredictable, thus negating the idea that Soviet ships were waiting at a specific ditching point to pick up and imprison survivors.

In the absence of those answers, some have filled the void with speculation portrayed as fact. That's dangerous not only because it becomes the source of misinformation but also because it plays with people's minds. People can be driven to irrational behavior that drives other people away.

For years after Reva Cullen was released from the state hospital in Evanston, she applied for various jobs in Utah, Colorado, Nevada, and Washington. The rejection letters in her archive mention nothing of her hospital stay, but it was clear that prospective employers felt some reason to keep her at arm's length. On October 17, 1972, Gerald Warner of the Utah Department of Employment Security, wrote a terse letter, stating, "On September 8, 1972, you quit your job with Utah Girl Scout Council because you weren't permitted to do the work for which you were employed. You also felt the employer had poor personnel practices. The situation was not so compelling as to leave you no alternative but to quit before you had other work to go to. You left work voluntarily without good cause." Warner wrote that he would deny the unemployment benefits she was seeking.

Days before that letter was sent, she received another letter from the Federation of Rocky Mountain States offering her $12,000 a year as a public information consultant. A pittance for someone with her level of professional experience. She had a meeting with an acquaintance at the University of Colorado News Service, but it yielded no job offer, only a letter from the friend urging her to keep in touch.

There came a point where Reva threatened a sexual discrimination lawsuit after one particularly blunt employment rejection letter arrived. She knew she was more than qualified for the job, yet the more she was rejected, the more bitter she became. The drinking resumed, Mike Hurwitz said. He traced her downward spiral back to the government's secrecy and stonewalling over Globemaster 49-244.

Although Reva didn't talk much with her family members about the ugly situation between her and Cullen's other wife, Ruth, it had to have weighed heavily in her thoughts. She lost one big federal court battle involving insurance benefits assigned to "Mrs. Paul T. Cullen." A separate court battle in Florida had generated national headlines that hardly cast Reva in a favorable light. But another question must have weighed in her mind: who Paul Cullen really was. The court cases had revealed a lot of information that Reva apparently hadn't known regarding Paul's duplicity and the fact that he had married her without the benefit of having divorced Ruth Cullen. He lied to her family. Did she really know the man she had married?

The Hurwitzes said she no doubt loved Paul to her dying day. But even so, knowing that a federal court had ruled she could not lay exclusive claim to the title of "Mrs. Paul T. Cullen" had to have added to Reva's anguish. Perhaps even worse would have been looking back on the trajectory of their relationship and the similarities of hers and Ruth's second-tier status. Paul Cullen had consigned Ruth to a life as a housewife, with no job and no career prospects of her own. She really had no identity other than as "Mrs. Paul T. Cullen." At the time of his disappearance, Reva was well on her way to having the same status as Ruth.

Looking back, from 1948 to 1951, instead of working as a journalist, interviewing generals, and witnessing nuclear test explosions, Reva's sole job was to be a general's wife, stuck attending garden parties and social gatherings with the other officers' wives at Barksdale. Newspaper photo captions no longer referred to her by her own name but rather as the general's wife. In April 1953, two years after Cullen's disappearance, Reva traveled to Washington, where she was hosted by Major and Mrs. William J. Lookadoo. The society page of the *Washington Evening Star* didn't even bother to publish Reva's name, referring to her only as Mrs. Paul T. Cullen of Laramie, Wyoming, who had been in town visiting her brother, Major David Hurwitz.[5] It was as if Reva's identity as an independent woman with her own professional aspirations had been erased by virtue of having married Paul Cullen.

In June 1948, she received a letter from an old friend from her Kwajalein days. He wrote that he was banging out the two-page, single-spaced letter to her while on a train between Seoul and Kwangju [Gwangju], asking how her newspaper and magazine career was going. Her response is unknown, but her journalism career at the time was in a deep sleep. She should have been on a train to some exotic city or on a ship bound for islands dotted by swaying palm trees. Instead, she sat at home, her identity now melded with that of Ruth, with both their first names now supplanted by that single word: "Mrs."

That said, Reva did score some major journalistic achievements after Paul Cullen's death, including a claim to being the first woman to break the sound barrier. The story, however, turned into something of a joke, as if the military were focused on what effect breaking the sound barrier would have on a woman's lipstick.[6]

Reva kept the "Mrs." title for the rest of her life. Eventually, she did find jobs in public relations and was able to get back into journalism, though hardly in the swashbuckling capacity of her younger years. The Hurwitz nieces and nephew said her strong belief that something nefarious had occurred on the Globemaster flight, and her inability to get answers no matter how good her military contacts were, only added to her frustrations and obsessions. She died on July 26, 1989, at age 73, never knowing about the others in the survivor community who were seeking the same answers, never knowing that the Air Force was slowly and quietly declassifying documents that would help her fill in the gaps. The one written attempt in her archives asking the Air Force for an official explanation of the Globemaster's disappearance yielded no new information or the slightest deviation from the misinformation-laden form condolence letters the Air Force had sent out back in 1951.

As for Ruth Cullen, she packed up her belongings in Washington and moved back to Denver to care for her aging father. She reengaged with the Galilee Baptist Church ministry founded by her father, Joshua Gravett, who died in 1956.[7] She remained there until her death in 1984. Aside from her lengthy interview with the New York *Daily News*, she stayed out of the headlines for the rest of her life.

The U.S. government has devoted significant resources to tracking down a wide variety of claims that American service members were spotted at this gulag or that prison in the Soviet Union since World War II. At least five volumes have been produced presenting the results of those inquiries.[8] To date, none have substantiated anything remotely associated with the Globemaster crew and passengers.

Close relatives by nature want to know more and more about what happened—or, more like, *how* could this have happened?—when a loved one dies. Some kind of innate tendency, sometimes even an obsession, surfaces to identify the root cause, perhaps to determine whether the death was preventable or to know whether the loved one suffered before dying. The push to assign blame and demand accountability becomes overwhelming.

An entirely separate Globemaster crash in November 1952 on the snow-covered slopes of Alaska led to the disappearance of fifty-one men. Weather conditions and a heavy snowpack made it almost impossible to locate the crash site, much less recover bodies. This was not an atomic mission, and there was no element of Soviet intrigue or sabotage to muddle the picture. The plane hit a mountainside in truly foul weather.

The family members wanted to know what had happened and whether there was any possibility that some of those onboard had survived. They just wanted to know something—anything—to fill the information gaps. The letters they wrote pleading for answers from one of the chief crash investigators, Dr. Terris Moore, prompted follow-up investigations that ultimately yielded the location of the crash site and recovery of clues. Those families' desperate search for answers is recounted in the 2015 book, *Letters from the Globemaster Families: The Lost C-124 of Mount Gannett, Alaska*.[9] I read the book in the faint hope that the author might have looked into the fate of Globemaster 49-244 (he did not), but reading it helped provide insights into the psychology of loss and the insatiable human demand for answers when a loved one disappears.

Seventeen years after the Globemaster incident, another military catastrophe occurred that again raised the specter of an act of war by the Soviet Union. The USS *Scorpion*, a Skipjack-class nuclear-powered submarine, sank on May 27, 1968, while on a secret mission surveilling a Soviet submarine in the middle Atlantic. All ninety-nine onboard were killed. Much speculation developed in the following decades that the Soviet sub had fired on the *Scorpion* after an American spy, John Anthony Walker, Jr., fed information to Moscow about the submarine's activities. Both governments deny such a confrontation occurred.

When the people who hold all the answers to what happened refuse to divulge what they know, that's where the logical leaps begin for the family members left behind: *Why are they hiding the truth? Who are they protecting?* Conspiracy theories start to sprout. If a misstatement of facts is discovered or, worse, someone is caught stating an outright lie, the conspiracy advances from theory to reality. Aha! They really are trying to hide something!

It appeared that some of the surviving family members of 49-244 were caught in that psychological loop, and it was almost entirely due to the government's refusal to release everything in its archives.

One of the family members who maintained a more dispassionate perspective on the case was Lawrence E. Rafferty, son of Captain Lawrence Rafferty, the passenger whose floating satchel full of documents provided the confirmation searchers needed that the wreckage was, in fact, that of 49-244. Larry the son was born May 12, 1951, six weeks after the plane went down. His mother opted not to affix "Jr." to his name since the father was no longer deemed to be alive.

Rafferty said he regarded Cullen as a prime target of suspicion, given his work with the Soviets in World War II and his marital duplicity. But he also noted the zeal with which General LeMay pursued the idea of attacking the Soviets before they could attack the West. One way of pushing the U.S. president to take aggressive action would be staging an overt act of war, such as downing a U.S. military plane with a general onboard, and blaming it on Moscow. Rafferty said he wouldn't put it past LeMay to have staged the entire Globemaster incident to create a pretext for war.

He said he believes that an incendiary device used by the CIA at the time was responsible for a fire onboard before the plane ditched. He did take seriously the note that was discovered on the beach in Ireland, believing that use of the word "liner" to refer to the C-124 was part of the vernacular at the time. He cited the fact that the military kept the existence of the note secret for decades as evidence that they were hiding something. Bolstering that conviction was the fact that some communications and documents from the ditching and subsequent search remained classified as of 2025.

In an encounter he had in Washington with officials of the Defense POW/MIA Accounting Agency, Rafferty questioned them about the early sightings of survivors by the B-29 overflying the ditching site. He quoted the officials as saying they knew nothing about it. They collected a DNA sample from him—something they do routinely when a prisoner of war/missing in action case remains unresolved. When officials of the agency got back to him several days later about potentially arranging a meeting to review documents, the officials said the meeting would be canceled because the Globemaster victims were not considered to be a POW/MIA case. He said the officials told him "there was no evidence of enemy action."

Rafferty said he responded, "No evidence of enemy action, and yet it was classified for sixty to sixty-five years? And we have language from the first boat on site saying that there was possible gunfire." Not to mention the fact that they were on a military mission, meaning they were "in action."

"They had orders. How can they not be somebody you're looking for?" Rafferty asked them. It was impossible to get posthumous medals awarded for the victims, and the process for obtaining a headstone placement for them at Arlington National Cemetery was beyond arduous.

Jim Hopkins said he had to devote years to obtain consent for a memorial ceremony at Arlington for his father. The Department of the Army administers such ceremonies. Hopkins also asked U.S. Senator Martin Heinrich of New Mexico to look into the official version of what happened in hopes of getting remaining documents declassified and clarifying the misinformation that accompanied the Air Force's explanation of the Globemaster's ditching. "What seems clear is that the Air Force version of the aircraft's disappearance in 1951 was a complete fabrication," Jim Hopkins wrote to the senator. "Of course, a robust skepticism is always necessary when coverups or conspiracies are being bruited about. Yet, the military's lies and obfuscations on the disappearance of the C-124 need to be revealed and the truth, if different from the 'official' version, be finally told."[10]

Heinrich's office failed to turn up new information, however.

Part of the problem Jim Hopkins had with placing a headstone for his father at Arlington was that an official marker had already been placed at a cemetery in Palestine, Texas, his father's hometown. The placement had to be officially canceled so that a new headstone could be placed in Arlington. Next came the question of how James Hopkins died and what would be the wording of his marker. Jim Hopkins ultimately obtained approval for the words "Cold War Lost at Sea" to be listed at the bottom of the headstone, which now sits near the top of a hill overlooking the cemetery facing eastward, as if facing the vast expanse of the Atlantic lapping at nearby Maryland's shores. But since death while serving in an official mission during the Cold War is not recognized as having been killed in war, no killed-in-action honors accompanied the ceremony. The recognition of Lieutenant Colonel Hopkins's service in World War II had to suffice.

On September 30, 2021, his family members walked behind a horse-drawn carriage bearing an empty coffin escorted by a full-honors military band and procession. A jet flown by a pilot of the 509th Bomb Wing, now based at Whiteman Air Force Base in Missouri, overflew the ceremony, which required the momentary suspension of flights to and from nearby Ronald Reagan Washington National Airport.

Reading a eulogy during the ceremony, an officer read an account pulled from the internet about the plane's ditching and aftermath. His account drew wry smiles from family members because it contained incorrect information that had circulated and recirculated as if it were fact. The Whiteman Air Force Base website account of the Hopkins ceremony also carried information drawn from the nongovernmental Bureau of Aircraft Accident Archives, which also had a misleading account of what happened, including a brash statement that all fifty-three aboard had survived.[11]

The context here underscores the danger when government withholds vital information or knowingly misleads the public in the aftermath of a mysterious event. Some family members of the victims go crazy as they string together amorphous bits and pieces of information, desperately trying to arrive at a narrative that will satisfy their understandable obsession with explaining what happened. Others turn into amateur sleuths, less interested in arriving at the truth as much as inventing a narrative that satisfies their need for an explanation. Journalists choose bits and pieces of these narratives to craft their own stories, misinterpreting the family members' confident assertions as fact, then reporting it and furthering the spread of misinformation. Then official sites, such as the Whiteman Air Force Base website, cite these supposedly authoritative sources as fact, and the loop is closed.[12] One person's made-up story all of a sudden becomes the official, government-certified version of what happened.

EPILOGUE

WITHOUT THE FULL RELEASE OF ALL AVAILABLE INFORMATION and documentation in the government's possession, it is impossible to state definitively how and why Globemaster 49-244 ditched and the survivors (as well as the dead) disappeared without a trace. I've tried to break this story down into an explanation based on the actors involved and what they were doing at the time to warrant scrutiny of their actions.

I break this down into means, motive, and opportunity. It's not good enough to blurt out that the Russians did it, and they had ships in the area to sweep up the survivors and whisk them away to a gulag, never to be seen again. Anyone making such a simplistic assertion needs to go to the extra steps of tracking down, and credibly verifying: Did the Russians have the means/capability to do such a thing? Did they have a motive? And how did the circumstances in the days, weeks, and months before the event create the opportunity for them to act?

The same criteria apply to General LeMay and his command staff. It's not good enough to blurt out that LeMay was sending nukes to Britain, and that's why the plane went down. Such an assertion requires an understanding of what preceded this mission: Did LeMay have the means—access to atomic weapons, an ability to transport them, and an ability to hide them if necessary from the SAC's British hosts? Did he have the necessary motive to do it? Did the opportunity present itself for LeMay to act at this specific moment?

The same questions apply to General Cullen: Means. Motive. Opportunity.

Let's start from before World War II ended. Cullen had the rare opportunity to serve as an aerial reconnaissance commander inside Russia.

He had direct and sustained contact with his Soviet military counterparts. He communicated with them his disgruntlement and frustrations about how his mission was being handled and mismanaged by his bosses (see Chapter 4). If ever there was a ripe moment for Cullen to be recruited to the other side, this was it. It was highly unprofessional of Cullen to talk the way he did to his Soviet counterparts, and it confirmed what others said about him that he was reckless, cocky, and talky. But that's not proof that he had become a spy. It just means he was someone worthy of far greater scrutiny than he received.

The same holds true of Cullen's reckless extramarital relationship and bigamy. He talked to both of his wives about his deployment to Britain, divulging top secret information. He apparently exchanged enough details with Reva Cullen to convince her from the day the Globemaster disappeared that the Soviets were involved and that atomic weaponry had been on the plane.

Did Cullen have the means to divulge top secret information that made its way to Soviet intelligence? Absolutely—even if he did it unwittingly through his characteristic recklessness. The Soviets didn't need to approach him directly. They might just have easily planted an acquaintance in the path of Ruth or Reva Cullen to strike up a conversation yielding the key information the spies needed. But keep in mind that Cullen received confirmation of his appointment to Britain only a few days before the flight. For the Soviets to be able to obtain that information and devise a plan on short notice to foil the deployment would have required extraordinary skills.

Did Cullen have the motive to divulge classified information? Yes and no. He certainly was disgruntled over the mission in Russia and the way Elliott Roosevelt was able to leapfrog over him in rank to steal the headlines. But in subsequent years, his rapid rise in the ranks and steadily escalating fame didn't follow the track of a disgruntled officer. Besides, Cullen wasn't an al-Qaeda suicide bomber. He would not have been likely to divulge information deliberately that was certain to prompt his own death. Did Cullen have the opportunity to make the ditching happen? Anyone possessing the top secret information Cullen had would have multiple opportunities, if so motivated, to arm the enemy with enough details to intercept the plane and bring it down. The question is whether Cullen had sufficient motive to do it. His record doesn't support it. But his record absolutely reflects a level of hubris and carelessness that could have compromised the mission and led to its downfall.

If not Cullen, then who? The other primary suspect should have been Kim Philby, the British superspy working for the Soviets from Washington at the time of the Globemaster ditching. Philby was a diplomat serving on a joint security committee that involved daily exchanges of top secret information with his American military and diplomatic counterparts. Since the Globemaster mission—along with Operation Evening Star and the deployment of M107 Fat Man bombs to Britain—required intricate coordination between the American and British government, Philby would have been ideally placed to participate in the discussions.

In spite of all of the discussions about atomic deployments and actual movements of M107s to Britain for use in the Evening Star exercises, there has only been a very strong hint that something of an atomic nature was aboard the Globemaster. No document has confirmed it. But it's important not to forget the presence of General Hunter Harris, Jr., performing inspections onboard the plane before 49-244 departed Walker Air Force Base. The former head of the U.S. Special Weapons Command simply had no business checking the tie-down cables of a KB-29 tank on a supposedly routine cargo flight. Harris had a motive for being there, and it is logical to conclude it was related to his work in atomic weaponry, not cargo tie-downs.

The investigation's focus on the discovery of radioactive materials that had washed up ashore in the Azores after the Globemaster ditching strongly suggested that something of a radioactive nature that wasn't on the official manifest had nevertheless been on the plane. Members of the 509th Bomb Wing had no business handling radioactive materials other than what they were trained to handle: the atomic core of a Fat Man.

What if the Russians did somehow obtain intelligence in advance that a flight was leaving the United States, bound for Britain, carrying the newly appointed SAC commander, plus an atomic attack force including a pilot who had flown on the Nagasaki mission? It would no doubt present the juiciest of scenarios for sabotage, interception, capture, or destruction.

Did the Russians have the means to obtain such intelligence in a timely enough fashion that they could scramble together a plan to meddle with the flight? Yes, if someone like Cullen or Philby with senior-level access to the information had conveyed it to a Russian spy with the ability to quickly utilize it. That's a lot of ifs. Did the Russians have the motive to obtain such intelligence? Absolutely. Getting it would have been their highest priority, because stopping the establishment of an SAC command in Britain and potentially intercepting a flight carrying atomic experts and weaponry was foremost on Stalin's mind. Opportunity? This was the moment for action, unquestionably.

But what about Russia's means to intercept or sabotage the Globemaster in midflight? Given the extremely short period of time that elapsed between the appointment of Cullen to command the SAC base in Britain and for the Globemaster flight to be organized, the Soviets would have needed to scramble like never before to process this intelligence, send it up the chain of command, then obtain approval for a plan designed to ensure the plane never reached its destination. The Russians had the technical means, yes, but could they pull it off that quickly? Not likely.

Planting a bomb onboard the plane would have brought it down quickly, but it wouldn't present an opportunity to capture the cargo or Cullen or the other experts onboard. But even if they obtained the intelligence about the flight only, say, two days before, they would have had the means to deploy ships and submarines to a specific area of the Atlantic. They had the means, using their own aerial-refueling capabilities, to send one or more MiG jet fighters to the North Atlantic to jam the Globemaster's communications and force it to divert. The MiGs could slowly force it to descend to a specific point, then ditch. At that point, the Soviet ships and submarines would be waiting.

Under such conditions—a nearly 300-mile southerly journey—the pilot and Cullen would have had the time to rig up an explosive charge in keeping with their standing orders to destroy their classified material or scuttle the plane in order to prevent its capture by the enemy. Those who survived the ditching would have had time to evacuate the plane and get a safe distance before it exploded and sank. No one can know what happened to the survivors. But one of the unfortunate aspects of the search operation was that, during the five times when evidence surfaced of survivors, broadcasts went out across the area to alert all ships, including a passenger ship and an American civilian airliner, to the geocoordinates of the sighting. If the Soviet ships were monitoring, they knew exactly where to go to hunt down the survivors and capture or kill them before any rescue vessels could arrive. Thus, no survivors, no bodies, no traces of those who had been aboard.

In 2016, delegations of the U.S.-Russia Joint Commission on POW/MIAs met at the Pentagon in Washington to exchange information and ask questions regarding unresolved cases from past wars, including the Cold War. At this meeting, Tim Shea, of the U.S. Defense Intelligence Agency, posed a pointed question to his Russian counterpart, General-Lieutenant Vasiliy S. Khristoforov, chief of the Department of Registration and Archival Funds of the Russian Federal Security Service. Shea described the times and dates of the final leg of the Globemaster's flight, along with the geocoordinates of its point of diversion and ditching site, along with other details. Then he stated:

> There were reports that Soviet submarines and surface ships were active in the area of the crash. The U.S. Side seeks access to relevant archival material located at the Russian Navy Archives in Gatchina which might shed light on the fate of this C-124 and its 53 passengers. Soviet Naval personnel almost certainly witnessed the aircraft crash and would most likely have recorded the event in their ships' logs. Any information found would help formulate a final and accurate explanation to the families as to the circumstances of loss of these 53 men.[1]

Khristoforov replied succinctly: "Send your request and we will look into it."

After several email exchanges, this author contacted Shea by phone in September 2019 about the wording of his query and what basis he had for details that never showed up in any investigation reports declassified since the plane's disappearance. He said the government had no information of its own regarding those details and cited uncorroborated information supplied by the surviving family members, who had pressured him to pose the question.

The Russians replied that they could find no information regarding Soviet vessels participating "in the search and rescue operations for the aircraft," Shea said in one email reply.

And that was the final word of what happened to Globemaster 49-244.

ACKNOWLEDGMENTS

THIS BOOK IS THE RESULT OF DISCUSSIONS OVER SEVERAL decades between my wife Catherine Hopkins, her father Jim, and me about the many ways a child's upbringing and entry into adulthood can be swayed by the tragic disappearance of a parent. In this case, the parent was Lieutenant Colonel James I. Hopkins, one of the most senior officers and the most experienced atomic pilot aboard Globemaster 49-244. For many years, the story of his disappearance was simple to explain because there was only one known version, supplied by the Air Force, that dismissed the entire affair as an unsurvivable midair explosion that killed all aboard instantly. End of discussion.

Surviving family members had no choice but to accept that version and move on with their lives. Wives remarried, which meant children had to adapt to a new man in the house. The hero fathers who died in service to their country were replaced by men of far lower stature and character. No one can know how lives would have turned out if the surviving family members had been told the truth from the start. But it is a certainty that lives were inextricably altered by this tragedy and cover-up.

Sometime around 2010, documents began circulating that suggested there was more—much more—to the story of 49-244. It is unfortunate that documents telling the real story of this episode were somehow mixed in with fictitious narratives that caused some surviving family members to adopt a horribly skewed version of events. And they adhere to those skewed versions with the convictions of true believers. Perhaps this book will change some minds or answer some lingering questions for them. They deserved better than what their government gave them.

Special thanks go out to Barbara, Carolyn, and Mike Hurwitz for the hours they spent recalling details of the adventurous life of their aunt, Reva Joy Hurwitz Cullen.

The American Heritage Center Archives at the University of Wyoming in Laramie was also indispensable in providing access to years' worth of letters, memos, and memorabilia that helped explain Reva's early romance with Paul T. Cullen and troubled life after his disappearance.

I also owe a debt of gratitude to Larry Rafferty and Keith Amsden for their patience as I tried to jog their families' memories of emotions and reactions from so many decades ago.

Researchers at the Library of Congress helped me locate obscure files and sift through mountains of documents as I searched for leads and clues.

Tammy Horton at the Air Force Historical Research Agency also provided invaluable help locating some of the more obscure files cited in this book, including some that don't appear on public listings.

Longtime friend and reporting collaborator Cathleen Farrell generously provided food and lodging during my stay outside Washington for Library of Congress research.

Tish Durkin (aka Combat Tish from our early days covering the Iraq War) provided editing expertise and enormous help with contact information for my research in Ireland.

In Dublin, Aaron Clayton donated his time to locate and copy documents related to the mysterious message found in a paint can in Renvyle. The image of the message is reproduced with the kind permission of the director of the National Archives of Ireland.

Irish journalist and documentary producer Pavel Barter provided invaluable counsel and help in the early stages of research as we both pursued answers and independently concluded that the disappearance of Globemaster 49-244 might remain an unsolved mystery despite our best efforts to come up with answers. Pavel provided an important sounding board as I sought to compare notes and confirm or dispel many of the legends that have surfaced about this mystery. He also drew much-needed attention to the injustice suffered by journalist Arthur Quinlan for the crime of accurately reporting the existence of an investigation into sabotage aboard 49-244.

Nick Waligorski's careful drafting skills converted my mangled collection of latitude-longitude geocoordinates into the far more intelligible maps that adorn these pages.

In St. Louis, journalist Paul Waldman provided invaluable advice in the earliest stages that helped shape the current narrative.

The wonderful reporters and editors at ESPN provided encouragement and inspiration through their exemplary long-form journalistic exploits. I'm particularly grateful to Mike Drago, Chris Buckle, Elaine Teng, Laura Purtell, John Mastroberardino, Willie Weinbaum, Jena Janovy, and Rayna Banks for the many ways, big and small, that they encouraged perseverance and made every effort to accommodate my quirky work schedule so I could complete this project.

Gregg Jones, celebrated author as well as my former roommate during the early days of the Afghanistan War in 2001, shared hundreds of documents from his own research into the 509th Composite Group for his book *Most Honorable Son*. Gregg provided essential guidance and made crucial introductions for me in the publishing world.

Our mutual literary agent, Andrew Stuart, and editorial consultant Paul Starobin were the ones who gently coaxed me into converting my first attempt at a historical fiction novel into this nonfiction product.

James Abbate, my editor at Kensington Publishing, served as one of my most energetic cheerleaders after I submitted my manuscript and nervously awaited feedback. Special thanks to copy editor Sheila Higgins for her meticulous attention to detail and to production editor Stephen Smith.

BIBLIOGRAPHY

BOOKS AND PRINT ARTICLES

Abella, Alex. *Soldiers of Reason: The Rand Corporation*. Houghton Mifflin Harcourt, New York, 2008.

Albertson, Trevor. *Winning Armageddon: Curtis LeMay and Strategic Air Command, 1948-1957.* Naval Institute Press, Annapolis, Maryland, 2019.

Albertson, Trevor D. "Ready for the Worst: Preemption, Prevention and American Nuclear Policy." *Air Power History* 62, no. 1 (2015), 30–39.

Alexander, Frederick C. *History of Sandia Corporation Through Fiscal Year 1963*. Sandia National Laboratories, New Mexico, 1963.

American Heritage Center Archives. "Reva Joy Hurwitz Cullen Papers, 1940-1979." University of Wyoming, Laramie, OCLC: 981528725.

Andrew, Christopher, and Vasili Mitrohkhin. *The Sword and the Shield: The Mitrokhin Archive and the Secret History of the KGB*. Basic Books, New York, 1999.

Axelrod, Alan. *The Real History of the Cold War: A New Look at the Past*. Sterling Publishing Co., New York, 2009.

Baggott, Jim. *The First War of Physics: The Secret History of the Atom Bomb 1939-1949*. Pegasus Books, New York, 2011.

Bird, Kai, and Martin J. Sherwin. *American Prometheus: The Triumph and Tragedy of J. Robert Oppenheimer.* Vintage Books, 2005.

Blight, James G., and David A. Welch. *On the Brink: Americans and Soviets Reexamine the Cuban Missile Crisis*. The Noonday Press, New York, 1989.

Blum, Howard. *In the Enemy's House: The Secret Saga of the FBI Agent and the Code Breaker Who Caught the Russian Spies*. HarperCollins, New York, 2018.

Boyne, Walter J. *Beyond the Wild Blue: A History of the U.S. Air Force 1947-1997.* St. Martin's Press, New York, 1997.

Campbell, Duncan. *The Unsinkable Aircraft Carrier: American Military Power in Britain*. Palladin Grafton Books, London, 1986.

Campbell, Richard H. *The Silverplate Bombers: A History and Registry of the Enola Gay and Other B-29s Configured to Carry Atomic Bombs*. McFarland & Company, Jefferson, North Carolina, 2005.

Carllton III, Paul K. *General Curtis E. LeMay on Leadership and Command*. School of Advanced Air and Space Studies, Air University, Maxwell Air Force Base, Alabama, 2010.

Conversino, Mark J. *Fighting With the Soviets: The Failure of Operation Frantic 1944-1945*. University of Kansas Press, Lawrence, Kansas, 1997.

Dando, L. S. *Report of Investigation*. U.S. Chemical Corps Engineering Agency, Edgewood Chemical Center, Edgewood, Maryland, Jan. 8, 1952.

Davenport-Hines, Richard. *Enemies Within: Communists, the Cambridge Spies and the Making of Modern Britain*. William Collins, London, 2018.

Department of the Air Force Historical Research Agency. "History of the 7th Air Division, March 1951." IRIS Number 00459200, Ref. N0824, Reel 10527.

———. IRIS Number 00465460 Ref. P0609, Reel 11372.

———. "History of the 509th Bomb Wing." IRIS number 459200, Reel N0824.

———. Strategic Air Command. "Appendix II to History of 7th Air Division, 20 March – 30 December 1951, United Kingdom." IRIS Number 00425681, Ref. P0390, Reel 11137.

———. Directorate of Flight Safety Research, Norton Air Force Base. "Aircraft Accidents for 1951, Major." IRIS Number 877715, Reel 46768.

———. "Frantic History." IRIS Ref. B5122, Reel 7217.

———. Untitled documents related to Operation Frantic, IRIS Ref. B5131, Reel 7226.

"Department of Defense Appropriations for 1952: Hearings Before a Subcommittee of the Committee on Appropriations, House of Representatives, Eighty-second Congress, First Session." U.S. Government Printing Office, Washington, D.C., 1951.

Dingman, Roger. "Atomic Diplomacy During the Korean War." *International Security*, The MIT Press, vol. 13, no. 3 (Winter 1988–1989), 50–91.

Divine, Robert A. *Since 1945: Politics and Diplomacy in Recent American History*. John Wiley & Sons, 1975.

Duke, Simon. *US Defence Bases in the United Kingdom: A Matter for Joint Decision?* The Macmillan Press Ltd., U.K., 1987.

Earley, Pete. *Comrade J: The Untold Secrets of Russia's Master Spy in America After the End of the Cold War*. Berkley, New York, 2007.

Farell, Don A. *Atomic Bomb Island*. Stackpole Books, Guilford, Connecticut, 2019.

Federal Bureau of Investigation. "Underground Soviet Espionage Organization [NKVD] in Agencies of the US Government." Oct. 21, 1946.

Feklisov, Alexander, and Sergei Kostin. *The Man Behind the Rosenbergs*. Enigma Books, New York, 2004.

Fried, Richard M. *Nightmare in Red: The McCarthy Era in Perspective*. Oxford University Press, New York, 1990.

Friedman, Norman. *The Fifty Year War: Conflict and Strategy in the Cold War*. Naval Institute Press, Annapolis, Maryland, 2000.

Gladwell, Malcolm. *The Bomber Mafia*. Little Brown, New York, 2021.

Hansen, Chris. *Enfant Terrible: The Times and Schemes of General Elliott Roosevelt*. Able Baker Press, Tucson, Arizona, 2012.

Hansen, Chuck. *U.S. Nuclear Weapons: The Secret History*. Orion Books, New York, 1988.

Harder, Robert O. *The Three Musketeers of the Army Air Forces*. Naval Institute Press, Annapolis, Maryland, 2015.

Haynes, John Earl, and Harvey Klehr. *Venona: Decoding Soviet Espionage in America*. Yale University Press, New Haven, Connecticut, 1999.

Haynes, John Earl, Harvey Klehr, and Alexander Vassiliev. *Spies: The Rise and Fall of the KGB in America*. Yale University Press, New Haven, Connecticut, 2009.

Herken, Gregg. *The Georgetown Set: Friends and Rivals in Cold War Washington*. Alfred A. Knopf, New York, 2014.

Hoffman, David. *The Billion Dollar Spy*. Doubleday, New York, 2015.

Hopkins, James K. *Into the Heart of the Fire: The British in the Spanish Civil War*. Stanford University Press, Stanford, California, 1998.

Hornfischer, James D. *Who Can Hold the Sea: The U.S. Navy in the Cold War 1945-1960*. Bantam Books, New York, 2022.

Humes, James. *The Wit & Wisdom of Winston Churchill*. HarperCollins, New York, 1994.

Infield, Glenn B. *The Poltava Affair: A Russian Warning: An American Tragedy*. Macmillan, New York, 1973.

Jacobsen, Annie. *Area 51: An Uncensored History of America's Top Secret Military Base*. Back Bay Books, New York, 2012.

Jones, Gregg. *Most Honorable Son: A Forgotten Hero's Fight Against Fascism and Hate During World War II*. Citadel, New York, 2024.

Kauffman, Christopher J. *Faith and Fraternalism: The History of the Knights of Columbus, 1882-1982*. Harper & Row, 1982.

Keeney, L. Douglas. *15 Minutes: General Curtis LeMay and the Countdown to Nuclear Annihilation*. St. Martin's Press, New York, 2011.

Kegley, Carles W., Jr., and Eugene R. Witkopf, eds. *The Nuclear Reader: Strategy, Weapons, War*. St. Martin's Press, New York, 1985.

Khlevniuk, Oleg V. *Stalin: New Biography of a Dictator*. Yale University Press, New Haven and London, 2015.

Kozak, Warren. *LeMay: The Life and Wars of General Curtis LeMay*. Regnery History, Washington, D.C., 2009.

Krauss, Robert, and Amelia Krauss, eds. *The 509th Remembered*. 509th Press, Buchanan, Michigan, 2005.

Kuter, L. S., Army Air Forces deputy chief of air staff. "Memorandum for Major General D.D. Eisenhower." Library of Congress Manuscript Division. Container 146, May 5, 1943.

LeMay, Curtis E., and MacKinlay Kantor. *Mission With LeMay*. Doubleday & Company, Garden City, New York, 1965.

Library of Congress. Manuscript Division. "The Papers of Henry H. Arnold." Container 146, May 5, 1943.

Library of Congress. Manuscript Reading Room, Papers of Curtis E. LeMay, Box B-195 (B-3111).

———. Box 11.

Lomas, Daniel W. B. *Intelligence Security and the Attlee Governments, 1945-51*. Manchester University Press, Manchester, U.K., 2017.

Macintyre, Ben. *A Spy Among Friends: Kim Philby and the Great Betrayal*. Bloomsbury, London, 2015.

Meilinger, Phillip S. *Bomber: The Formation and Early Years of Strategic Air Command*. Air University Press, Air Force Research Institute, Maxwell Air Force Base, Alabama, 2012.

Morgan, Ted. *Reds: McCarthyism in Twentieth-Century America*. Random House, New York, 2003.

Moss, Norman. *Klaus Fuchs: The Man Who Stole the Atom Bomb*. Sharpe Books, United Kingdom, 2018.

National Defense Research Committee, Office of Scientific Research and Development. "Fire Warfare: Incendiaries and Flame Throwers," 1946.

Nelson, Craig. *The Age of Radiance: The Epic Rise and Dramatic Fall of the Atomic Era*. Scribner, New York, 2014.

Newhouse, John. *War and Peace in the Nuclear Age*. Vantage Books, New York, 1988.

Office of Air Force History. *Strategic Air Warfare: An Interview with Generals Curtis E. LeMay, Leon W. Johnson, David A. Burchinal, and Jack J. Catton*. U.S. Air Force, Washington D.C., 1988.

Offley, Ed. *Scorpion Down: Sunk by the Soviets, Buried by the Pentagon: The Untold Story of the USS Scorpion*. Basic Books, New York, 2008.

Olsen, Margaret Hook. *Patriarch of the Rockies: The Life Story of Joshua Gravett*. Golden Bell Press, Denver, 1960.

O'Toole, Michael. *Cleared for Disaster*. Mercier Press, Cork, Ireland, 2006.

Parrish, Michael. *Soviet Espionage and the Cold War*. Oxford University Press, New York, 2001.

Payne, Robert. *The Rise and Fall of Stalin*. Simon & Schuster, New York, 1965.

Persico, Joseph E. *Roosevelt's Centurions: FDR and the Commanders He Led to Victory in World War II*. Random House, New York, 2013.

Philby, Kim. *My Silent War*. Grove Press, New York, 1968.

Pietrusza, David. *1948: Harry Truman's Improbable Victory and the Year That Transformed America*. Union Square Press, New York, 2011.

Polenberg, Richard. *War and Society: The United States, 1941-1945*. J.B. Lippincott, Philadelphia, 1972.

Prados, John. *The Soviet Estimate: U.S. Intelligence Analysis and Soviet Strategic Forces*. Princeton University Press, Princeton, New Jersey, 1986.

Reardon, Steven L. *History of the Office of the Secretary of Defense: The Formative Years, 1947-1950*. U.S. Department of Defense, Washington, D.C., 1984.

Records of the Joint Chiefs of Staff, Modern Military Records Branch. "Brief of Joint Outline Emergency War Plan (OFFTACKLE)." National Archives, Washington, D.C., May 26, 1949.

Reed, Craig W. *Red November: Inside the Secret U.S.-Soviet Submarine War*. William Morrow, 2010.

Remnick, David. *Lenin's Tomb: The Last Days of the Soviet Empire*. Vantage Books, New York, 1993.

Ricks, Thomas E. *The Generals: American Military Command from World War II to Today*. Penguin, New York, 2012.

Rocereta, Michael. *Letters from the Globemaster Families*. iUniverse, Bloomington, Indiana, 2015.

Roosevelt, Elliott. *As He Saw It*, 1st ed. Duell, Sloan and Pearce, New York, 1946.

Rosenberg, David Alan. "The Origins of Overkill: Nuclear Weapons and American Strategy, 1945-1960." *International Security*, vol. 7, no. 4 (1983), 3–71.

Ross, Steven T. *American War Plans 1945-1950*. Garland, New York, 1988.

Schlosser, Eric. *Command and Control: Nuclear Weapons, the Damascus Accident, and the Illusion of Safety*. Penguin, New York, 2013.

Schmuhl, Robert. *Mr. Churchill in the White House: The Untold Story of a Prime Minister and Two Presidents*. New York, 2024.

Shakespeare, Christian. *Kim Philby: Our Man in Moscow*. Self-published, 2015.

Sheinkin, Steve. *Bomb*. Flash Point, New York, 2012.

Smith, Michael. *The Anatomy of a Traitor: A History of Espionage and Betrayal*. Aurum Press, London, 1982.

Soldatov, Andrei, and Irina Borogan. *The Compatriots*. Public Affairs, New York, 2019.

Sparrow, James T. *Warfare State: World War II Americans and the Age of Big Government*. Oxford University Press, New York, 2011.

Tibbets, Paul W. *Return of the Enola Gay*. Mid Coast Marketing, Columbus, Ohio, 1988.

Truman, Harry S. *Two Years of Trial and Hope, 1947-1949*. Doubleday & Company, New York, 1956.

Unger, Debi, Irwin Unger, and Stanley Hirshson. *George Marshall: A Biography*. HarperCollins, New York, 2014.

U.S. Air Force. *The Airman's Handbook: A Ready Reference of Helpful Information and Counsel for All Airmen of the United States Air Force*, 7th ed. The Military Service Publishing Company, Harrisburg, Pennsylvania, 1955.

U.S. Department of Defense, Defense Threat Reduction Agency. "Defense's Nuclear Agency, 1945-1997." U.S. Government Printing Office, Washington, D.C., 2002.

U.S. National Archives. "Memorandum From President Harry S. Truman to Secretary of State James Byrnes." NAID: 294549769, Apr. 5, 1946.

Wallace, Robert, H. Keith Melton, and Henry Robert Schlesinger. *Spycraft: The Secret History of the CIA's Spytechs From Communism to Al-Qaeda*. Dutton, New York, 2008.

Weiner, Tim. *Legacy of Ashes: The History of the CIA*. Doubleday, New York, 2007.

Weisgall, Jonathan M. *Operation: Crossroads: The Atomic Tests at Bikini Atoll*. Naval Institute Press, Annapolis, Maryland, 1994.

Wellerstein, Alex. *Restricted Data: The History of Nuclear Secrecy in the United States*. University of Chicago Press, 2021.

Westoby, Adam. *The Evolution of Communism*. The Free Press, New York, 1989.

Woods, Randall B. *Shadow Warrior: The Life of William Egan Colby*. Basic Books, New York, 2013.

Yust, Walter, editor. *1951 Britannica Book of the Year*. Encyclopaedia Britannica, Chicago, 1951.

ONLINE

Abrahamson, James L. "The Sandia Pioneers." *American Diplomacy* (June 2002). https://americandiplomacy.web.unc.edu/2002/06/the-sandia-pioneers.

Albertson, Trevor D. "Ready for the Worst: Pre-emption, Prevention and American Nuclear Policy." *Air Power History* 62, no. 1 (2015), 30–39. https://www.afhistory.org/airpowerhistory/Air_Power_History_2015_spring.pdf.

Alexander, Frederick C., Jr. "History of Sandia Corporation Through Fiscal Year 1963." Defense Technical Information Center, December 1, 1963. https://ntrl.ntis.gov/NTRL/.

Allen, Michael E. "The Gulag Study." Joint Commission Support Directorate Defense POW/Missing Personnel Office, 2005. https://www.dpaa.mil/Portals/85/Documents/USRJC/The_Gulag_Study_5th_Ed.pdf.

Atomic Archive. "The Atomic Bombings of Hiroshima and Nagasaki." https://www.atomicarchive.com/resources/documents/med/med_chp10.html.

BBC.com. "Soviet Expansion into Eastern Europe, 1945-1948." https://www.bbc.co.uk/bitesize/guides/zt8ncwx/revision/5.

Bolger, Daniel P. "Reluctant Allies: The United States Army Air Force and the Soviet Voemno Vozdushnie Sily 1941-1945." University of Chicago, Jan. 1985. apps.dtic.mil/sti/pdfs/ADA169037.pdf.

Broad, William J. "How a Star Times Reporter Got Paid by Government Agencies He Covered." *The New York Times*, Aug. 9, 2021. https://www.nytimes.com/2021/08/09/science/william-laurence-new-york-times.html.

Casteel, Burton A., Jr. "SpetsNaz: A Soviet Sabotage Threat." U.S. Air Force Air Command and Staff College, Air University, Maxwell Air Force Base, Apr. 1986. https://apps.dtic.mil/sti/tr/pdf/ADA168375.pdf.

Churchill Archive. "CHUR 2/28/126." https://www.churchillarchive.com/catalogue-item?docid=CHUR2_28_126.

CIA Memorandum. "Soviet Use of Assassination and Kidnaping," Feb. 1964. https://www.cia.gov/readingroom/docs/CIA-RDP78T03194A000400010014-6.pdf.

Cornelius, George. "Air Reconnaissance—Great Silent Weapon," U.S. Naval Institute Proceedings, July 1959. https://www.usni.org/magazines/proceedings/1959/july.

Deaile, Melvin G. "The SAC Mentality: The Origins of Strategic Air Command's Organizational Culture." *Air & Space Power Journal* (Mar.–Apr. 2015), 48–73. https://www.airuniversity.af.edu/Portals/10/ASPJ/journals/Volume-29_Issue-2/F-Deaile.pdf.

Dean, A., and Jean M. Larsen. Yellowstone Park Collection, vol. 24–27, *Annals of Wyoming*, Brigham Young University. https://archive.org/stream/annalsofwyoming2427wyom/annalsofwyoming2427wyom_djvu.txt.

Dingman, Roger. "Strategic Planning and the Policy Process: American Plans for War in East Asia, 1945-1950." *Naval War College Review*, vol. 32, no. 7 (1979), Article 3. https://digital-commons.usnwc.edu/cgi/viewcontent.cgi?article=5542&context=nwc-review.

Edmondson, Catie. "A Reporter's Journey into How the U.S. Funded the Bomb." *The New York Times*, Jan. 17, 2024. https://www.nytimes.com/2024/01/17/us/politics/atomic-bomb-secret-funding-congress.html.

George, Alexander L. "Intelligence Value of Soviet Notes on Air Incidents 1950-1953." U.S. Air Force Project RAND Research Memorandum, Oct. 15, 1954. https://www.secretsdeclassified.af.mil/Portals/67/documents/RM1348%20Intelligence%20Value%20of%20Soviet%20Notes%20on%20Air%20Incidents%201950-1953.pdf?ver=2018-02-01-090339-050.

George, Alexander L. "Soviet Reactions to Border Flights and Overflights in Peacetime." U.S. Air Force Project RAND Research Memorandum, Oct. 15, 1954. https://www.rand.org/content/dam/rand/pubs/research_memoranda/2014/RM1346.pdf.

George Washington University National Security Archive. "Central Intelligence Group: Revised Soviet Tactics in International Affairs." Central Intelligence Agency, Jan. 6, 1947. https://nsarchive.gwu.edu/document/30007-78-central-intelligence-group-office-reports-and-estimate-ore-11-revised-soviet.

George Washington University National Security Archive. "Commanders Conference." Ramey Air Force Base, Puerto Rico, Apr. 25–27, 1950. https://nsarchive2.gwu.edu/nukevault/special/doc03a.pdf.

George Washington University National Security Archive. "Defence Policy and Global Strategy." Pentagon Conference, July 31, 1952. https://nsarchive2.gwu.edu/nukevault/special/doc04.pdf.

George Washington University National Security Archive. "Letter from George C. Kenney to Hoyt Vandenberg." April 29, 1950. https://nsarchive2.gwu.edu/nukevault/special/doc03d.pdf.

George Washington University National Security Archive. "SAC Historical Study No. 61, The Strategic Air Command, A Chronological History 1946-1956." Historical Division of the Office of Information, SAC Headquarters, undated. https://nsarchive.gwu.edu/document/21077-doc-4-thestrategicaircommandchron-48-56-p-207-ff-berlin-crisis.

Georgetown University National Security Archive. "Report of the Manager Santa Fe Operations U.S. Atomic Energy Commission." July 1950–Jan. 1954. https://nsarchive2.gwu.edu/nukevault/ebb507/docs/doc%207%20%2054.01.01%20Santa%20Fe%20Ops%20report.pdf.

Gerald R. Ford Presidential Library. Correspondence related to the disappearance of Navy PBY off the Lithuanian coast. https://www.fordlibrarymuseum.gov/sites/default/files/pdf_documents/library/document/0019/4520652.pdf.

Glenshaw, Paul. "Secret Casualties of the Cold War." *Smithsonian*, September 2017. https://www.smithsonianmag.com/air-space-magazine/secret-casualties-of-the-cold-war-180967122.

Global Security. "Weapon Storage Sites / Q Area." https://www.globalsecurity.org/wmd/facility/q_area-intro.htm#google_vignette.

Hansard, the official transcript of Parliament. Feb. 15, 1951. https://hansard.parliament.uk/Commons/1951-02-15/debates/fa7dd4bf-63ef-419a-82b1-73a914c6e263/Defence(GovernmentPolicy).

Hewlett, Richard G., with Francis Duncan, and Oscar E. Anderson, Jr. "Atomic Shield: A History of the United States Atomic Energy Commission, Vol. II, 1947-1952." University of California Press, Berkeley, 1990. https://archive.org/details/atomicshield-19470000hewl/page/473/mode/1up?q=mildenhall.

"History of the Office of the Secretary of Defense. Volume 1. The Formative Years, 1947 1950." Defense Technical Information Center, U.S. Department of Defense. https://apps.dtic.mil/sti/pdfs/ADA150543.pdf.

Holloway, Don. "Bombs Away" LeMay: America's Unapologetic Champion of Waging Total War." HistoryNet, 2022. https://www.historynet.com/bombs-away-lemay-americas-unapologetic-champion-of-waging-total-war.

Joint Chiefs of Staff. "Possible Employment of Atomic Bombs in Korea." Nov. 20, 1950. https://archive.org/details/PossibleEmploymentOfAtomicBombsInKorea.

Khan, Stephen. "'Atomic Plague: How the UK Press Reported Hiroshima." *The Conversation*, Aug. 6, 2020. https://theconversation.com/atomic-plague-how-the-uk-press-reported-hiroshima-144081.

Lomas, Daniel W. B. *Intelligence Security and the Attlee Governments 1945-1951*. https://www.academia.edu/56118198.

"Memorandum for the Secretary: U.S. Public Opinion on the Berlin Situation." National Archives, Harry S. Truman Library and Museum, July 29, 1948. www.trumanlibrary.gov.

Military Hall of Honor. "Col. Thomas J. Classen." 2021. https://militaryhallofhonor.com/honoree-record.php?id=312409.

Nuclear Compendium. "Nuclear Companion: A Nuclear Weapons History Hobby Showcase." MK3 section. https://nukecompendium.com/weapons/mk3/.

Office of the Assistant to the Secretary of Defense (Atomic Energy). "History of the Custody and Deployment of Nuclear Weapons, July 1945 through September 1977." Feb. 1978. https://nsarchive2.gwu.edu/news/19991020/history-of-custody.pdf.

Office of Strategic Services. "Simple Sabotage Field Manual." Washington, D.C., Jan. 17, 1944. https://www.cia.gov/static/5c875f3ec660e092cf893f60b4a288df/SimpleSabotage.pdf.

Penney, Howard W. "A Brief History of the Defense Mapping Agency." *PE&RS Journal*, May 1973. https://www.asprs.org/wp-content/uploads/pers/1973journal/may/1973_may_469-472.pdf.

Posey, Carl A. "How the Korean War Almost Went Nuclear in 1950." *Smithsonian*, July 2015. https://www.smithsonianmag.com/air-space-magazine/how-korean-war-almost-went-nuclear-180955324/.

Proceedings of the U.S.–Russia Joint Commission on POW-MIAs. June 17, 1996. www.dpaa.mil/Portals/85/Documents/USRJC/USsideUS-Russia_Joint_Commission_POW-MIAS.pdf.

Quinlivan, James T. "Soviet Strategic Air Defense: A Long Past and an Uncertain Future." The RAND Corporation, 1989. https://www.rand.org/pubs/papers/P7579.html.

Royal Air Force Mildenhall. "RAF Mildenhall History." https://www.mildenhall.af.mil/About-Us/Fact-Sheets/Display/Article/270389/raf-mildenhall-history/.

Rummel, R. J. *Statistics of Democide*. University of Hawaii, 2002. https://www.hawaii.edu/powerkills/SOD.CHAP13.HTM.

Schnabel, James F., and Robert J. Watson. "History of the Joint Chiefs of Staff, Volume III: The Joint Chiefs of Staff and National Policy 1950-1951, The Korean War, Part One." Office of the Chairman of the Joint Chiefs of Staff, Washington, D.C., 1998. https://www.jcs.mil/Portals/36/Documents/History/Policy/Policy_V003_P001.pdf.

"Science: Crossroads." *Time*, July 1, 1946. https://time.com/archive/6606119/science-crossroads/.

Smith, Raymond, and Zametica, John. "The Cold Warrior: Clement Attlee Reconsidered, 1945-7." *International Affairs, Royal Institute of International Affairs*, vol. 61, no. 2, Apr. 1985. https://www.jstor.org/stable/2617482.

Sommer, Barbara W. "Interview with Jane LeMay Lodge, Daughter of Gen. Curtis LeMay." History Nebraska, San Juan Capistrano, California, September 10, 1998. www.nebraskastudies.org.

"Stalin's American Air Force—Operation Frantic 1944." YouTube. https://www.youtube.com/watch?v=avtFo0Zv4Dk.

Steakley, Ralph. "Chronology of Events Relating to DESOTO Patrol Incidents in the Gulf of Tonkin on 2 and 4 August, 1964." U.S. Department of Defense. media.defense.gov/2021/Jul/14/2002762866/-1/-1/0/REL2_STEAKLEY.pdf.

Stearn, Jess. "The Generals' Wives Just Refuse to Fade Away." *Daily News*, November 30, 1952. https://www.newspapers.com/article/daily-news-ny-daily-news-front-page/151446229/ and 151122351.

U.S. Department of Defense, Defense Nuclear Agency. "Operation Crossroads 1946: United States Atmospheric Nuclear Weapons Tests." https://apps.dtic.mil/sti/tr/pdf/ADA146562.pdf.

U.S. Department of Defense, Defense Threat Reduction Agency. "Defense's Nuclear Agency 1947-1997." DRTA History Series, U.S. Government Printing Office, Washington, D.C. https://www.dtra.mil/Portals/125/Documents/History/Defenses-Nuclear-Agency-1947-1997.pdf.

U.S. State Department. "A Report to the President Pursuant to the President's Directive of January 31, 1950." https://history.state.gov/historicaldocuments/frus1950v01/d85.

U.S. State Department. "Draft Agreement Between the Governments of the United States, the United Kingdom, and Canada." Foreign Relations of the United States, 1948. https://history.state.gov/historicaldocuments/frus1948v01p2/d66.

Woulfe, Jimmy. "Legendary Journalist Arthur Quinlan Dies." *Irish Examiner* 92, December 24, 2012. https://www.irishexaminer.com/news/arid-20217817.html.

NOTES

INTRODUCTION

1 Still-classified investigation records pertaining to the Globemaster's disappearance are contained in the Headquarters of the U.S. Air Force (Air Staff); series title: General Investigative Files, 1948–1961, entry UD-UP 138, Record Group 341. This entry consists of seventeen boxes (Boxes 431–437, 467–476) and includes 42,500 pages of material. According to Nichole Stephenson, archive specialist at the National Archives, this entry consists of enclosures to Air Force Office of Special Investigation (AFOSI) investigative files that currently face an 11-year backlog for classification review and release.

CHAPTER 1

1 L. Douglas Keeney, *15 Minutes: General Curtis LeMay and the Countdown to Nuclear Annihilation* (St. Martin's Press, 2011), 20.

2 Oleg V. Khlevniuk, *Stalin: New Biography of a Dictator* (Yale University Press, 2015), 381.

3 The Joint Chiefs of Staff sought to downplay a claim in 1948 by the Soviet deputy foreign minister that the United States had lost its atomic monopoly, declaring that the Soviet ability to produce an atomic bomb would not come to fruition until 1952 at the earliest. Even famed nuclear physicist J. Robert Oppenheimer advised the U.S. military that any such Soviet atomic capability would not come "for a long time to come." The first Soviet atomic test explosion occurred on Aug. 29, 1949.

4 John Prados, *The Soviet Estimate* (Princeton University Press, 1982), 8.

5 Robert A. *Divine, Since 1945: Politics and Diplomacy in Recent American History* (John Wiley & Sons, 1975), 28–29.

6 From 1945 to March 1951, at least twenty-two downings of Western military aircraft have been attributed to hostile Soviet actions along the East-West dividing line in Europe. David Lednicer, "Aircraft Downed During the Cold War and Thereafter," November 8, 2015. https://sw.propwashgang.org/shootdown_list.html.

7 George Washington University National Security Archive, "Commanders Conference," Apr. 25–27, 1950. https://nsarchive2.gwu.edu/nukevault/special/doc03a.pdf.

8 Carl A. Posey, "How the Korean War Almost Went Nuclear in 1950," Smithsonian, July 2015. https://www.smithsonianmag.com. See also: Joint Chiefs of Staff, "Possible Employment of Atomic Bombs in Korea," Nov. 20, 1950. https://archive.org/details/PossibleEmploymentOfAtomicBombsInKorea.

9 Warren Kozak, *LeMay: The Life and Wars of General Curtis LeMay* (Regnery History, 2009), 305.

10 General Curtis LeMay, Oral History, Air Force Oral History Project, 592, p. 54.
11 Library of Congress, Manuscript Reading Room, Papers of Curtis E. LeMay, Box B-100: Commanders Conference, April 25–27, 1950.
12 Trevor D. Albertson, "Ready for the Worst: Preemption, Prevention and American Nuclear Policy," *Air Power History* 62, no. 1 (2015), 30–39.
13 Office of the Assistant to the Secretary of Defense (Atomic Energy), "History of the Custody and Deployment of Nuclear Weapons, July 1945 Through September 1977," Feb. 1978, 17. https://nsarchive2.gwu.edu/news/19991020/history-of-custody.pdf.
14 Global Security, "Weapon Storage Sites / Q Area." https://www.globalsecurity.org/wmd/facility/q_area-intro.htm#google_vignette.
15 L. Douglas Keeney, *15 Minutes: General Curtis LeMay and the Countdown to Nuclear Annihilation* (St. Martin's Press, 2011), 69–70.
16 Library of Congress, Manuscript Reading Room, Papers of Curtis E. LeMay, Box B-49.
17 Daniel W. B. Lomas, *Intelligence, Security and the Attlee Governments, 1945–51: An Uneasy Relationship?* (Manchester University Press, 2017), 163–169.
18 Woodrow J. Kuhns, "Assessing the Soviet Threat: The Early Cold War Years." CIA website.
19 National Security Archive, "Central Intelligence Group: Revised Soviet Tactics in International Affairs," Central Intelligence Agency, Jan. 6, 1947. https://nsarchive.gwu.edu/document/30007-78-central-intelligence-group-office-reports-and-estimate-ore-11-revised-soviet.
20 Curtis LeMay, *Mission with LeMay* (Doubleday & Company, 1965), 436.
21 "Brief of Joint Outline Emergency War Plan (OFFTACKLE)," Records of the Joint Chiefs of Staff, Modern Military Records Branch, National Archives, May 26, 1949, Section 42.
22 Ibid.
23 Joint Chiefs of Staff, Report of the Ad Hoc Committee, "Evaluation of Effects on Soviet War Effort Resulting From the Strategic Air Offensive," May 12, 1949, 8. Retrieved from the National Security Archive, George Washington University. https://nsarchive.gwu.edu/document/20287-national-security-archive-doc-02-report.
24 Royal Air Force Mildenhall, "RAF Mildenhall History." https://www.mildenhall.af.mil/About-Us/Fact-Sheets/Display/Article/270389/raf-mildenhall-history/.

CHAPTER 2

1 John Newhouse, *War and Peace in the Nuclear Age* (Vantage Books, 1988), 280, citing a WGBH Boston Public Radio interview with Sprague.
2 George Washington University National Security Archive, "Commanders Conference," Apr. 25–27, 1950. https://nsarchive2.gwu.edu/nukevault/special/doc03a.pdf.
3 "Air Force Lauds Omaha's Support," *Omaha World-Herald*, Mar. 29, 1951, 10.
4 Douglas Larsen, "B-36 'Atom Crew,'" Mar. 25, 1951, *Omaha World-Herald*, 85.
5 "SAC Puts Emphasis Upon Escort Fighters," *Omaha World-Herald*, Mar. 29, 1951, 63.
6 "Search Plane Sights Flares," *Omaha World-Herald*, Mar. 24, 1951, 1.
7 "Background for War: Man in the First Plane," *Time*, Sept. 4, 1950. https://time.com/archive/6794113/background-for-war-man-in-the-first-plane/.
8 Warren Kozak, *LeMay: The Life and Wars of General Curtis LeMay* (Regnery History, 2009), 280.
9 Jane LeMay Lodge, interviewed by Barbara W. Sommer, San Juan Capistrano, California, Sept. 10, 1998, courtesy of History Nebraska. www.nebraskastudies.org.
10 Estimates vary widely, but R. J. Rummel of the University of Hawaii provided a detailed

statistical breakdown of the casualties and aftermath in *Statistics of Democide*, Chapter 13, "Death by American Bombing and Other Democide," 2002. https://www.hawaii.edu/powerkills/SOD.CHAP13.HTM.

11 Kozak, *LeMay*, 226.

12 Ibid., 212.

13 General Curtis E. LeMay, interview by Robert F. Futrell, Thomas G. Belden, and J. Van Staaveren, June 8, 1972. Transcript, IRIS 00904608, DAFHRA.

14 Don Hollway, "'Bombs Away' LeMay: America's Unapologetic Champion of Waging Total War," HistoryNet, 2022. https://www.historynet.com/bombs-away-lemay-americas-unapologetic-champion-of-waging-total-war.

15 Kozak, *LeMay*, 281.

16 Ibid., 284.

CHAPTER 3

1 "Earth View and Aerial Maps," Britannica.com. See also: Howard W. Penney, "A Brief History of the Defense Mapping Agency," *PE&RS Journal* (May 1973).

2 "Army Planes Scout 'Enemy,'" *Pittsburgh Sun-Telegraph*, Sept. 7, 1933, 20.

3 "U.S. Surveys Canal," *Buffalo Courier Express*, Oct. 3, 1935, 2.

4 Elliott Roosevelt, *As He Saw It* (1st ed., Duell, Sloan and Pearce, 1946), 54.

5 Chris Hansen, *Enfant Terrible: The Times and Schemes of General Elliott Roosevelt* (Able Baker Press, 2012), 219.

6 Ibid., 223–225.

7 Robert Schmuhl, *Mr. Churchill in the White House* (Liverlight Publishing, 2024), 32–33.

8 Roosevelt, *As He Saw It*, 55.

9 Library of Congress, Manuscript Division, "The Papers of Henry H. Arnold," Container 146 (May 5, 1943), 615–629.

10 The Associated Press, "Air Photographers Paved Invasion Path," *The Duluth News*, June 6, 1943, 2.

11 C. L. Sulzberger, "Vichy Shift a Peril to African Airline," *The New York Times*, Apr. 16, 1942, 1.

12 Commander George Cornelius, "Air Reconnaissance—Great Silent Weapon," U.S. Naval Institute Proceedings, July 1959. https://www.usni.org/magazines/proceedings/1959/july.

13 In an ironic twist of history, Coldwater Creek would, years later, become contaminated with radioactive waste illegally dumped from a facility a few miles away where uranium was being processed and refined to make the first atomic bombs under the top secret Manhattan Project.

14 "Africa Mapped by Air Months Before Invasion," *Chicago Tribune*, June 6, 1943, 8.

CHAPTER 4

1 Mark J. Conversino, *Fighting With the Soviets: The Failure of Operation FRANTIC, 1944-1945* (University Press of Kansas, 1997), 31, 60–61.

2 Elliott Roosevelt, *As He Saw It* (1st ed., Duell, Sloan and Pearce, 1946), 185.

3 Daniel P. Bolger, *Reluctant Allies: The United States Army Air Force and the Soviet Voemno Vozdushnie Sily 1941-1945* (University of Chicago, Jan. 1985), 68. apps.dtic.mil/sti/pdfs/ADA169037.pdf.

4 Office diary of General Fred Anderson, Hoover Institution, Stanford University, Box

2, Feb. 8, 1944, as cited in Chris Hansen, *Enfant Terrible: The Times and Schemes of General Elliott Roosevelt* (Able Baker Press, 2012), 360.

5 Ibid., 362.

6 Glenn B. Infield, *The Poltava Affair: A Russian Warning: An American Tragedy* (Macmillan, 1973), 54.

7 Hansen, *Enfant Terrible*, 230.

8 Infield, *The Poltava Affair*, 26.

9 Brigadier General L. S. Kuter, Army Air Forces deputy chief of air staff, "Memorandum for Major General D.D. Eisenhower," Library of Congress, Manuscript Division. See also: Library of Congress, Manuscript Division. "The Papers of Henry H. Arnold," Container 146 (May 5, 1943).

10 Ibid.

11 Daniel P. Bolger, *Reluctant Allies: The United States Army Air Force and the Soviet Voenno Vozdushnie Sily 1941–1945* (University of Chicago, Jan. 1985), 199–200. https://apps.dtic.mil/sti/pdfs/ADA169037.pdf.

12 Ibid., 188.

CHAPTER 5

1 Chuck Hansen, *U.S. Nuclear Weapons: The Secret History* (Orion Books, 1988), 121–125.

2 Atomic Archive, "The Atomic Bombings of Hiroshima and Nagasaki." https://www.atomicarchive.com/resources/documents/med/med_chp10.html.

3 Atomic Heritage Foundation Nuclear Museum, "Theodore Hall, Soviet Spy, Los Alamos, NM." https://ahf.nuclearmuseum.org/ahf/profile/theodore-hall.

4 Paul W. Tibbets, *Return of the Enola Gay* (Mid Coast Marketing, 1988), 162.

5 Ibid., 189–190.

6 Robert O. Harder, *The Three Musketeers of the Army Air Forces* (Naval Institute Press, 2015), 113–114.

7 Charles W. Sweeney with James A. Antonucci and Marion K. Antonucci, *War's End: An Eyewitness Account of America's Last Atomic Mission* (Avon Books, 1997), 18.

8 Harder, *The Three Musketeers*, 175–187.

9 Sweeney et al., *War's End*, 175.

10 James I. Hopkins personnel file retrieved from the National Archives' National Personnel Records Center, St. Louis, Missouri.

11 In fact, Sweeney did not know he had been designated to command the Nagasaki mission until Aug. 6, 1945, the day of the Hiroshima bombing and three days before the Nagasaki attack. Sweeney states this in his own narrative. See Sweeney et al., *War's End*, 18.

12 Military Hall of Honor, Colonel Thomas J. Classen, 2021. https://militaryhallofhonor.com/honoree-record.php?id=312409.

13 Don A. Farrell, *Atomic Bomb Island* (Stackpole Books, 2019), 179–180.

14 Sweeney et al., *War's End*, 188–190.

15 Robert Krauss and Amelia Krauss, eds., *The 509th Remembered* (509th Press, 2005), 20.

16 Harder, *The Three Musketeers*, 185.

17 Tibbets, *Return of the Enola Gay*, 250.

18 Harder, *The Three Musketeers*, 185.

19 Sept. 8, 1950, letter to the U.S. Air Force headquarters by Major General A. W. Kissner, recovered from the personnel file of Lieutenant Colonel James I. Hopkins.

20 Lieutenant Colonel James I. Hopkins personnel record, recovered from the National Personnel Records Center, St. Louis, Missouri.

CHAPTER 6

1 Paul W. Tibbets, *Return of the Enola Gay* (Mid Coast Marketing, 1988), 253.
2 "Science: Crossroads," *Time*, July 1, 1946. https://time.com/archive/6606119/science-crossroads/.
3 Tibbets, *Return of the Enola Gay*, 126–131.
4 Ibid., 192–193.
5 Ibid., 186–187.
6 Personal correspondence of General Curtis E. LeMay, Library of Congress, Manuscript Reading Room, Box 11: Letter from Brigadier General Lauris Norstad, April 17, 1945. Although Norstad was voluminous in his multipage, single-spaced letters, LeMay tended to respond with business-like, single-page responses of just a few paragraphs.
7 Tibbets, *Return of the Enola Gay*, 258.
8 Undated ABC Radio interview, conducted prior to the July 1, 1946, Able test, a recording of which was recovered by Hopkins's son, James K. Hopkins, and restored by sound engineer Phil Ford.
9 Bordentown (New Jersey) Regional High School, Alumni Hall of Fame, "Harold H. Wood Class of 1933." https://brhs.bordentown.k12.nj.us/apps/pages/index.jsp?uREC_ID=444485&type=d&pREC_ID=958571.
10 William C. Harrison, Jr., Obituary, *Fort Worth Star-Telegram*, May 7, 2003, 32.
11 "Bikini A-Bomb Ripped Ship's Turrets—Powder Unexploded," *St. Louis Star-Times*, Oct. 10, 1946, 14. https://www.newspapers.com/image/205506748/?match=1&terms=%22operation%20crossroads%22.
12 Defense Nuclear Agency, Department of Defense, "Operation Crossroads 1946: United States Atmospheric Nuclear Weapons Tests," 6. https://apps.dtic.mil/sti/tr/pdf/ADA146562.pdf.
13 SAC Historical Study No. 61, "The Strategic Air Command, A Chronological History 1946-1956," Historical Division of the Office of Information, SAC headquarters, undated, p. 51, as posted on the National Security Archive, Washington University. https://nsarchive.gwu.edu/document/21077-doc-4-thestrategicaircommandchron-48-56-p-207-ff-berlin-crisis.
14 Tibbets, *Return of the Enola Gay*, 264.
15 Ibid.
16 Jonathan M. Weisgall, *Operation Crossroads: The Atomic Tests at Bikini Atoll* (Naval Institute Press, 1994), 187.
17 Office of Air Force History, "Strategic Air Warfare: An Interview with Generals Curtis E. LeMay, Leon W. Johnson, David A. Burchinal, and Jack J. Catton," United States Air Force, 1988, 78–79.
18 L. Douglas Keeney, *15 Minutes: General Curtis LeMay and the Countdown to Nuclear Annihilation* (St. Martin's Press, 2011), 33.

CHAPTER 7

1 "Communist Party of Texas 1940 State Platform," Internet Archive. https://archive.org/details/1940StatePlatform_621/mode/2up.
2 "Annals of Wyoming," A. Dean and Jean M. Larsen Yellowstone Park Collection, Brigham Young University, vol. 24–27. https://archive.org/stream/annalsofwyoming2427wyom/annalsofwyoming2427wyom_djvu.txt.
3 Matsonia passenger list, "Civilian employees American Red Cross, pursuant orders, W.D. Ex. Priority No. 4565 A&H," submitted to immigration authorities in Honolulu, Hawaii, on Jan. 6, 1945. Accessed via Ancestry.com.
4 This and all subsequent references to Reva Joy Hurwitz's correspondence are based on

letters archived at the University of Wyoming American Heritage Archive, Box 1: Reva Joy Hurwitz Cullen archive, Laramie, Wyoming., Laramie.

5 Ibid. Letter to Garvin Hurwitz dated Dec. 20, 1945.

6 Transcript by Richard Kucera of the documentary *Radio Bikini* by Robert Stone, The American Experience, Public Broadcasting System, 1988. https://nuclearweaponarchive.org/News/Kucera.html.

7 Cullen archive, Box 1. Letter to family dated June 6, 1946.

8 Ibid. Letter to family dated July 27, 1945.

9 Ibid.

10 Ibid.

11 Ibid. Letter to family dated Aug. 7, 1946.

12 Ibid.

13 Ibid. Letter to family dated Aug. 19, 1946.

14 Ibid. Letter to family. Undated, but references indicate it was the first anniversary of V.J.Day, Aug. 14, 1946.

CHAPTER 8

1 International News Service, "Atomic Energy Experiments Explain 'Flying Saucers,' Says Scientist; More in Sky," *Albuquerque Journal*, July 6, 1947, 1.

2 United Press, "'Flying Saucers' To Be Checked by Army," *Merced Sun-Star*, July 3, 1947, 1.

3 The Associated Press, "Flying Disc Found; In Army Possession," *The Bakersfield Californian*, July 8, 1947, 1.

4 Air Force Captain James McAndrew, "The Roswell Report: Case Closed," U.S. Government Printing Office, Oct. 2010, 23. https://media.defense.gov/2010/Oct/27/2001330219/-1/-1/0/AFD-101027-030.pdf.

5 Donovan Webster, "In 1947, a High-Altitude Balloon Crash Landed in Roswell. The Aliens Never Left," *Smithsonian*, July 5, 2017. https://www.smithsonianmag.com/smithsonian-institution/in-1947-high-altitude-balloon-crash-landed-roswell-aliens-never-left-180963917/.

6 James Michael Young, "The U.S. Air Force's Long Range Detection Program and Project MOGUL," *Air Power History*, vol. 67, no. 4 (Winter 2020), 25–32. https://www.jstor.org/stable/26965566.

7 Air Force Captain James McAndrew, "The Roswell Report."

8 Ibid.

9 Author interview with James I. Hopkins's son, James K. Hopkins, on Mar. 20, 2022.

CHAPTER 9

1 America's National Churchill Museum, Winston Churchill, "The Sinews of Peace, 1947," Fulton, Missouri, March 5, 1947. https://www.nationalchurchillmuseum.org/sinews-of-peace-iron-curtain-speech.html.

2 James C. Humes, *The Wit & Wisdom of Winston Churchill* (HarperCollins, 1994), 48.

3 Raymond Smit and John Zametica, "The Cold Warrior: Clement Attlee Reconsidered, 1945-7," *International Affairs*, vol. 61, no. 2 (Apr. 1985), 237–252. https://doi.org/10.2307/2617482.

4 Ibid., 135.

5 National Archives, "Memorandum from President Harry S. Truman to Secretary of State James Byrnes," NAID: 294549769, Apr. 5, 1946, 19–24.

6 Piotr Wrobel, *Historical Dictionary of Poland 1945-1996* (Routledge, 2014).

7 BBC.com, "Soviet expansion into Eastern Europe, 1945-1948." https://www.bbc.co.uk/bitesize/guides/zt8ncwx/revision/5.

8 The Associated Press, "Justice Swift Considers Defi to Soviet Head," *Sun Journal*, May 26, 1946, 1.

9 Christopher J. Kauffman, *Faith and Fraternalism: The History of the Knights of Columbus, 1882-1982* (Harper & Row, 1982), 363.

10 Warren Kozak, *LeMay: The Life and Times of General Curtis LeMay* (Regnery History, 2009), 283.

11 "Memorandum for the Secretary: U.S. Public Opinion on the Berlin Situation," National Archives, Harry S. Truman Library and Museum, July 29, 1948, 2. https://trumanlibrary.gov.

12 Dutch Communist radio broadcast summarized in "Memorandum from George Elsey to Rose Conway, with Attachment and Related Material," National Archives, NAID: 294549816, Feb. 3, 1949, 4.

13 "Report, Central Intelligence Agency Daily Summary," Summary of Telegrams, National Archives, NAID: 294549869, Feb. 20, 1951.

CHAPTER 10

1 Paul W. Tibbets, *Return of the Enola Gay* (Mid Coast Marketing, 1988), 171–172.

2 National Archives News, "Remembering the 1973 NPRC Fire." https://www.archives.gov/news/articles/2023-nprc-fire-anniversary.

3 Jess Stearn, "The Generals' Wives Just Refuse to Fade Away," *Daily News*, Nov. 30, 1952, C22–23.

4 Warren Kozak, *LeMay: The Life and Wars of General Curtis LeMay* (Regnery History, 2009), 282.

5 Author interview with Carolyn Elizabeth Hurwitz, Nov. 8, 2024.

6 Copy of the marriage certificate, Record No. 007 2278, obtained via Ancestry.com and Familysearch.com.

7 University of Wyoming American Heritage Archive, Box 1: Reva Joy Hurwitz Cullen archive, Laramie, Wyoming.

8 "Hearing Reveals General's Mixed-Up Marital Status," *Tampa Bay Times*, Mar. 27, 1953, 7.

9 Ibid.

10 Michael Smith, *The Anatomy of a Traitor: A History of Espionage and Betrayal* (Aurum Press, 2017).

CHAPTER 11

1 Roger Dingman, "Strategic Planning and the Policy Process: American Plans for War in East Asia, 1945-1950," *Naval War College Review*, 8. https://digital-commons.usnwc.edu/cgi/viewcontent.cgi?article=5542&context=nwc-review.

2 Federal Bureau of Investigation, "Underground Soviet Espionage Organization [NKVD] in Agencies of the US Government," Oct. 21, 1946, 7. See also: Harry S. Truman Library, White House Central Files (Confidential File), "Justice" (7), box 22, as cited in "Venona: Soviet Espionage and The American Response 1939-1957." CIA.gov.

3 David Clay Large, *Between Two Fires* (Norton, 1990), 270–271.

4 Kim Philby, *My Silent War* (Grove Press, 1968), 131–132.

5 Evidence of infiltration of the committee can be found in minutes kept by the State Department historian from the 1948–1950 period. The name of one of the Cambridge

Five, Donald MacLean, appears in the minutes of a Jan. 6, 1948, top secret meeting. "Draft Agreement Between the Governments of the United States, the United Kingdom, and Canada." See also: "Foreign Relations of the United States, 1948, General; the United Nations, Volume I, Part 2." https://history.state.gov/historicaldocuments/frus1948v01p2/d66.

6 Ben Macintyre, *A Spy Among Friends: Kim Philby and the Great Betrayal* (Bloomsbury, London), 2015, 19–22.

7 Norman Moss, *Klaus Fuchs: The Man Who Stole the Atom Bomb* (Sharpe Books, U.K., 2018), 100.

8 Central Intelligence Agency, "Venona: Soviet Espionage and The American Response 1939-1957," Loy W. Henderson 1939 memorandum recounting General Walter Krivitzky's defection and description of the Soviet spy network in the United States, p. 6 of the memo.

9 Kim Philby, *My Silent War* (Grove Press, New York, 1968), 212.

10 Alexander Feklisov and Sergei Kostin. *The Man Behind the Rosenbergs* (Enigma Books, New York, 2004), 66: "Without the choice of people like Klaus Fuchs, Allan Nunn May, and other secret agents of Soviet intelligence whose identity has not yet been revealed, without the sense of danger that Niels Bohr or Robert Oppenheimer felt in having the atomic superweapon under one country's control that could easily shatter such a fragile peace, we would have had few chances of avoiding another world war."

11 Ben Macintyre, *A Spy Among Friends* (Bloomsbury, London), 39. Kim Philby's mother, Dora, wrote to her husband in Saudi Arabia: "I do hope Kim gets a job to get him off this bloody communism. He's not quite extreme yet, but may become so."

12 Simon Duke, *US Defence Bases in the United Kingdom: A Matter for Joint Decision?* (The Macmillan Press Ltd., U.K., 1987), 63–65.

13 "'Atomic Plague': How the UK Press Reported Hiroshima," *The Conversation*, Aug. 6, 2020. https://theconversation.com/atomic-plague-how-the-uk-press-reported-hiroshima-144081.

14 Feklisov and Kostin, *The Man Behind the Rosenbergs*, 164.

15 Ibid., 182.

16 He returned to America during the Cuban Missile Crisis, serving as the liaison with an American television reporter and relaying word from the Kremlin on terms for resolving a crisis that, without Feklisov's intervention, might have led to a direct U.S.–Russian nuclear confrontation.

CHAPTER 12

1 Office of Air Force History, "Strategic Air Warfare: An Interview with Generals Curtis E. LeMay, Leon W. Johnson, David A. Burchinal, and Jack J. Catton," United States Air Force, 1988, 78.

2 U.S. Department of Defense, Defense Threat Reduction Agency, "Defense's Nuclear Agency, 1945-1997," U.S. Government Printing Office, Washington, D.C., 2002, 53.

3 David Pietrusza, *1948: Harry Truman's Improbable Victory and the Year That Transformed America* (Union Square Press, 2011), 276.

4 NSC 68, "A Report to the National Security Council," https://info.publicintelligence.net/US-NSC-68.pdf, 3.

5 Ibid. 62.

6 Warren Kozak, *LeMay: The Life and Wars of General Curtis LeMay* (Regnery History, 2009), 313.

7 George H. Quester, "Origins of the Cold War: Some Clues From Public Opinion," *Political Science Quarterly*, vol. 93, no. 4 (Winter 1978–1979), 647–663, republished by JSTOR. https://www.jstor.org/stable/2150108?seq=10.
8 Steven R. Prebeck, *Past Cases of Preventive War* (Air University Press, 1993).
9 David Pietrusza, *1948: Harry Truman's Improbable Victory and the Year That Transformed America* (Union Square Press, 2011), 274.
10 NSC 68, 34.

CHAPTER 13

1 Library of Congress, Manuscript Reading Room, Papers of Curtis E. LeMay, Box B-195 (B-3111): March 1951 letter to Major General Archie Old from Major General S. E. Anderson regarding KB-29 shortages and the possibility of using Cullen's plane for tank transport.
2 George Washington University National Security Archive, "Commanders Conference," Apr. 25–27, 1950, 225. https://nsarchive2.gwu.edu/nukevault/special/doc03a.pdf.
3 Ibid., 226–227 (italics added).
4 The creation of that early warning system is outlined in detail in L. Douglas Keeney's *15 Minutes: General Curtis LeMay and the Countdown to Nuclear Annihilation* (St. Martin's Press, 2011).
5 George Washington University National Security Archive, "Commanders Conference," 230–231.
6 Ibid., 239–240.
7 Ibid., 517.
8 Ibid., 10.
9 Ibid., 3.
10 Ibid., 4.
11 Ibid., 14–15.
12 A handwritten note preserved in the Gerald R. Ford Presidential Library recounts the tale of a freed American prisoner, John Noble, who said he encountered a German prisoner who witnessed eight Americans captured after the Apr. 8, 1950, downing off the German Baltic Coast. The account couldn't be confirmed. There were similar, unconfirmed accounts from a Russian prison of Americans believed to have been captured and taken prisoner after the Globemaster disappearance in the Atlantic. https://www.fordlibrarymuseum.gov/sites/default/files/pdf_documents/library/document/0019/4520652.pdf.
13 George Washington University National Security Archive, "Commanders Conference," 203.
14 The B-50 did have one distinct advantage over the B-29, which required the conspicuous digging of a loading pit in order to fit a Fat Man into the Silverplate B-29's bomb bay. For any Britons watching, the pit construction was a clear sign of what was being planned. The B-50 was designed to be lifted with hydraulic jacks to make preparations less conspicuous.
15 George Washington University National Security Archive, "Commanders Conference," 205–206.
16 Summary of British position during "Defence Policy and Global Strategy" conference at the Pentagon, July 31, 1952, 2. Retrieved from the National Security Archive. https://nsarchive2.gwu.edu/nukevault/special/doc04.pdf.

17 George Washington University National Security Archive, "Commanders Conference," 217.
18 Ibid., 223.
19 Ibid., 224.
20 Letter from George C. Kenney to Hoyt Vandenberg, National Security Archive, Apr. 29, 1950. https://nsarchive2.gwu.edu/nukevault/special/doc03d.pdf.
21 Trevor D. Albertson, "Ready for the Worst: Pre-emption, Prevention and American Nuclear Policy," *Air Power History* 62, no. 1 (2015), 34. https://www.afhistory.org/airpowerhistory/Air_Power_History_2015_spring.pdf.
22 Steven T. Ross, *American War Plans 1945-1950* (Garland, 1988), 102.
23 George Washington University National Security Archive, "Defence Policy and Global Strategy," July 31, 1952, 2.
24 U.S. Department of Defense, Defense Threat Reduction Agency, "Defense's Nuclear Agency, 1945-1997," U.S. Government Printing Office, Washington, D.C., 2002, 368.
25 Office of Air Force History, "Strategic Air Warfare: An Interview with Generals Curtis E. LeMay, Leon W. Johnson, David A. Burchinal, and Jack J. Catton," United States Air Force, 1988, 92.
26 Curtis E. LeMay, *Mission With LeMay* (Doubleday & Company, 1965), 481–482.
27 Trevor Albertson, *Winning Armageddon: Curtis LeMay and Strategic Air Command, 1948-1957* (Naval Institute Press, 2019), 12–13.
28 Albertson, "Ready for the Worst," 33.
29 LeMay, *Mission With LeMay*, 436.

CHAPTER 14

1 LeMay stated after his U.S. Air Force retirement that he believed he had full authority under certain circumstances, namely, the annihilation of the civilian command, to launch a nuclear attack with or without the president's approval. See Office of Air Force History, "Strategic Air Warfare: An Interview with Generals Curtis E. LeMay, Leon W. Johnson, David A. Burchinal, and Jack J. Catton," United States Air Force, 1988, 92.
2 Phillip S. Meilinger, *Bomber: The Formation and Early Years of Strategic Air Command* (Air University Press, Air Force Research Institute, Maxwell Air Force Base, 2012), 83.
3 General Curtis LeMay and Bill Yenne, *Superfortress: The Boeing B-29 and American Airpower in World War II* (Westholme Publishing, 2007), 167.
4 DAFHRA, IRIS Number 877715, Reel 46768, p. 251.
5 Ibid., 252.
6 Robert Krauss and Amelia Krauss, eds., *The 509th Remembered* (509th Press, 2005), 20.
7 In the investigations that followed the plane's disappearance, references were made to flights that immediately preceded 49-244 that cited tail numbers 49-240 and 49-241.
8 "Weekly Statistical Report of Operational Missions," Walker Air Force Base, Mar. 1951. Document obtained from the Strategic Air Command archives by Keith Amsden.

CHAPTER 15

1 The History Channel, "LeMay and Kennedy Argue Over Cuban Missile Crisis," audio recording of Oval Office discussion on Oct. 19, 1962. https://www.history.com/speeches/lemay-and-kennedy-argue-over-cuban-missile-crisis.
2 John F. Kennedy Presidential Library and Museum, *A Pretty Bad Fix: Transcript*, Atomic Gambit podcast, Oct. 18, 2022. https://www.jfklibrary.org/about-us/social-media-podcasts-and-apps/atomic-gambit/episode-2-a-pretty-bad-fix/transcript.

3 L. Douglas Keeney, *15 Minutes: General Curtis LeMay and the Countdown to Nuclear Annihilation* (St. Martin's Press, 2011), 83.
4 Drew Pearson, "The Washington Merry-Go-Round," *The Decatur Daily*, Aug. 31, 1950, 4.
5 "Matthews Favors U.S. War for Peace," *The New York Times*, Aug. 26, 1950, 1, 6. See also: "Commanding General's Diary," Library of Congress, Curtis B. LeMay, Box B-103, Aug. 26, 1950.
6 Harry S. Truman, *Two Years of Trial and Hope, 1947-1949* (Doubleday & Company, 1956), 383. Accessed via Internet Archive. https://archive.org/details/memoirsbyharryst012833mbp/page/382/mode/2up.
7 House Committee on Un-American Activities, annual report, 1950, 33. Accessed via Internet Archive. https://archive.org.
8 Truman, *Two Years of Trial and Hope*, 385–386.
9 Ibid., 385.
10 Daniel W. B. Lomas, *Intelligence Security and the Attlee Governments, 1945-51: An Uneasy Relationship?* (Manchester University Press, 2017), 163–172.
11 Robert A. Divine, *Since 1945: Politics and American Diplomacy in Recent American History* (John Wiley & Sons, 1975), 39.
12 "Military Expenditure (% of GDP)." Our World in Data, 1951. https://ourworldindata.org/grapher/military-spending-as-a-share-of-gdp-gmsd?time=earliest.
13 Oleg V. Khlevniuk, *Stalin: New Biography of a Dictator* (Yale University Press, 2015), 431.
14 Memorandum of Conversation, Aug. 5, 1951, 2. https://nsarchive2.gwu.edu/NSAEBB/NSAEBB159/usukconsult-2a.pdf.
15 Library of Congress, Manuscript Reading Room, Papers of Curtis E. LeMay, Box B-49: "Headquarters Eighth Air Force" letter from Major General S. E. Anderson to LeMay, Mar. 13, 1951.
16 "Nuclear Companion: A Nuclear Weapons History Hobby Showcase," MK3 section. https://nukecompendium.com/weapons/mk3/. See also: Frederick C. Alexander, Jr., "History of Sandia Corporation Through Fiscal Year 1963," Defense Technical Information Center, Dec. 1, 1963. https://ntrl.ntis.gov/NTRL/.
17 "Memorandum for the Secretary of Defense: The Military Effectiveness and Desirability of Employing Atomic Weapons Tactically in Korea," Daniel Ellsberg files, Internet Archive. https://archive.org/details/TheMilitaryEffectivenessAndDurabilityOfEmployingAtomicWeaponsTacticallyInKorea/page/n1/mode/2up.
18 Hansard, the official transcript of Parliament, from Feb. 15, 1951. https://hansard.parliament.uk/Commons/1951-02-15/debates/fa7dd4bf-63ef-419a-82b1-73a914c6e263/Defence(GovernmentPolicy).
19 Churchill Archive, Letter from President Truman to Churchill, Feb. 16, 1951. https://www.churchillarchive.com/catalogue-item?docid=CHUR2_28_127-128.
20 Churchill Archive, Letter from Truman to Churchill, Mar. 24, 1951. https://www.churchillarchive.com/catalogue-item?docid=CHUR2_28_126.
21 Melvin G. Deaile, "The SAC Mentality: The Origins of Strategic Air Command's Organizational Culture, 1948–51," *Air & Space Power Journal*, Mar.–Apr. 2015, 65.
22 Steven L. Reardon, "History of the Office of the Secretary of Defense: The Formative Years, 1947-1950," U.S. Department of Defense, 1984, 428.
23 Ibid., 430.
24 Ibid., 342.

CHAPTER 16

1 The American Presidency Project, "Proclamation 2914—Proclaiming the Existence of a National Emergency." https://www.presidency.ucsb.edu/documents/proclamation-2914-proclaiming-the-existence-national-emergency.

2 Library of Congress, Manuscript Reading Room, Papers of Curtis E. LeMay, Box B-103: Curtis LeMay, "Memorandum for the Record," Jan. 3, 1951. (Declassified June 18, 1979.)

3 Library of Congress, Manuscript Reading Room, Papers of Curtis E. LeMay, Box B-103: "Commanding Generals Diary for 18 Dec 50 & 19 Dec."

4 The author was instructed to contact Ernie Emrich, classified documents director at the Library of Congress Manuscripts Reading Room, for an explanation. Emrich permitted his email to be shared with the author, but repeated messages to Emrich went unanswered, nor was there even an acknowledgment of receipt.

5 Library of Congress, Manuscript Reading Room, Papers of Curtis E. LeMay, Box B-103, Jan. 27, 1951.

6 Library of Congress, Manuscript Reading Room, Papers of Curtis E. LeMay, Box B-103, Feb. 5, 1951.

7 McConnell was a rising star within the Air Force, and after Cullen's death in the Globemaster disappearance, McConnell was appointed to command the Seventh Air Division. He continued to rise through the ranks, ultimately becoming the sixth Air Force Chief of Staff.

8 Library of Congress, Manuscript Reading Room, Papers of Curtis E. LeMay, Box B-103: Brigadier General W. C. Sweeney, "Memorandum for the Record," Dec. 22, 1950 (Top Secret/Declassified).

9 Ibid.

10 Library of Congress, Manuscript Reading Room, Papers of Curtis E. LeMay, Box B-103: "Diary Notes 26 Dec 1950."

11 Library of Congress, Manuscript Reading Room, Papers of Curtis E. LeMay, Box B-103, Nov. 6, 1950.

12 Library of Congress, Manuscript Reading Room, Papers of Curtis E. LeMay, Box B-103: "Overseas Assignment of Negro Personnel," Nov 1949–Apr. 1950.

13 Library of Congress, Manuscript Reading Room, Papers of Curtis E. LeMay, Box B-103: "Overseas Assignment of Negro Personnel," Dec.14, 1950. (Typos and ellipses are part of the quotation.)

14 Library of Congress, Manuscript Reading Room, Papers of Curtis E. LeMay, Box B-103: "Overseas Assignment of Negro Personnel," Jan. 17, 1951.

15 Library of Congress, Manuscript Reading Room, Papers of Curtis E. LeMay, Box B-103: "Overseas Assignment of Negro Personnel," Jan. 25, 1951.

16 Office of Strategic Services, "Simple Sabotage Field Manual," Jan. 17, 1944. https://www.cia.gov/static/5c875f3ec660e092cf893f60b4a288df/SimpleSabotage.pdf.

17 Library of Congress, Manuscript Reading Room, Papers of Curtis E. LeMay, Box B-103: "Commanding Generals Diary for 14 Feb 51."

18 Colonel William M. Smith, U.S. Air Force Chief of Operations, "Memorandum for General Eaton, Subject: S. Res. 8 (Wherry)," Feb. 19, 1951.

19 LeMay diary entry for Feb. 22, 1951 (Top Secret/Declassified).

20 Lieutenant Colonel Paul K. Carlton, "Memo for General LeMay," Mar. 1, 1951.

21 LeMay diary entry for Mar. 9, 1951.

22 Diary entry for Mar. 4, 1951. Assistant's multiple typographical errors have been cleaned up for readability.

23 Diary entry for Mar. 18–19, 1951 (Top Secret/Declassified). Assistant's multiple typographical errors have been cleaned up for readability.

24 Library of Congress, Manuscript Reading Room, Papers of Curtis E. LeMay, Box B-49: "Headquarters Eighth Air Force" letter from Major General S. E. Anderson to LeMay, Mar. 13, 1951. See also: Two entries from July 8, 1950, one specifically mentioning an M107 bomb dropped (and lost) in an Arizona canyon during a practice bombing raid from Riggs Air Force Base, plus a separate diary entry from LeMay on July 8 discussing with Vandenberg the possibility of sending "bombs minus nuclear component" to Third Air Division units.

CHAPTER 17

1 Statement by Air Force Lieutenant Colonel George W. Von Arb included in the post-disappearance investigative report filed with the Strategic Air Command in Apr. 1951. DAFHRA IRIS Number 877715, Reel 46768, p. 238.

2 General Hunter Harris biography, U.S. Air Force. https://www.af.mil/About-Us/Biographies/Display/Article/106828/general-hunter-harris/.

3 *The Airman's Handbook* (7th ed., The Military Service Publishing Company, 1955), 422.

4 Ibid., 424.

5 "Report of Special Accident Investigation of C-124A Aircraft," addendum to material supplied in DAFHRA IRIS Number 877715, Reel 46768, no page number listed.

6 "Flight Plan: All Entries in Nautical Miles," handwritten navigator's log addendum to DAFHRA IRIS Number 877715, Reel 46768, p. 248.

7 "Preliminary Report on C-124A, No. 49-244," Apr. 10, 1951, DAFHRA IRIS Number 877715, Reel 46768.

8 Testimony of Colonel Avery J. Ladd, commanding officer, Second Strategic Support Squadron, Walker Air Force Base, Roswell, New Mexico, Mar. 24, 1951. Addendum to DAFHRA IRIS Number 877715, Reel 46768.

CHAPTER 18

1 Department of the Air Force Historical Research Agency (DAFHRA), Maxwell Air Force Base, Alabama, "Aircraft Accidents for 1951, Major," IRIS Number 877715, Reel 46768, p. 417.

2 Ibid., 240.

3 Ibid., 233. Water conditions at the time were estimated to be a temperature of 50 degrees Fahrenheit with eight-foot swells spaced seventy-two feet apart.

4 Ibid., 255. "Inventory of material salvaged by US Navy from search area covered in searching for C-124 aircraft number 5882 [49-244]." Note: Some official documents referred to the flight by its unique radio call sign for this flight, 5882, rather than the plane's tail number.

5 Ibid., 253.

6 Ibid., 249.

7 F. E. Smith, "Survival at Sea," Royal Naval Personnel Research Committee, Medical Research Council, U.K., May 1976. Accessible from the National Technical Reports Library. https://ntrl.ntis.gov/NTRL.

8 Don Wagner, "Last Flight, The Missing Airmen, March 1951." Note: This account is unsourced and contains descriptions unsupported by official investigation findings. https://thekwe.org/topics/airplane_crashes/globemaster_ireland/globemaster_ireland_last_flight_of_49244.pdf.

CHAPTER 19

1 DAFHRA IRIS Number 877715, Reel 46768, p. 441.
2 The Associated Press, "U.S. Plane Crashes With 53; Flares in Atlantic Spur Hope," *The New York Times*, Mar. 24, 1951, 1.
3 DAFHRA, IRIS Number 877715, Reel 46768, pp. 396–427.
4 This document is part of a series collected from DAFHRA by surviving family members of those who disappeared aboard 49-244. The origin is part of reels that no longer appear in archive searches, but family members provided a hard copy to the author.
5 The Associated Press, "Clue Shifts Hunt for Air Survivors," *The New York Times*, Mar. 25, 1951, 38.
6 The Associated Press, "U.S. Plane Crashes with 53; Flares in Atlantic Spur Hope," *The New York Times*, Mar. 24, 1951, 1, 4.
7 DAFHRA, IRIS Number 877715, Reel 46768, p. 404.
8 This document is part of a series collected from DAFHRA by surviving family members of those who disappeared aboard 49-244. The origin is part of reels that no longer appear in archive searches, but family members provided a hard copy to the author.
9 Ibid.
10 Ibid.
11 DAFHRA, "47th Air Division History, March 1951," IRIS Number 465460, Ref. P0609, Reel 11372, pp. 71–73.
12 Proceedings of the U.S.-Russia Joint Commission on POW-MIAs. www.dpaa.mil/Portals/85/Documents/USRJC/UssideUS-Russia_Joint_Commission_POW-MIAS.pdf.
13 The flight plan originally called for a stopover in Gander, but pilot Bell altered the plan before takeoff from Barksdale.
14 Weather ship *Charlie* log, 8 p.m. to midnight entry. Hard copy provided by Irish journalist Pavel Barter.
15 United Press International, "Plane Missing Over Ocean Blown to Bits, Officer Says," *The New York Times*, Mar. 30, 1951, 3.
16 The Associated Press, "Searchers Find No Trace of 53 on Big U.S. Plane Missing at Sea," *St. Louis Post-Dispatch*, Mar. 25, 1951, 1.
17 DAFHRA "Aircraft Accidents for 1951," IRIS Number 877715, Reel 46768, pp. 203–204. This listing includes not only the SAC affiliation and assignment of all aboard but also the individuals' rank, rating, and service number.
18 The Associated Press, "Clue Shifts Hunt for Air Survivors," *The New York Times*, Mar. 25, 1951, 38.
19 Ibid., 227.
20 United Press International, "Missing Plane May Have Had Atomic Cargo: Sabotage Is Hinted in Case of Overdue U.S. Globemaster," *Valley Morning Star*, Harlingen, Texas, Mar. 27, 1951, 1.

CHAPTER 20

1 DAFHRA IRIS Number 877715, Reel 46768, pp. 278–336.
2 Author interview with Keith Amsden, Oct. 4, 2024.
3 DAFHRA, IRIS Number 877715, Reel 46768, p. 318.
4 Ibid., 238.
5 Ibid., 629–659.
6 United Press International, "Faulty Planes Inspection Rap," *Waco Times-Herald*, July 26, 1945, 1.

7 Stephan Wilkinson, "The Scandal That Led to Harry S. Truman Becoming President and Marilyn Monroe Getting Married," 2024. www.historynet.com/curtiss-wright-scandal.
8 Author interview with herbicide specialist Charles M. Bartlett, the Fort Deitrich, Maryland, operations officer who headed development of Agent Orange, Aug. 1999.
9 The serial numbers of C-124s were based on the year when the plane's production began, with forty-nine signifying 1949, followed by a hyphen and the plane's place in the production line.
10 Inspector General U.S. Air Force, "Report of Special Accident Investigations of C-124A Aircraft," Department of the Air Force, July 9, 1951, 1–6. DAFHRA IRIS Number 877715, Reel 46768, pp. 554–622.
11 Ibid., 436–437.
12 Testimony of Lieutenant Colonel Avery J. Ladd, commanding officer of the Second Strategic Support Squadron, Walker Air Force Base, Roswell, New Mexico, Mar. 24, 1951. DAFHRA, IRIS Number 877715, Reel 46768, p. 635.
13 Ibid., 441–442.
14 Ibid., 443–444. The document refers to John C. McBlaine, but Air Force records refer to General John F. McBlain as the SAC inspector general at the time.
15 Ibid., 451.
16 Some surviving family members of the victims have advanced speculation that the weather ship *Charlie* had intercepted a Mayday call from the plane, reporting a fire onboard, around the time it veered off course. No such reference appeared anywhere in the investigation report. In fact, the investigation directly refuted the idea that a fire onboard had prompted the diversion and ditching.
17 DAFHRA IRIS Number 877715, Reel 46768, p. 712.
18 Weston Solutions, "Final Work Plan, Military Munitions Response Program," Military Munitions Response Program Remedial Investigations U.S. Army Garrison, West Point, New York, 228, 321, 331, 334.
19 D. P. Jensen, Douglas Aircraft Company, Inc. Testing Division, "Crash Investigation C-124A, No. 49244 (Spectographic Laboratory)," July 7, 1951. DAFHRA IRIS Number 877715, Reel 46768, pp. 291–319.
20 Ibid., 285–289.
21 Ibid., 235.
22 Cable from Office of Special Investigations, Westover Air Force Base in Massachusetts to the deputy inspector general for technical inspections and flight safety at Norton Air Force Base, Apr. 9, 1951.
23 During the year prior to this flight, the military phased out the Mark 3 Fat Man of the type used in the Nagasaki bombing, transitioning to a heavier but easier-to-arm Mark 4 Fat Man. The weight difference between the two models was about 500 pounds.
24 DAFHRA IRIS Number 877715, Reel 46768, p. 730.
25 Ibid., 451.
26 Ibid., 311.
27 Ibid., 313.
28 L. S. Dando, "Report of Investigation," U.S. Chemical Corps Engineering Agency, Edgewood Chemical Center, Jan. 8, 1952, 2.
29 National Defense Research Committee, Office of Scientific Research and Development, "Fire Warfare: Incendiaries and Flame Throwers," 1946, 21.

CHAPTER 21

1 Robert F. Futrell, *The United States Air Force in Korea 1950-1953* (Duell, Sloan and Pearce, 1961), 376–380, as cited in James T. Quinlivan, "Soviet Strategic Air Defense: A Long Past and an Uncertain Future" (The RAND Corporation, 1989), 10–11.
2 John Prados, *The Soviet Estimate: U.S. Intelligence Analysis and Soviet Strategic Forces* (Princeton University Press, 1986), 30.
3 Paul Glenshaw, "Secret Casualties of the Cold War," *Smithsonian*, Sept. 2017. https://www.smithsonianmag.com/air-space-magazine/secret-casualties-of-the-cold-war-180967122.
4 Ibid.
5 Catie Edmondson, "A Reporter's Journey Into How the U.S. Funded the Bomb," *The New York Times*, Jan. 17, 2024. https://www.nytimes.com/2024/01/17/us/politics/atomic-bomb-secret-funding-congress.html.
6 "Department of Defense Appropriations for 1952: Hearings Before a Subcommittee of the Committee on Appropriations, House of Representatives, Eighty-second Congress, First Session," U.S. Government Printing Office, July 2, 1951, 647.
7 National Personnel Records Center, personnel file of Lieutenant Colonel James Iredell Hopkins, Mar. 20, 1951.
8 DAFHRA, "History for March 1951," Headquarters Bombardment Wing, Medium, 509th Provisional APO #179, U.S. Air Force, compiled by Capt. William F. Byess, 2nd Lieutenant Jacob S. Refson, Staff Sgt. John V. Ruppersburg, and Private First Class Francis L. Moran, IRIS no. 459200, reel 10527, p. 16.
9 Frederick C. Alexander, "History of Sandia Corporation Through Fiscal Year 1963" (Sandia National Laboratories, 1963), 28.
10 DAFHRA History for March, 17.
11 United Press International, "B-29 With 12 Aboard Missing," *The Duncan Banner*, Mar. 11, 1951, 1.
12 DAFHRA History for March, 30.
13 Boldface added.
14 DAFHRA History for March, 59.
15 Ibid., 89.
16 Ibid., 167.
17 Major Paul K. Carlton III, "General Curtis E. LeMay on Leadership and Command," School of Advanced Air and Space Studies, Air University, Maxwell Air Force Base, Alabama, 2010, 47–48.
18 Library of Congress, Manuscript Reading Room, Box 11: Personal correspondence of Major General Curtis LeMay, July 1945.

CHAPTER 22

1 Author interview with Lawrence E. Rafferty, son of Captain Lawrence Rafferty, Nov. 22, 2024.
2 The Associated Press, "2 Wives Claim General's Funds," *Tampa Times*, Oct. 13, 1951, 8.
3 "Test of Late General's 1948 Divorce Looms Here," *Tampa Bay Times*, Feb. 3, 1952, 11.
4 "Estado de Chihuahua Acto de Matrimonio," document 007 2278, Mar. 22, 1947, 277. Reproduced and recovered via Ancestry.com.
5 Author interview with Carolyn Hurwitz on Dec. 5, 2024.
6 Mike Morgan, "Two Wives Claim Pension of General Killed in Crash," *The Tampa Tribune*, Oct. 12, 1951, 1.

7 "Hearing Reveals General's Mixed-Up Marital Status," *Tampa Bay Times*, Mar. 27, 1953, 7.

8 Jess Stearn, "The Generals' Wives Refuse to Fade Away," *Daily News*, Nov. 30, 1952, 96–97.

9 United Press, "Two 'Widows' Battle for Title as Heir to Estate of General," *Times-News*, Mar. 27, 1953, 5.

10 The Associated Press, "Insurance Firm Wins Decision," *Billings Gazette*, Sept. 3, 1953, 13.

11 "News of Record," *The Tampa Tribune*, Aug. 19, 1951, 34.

12 Stearn, "The Generals' Wives Refuse to Fade Away."

CHAPTER 23

1 William J. Broad, "How a Star Times Reporter Got Paid by Government Agencies He Covered," *The New York Times*, Aug. 9, 2021. https://www.nytimes.com/2021/08/09/science/william-laurence-new-york-times.html.

2 United Press, London, "Missing Plane May Have Had Atomic Cargo," *Valley Morning Star*, Mar. 27, 1951, 1.

3 *Daily News*, Mar. 27, 1951, 411.

4 *The Salt Lake Tribune*, Mar. 27, 1951, 7.

5 For examples, see https://www.archives.gov/files/research/jfk/releases/2018/docid-32303616.pdf and https://catalog.archives.gov/id/135840735.

6 "Hint Sabotage on Lost Plane," *Daily News*, Mar. 27, 1951, 343.

7 DAFHRA, IRIS Number 877715, Reel 46768, "At Headquarters, 3rd Air force, APO 125," 322–326. News agencies picked up on the Press Association report. See also: United Press, "Search Resumed for Globemaster Lost in Atlantic," *Los Angeles Daily News*, Apr. 2, 1951, 26.

8 DAFHRA, IRIS Number 877715, Reel 46768, p. 322.

9 Ibid., 323.

10 Ibid., 326.

11 Arthur Quinlan, "Interview With Che Guevara Lynch," Society for Irish Latin American Studies. https://www.irlandeses.org/quinlan.htm.

12 Jimmy Woulfe, "Legendary Journalist Arthur Quinlan Dies, 92," *Irish Examiner*, Dec. 24, 2012. https://www.irishexaminer.com/news/arid-20217817.html.

13 Garrett Brennan, letter dated May 2, 1951, and stamped "Confidential" to the Secretary, Department of Justice in Dublin, *Message found, 28/4/1951, on the beach at Renvyle, Clifden, County Galway, purporting to relate to U.S. Globemaster plane, missing since 23/3/1951.* National Archives of Ireland, Document Reference Code JUS/8/994.

14 Michael O'Toole, *Cleared for Disaster* (Mercier Press, 2006, as cited in Carl Nally and Dermot Butler, *States of Denial*, Mercier Press, 2013), 66–69.

CHAPTER 24

1 William Weinbaum and Tod Robberson, "The Battle Within," ESPN.com, Nov. 7, 2024. https://www.espn.com/espn/feature/story?id=41849751&_slug_=pat-tillman-friendly-fire-death-20-years-trauma-platoon.

2 Paul Glenshaw, "Secret Casualties of the Cold War," *Smithsonian*, Dec. 2017. https://www.smithsonianmag.com/air-space-magazine/secret-casualties-of-the-cold-war-180967122/.

3 Barbara Crosette, "Yeltsin Says U.S. Servicemen Were Held by Stalin," *The New York Times*, June 13, 1992, 6.

4 Based on author's interviews with Reva Cullen's nieces, Carolyn and Barbara Hurwitz, and nephew Mike Hurwitz.

5 Evelyn M. Dent, "Service News: Leggetts Take Over Holloways' House," *Washington Evening Star*, Apr. 26, 1953, 86.

6 Judy Rollins, "World Was Beat for Woman of Many Experiences," *The Salt Lake Tribune*, Feb. 16, 1971, 6.

7 Margaret Hook Olsen, *Patriarch of the Rockies: The Life Story of Joshua Gravett* (Golden Bell Press, 1960), 156.

8 Chief Petty Officer Michael E. Allen, Joint Commission Support Directorate Defense POW/Missing Personnel Office, "The Gulag Study," 2005. https://www.dpaa.mil/Portals/85/Documents/USRJC/The_Gulag_Study_5th_Ed.pdf.

9 Michael Rocereta, "Letters from the Globemaster Families," iUniverse, 2015.

10 James K. Hopkins letter to U.S. Senator Martin Heinrich, July 24, 2018.

11 Bureau of Aircraft Accident Archives, "Crash of a Douglas C-124A Globemaster II into the Atlantic Ocean: 53 killed." https://www.baaa-acro.com/crash/crash-douglas-c-124a-globemaster-ii-atlantic-ocean-53-killed.

12 Technical Sergeant Heather Salazar, 509th Bomb Wing, Whiteman Air Force Base, "A Splendid Ceremony: Team Whiteman Honors Original Striker at Arlington," Oct. 18, 2021. https://www.whiteman.af.mil/News/Article/2814053/a-splendid-ceremony-team-whiteman-honors-original-striker-at-arlington/.

EPILOGUE

1 Minutes of the 20th Plenum of the U.S.-Russia Joint Commission on POW/MIAs May 23-24, 2016, Pentagon Conference Center, Washington, D.C. https://www.dpaa.mil/portals/85/Documents/USRJC/20th_Plenum_Minutes.pdf.

INDEX